Arab Women Novelists

SUNY Series in Middle Eastern Studies
Shahrough Akhavi, Editor

Arab Women Novelists

The Formative Years and Beyond

Joseph T. Zeidan

State University of New York Press

Published by
State University of New York Press, Albany

Printed in the United States of America

For information, address State University of New York
Press, State University Plaza, Albany, N.Y., 12246

Production by E. Moore
Marketing by Bernadette LaManna

Library of Congress Cataloging-in-Publication Data

Zeidan, Joseph T., 1944–
Arab women novelists: the formative years and beyond/Joseph T. Zeidan.
p. cm.
Includes bibliographical references and index.
ISBN 0-7914-2171-6 (acid-free).—ISBN 0-7914-2172-4 (pbk.: acid-free)
1. Arabic fiction—Women authors—History and criticism. 2. Arabic fiction—20th century—History and criticism. 3. Women authors, Arab—Political and social views. 4. Feminism and literature—Arab countries. 5. Women in literature. 6. Women—Arab countries—Social conditions. I. Title.
PJ7525.2.Z45 1995
892'.736099287—dc20 94-1007
CIP

10 9 8 7 6 5 4 3 2 1

To my brother Ḥabīb (1937–1976).
It is never too late to say
thank you.

Contents

ACKNOWLEDGMENTS

While writing this book I have been fortunate to have received assistance and encouragement from many sources. The first phase of this study was undertaken at the University of California, Berkeley in the 1980s under the supervision of Mounah Khouri, William Brinner, and John Dillon. Their kind help and superb guidance was much appreciated. To Frederic J. Cadora I owe a special debt of gratitude for his continuing gracious support of my work from the moment I joined the Department of Near Eastern, Judaic, and Hellenic Languages and Literatures at The Ohio State University. His encouragement as well as financial support from the College of Humanities at The Ohio State University enabled me to bring this study to fruition.

Among the friends and colleagues who were kind enough to read the manuscript in whole or in part and who provided me with useful comments and suggestions, I extend particular thanks to Steve Skelley, Barbara DeMarco, Mustafa Ahmed, Aida Bamia, Richard Davis, and Sabra Webber. In addition, I have benefited greatly from the generous assistance of Dona Straley and Patrick Visel of the Middle East Studies Library at the Ohio State University.

During the production of the manuscript the efforts of several individuals made the completion of this study possible. Cathy Calhoun and Martha Klironomos assisted in typing the early draft, allowing me to get preliminary thoughts down on paper. I am particularly grateful for the sustained efforts of Rebecca Thomas, who edited the manuscript and who stayed the course with me until its completion. I also extend my deep appreciation to Sandra Welch, who tirelessly typed and retyped every draft of the manuscript and took a personal interest in this project. Her insightful observations and editorial assistance were most welcome.

Last, but certainly not least, greatest thanks are due to my wife, Leila, for her constant encouragement and affectionate understanding, and to my children, Tariq and Samar, for their love and patience through the process.

Transliteration System

Anglicized spellings of commonly used names and locations have been retained for the ease of use in an English language text. In such cases where I have found it necessary to transliterate vocabulary, names, or titles from the Arabic I have conformed to the following transliteration system:

ء	ʾ	س	s	ل	l	Short	َ	= a
ب	b	ش	sh	م	m		ُ	= u
ت	t	ص	ṣ	ن	n		ِ	= i
ث	th	ض	ḍ	ه	h			
ج	j	ط	ṭ	و	w	Long	ا	= ā
ح	ḥ	ظ	ẓ	ي	y		و	= ū
خ	kh	ع	ʿ	ة	h/t		ي	= ī
د	d	غ	gh					
ذ	dh	ف	f	Doubled:	ِيّ = iyy		ُوّ = uww	
ر	r	ق	q	Final Nisbah:	ِيّ = i			
ز	z	ك	k	Diphthongs:	َو = aw		َي = ay	

INTRODUCTION

Although the contributions of women writers to modern Arabic literature constitute one of the most important features of that literature, to date no map for interested scholars details the emergence and development of their work. In the last half-century, Arab women writers have not only entered the field of literature in ever-increasing numbers, but have also distinguished themselves with an impressive richness and diversity in their writing. They have demonstrated their talents mainly in the genres of the novel, poetry, and the short story and will no doubt soon produce many new works in others (such as drama) as well—especially as their public mobility and access to education improve further. Part of the reason for this is undoubtedly the fact that many early primary sources that such a study requires are out of print or not widely available. The difficulty of obtaining primary sources and the scarcity of scholarly works on them created quite a challenge in terms of this study. I can only hope that, as interest in Arab women writers increases, more of their work will be available to us and more books and articles will be written about them. This book is one effort toward that goal, and assesses the contributions of women to the Arabic novel (both in subject matter and in form) up to the early 1980s.

Because of the nature of the topic—the "formative years"—the focus here is narrowed to representative writers chosen from the Arab East (Egypt, Lebanon, Syria, and Palestine) where the pioneering women's fiction was produced. The number of women writers emerging in Iraq, Saudi Arabia, Kuwait, and North Africa is increasing rapidly. Any study of Arab women's literary activity beyond the formative years will undoubtedly include North African authors, who participated in the spirit of Arab revivalism that swept postcolonial North Africa. Admittedly, the idea of "formative years" as a single entity for women's fiction in the Arab world is an artificial construct; the "Arab world" is not a single monolithic entity whose different components (be they religious, political, or social) are homogeneous in their experiences and in how these experiences affect society. Therefore, what in this book is addressed as the formative years is not uniform over the broad expanse of the Arab world. For Morocco, Tunisia, and Algeria, for example, the formative years of women's fiction writing may begin several decades later than the formative years of Egyptian women's writing. The writers addressed in this book have, however, had an effect on the formative years of women writers in other parts of the Arab world, and as such, have earned a special place in the history of Arabic literature.

I choose to discuss only novels written in Arabic despite the fact that some interesting novels have been written in French and English.[1] My choice to include only those novels written in Arabic is based upon my interest in the interaction between Arabic novels and Arab society and between women writers and the Arabic language itself. In the first place, the shift from writing novels in a European language to writing novels in the Arabic language may be seen as being emblematic of Arab society's shifting emphasis from the focus on foreign customs to addressing local Arab issues. In addition, novels published in Arabic are read mostly by Arab audiences and are thus much more likely than other novels to be written specifically for Arab readers and to have noticeable effects on Arab culture and politics. This, in turn, means that they more directly comment upon and attempt to affect the status of Arab women and of Arab women's writing in the writers' own cultures. In addition, Arabic literature is subject to the rules of a tradition that holds the Classical Arabic language to be sacred (meaning that changes in the formal language are discouraged). This creates quite a challenge for women writers who, if they are to find their voices, must change this patriarchal language that marginalizes them and at the same time must make the language acceptable enough to be published and read by a significant audience.

The focus on women novelists is not intended to imply that

gender in itself determines the nature of literary creation; rather, it underscores differences in experience, differences that are manifested in literature. For such an undertaking it is absolutely necessary to call upon feminist literary theory because it supports a focus on women's literature where women are at the center of the discussion, and it is a highly developed field with many and varied resources available to scholars. However, feminist literary theory is still mostly the domain of Western feminism, and we must therefore remain mindful of the problems involved in applying theory developed in the West to literature produced in the Arab world. Despite the impact of Western culture on Arabs in most aspects of life, I still believe that there is a tremendous risk involved in applying Western feminist theories and critical concepts to Arab women's literature. That does not mean that those theories cannot be valuable tools for interpreting certain literary phenomena and techniques. The danger lies in imposing these theories indiscriminately on a literature which, compared to Western literature, may have a different historical-cultural context.

Fortunately, feminist theory, although certainly not universally "true" in any single development or application, has a built-in allowance for (and indeed, an insistence on) the contextualization of theory, theorists, and subjects of study. This means that it is highly adaptable. For example, in this book I characterize certain works written by Arab women as "individualistic," a quality that has been associated with Western patriarchal values. In the West, many social problems are trivialized and ignored based on rhetoric about individual opportunity and responsibility for one's own "success"; consequently, feminists and other groups have struggled to organize around collective identity to resist discrimination based on individual "freedom." However, "individualistic" works by Arab women can be read as feminist in the context of Arab culture. In that culture, collective ethnic and religious identity-conformity behaviors are highly valued by the power structure, and therefore sexism is institutionalized through those values. For women to resist oppression, they must resist the institutions that depend on it, and in fact the Arab women's struggle against the patriarchal system began with the assertion of their individuality and their individual rights—as reflected in the works by Arab women during the 1950s and 1960s. Later works show an increase in concern for national identity among these writers, and again we must understand the context. Although this too is often viewed in the West as antifeminist (because of the real presence in Western societies of nationalism based on a hierarchy of cultures), and this focus on national identity does seem to result in less attention overall to feminist concerns in the writings discussed, many of the writers were able to successfully deal with both in their works. Again, the two are compatible here in the context of the national identity crisis in the Arab world, which has been brought on by external pressure to remain separated by geographic boundaries and to submit to other nations' anti-Arab prejudices and activities, as opposed to the situation in the West, in which some cultures base nationalistic feeling on their alleged superiority to others. Thus feminist theory can be adapted to various circumstances to interpret and counter oppression in its many forms.

Although the roots of Arab women's literature extend back to the pre-Islamic dawn of Arab society, at the beginning of the Arab cultural reawakening *al-nahḍah* the literary contributions of women were nonetheless still meager as a result of social, religious, and economic factors. These factors have not disappeared by any means; for example, the veil has made a comeback recently in some Arab countries, and others never abandoned it. (Indeed, any practice associated with religion is difficult to change.) Chapter One provides some discussion of the history of the status of women in the Arab world and of the modern women's movement there. That movement began to gather momentum early in the nineteenth century when increased contact with the West led Arab intellectuals to question the position of Arab women. These scholars began to debate the reasons for the practices of veiling and denying education to women, and they focused on the question of whether Islam itself required these or whether the patriarchal system had imposed the restrictions on pseudo-religious grounds. Chapter One traces the ensuing struggle over women's rights in the Arab world, particularly the gradual improvement in women's access to education—the first area in which women made significant gains (though less due to decreasing sexism than to the spreading belief that inclusive education was necessary for a strong nation). Progress with respect to the vote and election of women to political office was slower and more sporadic, but was also an important facet of the movement and is outlined in this chapter as well.

Not surprisingly, Arab women writers were scarce until fairly recently, and what writings they did produce usually imitated the norms established by the existing male-dominated literary tradition, but these provided the foundations for the modern literary accomplishments of Arab women and are the subject of Chapter Two. Included in this chapter is a discussion of nonfiction genres such as poetry, although the primary focus of this study is the novel. I found it necessary to include these because it was in these forms that Arab women writers began to develop a distinct æsthetic. This happened as these women began to feel a sense of solidarity with their predecessors (who were even fewer) and developed a more political awareness of themselves as women. Deriving strength from bonds with other women, they found ways to subvert the system that denied them access to education and intellectual society, which are vital to any writer. By forming their own literary societies and establishing salons and journals, a number of privileged Arab women writers were able to bring some mainstream cultural activities to their normally isolated domains, and they could gain at least some exposure to the outside world and to literary criticism and discussion. Ironically, Christian women were disproportionately well-represented among the more successful women writers, as so many of them were educated in Western missionary schools. This meant that, in relation to their Muslim counterparts, they were more likely to have read a great deal and to have learned values that reflected women's greater freedom in the West. Overall, the work produced by the writers discussed in Chapter Two remained rather meager; however, considering their education levels, their limited mobility, and lack of attention and credit given them by literary critics of the time, their work stands as a symbol of these writers' remarkable talents and determination to overcome the barriers placed before them.

Chapter Three surveys the 1950s and 1960s, at which time women's novels gained momentum and women writers emerged in greater numbers. This was a fairly natural progression in that, as individual Arab states won their independence and looked for ways to strengthen themselves nationally, education became much more widely available to girls and women. In the wave of individualism that tends to follow struggles for national independence, Arab women writers approached their work from individualistic perspectives and produced literature that greatly resembled that of earlier Western feminists. They began writing about their own lives often in first-person narration, a sign that they were breaking away from the established literary traditions to which the previous generation had adhered so closely. Their writing was characterized by protest against male domination and by an insistence that men be held accountable for this situation. Key themes were individualism, the drive to assert a personal and distinctly female identity, and demands for the social, sexual, and political rights of women. (The subject matter tended to center around a few main issues, as those in a position to write were almost always from privileged backgrounds and were most concerned with issues affecting them directly.) Of course, they did not escape the internal conflict such themes bring about, and this was evident in their work. They had to come to terms with their ambivalence toward their own bodies—symbols of their individual existence, but also constructed as objects by their culture and therefore simultaneously limiting to them as individuals. They experienced conflict with regard to their mothers as well, because their mothers represented both the writers themselves and the traditions they were trying to escape. They also wrestled with the dilemma of how to live if there was no place in society where nontraditional women were fully accepted. Most of them paid a high price personally for pursuing writing careers. And still there remained the problem of harsh critics who attacked not only women's writings, but the writers themselves in ways they would have never done had the writers been men. Fortunately, general acceptance of women writers improved as more women were published, evidenced by the increased demand for, and discussion of, women's literature. Many publishers even began to put these authors' photographs on the back covers of their books—a phenomenon that, though perhaps problematic in some ways (since this was not the practice for male authors and one wonders why it was established in the first place), at least testifies to the publishers' confidence that making female authorship obvious would not hurt the sale of the books.

Finally, Chapter Four discusses trends beginning in the late 1960s, and especially after the 1967 Arab-Israeli war, when women's literature underwent another shift in emphasis and attitudes. As a result of the military disaster and a new interest in the Palestinian problem, women novelists began to place greater stress on international politics. This shift caused women novelists some difficulties. Historical details became so important in some novels that characterization suffered, as did credibility when the writers attempted to describe experiences about which they knew very little (such as fighting in the war). Nevertheless, they concentrated on the question of national identity and effected changes in the way the public viewed and acted on the threat to the Arab world. For example, some women writers subscribed to the philosophy that national problems are the responsibility of every citizen and that true citizenship requires one to actively assume that responsibility rather than wait passively or escape the turmoil. In general, the struggle for women's freedom and national identity were being linked in a way they had not been before—they were no longer simply parallel, but were interdependent struggles. There were some writers who placed such emphasis on the need for national solidarity that it came to overshadow their former insistence on individual identity; in fact, in the face of the national crisis and the need for solidarity, some of these writers ceased to look upon men as the primary oppressors. Instead, they saw both men and women as being oppressed by existing political and social conditions and constantly threatened by hostile foreign forces.

However, the trend seems to be the integration, to greater or lesser degrees, of feminist and nationalist concerns in Arab women's novels, and we can only guess how this will affect the development of these novels. Will the number of Arab women novelists increase as women are motivated and encouraged by political conditions? How will these novels affect and reflect the movements for national solidarity and women's rights? And how will these novelists change the face of Arabic literature?

1. Women in Arab Society: A Historical Perspective

The following contradictory statements represent diametrically opposed views of women in Arabia: "When Islam appeared in Arabia, women held a very low position in society" (Siddiqi 1952: 17) and "On the whole, their position was higher and their influence great" (Nicholson 1969: 87). The contradictory views expressed by scholars concerning the status of women in the pre-Islamic period (*al-Jāhiliyyah*) stem largely from a mistaken conception of "Arabia" as a homogeneous society and a failure to recognize the existence of separate tribal entities with widely differing philosophies in many areas.

To shed light upon the position of women among the diverse societies in the Arabian peninsula, it is instructive to compare the two most influential societies—Mecca and Medina. The patriarchal features of Meccan society were already well-established by the time Islam emerged in the seventh century. Muḥammad himself belonged to a patrilineal clan.[1] In Medina, on the other hand, society was still matrilineal; women played a decisive role, so much so that one of Muḥammad's successors, the Caliph ʿUmar, complained: "We of Quraysh used to dominate [our] women; but when we came among the Ansar, they proved to be a people whose women dominated them; and our women began to copy the habits of the women of the Ansar" (Riencourt 1974: 188).[2] Despite the strikingly different perceptions of the position of women in the two societies, it would be futile to attempt a detailed list of their rights and duties because the data available to us are simply too sketchy and selective to justify any conclusions. The task becomes even harder if we try to deal with the status of women in other urban settlements and in the nonurban tribes, about whom we know even less. Consequently, the available information on women in pre-Islamic Arabia must be approached with a great deal of caution.

There is evidence to indicate that pre-Islamic women had their say in the specific areas of marriage and divorce.[3] The poetess al-Khansā' (c. 600–670) dared to turn down Durayd Ibn al-Ṣummah's proposal of marriage, despite her brother's intervention on behalf of her suitor (A. Ḥasan 1970: 15–16). Certainly not every woman of the pre-Islamic period enjoyed al-Khansā''s independence; nonetheless, it would be misleading to disregard her case as merely an exception to the general rule, for, in fact, a powerful and respected class of women emerged in the *Jāhiliyyah* that included priestesses, fortune tellers, and self-proclaimed prophetesses.[4] In Mecca itself, the key to the Ka'bah, the holiest shrine of the pre-Islamic Arabs as well as of the Muslims, was kept for a long time in the hands of a woman, Bint Khalīl al-Khuzā'ī.[5]

With the coming of Islam and the synthesis and codification in the Qur'ān and *ḥadīth* (tradition) of elements of social practice drawn, perhaps, not simply from among various tribal practices but from the social and religious practices encountered while engaged in trade with people from most of the known world, Muslim women's rights and duties were formalized. For a variety of reasons, Islam has been blamed for the inferior status of Muslim women. Although a basic precept of the Qur'ān is the equality of men and women in relation to God, both on earth and in the afterlife, it is also true that Muslims, like the other Abrahamic traditions, conceived of women as inherently fragile and thus in need of continuous guidance and supervision by men. After the beginnings of Islam, some of its teachings on women were abrogated by a social system repressive to women. For example, although Islam granted women the right to own property and to dispose of it without male interference and the right to education, women were often unaware of these rights. Because women were almost entirely secluded from the external world, without the mobility and freedom to mingle with men, in practice they depended on the integrity of the few men with whom they did have contact—fathers, brothers, and husbands.

In the sphere of conjugal life, Islam abolished some of the marriage patterns that had existed in the *Jāhiliyyah*.[6] Though polygamy was allowed, it was not recommended,[7] because the husband was required to treat his wives equally both in sexual and financial matters. The practice of polygamy was not seriously questioned until the beginning of the twentieth century. Muḥammad ʿAbduh (1849–1905), one of a number of distinguished Muslim reformers, in a revolutionary *fatwā*,[8] concluded that one could eliminate polygamy without violating the principles of Islam because no man could really treat his wives equally. The movement to restrict polygamy, initiated by ʿAbduh and continued by other modern commentators, was met overwhelmingly (though not exclusively)[9] by harsh opposition from religious quarters.[10]

One of the most controversial issues that some Muslim scholars have associated with Islam as a religion has been veiling. Veiling has been perceived by its supporters as a shield for preserving women's chastity and honor, but by its opponents as a detestable symbol of women's sexual segregation and social passivity throughout the history of Islam. The outcry against the veil and everything it represented was to become one of the essential features of the Muslim women's emancipation movement in the early twentieth century.

There does exist evidence to support the idea that Islam was responsible for the institution of the veil: ʿUmar ibn al-Khaṭṭāb, one of the early converts, urged the Prophet to segregate his wives from men, especially when the Prophet's house became a popular place for gatherings of the believers.

Before the revelations of the *Āyat al-Ḥijāb* of the Qur'ān, not only the Prophet's wives but also the women of Medina were unveiled.[11] The fact that the *āyah* was addressed to the Prophet's wives supported the claim of later opponents of the veil that veiling was intended only for the Prophet's wives.

Debate over the attitude of Islam toward women's education has been another major issue since the begining of the twentieth century. The debate stemmed largely from contradictory *ḥadīths*.

Those who support the granting of education to Muslim women cite general *ḥadīths* applicable to both sexes, e.g., "The quest for knowledge is a (religious) duty for every Muslim" (al-Khūlī n.d.: 211), or the *ḥadīth* that shows the Prophet's interest in learning for women in particular: "Any man who had a girl (slave) and taught and educated her well, then set her free and married her, would be twice rewarded" (Riḍā n.d.: 18).

'Ā'ishah's active role in Islam provides evidence that women at this early date could hold respected positions in the field of religion. 'Ā'ishah was an authority on matters regarding the Prophet and on the interpretation of the *ḥadīth* both during the Prophet's lifetime and after his death, to such an extent that she transmitted 2,210 *ḥadīths* about the Prophet even though she was only nineteen when he died. The Prophet himself asked Muslims to take half their religion from 'Ā'ishah (*"Khudhū niṣf dīnakum 'an hādhihi al-ḥumayrā"*) (Wajdī 1936: 485). Islamic scholars have affirmed that 'Ā'ishah was more accurate than Abū Hurayrah, the most famous transmitter of *ḥadīth*. 'Urwah ibn al-Zubayr confessed: "I have not seen anybody who was more knowledgeable in jurisprudence (*fiqh*) or medicine or poetry than 'Ā'ishah" ('Afīfī n.d.: 143). We know 'Ā'ishah could read, although we do not know if she could also write.[12] We have evidence that another of the Prophet's wives, Ḥafṣah bint 'Umar, could do both, and that the Prophet encouraged her to continue her learning after their marriage (Kaḥḥālah 1977: vol. 1, 32).

On the other hand, 'Ā'ishah also transmitted a *ḥadīth* in which the Prophet said: "Do not take them [women] to places of learning (*ghuraf*) and do not teach them writing. Rather teach them spinning and *Sūrat al-Nūr*" (Kaḥḥālah 1977: vol. 1, 32). This *ḥadīth* was later used by some writers to support their claim that Islam did not favor education for women. The Caliphs 'Umar ibn al-Khaṭṭāb and 'Alī ibn Abī Ṭālib supported this view. To Ibn al-Khaṭṭāb was attributed the statement: "Keep women away from writing and do not let them join places of learning, and seek help against them by telling them 'no' because 'yes' will do them harm" (Kaḥḥālah 1977: vol. 1, 33). We are also told that 'Alī ibn Abī Ṭālib, when he passed a man teaching a woman handwriting (*khaṭṭ*) said, "Do not add to the evil (another) evil" (Kaḥḥālah 1977: vol. 1, 34).

The position of women in Islam has been the subject of heated controversy among Muslim intellectuals ever since they were exposed to modern Western civilization. Before that exposure,

Muslims seemed to be content with the traditional social norms that shaped their lives. For example, although the French invasion of Egypt (1798–1801) provided an opportunity for some Egyptian intellectuals to see firsthand some aspects of French science and the French way of life, nonetheless French occupation did not make a profound impact on Egyptian customs and manners, partly because French rule lasted only for a short period and partly because traditional customs and manners were so deeply rooted in Egyptian life, especially because they were associated with Islam.

When the noted Egyptian historian ʻAbd al-Raḥmān al-Jabartī (1745–1825) wrote the history of the French invasion, he recorded his personal impressions of the women who accompanied the French army. Generally speaking, these were the impressions of a man who had many reservations about what he was observing. Al-Jabartī accused the French of corrupting Egyptian Muslim women because they provided the Egyptians with bad examples. Even the daughter of the greatest religious notable, the Shaykh al-Bakrī, had mixed with the French and had dressed like a French lady. She was executed for it when the Turks returned to Egypt (al-Jabartī 1904–5: 35–36).

However, one episode in particular suggests that Egyptian women viewed the situation quite differently.[13] The French historian Clot Bey told the following story, as he heard it in France from Napoleon himself:

> General Menon married a woman from Rashīd, and treated her as if she were French, for he gave her his hand as they entered the dining room, and chose the best seat for her, and offered her the best and most delicious food. Whenever the napkin fell from her lap he rushed to pick it up and return it to its place. When this woman told her friends about these matters in one of Rashīd's bathhouses, a ray of hope shone for these women that their conditions and customs might change. They wrote a petition to the Supreme Sultan, Bonaparte, asking them to force their husbands to treat them as Menon treated his wife. (I. Khalīfah 1973: 6)

Saʻīdah Ramaḍān questioned the credibility of this story. She noted that the event was not mentioned in al-Jabartī's works (Ramaḍān 1976: 124).

Possibly the first Egyptian intellectual who had a chance to experience European habits and morals firsthand and in Europe itself was Rifā'ah Rāfi' al-Ṭahṭāwī (1801–1873). Part of the significance of his experience for us stems from the fact that al-Ṭahṭāwī was a religious figure who had graduated from al-Azhar University. He had gone to France in 1826 to serve as a religious guide (*imām*) to the first group of Egyptian students sent there by Muḥammad 'Alī (r. 1805–1849). While there, al-Ṭahṭāwī found the time and energy to learn French, and embarked upon a thorough study of French thought and history. One of the aspects of the French way of life that drew his attention during his stay was the status of women in that society. Upon his return to Egypt, al-Ṭahṭāwī undertook the task of recording the observations made during his five years in France (1826–1831). The result was his book *Takhlīṣ al-Ibrīz ilā Talkhīṣ Bārīz*. His attitude was ambivalent. Some aspects of French civilization fascinated him, but the whole experience was an overwhelming and shocking one for a traditional scholar who had had to bridge in a relatively short time the gap between his religious training at al-Azhar and the secular society of France.

Al-Ṭahṭāwī argued that unveiling and social contact between men and women did not necessarily lead to corruption: "It would be wrong to regard the virtue of women as being dependent on the presence or absence of the veil. Rather, virtue (stems from) good . . . upbringing (*tarbiyah*), loving only one (person) and no others, and harmony between the spouses" (317–318). Al-Ṭahṭāwī had a surprisingly positive reaction to the Western practice of allowing men and women to dance together, a symbol of the free interaction of the sexes: "Dancing (in the view of Westerners) is an art; it is like boxing. Not every dancer can master the intricacies of the movements. All people in France are fond of dancing, as if it were a form of elegance (*'ayāqah*) and chivalry (*futuwwah*), and not of moral depravity. For this reason dancing has never departed from the laws of decency, unlike dancing in Egypt where it is the specialty of women to awaken sexual desire in men" (139).

Despite al-Ṭahṭāwī's admiration of the way the French treated their women, he was sometimes dissatisfied with them because they allowed their women to dominate them (316). He also avoided tackling the question of veiling in Egypt. It seems that the time was not yet right for discussion of this matter.

Al-Ṭahṭāwī's real contribution to the advancement of women

is to be found in two of his works: *Mabāhij al-Albāb al-Miṣriyyah fī Manāhij al-Adāb al-ʿAṣriyyah* and *al-Murshid al-Amīn li-al-Banāt wa-al-Banīn*. The latter was written as a textbook[14] for boys and girls in the newly established schools of Egypt, in response to a request in 1837 from the Schools Bureau (Diwān al-Madāris) in which al-Ṭahṭāwī was a central figure. He devoted a chapter of the textbook to the thesis that "it is preferable not to discriminate in teaching boys and girls the basics of good education" (al-Ṭahṭāwī 1872: 66). He argued that education had a great impact on happiness in married life, for education and good manners on the mother's part determine how the children would be raised. Also, should circumstances demand it, education would prepare women to work at traditionally male jobs, at least insofar as those jobs suited her capabilities and energy.[15]

The nineteenth century might have ended without the issue of women's emancipation becoming a public concern had it not been for Qāsim Amīn (1863–1908), the original theorist of women's emancipation in the Muslim world. He went to Paris for his advanced law studies and stayed there for four years (1881–1885), not only trying to pursue his academic studies but also educating himself in the history of Western thought. The aspect of French intellectual life which impressed him most deeply was the freedom of expression:

> Real freedom allows one to express every idea, to propagate every doctrine, and to spread every thought. In free countries one can declare openly that he does not have a homeland, can blaspheme God and His prophets, can speak evil about his people's laws and manners and customs, can ridicule the principles on which their social life is based; he can say and write what he pleases about these subjects. Nobody will think, even if his opinion differs, that this reduces the speaker's personal honor in any way provided his words stem from good intentions and genuine convictions. How much time will pass before Egypt reaches this degree of freedom? (ʿAmārah 1976: vol. 2, 52)

Qāsim Amīn's works reveal the influence of Western sources. The origins of his social philosophy can be traced back to the liberal intellectual heritage of the nineteenth century, especially to the writings of Herbert Spencer, John Stuart Mill, Friedrich Nietzsche, Charles Darwin, and Karl Marx (L. ʿAwaḍ 1966: 74). His intellectual development progressed through three major stages. In the first stage, he reacted against the accusation that the teachings of Islam were hostile to women, brought against Islam by the Frenchman Duc d'Harcourt. In 1893, after three visits to Egypt, d'Harcourt wrote a book entitled *Egypte et les Egyptiens*, in which he criticized Egyptian manners and customs and related them to the long history of despotism that had afflicted Egypt. He held Islam responsible for the veil and for the inferior status of Egyptian women. When Qāsim Amīn read this book he was so shocked that he fell sick for ten days. He then determined to express a rebuttal (Khākī 1973: 64–71), and in the following year wrote *Les Egyptiens: Reponse à M. Le Duc d'Harcourt*,[16] in which he angrily refuted d'Harcourt's claim that Islam was to blame for the misfortunes of Egyptian women. Qāsim Amīn defended the veil and the idea of segregation of the sexes: "Our religion ordered that men would have their own gathering place which no woman would enter, and that women would assemble without any man among them. It intended, by doing so, to protect both man and woman against the women weakness which they have within themselves, and to eliminate thoroughly the source of evil" (ʿAmārah 1976: vol. 1, 293).

The second stage was marked by the publication of his book *Taḥrīr al-Mar'ah*[17] (*The Emancipation of Women*, 1899), a landmark in the history of the emancipation of Arab women in modern times, inasmuch as it represented, for the first time in Arab history, a systematic analysis of the Muslim woman's quest for liberation.[18]

The contrast of Qāsim Amīn's views during this stage with those from his earlier stage was striking. His demands for reform fell into two categories: the first pertained to customs, manners, and education; the second revealed his own understanding of Islam's attitude toward women. His point of departure was the assumption that women were equal to men. Men's apparent physical and mental superiority, he said, were explained by the freedom men enjoyed throughout history to develop their potential fully. Women, on the other hand, had been deprived of the same opportunity (ʿAmārah 1976: vol. 2, 119). Qāsim Amīn believed that the first step in creating a strong nation was to strengthen the basic social unit, the family, which could not function properly without an educated wife and mother: "This inferiority in the situation of women is the key obstacle in our path, preventing us from moving towards that which is in our best interests. Thus the education of women is not a luxury which can await the passage of time or a lengthy preparation, as many people falsely imagine who are out beating drums about the virtues of educating men before women. Instead it is necessary, a dire necessity, on which we must begin at once and to which the needed resources must be allocated. It is a critical requirement, which if done will make any other reform easier, but which if not done will undermine any other reform ('Amārah 1976: vol. 2, 79–80). Veiling, Qāsim Amīn proclaimed, was merely a custom and not a religious duty. It had been copied from other nations by Muslims and given religious significance ('Amārah 1976: vol. 2, 45). In defense of his point of view, Qāsim Amīn cited the example of women who lived in the desert and countryside where veiling was not practiced, and where the interaction between the sexes obviously had not led to corruption ('Amārah 1976: vol. 2, 59). He was very conciliatory on the matter of unveiling; he did not ask women to discard the veil at once; rather, he called for careful preparation of young girls for eventual unveiling ('Amārah 1976: vol. 2, 68).[19]

He noted the relationship between women's economic independence and their social emancipation, blaming the exclusion of Muslim women from economic activities as the main reason for their loss of rights. By virtue of her economic dependence on men "she became like a domestic animal, and was treated as such; its owner provided it with the necessities of life out of favor, and thus he had the right to use it as an amusement" ('Amārah 1976: vol. 2, 84–88).

Qāsim Amīn realized that education, the easing of veiling rules, and giving women the right to work under certain circumstances would not in themselves solve the entire problem. He also dealt with marriage, polygamy, and divorce. He discussed these in the light of the *āyah*: "And of signs is this: He created for you helpmates from yourselves that ye might find rest in them, and He ordained between you love and mercy" (Pickthal n.d.: 21). Qāsim Amīn insisted on the need for harmony and affection between husband and wife, and for this reason was opposed to "blind" marriages, an issue especially important for those members of the Egyptian intelligentsia who had been educated in the West, some of whom, Qāsim Amīn maintained, would prefer bachelorhood to marrying wives they had not seen.

Qāsim Amīn bitterly opposed polygamy and considered it "a barbarian custom," rooted in the pre-Islamic period, which did not suit modern times and was a great insult to the humanity of women ('Amārah 1976: vol. 2, 90). He also criticized the hasty way in which some men divorced their wives ('Amārah 1976: vol. 2, 101) and went so far as to demand that women be given the right to initiate divorce proceedings ('Amārah 1976: vol. 2, 106).

There can be no doubt that Qāsim Amīn was inspired by the example of Western women: "Anyone who has observed the women's movement in the West and their activities cannot doubt that they have done great deeds without which civilization would be impossible: one does not find a single branch of manufacture in which women do not work shoulder to shoulder with men; nor can one find philanthropic works in which women were not among the initiators; nor do political events occur unless women have a role" ('Amārah 1976: vol. 2, 80). To corroborate his arguments, Qāsim Amīm not only cited major figures of Western thought, he also demonstrated a profound knowledge of the primary sources of Islam, an unusual accomplishment for a writer of almost completely secular outlook. His bravura performance led some scholars to suggest that someone else had contributed—perhaps extensively—to the writing of *Taḥrīr al-Mar'ah*.[20]

The third stage of Amīn's intellectual development is embodied in his book *al-Mar'ah al-Jadīdah* (*The New Woman*, 1900), an expansion upon his earlier thesis that the emancipation of women was necessary if Muslim society were to function more effectively and that this was compatible with Islam. (Nevertheless, he based his argument less on Qur'ānic citation and *ḥadīth* than on the tenets of Western liberal philosophy.)

In *al-Mar'ah al-Jadīdah* Qāsim Amīn became more outspoken, both in his advocacy of women's rights and on the virtues of an intellectually freer society:

> People (in Egypt) got used to freedom little by little and began to feel that the confusion they felt in their lives could not be attributed to it. Love of freedom became rooted in many souls among us, to such an extent that we could no longer find meaning in life without it. The same will hold true in the

> case of freedom for women. In the first generation there will be many complaints and people will think that a great catastrophe has occurred because women will be experiencing freedoms which are almost completely new to them. Then, in the course of time, women will get used to exercising their freedoms and little by little they will (also) become aware of the obligations, and their mental and spiritual faculties will be elevated. ('Amārah 1976: vol. 2, 156–157)

Earlier, Qāsim Amīn had advocated elementary education for women; now he was demanding political and social equality. To a far greater extent than in *Taḥrīr al-Mar'ah*, he held up the countries of Western Europe as examples of societies in which women were free. He proposed a transformation of Egyptian society which should end, at least in this respect, in its becoming like that of Europe. He returned to his fundamental thesis concerning the benefits Islamic society would gain from the emancipation of women: "There is a correlation between the political situation and that of the family in every country. . . . Look at the Eastern countries. You will find that woman is in bondage to man, and man is in bondage to the ruler. He is an oppressor in his house, and oppressed when he leaves it! Then look at the European countries. You will find that their governments are based on freedom and respect for personal rights, and that the status of women there has therefore been elevated to a high degree of esteem and freedom in thought and work" ('Amārah 1976: vol. 2, 126). Qāsim Amīn's work is exemplary, both in the arguments it presents and in its overall approach to the basic problems of Arab (Muslim) society. For Qāsim Amīn, liberalism, and most important the emancipation of women, were not only worthwhile goals in themselves, but also were the most effective response to the threat of colonial domination. It is in this light that we must understand his stress on the role of women as mothers and, to a lesser degree, as wives. After the failure of 'Urābi's rebellion (1882), which led to the British occupation of Egypt, Qāsim Amīn and most of the Egyptian intelligentsia realized that the only way to confront colonialism was to rejuvenate Egyptian society by attacking its social evils, one of the worst of which was the subjugation of women, which left half the nation paralyzed.

The connection between emancipation of women and resistance to colonialism gave the issue a sense of urgency and collective national importance that left little room for individualism. Education for women was intended not as a means of their self-fulfillment, but mainly as a way to help make the society healthier and thus better able to withstand the political onslaught from Europe.[21]

Qāsim Amīn's views, as expressed in *Taḥrīr al-Mar'ah* and to a lesser degree in *al-Mar'ah al-Jadīdah,* caused a heated and bitter controversy in Egypt and throughout the Arab world.[22] The Khedive 'Abbās Ḥilmī II (r. 1892–1914) was enraged by Qāsim Amīn's books and suspected that the British had encouraged him to write them. He therefore refused to accept a copy of *al-Mar'ah al-Jadīdah* from Qāsim Amīn and banned the author from entering the palace under any circumstances (Khamīs 1978: 79–80).

After Qāsim Amīn, the feminist movement found another supporter in Aḥmad Luṭfī al-Sayyid (d. 1963), the founder of the People's Party (Ḥizb al-Ummah) and the editor of its newspaper *al-Jarīdah.* He believed that equality between men and women, as practiced in the countryside, was a deep-rooted Egyptian tradition, while the subordination of women was found only in urban areas of the country ('Awaḍ 1966: 80). Al-Sayyid's most remarkable contribution was to promote women's education at the university level.[23]

Nonetheless, al-Sayyid's attitude toward women's education was not really radical. Although he maintained that educational opportunities for women should be limitless, in practice he supported teaching them specifically only what were traditionally conceived to be feminine subjects, such as home economics, literature, and needlework (al-Sayyid 1937: 36). By choosing only these subjects, al-Sayyid revealed that he still thought of women mainly in the roles of wife and mother. Like Qāsim Amīn and other Egyptian intellectuals, he linked the education of women to happiness in married life. In one of his articles, al-Sayyid stated that educated young Egyptian men sought marriage only with educated women, and that they sometimes stipulated even more specific criteria.[24] This article, written in 1909, illustrated the rapid rise of upper- and middle-class intellectuals who were educated either in Egypt or in the West in the early twentieth century and their discontent with the educational conditions of women in Egypt.

It may be seen, then, that the movement for women's emancipation grew, in large part, out of a male vision of how to transform the Arab world. But we cannot overlook the importance of the role, however limited, of some women who, despite serious social handicaps, labored intensely for the advancement of the cause. The prominent female writer Malak Ḥifnī Nāṣif (1886–1918), better known by her pen name Bāḥithat al-Bādiyah, was one of the most outspoken writers on the subject of women in the early part of the twentieth century. Her father, Ḥifnī Nāṣif, was one of 'Abduh's disciples; he held a high administrative position and taught Arabic literature at the Egyptian University. He sent his daughter to a French missionary school, after which she attended the public al-Saniyyah school, becoming one of the first Egyptian women to obtain both primary and high school teaching certificates. Thereafter she taught in girls' public schools. She was the most effective woman to take part in the controversy surounding Qāsim Amīn and his views; she wrote a number of articles in al-Sayyid's newspaper *al-Jarīdah*, in which she described the miserable conditions under which Egyptian women lived.[25] She was more moderate than Qāsim Amīn, especially in her views on the veil, marriage, and divorce. As al-Sayyid wrote, "she took customs and religion into consideration in her demands" (al-Sayyid 1910: 17).

Nāṣif held that the Egyptian woman was deprived of all rights throughout every stage of her life. When she was born, the world met her with disappointment because she was not a boy. While growing up she was forbidden education beyond the basics of reading and writing, because she was destined to limit herself to domestic matters. In her house she became a helpless prisoner, deprived even of the right to choose the kind of clothes she wanted to put on. When she married she became a victim of her oppressive husband, who would not only prevent her from eating with him at the same table but also treated her like a slave (Nāṣif 1910: 62–63).

Like Qāsim Amīn, Nāṣif was convinced that the first step towards women's emancipation was education. Responding to the charge leveled by some men that women who were allowed to work would compete with men and take jobs from them, Nāṣif countered that men had infringed upon traditionally "feminine" jobs by inventing modern textile machines that replaced women workers. Rather than leave women idle, she said, men should let them use their spare time for worthwhile activities such as education (Nāṣif 1910: 98–99).

Nāṣif considered the existing division of labor to be a mere matter of convention: "Men emphatically tell us that we (women) were born for the house and they to earn a livelihood. I wish I knew what decree was issued by God to ordain that, and how they came to know about it (the decree) since it was not mentioned in any [religious] book" (100–101). Nāṣif went on to say that men had oppressed women for centuries, damaging their minds and bodies and then claiming that women were inherently weaker than men both physically and mentally. Nāṣif believed that women had the right to work under certain circumstances if they wished to: "I do not mean to urge women to abandon housework or the raising of children and indulge themselves in learning law or jurisdiction or driving trains. However, if someone wants to work in one of these professions the principle of personal freedom rules that no one should oppose her. They [men] may say that pregnancy and delivery force us to leave work, and they use that as an argument against us. There are, however, those women who never married, or those who are sterile and to whom pregnancy and delivery will never occur, or those whose husbands need their help" (99). Although Nāṣif did not favor the veil, she did not argue for its abolition. In her reponse to 'Abd al-Ḥamīd Ḥamdī,[26] a vehement advocate of unveiling, she asked him to take into account the fact that most Egyptian women were ignorant and unprepared for such a drastic step: "Innovation (*ṭafrah*) is impossible. Egypt's women are accustomed to the veil. If you order them to discard it at once, you will see what kind of disgrace they bring upon themselves. The result will be a disaster for both homeland and religion" (10). Although Nāṣif thought that unveiling would win out as soon as society was ready for it, she uncompromisingly rejected the idea of adopting European customs and values. At the end of that road she saw the destruction of Egyptian national identity (Nāṣif 1910: 13). This concern about foreign cultural infiltration also led her to attack missionary schools and to propose reforms in the Egyptian public schools (Nāṣif 1910: 17).

Nāṣif attacked the idea that girls were ready for marriage as soon as they reached puberty; she thought that the minimum age of marriage for girls should be sixteen (31–35). She opposed arranged marriages and polygamy (110, 27–30), two evils from which she had suffered personally.[27]

In 1911, Nāṣif presented to the Islamic Conference held in Cairo ten demands concerning the rights of women. These included free access for women to mosques, compulsory primary education for girls as well as for boys, the establishment of a school of medicine for women equal in standards to the one for men, and the establishment of professional schools and schools of economics for girls. Nāṣif also called for an increase in the number of dispensaries and free hospitals, for protection of women by the police on public highways, for restriction of polygamy, and for denial of divorce without the wife's side being heard.[28] The members of the congress unanimously rejected these demands.

The verbal battle sparked by Qāsim Amīn extended well beyond the borders of Egypt. In Iraq, Qāsim Amīn's ideas provoked a response from some talented poets and minor theorists. Jamīl Ṣidqī al-Zahāwī (1863–1936) led those who advocated unveiling and women's rights. After visiting several Arab countries where the issue of women was being hotly debated, al-Zahāwī wrote his first article, "al-Mar'ah wa-al-Difā' 'anhā" ("Defending Women," 1910), in the Egyptian newspaper *al-Mu'ayyad*.[29] In this article he attacked the veil and the inferior status of Muslim women: "I wonder how a man, who is incomplete without a woman, can persist in insulting her and depriving her of her rights. I wonder how a man, who cannot be complete without a woman, can humiliate the other part of himself. How can a man say that he wants to enjoy freedom, that greatest of all human rights, which is universal to both sexes, while the woman remains his property, created for his pleasures, and while as soon as he has used her up he assumes the right to replace her with another property as he sees fit, or even two or three or four" (al-Darbandī 1968: vol. 1, 256).[30] Al-Zahāwī paid dearly for his daring views. Religious and conservative circles reacted with fury. They implored the governor of Baghdad, Ḥusayn Nāẓim Pasha, to punish al-Zahāwī for his blasphemy. Quick to react, the governor fired al-Zahāwī from his teaching post at the Law School (Madrasat al-Ḥuqūq) in Baghdad and put him under house arrest (al-Hilālī 1972: 14).[31] Thoroughly incensed, one of the leading religious scholars responded to al-Zahāwī's article with a pamphlet bearing the threatening title *al-Sayf al-Bāriq fī 'Unq al-Māriq* (*The Shining Sword at the Apostate's Neck*).[32] Despite the furor, al-Zahāwī remained firm in his conviction that women were entitled to their rights, and he used his poetry to express his views.[33] He was aided in his struggle by another well-known Iraqi poet, Ma'rūf al-Ruṣāfī (1875–1945), who devoted part of his *dīwān* to women's issues.[34] Among other things, al-Ruṣāfī denied that veiling was an integral part of Islam (al-Ruṣāfī 1972: vol. 2, 157).

In fact, the veil proved to be a major source of dispute for Iraqi polemicists.[35] Some minor poets defended the veil as a moral and religious symbol.[36] Tawfīq al-Fukaykī claimed that Western orientalists were carrying the banner of unveiling with the aim of corrupting Muslim morals. On the other side, Muṣṭafā 'Alī argued that the veil was a non-Arabic custom that was adopted from the Persians (Dāwūd 1958: 100–101). It is interesting to note that some male participants in this debate assumed female names, such as Dr. Sāmī Shawkat, who used the penname Fatāt Ghassān. Actual women writers were totally absent from the Iraqi arena (Dāwūd 1958: 102).

In Lebanon, as early as 1847, Buṭrus al-Bustānī (1819–1883), one of the most outstanding figures of the Arab renaissance, called for education of women. In a speech that created considerable controversy among the Lebanese intelligentsia, al-Bustānī launched a fierce diatribe against the prevailing notion that education was dangerous to both men and women, especially the latter, because it could lead to atheism or to madness. He proceeded to enumerate the prerogatives of women and stress their inalienable right to education in order to enjoy life and become men's equals in feeling, opinion, and work: "Women without education are a great evil, if not the greatest evil imaginable" (F. I. al-Bustānī 1950: 23). Al-Bustānī had intended to establish the first girls' school in Lebanon along the same lines as his al-Madrasah al-Waṭaniyyah (The National School, 1863), the first indigenous boys' school in modern Lebanon or Syria. But the soil, he realized, was not yet ready for such a seed (Ṣā'igh 1964: 82).[37]

During this period in Lebanon, we hear the lone female voice of Madame Manṣūr Shakkūr. In an article in the journal *al-Jinān*, published in 1874, she urged women to seek knowledge not only to prepare themselves for the task of raising a new educated generation, but also to attain a higher status in society (al-Maqdisī 1967: 270). After al-Bustānī, there emerged in Lebanon Jurjī Niqūlā Bāz (1881–1959), whose activities gained him the titles Naṣīr al-Mar'ah (Supporter of Women) and the "Mobile Feminist Encyclopedia" (Ibrāhīm 1966: 12). He espoused the cause of women's rights, particularly education, in his magazine *al-Ḥasna'* (*The Fair Lady*,

1909–1912), which he intended to be "the voice of the feminine renaissance and its monthly platform" (Dāghir 1972: vol. 1, 160). In addition to his journalistic activities, Bāz wrote biographies of some well-known contemporary female figures, among them Miriam Jahshān, Mary 'Ajamī, Mary Yannī, Nāzik al-'Ābid, and Asmā Abī al-Luma'. In his *Iklīl Ghār li-Ra's al-Mar'ah* (*Laurel Wreath on Woman's Head*, 1927), Bāz dealt with the contributions of women to civilization in the fields of science, religion, invention, journalism, nursing, and national and philanthropic efforts. His book *al-Nisā'iyyāt* included articles by contemporary Lebanese, Syrian, and Egyptian women concerning the women's renaissance in the Arab world.

In discussing the position of Lebanese women, we must bear in mind both the similarities and the differences between the Christian and Muslim communities. Christian women did not have to struggle against the veil[38] or total sexual segregation except in extreme cases, although they faced many other obstacles characteristic of the patriarchal society in which they also found themselves. Christian advocates of women's rights therefore tended to concentrate their efforts on issues of a woman's subjugation to male relatives, her right to choose her future husband, and above all her right to equal education. In his book *Khārij al-Ḥarīm* (*Outside the Harem*, 1917), Amīn al-Rīḥānī (1876–1940) dealt with the obstacles that prevented the Arab woman from leading a full life. Elsewhere he summed up his views: "A woman who is forced to love against her will is quiet, obedient, and enduring; she cultivates in herself, her offspring and her nation the seeds of slavery. Therefore, the Eastern woman must first of all free herself, and in accomplishing this glorious goal it is all to the good if she continues to benefit from some or all of her traditional morals" (al-Rīḥānī 1967: 139–140).[39] The first Muslim intellectual to publicly advocate women's emancipation in Lebanon was Muḥammad Jamīl Bayhum. He felt compelled to take this stand as a result of his experiences in the West: "A result of this early direct contact with the West was a conflict between my inherited ideas and acquired criteria on the one hand, and my new observations and what I accidentally heard on the other. When I returned to my country, this conflict made me a carrier of new ideas and an advocate of reformist goals. The most prominent of these was a longing to liberate and educate women, and to prepare them through education to face a coming age which will be different from ours" (Bayhum 1962: 9). Bayhum's first book on this subject was *al-Mar'ah fī al-Tārīkh wa-al-Sharā'i'* (*Women in History and Laws*, 1921). Because this book did not cover any controversial issues concerning women such as the issue of the veil and the political rights of women, not only was it welcomed in the Arab world but it also found admirers among Muslims in other countries, such as India and Afghanistan, where it was translated into Urdu and Pushtu.[40] Pleased at this positive reaction, Bayhum continued to write books dealing with women. He wrote *al-Mar'ah fī al-Tamaddun al-Ḥadīth* (*Women in the New Civilization*) and *Fatāt al-Sharq fī Ḥaḍārat al-Gharb* (*Young Women of the East in Western Culture*, 1952),[41] in which he expanded upon the subject of equality between the sexes. There were, he said, six areas in which equality had to be achieved: human nature (*fiṭrah*), personal freedom, educational opportunity, work, political rights, and social rights (Ṭarabīshī 1980: 85). But Bayhum's efforts on behalf of the cause of Arab women, however sincere, were not remarkable. His moderation, his fondness for history rather than socioeconomic analysis, and his desire to please everybody made his books slip by without provoking controversy.

The case was different with the writings of Naẓirah Zayn al-Dīn (1908–1976),[42] who initiated one of the most dramatic and intense intellectual debates in the history of modern Arab women. In 1928 a very daring (not to mention lengthy) book was published in Beirut. The title was impressive: *Al-Sufūr wa-al-Ḥijāb: Muḥāḍarāt wa-Naẓarāt Marmāhā Taḥrīr al-Mar'ah wa-al-Tajaddud al-Ijtimā'ī fī al-'Ālam al-Islāmī* (*Unveiling and the Veil: Lectures and Outlooks Whose Goal Is Women's Emancipation and Social Renewal in the Islamic World*). The author was twenty-year-old Naẓīrah Zayn al-Dīn.

According to Zayn al-Dīn, what motivated her to write the book was her concern over the misery of the "Eastern Woman" and her realization that the restrictions imposed upon her had no justification in the Islamic religion. Her discontent with existing conditions was sharpened when the Syrian government under the French mandate intervened in 1927 to suppress a newly emerging movement toward unveiling (Zayn al-Dīn 1928: 1). Thus the veil was the main target of her criticism and argumentation. In Zayn al-Dīn's village, veiling was not practiced (44), and her father had allowed her to follow local tradition.

Zayn al-Dīn's book reveals her as a devoted follower of al-Afghānī (47–48, 106–107), Qāsim Amīn (23–24, 42–43, 49–50, 153–154, 168, 267–268), and ʿAbduh (27, 70, 117). She was also inspired by the drastic transformation Mustafa Kemal brought about in Turkey after the First World War, which included, among other things, the widespread abandonment of the veil (7, 22).

Naẓīrah Zayn al-Dīn divided her book into two major sections. The first deals with veiling from three different perspectives: religious, intellectual, and social. The second consists of arguments against advocates of the veil, mainly religious notables, using their own weapons to discredit them.

The veil in Islam, Zayn al-Dīn argued, was a harmful custom inherited from pagan times and with no basis in the teachings of Islam. It also led to corruption, suffering, and moral decay. In those countries where veiling was not practiced, Zayn al-Dīn said, women were able to obtain their rights and work for the advancement of their societies. A nation half of whose members were paralyzed could not "compete, overcome or excel" (33).

Zayn al-Dīn refuted the theory that the imposition of the veil on women was evidence of their inherent frailty. She argued that women were mentally the stronger sex, but men, by virtue of their physical superiority, had been able to subjugate women until women lost their original gift (67–69). She looked at the teachings of Islam in a new light to show that even in those three instances in which the Qur'ān had preferred men to women (inheritance, witness, and polygamy), it was men rather than women who had proven themselves deficient through their greed and aggressiveness (90–94). In a detailed interpretation of the Qur'ānic verses that refer to the veil, Zayn al-Dīn concluded that the full veil (i.e., covering the whole body, including the face) was meant only for the Prophet's wives (*Sūrah* 33:23, 53). Concerning the other two verses (*Sūrahs* 33:59 and 24:30), she said that there was no unanimity among Muslim scholars as to whether the call for covering the body referred also to covering the face and hands (179–215).

Zayn al-Dīn had little respect for the interpreters and commentators on the Qur'ān and the *ḥadīth*. In her opinion, most of them were presumptuous, ignorant of science, and confused: "When I embarked upon preparing my defence of women, I looked into the utterances of interpreters and jurisprudents concerning the subject, and I did not find among them an exclusive unanimity that I could follow on any matter. Rather, whenever I came across a saying, I found other sayings which opposed or contradicted it" (37).[43] Zayn al-Dīn's distrust of the interpreters of the Qur'ān led her to go back to the original sources of Islam (the Qur'ān and the *ḥadīth*) and to try to understand them in the light of reason (*'aql*), a key word in her argument: "In the sayings of our fathers and ancestors there is both right and wrong; there is no way to distinguish between the two except by reason, and reason cannot distinguish except through thinking and free investigation" (50).[44] Zayn al-Dīn used the historical incident in which women pledged allegiance to the Prophet after his conquest of Mecca to show that Muslim women had the right to take part in elections (396–397).

In contrast to Qāsim Amīn, Zayn al-Dīn did not advocate a gradual or postponed abandonment of the veil. She urged the immediate unveiling of women regardless of age or level of education (169–171): "The face is the mirror of the soul. The noble woman works hard to make her soul always pure, and her purity is reflected in her face" (254). Zayn al-Dīn's ideas shocked the religious and conservative circles, and their reaction was one of overwhelming fury. Their first accusation was that Zayn al-Dīn was not capable of writing such a comprehensive book, replete with arguments and documentation from the primary sources of Islam. In fact, they proclaimed, the book must have been written either by her father, the learned Sa'īd Zayn al-Dīn (who had once been the first chief judge of the Lebanese Court of Appeal), or else by a team of "Sunni and Shi'i Muslims, Christians, teachers, lawyers and missionaries."[45]

Unlike the debates that had earlier raged about the question of women's rights, no participant in the battle around Zayn al-Dīn's work ever denied women's right to education. Rather, they denied that the veil was an obstacle to such education, pointing to the veiled Malak Ḥifnī Nāṣif of Egypt to prove their argument (Ḥamdān 1928: 20–21).[46]

The main dispute centered on the objectives and goals of women's education. According to her critics, men and women had separate spheres of life, and neither sex should interfere in the sphere of the other. Women's education should thus be restricted to those areas of learning that had to do with administering households and raising children (Ḥamdān 1928: 21, 61; al-Ghalāyīnī 1928: 104).

Much of the wrath of these critics was not directed against the person of Zayn al-Dīn because her authorship itself was disputed. Rather, they aimed their brickbats at heretics and agents of Western imperialism—in their opinions, the book's real authors. They believed that these parties had written the book in an attempt to undermine Muslim society and thus perpetuate the foreign domination of Muslim countries (al-Ghalāyīnī 1928: 14–20; Ṣabrī 1935: 68).

Zayn al-Dīn never denied that her father had played a role in the writing of the book. She admitted that she had read the first draft of it to him and to another "enlightened shaykh" who had advised her to integrate religious argumentation into her rational discourse because religion and reason were harmonious. Zayn al-Dīn refused to be intimidated by the avalanche of books, pamphlets, and articles that criticized and sometimes ridiculed her views.[47] In the following year she wrote another lengthy work, *al-Fatāh wa-al-Shuyūkh: Naẓarāt wa-Munāẓarāt fī al-Sufūr wa-al-Ḥijāb* (*The Young Woman and the Religious Elders: An Outline and Discussion of Unveiling and the Veil*, 1929), in which she reinforced her earlier attitude toward the veil and related issues. The book consisted of three parts. In the first part she argued with some of her critics; in the second, she quoted favorable reviews of her first book; and in the third, she refuted the arguments of her opponents, as represented by the writing of Shaykh al-Ghalāyīnī. She also repeated her claim to sole authorship of the first book.

Zayn al-Dīn strongly believed that women had not only the right, but even the exclusive right, to interpret those Qur'ānic verses in which women were addressed, especially because men misinterpreted them for selfish reasons (Zayn al-Dīn 1929: vol. 3, 126). Like her predecessor Qāsim Amīn, Zayn al-Dīn reaffirmed that what she meant by unveiling was only the uncovering of the face and hands, or abiding by *al-ḥijāb al-sharʿī* ("the legal veil"). Zayn al-Dīn's two books stirred public opinion not only in the Arab world,[48] but also in Arab communities in North[49] and South America.[50]

In Syria the situation was less volatile than in Egypt or

Lebanon. We search in vain for counterparts of Egypt's Qāsim Amīn and Malak Ḥifnī Nāṣif or to Lebanon's Jurjī Niqūlā Bāz, Muḥammad Jamīl Bayhum or Zayn al-Dīn. The role of Syrian feminists and antifeminists seems to have been merely to react to what was taking place elsewhere. We do find some minor figures who contributed to the cause of women insofar as they favored education for them. These figures, however, limited themselves mostly to saying that women should be taught reading, writing, elementary mathematics, and geography, and they justified this as a means of producing better wives and mothers. Muḥammad Kurd 'Alī (1876–1953), one such figure, was not particularly enthusiastic about allowing women to take part in public life.[51] Whereas some poets in Syria called for discarding the veil,[52] others defended it.[53]

In Tunisia, however, Qāsim Amīn's denunciation of the veil found a devoted follower in al-Ṭāhir al-Ḥaddād (1899–1935), as reflected in his book *Imra'atunā fī al-Sharī'ah wa-al-Mujtama'* (*The Status of Our Women as Reflected in Law and Society*, 1930). Like Qāsim Amīn, al-Ḥaddād argued that Islam encouraged education for both sexes (al-Ḥaddād 1972: 201) and that women should be allowed to learn a skill or a profession to support themselves and their families (208). In discussing the Qur'ānic verses about women, al-Ḥaddād claimed that the references therein were not intended to be immutable but were intended for women in the Prophet's time alone. They could be reinterpreted in the light of modern needs, without violating the essence of Islam. He pointed out that the abolition of slavery, for example, though not ordered in the Qur'ān, had not affected its basic teachings (40). Al-Ḥaddād insisted that marriage was the business of a man and his wife and that divorce was a matter for the state to govern through the judiciary (138–141). He devoted one chapter to the veil and another to unveiling. The veil, al-Ḥaddād believed, was incompatible with the principle of giving the couple the chance to get to know each other before marriage. It also led to segregation of the sexes, to seclusion of women, and to men abandoning their homes to seek entertainment in public places. Furthermore, it held women back from the most basic education, without which they could not run their households. Al-Ḥaddād held the veil responsible for the deteriorating health of children, because they ended up imprisoned like their mothers (182–187). It is obvious that al-Ḥaddād borrowed most of his arguments from Qāsim Amīn. In doing so, he had a remarkable impact on North Africa,[54] even though his contribution to the cause of women in the rest of the Arab world was decidedly minimal.

Thus we see that the first area in which the women's movement actually bore fruit was education, although this was due more to men's personal and nationalist concerns than to the acceptance of truly feminist philosophy. No major figure in the modern era actually opposed education for women; the dispute centered on the nature of the education and the ends to which it should be directed. Even al-Ṭahṭāwī, al-Sayyid, and Bayhum agreed, although each for his own reasons, that women's education should be limited to certain areas, and that the ultimate goal should be either to produce better mothers to create a strong nation or better wives to create happy marriages.

Yet even a primary level of education was not easily attained, especially in the first stages of the Arab renaissance. The story of the first professional school for girls in Egypt is a remarkable example. In 1830, the Frenchman Dr. Clot Bey persuaded Muḥammad 'Alī to establish a special school for midwives to improve the health conditions and to reduce the high infant mortality rate. By 1832 not one single father in all Egypt had agreed to send his daughter to this school in spite of the attractive benefits of free tuition, lodging, and clothing. Faced with no alternative, Muḥammad 'Alī turned to his military units, urging them to enroll their daughters or else pay a penalty. They unanimously chose to pay as the lesser of two evils. Dr. Bey succeeded in recruiting eunuchs and ten slave girls, but this experiment failed within two years. He was finally forced to seek his trainees only in orphanages or from among young female slaves.[55]

The successful establishment of girls' schools in Egypt was achieved, in fact, by Western missionaries. The first school was set up by French nuns of the Order of Bon Pasteur (1844), followed by the American Mission School (1856), and the sisters of the Italian Franciscan Order (1873); all of these were established in Cairo (Taymūr 1952: 49). Most of the female students in the missionary schools were Copts,[56] because, for religious and cultural reasons, Muslims hesitated to take advantage of the opportunity (Cooper 1914: 165–166).[57]

Finally in 1873, al-Ṭahṭāwī, in his capacity as an influential member of the Schools Bureau, persuaded Khedive Ismā'īl (r.

1863–1879) to establish the first government girls' school, al-Madrasah al-Saniyyah. Ismā'īl's wife Jashmah Āfat took upon herself all the costs of the school. Its curriculum included reading and writing, basic mathematics, handicrafts and housekeeping (A. Shafīq 1934: 49). The school started with 200 female students, the number of enrollees doubling the following year (D. Shafīq 1955: 84). Other schools followed, but they offered girls only primary education; finally, in 1925, female students were allowed to pursue secondary studies (Woodsmall 1936: 176).[58] The goal of university education for women was achieved in 1928, when the Egyptian University in Cairo officially opened its doors to women. Six female students were admitted to the School of Medicine that year, and in 1929 more women were admitted to the School of Humanities.[59]

Women in Greater Syria, especially Lebanon, faced more favorable educational conditions after the turn of the century. European powers, having demanded special privileges from the Ottoman Empire, proceeded to compete with each other in establishing schools for boys and girls even in the most remote corners of the country. By World War I, the number of schools exceeded 1,300 (Ṭūbī 1966: 21).[60] A great many Muslim girls attended them because they were boarding schools and were strict about segregation of the sexes. The initial reaction of the Ottoman Empire to this cultural threat was to establish Qur'ānic schools (*katātīb*) in which religion and Arabic were taught. Separate schools of this type were also established for girls (Ṭūbī 1966: 20). When the Ottoman Constitution was proclaimed, it recognized the right of girls to primary education. The first regular primary schools for girls in Greater Syria were established in 1908. Missionary schools flourished during the French and British mandates, a phenomenon that disturbed the nationalist and Muslim religious circles and provoked them also to involve themselves in establishing indigenous schools for both sexes.

In Syria proper (excluding Lebanon, Jordan, and Palestine), in 1922, only three female students were admitted to Damascus University. In 1946–1947 this number reached forty-nine. By 1973–1974, 20.8 percent of the student body was female (al-Razzāz 1975: 27). Syria, like Egypt, still faces a persistent problem of illiteracy; in 1960 the illiteracy rate among both men and women was 82 percent (30).

Under Ottoman rule, Iraqi women had been deprived of the

right to education except in a few cases when they had the chance to attend the *Katātīb* or a non-Muslim community school. In 1899 the first official primary school for girls was established in Baghdad by the Ottoman ruler Wāmiq Pasha (Dāwūd 1958: 45). In 1918 an Iraqi woman, Zahrah Khiḍr, undertook the task of establishing a private school for girls (48). *Dār al-Mu'allimāt* (Female Teacher's Seminary), established in 1928, was a giant step in advancing women's education. Its alumnæ include a good number of women writers and activitists, including Nāzik al-Malā'ikah (b. 1923) and Lamī'ah 'Abbās 'Amārah (b. 1929).

The relative increase in education acquired by Egyptian women, their gradually developing consciousness of their collective power, and the political turbulence that eased some of the restrictions imposed on them, all contributed to the emergence of women's societies and organizations. The pioneers of feminist activism belonged to the urban upper and middle classes. These women were the first to benefit from the newly established educational institutes and to have the freedom to pursue their studies abroad, especially in Europe.

The year 1919 was a landmark not only in the national history of Egypt but also in the development of political and social awareness within the women's movement.[61] In that year, only three days after the end of World War I, an Egyptian delegation, led by Sa'd Zaghlūl, went to the British Resident demanding immediate independence for Egypt and the right to present their demands at the Paris peace talks. The British were unwilling even to listen to the idea and responded by forcing Sa'd Zaghlūl and his colleagues into exile. The Egyptian public reaction was overwhelming. Disregarding their different social, religious, and political affiliations, the Egyptian people exploded into violent demonstrations throughout 1919.

At the same time, women decided they would also demonstrate, in spite of all male objections. This led to the unprecedented scene of a thousand veiled women gathering and attempting to march through the streets of Cairo in protest. The British soldiers interfered and forced them to disperse. Among the organizers of women's demonstrations was a dynamic and tireless figure, Hudā Sha'rāwī (1879–1949), who was to play a major role in women's struggle for social and political equality. Her father was Muḥammad Sulṭān Pasha, the president of the First Chamber in

Egypt, who had disassociated himself from 'Urābī's movement in 1882 and had consequently been the one who governed Egypt during Khedive Tawfīq's brief absence. Sha'rāwī was educated at home by special tutors in various disciplines including music and languages (Arabic, French, and Turkish). Her father died when she was thirteen and she was forced by tradition to marry her wealthy cousin and legal guardian, 'Alī Sha'rāwī, who was already married and had several children. After her husband's death in 1922, Hudā Sha'rāwī had the leisure and financial resources to devote her entire life to the cause of women's emancipation. She had not been passive in the traditional manner even before this; during her husband's life she had sometimes left home without his consent to lead the women's demonstrations.[62]

On March 16, 1923, Hudā Sha'rāwī called a group of activist women together in her home for a meeting. This meeting resulted in the founding of the first nationwide feminist union in the country, al-Ittiḥād al-Nisā' al-Miṣrī (The Egyptian Feminist Union), with Sha'rāwī as its president. The union immediately affiliated itself with the International Alliance for Women's Suffrage.[63]

To help accomplish its aims, the Egyptian Feminist Union started the fortnightly periodical *L'Egyptienne* in 1925. It was directed and edited by Sīzā Nabarāwī, the union's secretary and a close friend of Sha'rāwī. This was followed in 1937 by the Arabic fortnightly *al-Miṣriyyah* (*The Egyptian Woman*), edited first by Fāṭimah Ni'mat Rāshid, then by Hudā Sha'rāwī, and later by Īvā Ḥabīb al-Miṣrī. Both magazines were forced to discontinue publication after a short time due to lack of public support; however, in its time, the union was able to recruit some leading men of letters, including Ṭāhā Ḥusayn (1889–1973) and Muḥammad Ḥusayn Haykal (1888–1956), to act as its legal advisers (*Taqrīr* 1951: 6). The activities of the Egyptian Feminist Union extended beyond the borders of Egypt. After the League of Nations decided to discuss the question of Palestine, the union's president, Hudā Sha'rāwī, invited women of other Arab states to convene in Cairo to discuss the Palestine problem. The resulting conference, in which delegates of seven Arab states took part, was held on October 15, 1938. Another Arab women's conference was held in Cairo in 1944 to discuss the social, economic, and political condition of Arab women. The outcome of this conference was the founding of an

Arab Feminist Union, of which Sha'rāwī was also elected president (Arafa 1973: 24).

Hudā Sha'rāwī gained her fame not only as a founder and president of women's organizations but also as a leader in the movement to discard the veil in Egypt. In 1923, she headed an Egyptian women's delegation to an International Women's Conference in Rome. As her ship drew into port in Alexandria, she took off the veil covering her face. Sha'rāwī's secretary, Sīzā Nabarāwī, and other members of the Feminist Union immediately imitated this dramatic and courageous act. Unfortunately, the gesture failed to attract as much attention as intended because at the same time that Hudā Sha'rāwī's followers had arrived at the port of Alexandria, the Egyptian masses who had gathered were not paying attention as they had turned to welcome their leader, Sa'd Zaghlūl.[64] Nevertheless Sha'rāwī's daring act had its repercussions and was later imitated by other upper- and middle-class women.

Sa'd Zaghlūl also sympathized with the movement to discard the veil. During the 1919 Revolution women were continuously coming to Zaghlūl's house to nurse those wounded in the clashes between the Egyptians and the British. Zaghlūl suggested the formation of a women's committee among the supporters of his political party, al-Wafd. The Cairo committee was headed by Sharīfah Riyāḍ, and Hudā Sha'rāwī was a member of it ('Abd al-Bāqī 1977: 273, Shafīq 1955: 129). Zaghlūl's wife Ṣafiyyah served as honorary president of the nationwide women's Wafd committee, which remained active until the 1952 revolution, when all parties were dissolved. Zaghlūl himself, on several occasions, urged female participants at his political gatherings to discard the veil. At one such meeting, he took the initiative and with his own hand lifted the veil of one of the women present. The rest of the women attending quickly followed suit and removed the veils covering their own faces (Al-Jawharī and Khayyāl 1980: 241).[65]

Despite the significant role Egyptian women had played in the political turmoil of 1919, they were denied both the vote and membership in political parties. Hudā Sha'rāwī tried to avoid this issue by claiming that the vote was still a premature demand (Kaḥḥālah 1977: vol. 1, 89). But in 1942 her friend Fāṭimah Ni'mat Rāshid founded a party exclusively for women: al-Ḥizb al-Nisā'i al-Qawmī (The National Feminist Party). This party not only reiterated all the earlier demands of women but also added a new one: the demand for political rights. The early dissolution of this party led another feminist activist, Durriyyah Shafīq, in 1949 to form a more vocal one called Ḥizb Bint al-Nīl (The Nile Daughter's Party). Shafīq published a magazine, *Bint al-Nīl* (*Daughter of the Nile*), in Arabic and French, as well as a children's magazine called *al-Bulbul* (*The Nightingale*). This party demanded the abolition of polygamy, the adoption of European divorce laws, and the right of women to vote and to be elected to parliament (Khamīs 1978: 87). In 1951, Shafīq's party marched on the parliament with some members of the Feminist Union and a number of young men in a demonstration demanding equal rights for women. A few days later the same party organized another demonstration in front of the ʿĀbdīn Palace and presented to the king a petition bearing their demands, written in blood (Khamīs 1978: 91).

However, Egyptian women had to wait until 1956 to be granted any constitutional political rights. In 1957 two women were elected to parliament.[66] From that point on Egyptian women began on a small scale to exercise their right to vote and to hold office. In 1962, for the first time in modern Egyptian history, a woman, Dr. Ḥikmat Abū Zayd,[67] was appointed minister of social affairs. The National Charter of May 1962 proclaimed the equality of men and women: "Woman must be regarded as equal to man and must therefore shed the remaining shackles that impede her free movement so that she may take a constructive and profound part in shaping life."[68] In Lebanon, it was Christian women who first founded feminist charitable organizations. As early as 1880, Emily Sursuq founded the Jamʿiyyat al-Banafsajah (The Violet Society) to help the needy. Some months later she established a school for orphan girls (Ibrāhīm 1966: 26; Ṣa'igh 1964: 85–86).[69] Such societies took their inspiration mainly from the charitable activities of communities of nuns from various religious orders. Muslims soon followed the Christian lead; shortly before World War I the Turkish governor of Beirut, ʿAẓmī Bey, founded Nādī al-Fatayāt al-Muslimāt (The Muslim Women's Club) to promote educational and cultural activities among Muslim women. These included teaching Arabic, French, and music. The club's monthly cultural programs were attended by men as well as women, in the same hall but separated by an aisle.[70]

Most of the women's societies were organized on a religious basis; for example, al-Jamʿiyyah al-Masīḥiyyah li-al-Shābbāt (The

Young Women's Christian Association) founded in 1920 (Ibrāhīm 1966: 29), Jam'iyyat al-Shābbāt al-Muslimāt (The Association of Young Muslim Women) founded in 1948 (55), and Jam'iyyat Nahḍat al-Mar'ah al-Durziyyah (The Association for the Awakening of Druze Women) founded in 1962 (73), each representing one of the three major religions in Lebanon. Over twenty-three such women's societies from both Lebanon and Syria held a meeting in 1928 to found an umbrella organization, al-Ittiḥād al-Nisā'i al-Sūrī al-Lubnānī (The Syro-Lebanese Feminist Union), headed by Labībah Thābit (Ṣā'igh 1964: 150–151).[71]

Another umbrella organization was founded in Lebanon in 1943, Jāmi'at Nisā' Lubnān (The League of Lebanese Women). This association, headed by Najlā' Ṣa'b, played an active role in the events that led to Lebanon's independence including holding political meetings and demonstrations. In 1950, after independence, it elected an executive committee to work to guarantee women's political rights in the country. This committee presented to the newly elected president a petition demanding political equality for women as well as the right to hold public positions. In 1953 Lebanese women won the unrestricted right to vote.[72]

Most of the early women's associations were active in both Syria and Lebanon. The Syro-Lebanese Feminist Union had branches in Beirut, Damascus, Tripoli, Ḥamāh, and Zaḥlah. In July 1930, the union held a conference in which women from India, Iraq, Turkey, Iran, and the Arabian Peninsula, as well as women of Lebanon and Syria, took part. At this conference it was decided that women should have the right to work side by side with men, that prospective spouses should be allowed to get to know each other before commitment to marriage, that domestic industries should be encouraged, that Arabic literature should be revived, that girls should receive compulsory primary education, and that the Arab world should work toward a unified culture (Kaḥḥālah 1977: vol. 1, 120–121).

Women's organizations in Syria proper included al-Nādī al-Adabī al-Nisā'ī (The Women's Literary Club, 1920),[73] Dawḥat al-Adab (The Tree of Literature, c. 1928), Ittiḥād al-Jam'iyyāt al-Nisā'iyyah (The Union of Feminist Associations, 1944) (al-Razzāz 1975: 124–126). These Syrian groups held in common certain goals, among them education for women, the preservation of the national identity by resisting the "negative" aspects of Westernization, the protection of native manufacturers, and the raising of women's consciousness. By 1965 the number of such women's organizations in Syria had reached fifty, most of them located in Damascus (127–128).

Syrian women involved themselves in politics more than did their Lebanese counterparts. Syrian women took part in the resistance to French rule in 1921 (it is recorded that at least one woman was killed in 1921 and at least ninety-five women were killed in the 1925 clashes between the French and the Druze) (152–153). While the Franco-Syrian Treaty was being presented in the Syrian parliament in November 1934, a crowd of veiled Muslim women marched to the parliament building to protest it. The treaty was later withdrawn (Woodsmall 1936: 363).

The women of Iraq advanced more slowly in terms of organizing themselves and participating in public life. The largest women's organization there was the one founded in Baghdad in the 1930s, Nādī al-Nahḍah al-Nisā'iyyah (The Club for the Awakening of Women). It had about sixty members, all of them upper-class women. Among other things, it established an orphanage, a school, and a library for poor girls (Kaḥḥālah 1977: vol. 1, 122).[74]

In 1951 al-Ittiḥād al-Nisā'i al-'Irāqī (The Iraqi Feminist Union) presented a petition to the government demanding changes in the constitution to guarantee women their rights (al-Darbandī 1968: vol. 2, 253–254). It was not until 1958 that Premier Nūrī al-Sa'īd raised the issue of reforms that were needed in Iraq, among them granting women a restricted right to vote (Dāwūd 1958: 235).

By and large, Arab feminists came from the urban upper and middle classes, and the rights they demanded were determined by their own interests. The particular needs of women in the rural and desert areas were totally ignored. To illustrate this point one need only recall the bitter and prolonged battle around the veil, on which so much ink and intellectual energy was expended. To nonurban women (who were, and still are, a majority among Arab women) this battle was merely academic. Veiling had never been practiced outside the cities, but not even the staunchest advocates of the veil had claimed that rural women were violating a sacred principle of Islam. Some of the nationalist movements seized upon the veil, which some considered a symbol of the subjugation and degradation of women, and tried to make it a symbol of national independence and a shield against Western cultural penetration.

This gave the veiling dispute a nationalist dimension in addition to its religious one, adding fuel to a raging fire.[75]

In most Arab countries an impressive cadre of women professionals has emerged, holding key positions in public life. At least five Arab states, (Egypt, Syria, Iraq, Jordan, and Tunisia) have or have had women cabinet members. The issue of women's education remains controversial, however, with some still insisting that women's education be restricted to specific areas. Women have essentially won the battle for education in the Arab world today, but progress in other areas is still being held up by conservative elements of the societies, and the process of women's emancipation is far from complete.

In the twentieth century, the earliest advocates of women's emancipation were men, especially Qāsim Amīn, who emerges as a central figure in this arena. These men were not usually motivated by concern for women's rights *per se.* They pressed for reforms in the status of women because they felt that these reforms would strengthen Arab society at a time when it was under attack from the West. In this respect, nationalism was beneficial to feminism, although later it sometimes became a hindrance because conservatives claimed that antifeminist practices such as veiling were signs of national identity. Though the Islamic religion granted women a number of rights, and supporters of women have been able to quote these to their advantage, it has often been interpreted by traditionalists in such a way as to constitute another obstacle.

The battle itself has revolved around two major issues. One is the veil, which has been considered an important symbol by both sides. The other is education, whose importance is real as well as symbolic. Early advocates of women's emancipation realized that education was necessary to create a generation of women able to articulate the reforms they wanted and to fight for those reforms, and that any reforms achieved without education for women would be useless.

The first generation of modern Arab women writers both resulted from and responded to the military and colonial pressure of the West with their attendant cultural, including intellectual, hegemony. Growing awareness of feminist debates in the West (where middle- and upper-class women, were fighting for similar rights, in some cases less successfully) sparked a new reflectivity about and dialogue on the situation of women. Women (and men) now pursued this "discussion" in works of fiction as well as nonfiction, in poetry and in prose, as in their more traditional creative resources—music and oral literature.

2. The Pioneering Generation

Some Arab scholars[1] have not been satisfied with the usual explanation for the scarcity of surviving women's poetry in Arabic literature from the pre-Islamic period; that is, that most of this poetry has simply been lost.[2] But for the whole pre-Islamic literary period (almost two centuries) the only major female literary figure was al-Khansā' (c. 600–670).[3] The project of gathering together the pre-Islamic poetry and writing it down began only in the eighth century, and masterpieces collected (the *Mu'allaqāt*, for example) were exclusively those of men. Such anthologies as Ibn Sallām's al-Jumaḥī's *Ṭabaqāt al-Shu'arā'*, al-Mufaḍḍal al-Ḍabbī's *al-Mufaḍḍaliyyāt*, al-Marzubānī's *Mu'jam al-Shu'arā'*, Abū Tammām's *al-Ḥamāsah*, and al-Buḥturī's *al-Ḥamāsah* included only a few selections of women's poetry. Some anthologies were devoted exclusively to women's poetry, a few of which were mentioned in Ibn al-Nadīm's *al-Fihrist*, but much of this material has been lost. One of these anthologies was al-Marzubānī's *Ash'ar al-Nisā'*, of which only one-tenth has survived. Yet this surviving portion includes biographies of thirty-eight women poets, most of whom are not mentioned in other sources. Still, these facts do not satisfy some scholars of Arabic literature as an explanation for the general lack of women's poetry. These scholars maintain, rather, that the first collectors of pre-Islamic poetry were looking for certain qualities, which they found only in men's poetry. These qualities included abstruse poetic diction, a wide variety of subject matter within the same poem, and frequent references to historical events (al-Ḥūfī 1963: 604–605). They further maintain that those early collectors who undertook the project of gathering and writing down the pre-Islamic poetry in the eighth century were influenced too much by the inferior status of women in their own era and were thus reluctant to record women's poetry from the pre-Islamic period (605).

We do know that the main field in which the women of the *Jāhiliyyah* demonstrated their poetic gifts was elegy[4]—so much so that it came to be considered their special domain. Arabs trained their daughters to excel in it, in some cases by having them practice composing elegies upon their still living fathers (Bayhum 1962: 64). Even in its special province, the poetry of women exalted "manly" traits such as courage in the battlefield, leadership, and generosity. Even in elegies addressed to sons and husbands, there was an astonishing lack of intimate motherly love or conjugal passion. Men were characterized by endurance and determination to overcome or withstand the tragedy of death, whereas women were depicted as self-pitying, helpless, and appealing to males for succor. But even in their field of "speciality," male poets were favored by the critics. Al-Jumaḥī, for instance, put al-Khansā' in second place succeeding a male poet (al-Mutammim ibn Nuwayrah) among poets of elegy (al-Jumaḥī n.d.: 48).

Though the magnitude and value of the female contribution to Arabic literature varied with time and has been assessed differently over time, that contribution was never entirely absent, from the *Jāhiliyyah* to the fall of the Abbasid dynasty (1258 C.E.)—a fact that, as we will see in this chapter, drew the attention of some figures in the pioneering generation and inspired them to follow in their footsteps. One thing that was more or less consistently true was that women writers, to gain recognition, had to adjust to literary norms and standards established by men. For example, the works of al-Khansā' were evaluated by all literary critics according to the criteria set up by *al-Shu'arā' al-Fuḥūl*, the (male) master poets. It is significant that the word for literary excellence (*fuḥūlah*) was derived from *faḥl*, which originally meant a sexually superior male. The poet Bashshār ibn Burd (714–784) noted masculine qualities in al-Khansā''s poetry. When he stated that no woman wrote poetry without a trace of weakness, he was asked whether his judgment fit al-Khansā'. Bashshār replied: "that [woman] defeated the [male] master poets (*fuḥūl*); she had four testicles" (al-Ḥūfī 1963: 687).

This term, *fuḥūlah*, which has been used throughtout the history of Arabic literature, was singled out as a target by the Iraqi female Nāzik al-Malā'ikah in her fierce attack on the Arabic language and on the inferior status of women in general. Al-Malā'ikah denounced Arabic as a sexist language that belittled women in its vocabulary and grammar (1953: 2–3).[5]

After the advent of Islam in the seventh century, women continued to contribute to Arabic letters, mainly in the sphere of poetry, with varying degrees of artistic accomplishment. In the following centuries a number of gifted female poets emerged, but they did not always receive the credit they deserved. Laylā al-Akhyaliyyah (d. c. 700), for instance, was not included in any category of Muslim poets in al-Jumaḥī's *Ṭabaqāt al-Shu'arā'*, although the author admitted that al-Akhyaliyyah, known for her love poetry, was superior to al-Nābighah al-Ji'dī who was ranked third (al-Jumaḥī n.d.). Al-Aṣma'ī, too, preferred al-Akhyaliyyah to al-Ji'dī (al-Aṣma'ī 1971: 17).[6]

As we have seen in Chapter One, one of the most important features of the Arab *al-Nahḍah* (the Arabs' renaissance), which most scholars date back to the nineteenth century (although it became more vigorous in the following century) was the realization of the need to transmit knowledge by means of education. This awareness, initiated by the male figures of the renaissance, very soon began to entail rethinking the educational status of women in Arab society and realizing the necessity to include them in the pursuit of knowledge. But even such an enlightened intellectual as the Lebanese Buṭrus al-Bustānī did not forget to qualify his views regarding the very nature of women's education and the necessity to confine it. Women, al-Bustānī said in a lecture given in 1849, are entitled to learn all disciplines needed to enable them better to carry out their duties as individuals as well as members in the society. Among these disciplines, al-Bustānī singled out one to highlight and discuss: writing. He referred to writing as a noble craft (*ṣinā'ah sharīfah*) and argued its significance for women, even if some of them may have misused this medium. Having advocated the cause of Arab women brilliantly throughout that lecture, al-Bustānī paused to reassure his male audience and warn women at the same time: "Before concluding this discussion I would like to say a word to the cultured woman: being such a useful and important member in the world and society does not need to let woman fall into the plight of vanity and pride or lead her to feel superior to her man even if she is more knowledgeable than he, since nonessentials do not nullify the intrinsic" (1950: 20–21). The Egyptian al-Ṭahtāwī, too, was cautious in his call to let women have access to education, maintaining that they had to preserve, in the process, their "feminine modesty" (*ḥayā'*): "The *ḥayā'* is a praiseworthy trait in them, and it is appropriate for those who educate girls and take care of their affairs to leave their *ḥayā'* unchanged since it is their ornament" (1872: 49). Knowledge at the hand of women was largely perceived to be a threat to the moral order of the Arab patriarchal society in the nineteenth century. Henry H. Jessup, an American missionary who spent fifty-three years working in the field of education in Lebanon, noted that "the mass of Mohammedans [sic] are nervously afraid of entrusting the knowledge of reading and writing to their wives and daughters, lest they abuse it by writing clandestine letters to improper persons" (Jessup 1873: 17). Another missionary educator from the same period makes a more comprehensive statement that could be, I believe, applied to many Arab Muslims and Christians: "It is considered a disgrace for a female to know how to read and write, and a serious obstacle to her marriage, which is the principal object of the parents' heart" (1873: 129).

In the latter part of the nineteenth century, however, women's voices began to be heard. Their literary activities were concentrated in three areas: women's societies, journalism, and literary salons. The concentration of Arab women upon these fields reflects their awareness of the need to work collectively to achieve their objectives and a recognition that individual efforts could not bear fruit in a sexually segregated society. These were attempts to open channels to the mainstream culture dominated by men. Instead of venturing into the public world of men, pioneering Arab women devised means by which they brought men into their private domain.

Literary Societies

Alongside the many women's societies with practical philanthropic objectives, as we have seen in Chapter One, emerged literary societies concerned with women's intellectual well-being. One such literary association was founded in 1880 in Beirut, by the Lebanese writer Maryam Nimr Makāriyūs (1860–1888).[7] Called Bākūrat Sūriyā (The Dawn of Syria), it held lectures on social issues and conducted literary discussions.[8] In the same year another association, Jam'iyyat Zahrat al-Iḥsān (The Flower of Charity Association), was founded by some educated women from the Christian Orthodox community in Beirut. Its declared aim was to educate girls and raise their moral standards (Zaydan n.d.: 72). The Muslim women of Beirut had to wait until 1914 to witness the founding of their own association Jam'iyyat Yaqẓat al-Fatāh al-'Arabiyyah (The Association of the Arab Woman Awakening), which worked for the promotion of education among women (Zaydān n.d.: 73). In Syria, a women's association called Nūr al-'Afāf (The Light of Virtue) was founded in 1898 in Ḥims. It gave priority to cultural affairs and literary matters (Kaḥḥālah 1979: vol. 1, 116).

More societies were established after World War I, among them al-Nādī al-Adabī al-Nisā'ī (The Women's Literary Club) in Damascus, established in 1920 by Mary 'Ajamī (1888–1965) and Nāzik al-'Ābid Bayhum (1887–1960) (Kaḥḥālah 1979: vol. 1, 118), the wife of Muḥammad Bayhum. This club was aimed at strengthening the relationships among women by holding public meetings and giving its members a platform from which to give lectures. One of its achievements was the establishment of a public library for women (al-Razzāz 1975: 132). In 1928 a group of educated women gathered at the Bayhums' house in Beirut to elect the executive committee of another women's literary club intended to advance cultural standards among women (Kaḥḥālah 1979: vol. 1, 118).[9]

In 1942 al-Nadwah al-Thaqāfiyyah (The Cultural Club) was founded in Damascus. Its goals were to improve the social and cultural condition of women and to increase their involvement in the arts. This long-lived club is still active and has maintained an annual cultural season since 1950, during which lectures are given by individuals of both sexes.

JOURNALS

The tradition of Arab women's journalism started with Hind Nawfal of Lebanon, who established the monthly *al-Fatāh* (1892) in Alexandria. Hind Nawfal came from a family with a history of involvement in journalism and translation: her father and uncle worked in these fields for the Egyptian government (Khalīfah 1973: 36). In her editorial in the first issue of *al-Fatāh*, Nawfal announced that the journal would follow the example of publications in the West and urged her readers to look upon journalism as a respectable occupation. She recommended *al-Fatāh* to her female readers as the only journal that would advocate for them and asked for their editorial participation, because "it would not reduce their value as women nor ruin their virtue." She pointed out that "some of the most learned and cultured women in the West... are editors of newspapers" (39). Hind Nawfal discussed these women further and gave interesting statistics about them. The number of French women engaged in writing, she said, included 121 novelists, 217 textbook writers, 280 poets, 425 essayists, 32 playwrights, and 237 journalists (39–40).

From the very beginning, Nawfal's journal, like most women's periodicals to follow, avoided political and religious issues and focused instead on defending women and on discussing their role in history and their achievements in modern times. It taught home economics, child rearing, and the arts of sewing, embroidery, and drawing (38).

The field of women's journalism, begun with *al-Fatāh*, has grown impressively. Between 1892 and the present day the number of women's journals established in Egypt alone (even excluding the local journals of schools and the newsletters of feminist organizations) is at least fifty.[10]

The pioneers of women's journalism in Egypt were non-Muslims and non-Egyptians who had some exposure to Western culture and either had a family background in journalism (as with Hind Nawfal) or else enjoyed a great deal of personal freedom and political immunity (as with Alexandra Avierinoh, who held Italian citizenship). A large number of these journals published in Egypt were established by Lebanese women, including *al-Fatāh*, *Anīs al-Jalīs*, *al-ʿĀʾilah*, *al-Marʾah*, *al-Saʿādah*, *al-Zahrah*, *Majallat al-Sayyidāt wa-al-Banāt*, *Fatāt al-Sharq*, *al-Jins al-Laṭīf*, *al-Aʿmāl al-*

Yadawiyyah, and *Rūz al-Yūsuf*. One reason so many Lebanese published in Egypt rather than in their own land was that Egypt, in the first half of this century, was the center of Arab intellectual life and the Arab press, as well as being the center of distribution for many established publications. This, combined with relative political tolerance and the large population and consequent relatively large number of potential readers, made Egypt, and especially Cairo, the ideal center for publishing.[11]

These pioneers, many of whom were Lebanese Christians who had emigrated to Egypt along with their families due to economic, political, and religious factors in the early 1860s, faced a number of problems in the implementation of their philosophy. Because of the high rate of illiteracy among the Egyptian women,[12] women's journals had to adapt their approach and content to the fact that a significant proportion of their readership was composed of conservative men. Furthermore, these journals had to go through men's censorship in the household before reaching women, and in many cases men were the ones who read them to the illiterate women (Khalīfah 1973: 38). This prevented women's journals from directly tackling controversial issues such as the conflict between men's interpretation of Islam and women's aspirations or the role of women in public life. Instead, they focused on the need for female education, on domestic affairs, handicrafts, fashion, hygiene, and entertainment. Because their circulation was limited, they were often forced to rely financially on advertising and on government subsidies.[13] Despite these handicaps, the pioneering journals served both as a platform for women to voice their opinions and as a training ground where they learned to express themselves more effectively. As early as 1898, Labībah Sham'ūn issued an appeal in *Anīs al-Jalīs* for the right of women to participate in literary culture: "We do not demand that woman become a partner of the blacksmith and the carpenter, or a commander of navies or a governor of states and nations. Rather, we want her to learn the arts that she can absorb and from which she can benefit. Therefore what harm is there if she is both a poet and a scientist?" (Khalīfah 1973: 26). Because of the spread of educational opportunities for Egyptian women,[14] they were able to follow the Syro-Lebanese women's lead and found journals of their own. They began to cover a wider range of subjects, and their tone became more daring. The first Egyptian woman to enter this field was Jamīlah Ḥāfiẓ who published her short-lived journal *al-Rayḥānah* in Ḥilwān, near Cairo, in 1907. The tone of the journal was highly political, advocating the policy of "Egypt belongs to its people," a slogan that became very powerful in Egypt in the following decade. The political orientation of this journal, which deprived it of any financial support from the government and evoked a low response on the part of the female audience, led to its early closure.

The tendency to establish journals to promote certain political, social, and religious causes advocated by parties or organizations became more prevalent in Egypt between the 1920s and 1940s. One of the most outspoken women against the British presence in Egypt, who devoted much energy and time to recruiting women from the popular quarters of Cairo against the British between 1919 and 1923, was Labībah Aḥmad (d. 1951), the founder of the monthly *al-Nahḍah al-Nisā'iyyah* (Khalīfah 1973: 65). This journal became the organ of *Jam'iyyat Nahḍat al-Sayyidāt al-Miṣriyyāt* (The Association of the Egyptian Women's Awakening), which preached freedom, fraternity, and equality and called for the improvement of conditions of the Egyptian family and women's schools and for raising women's moral and religious standards (al-Subkī 1986: 107–109). Later, this journal became closely associated with the religious political party the Muslim Brethren. A totally different platform with largely secular doctrine was Munīrah Thābit's *al-Amal,* which included among its declared objectives, not only granting women the right to vote and the right to be elected to parliament, but also the independence of Egypt along the principles of the *Wafd* party (110–112). To counter the *Wafdi* publication, Tafidah 'Allām launched her monthly *Ummahāt al-Mustaqbal,* defending the policy of Ismā'īl Ṣidqī who was then the prime minister of Egypt and the archenemy of the *Wafd.* The Egyptian Feminist Union, in an attempt to propagate its principles through the press, chose to launch in 1925 its first organ, *L'Egyptienne* in French. Only in 1937 did the union find it proper to publish its Arabic-language organ *al-Miṣriyyah.* In one interesting case, a woman's journal proved to be ideologically solid enough to form an association which eventually become a political party. In 1945 Durriyyah Shafiq founded her monthly *Bint al-Nīl*; in 1949 the *Bint al-Nīl* Union emerged, and in 1951 the *Bint al-Nīl* party was formed under the leadership of Durriyyah Shafiq (see Chapter One). All three platforms, by and large, promoted the same principles with different degrees of urgency. On the family level, they called for abolishing polygamy and restricting divorce; politically, they advocated granting women full political rights such as voting and being elected to office (Khamīs 1978: 86–87).

From the very beginning men were closely involved in the women's press in Egypt. One of the pioneering journals, *Mir'āt al-Ḥasnā'*, was published in Cairo by Salīm Sarkīs, a male journalist disguised by the fictitious female name Maryam Maẓhar.[15] In some cases, men assumed major roles in editing women's journals behind the scenes, as was the case in Alexandra Avierinoh's *Anīs al-Jalīs* when Najīb al-Ḥaddād actively participated in publishing this magazine until his death, at which point his brother, Amīn al-Ḥaddād, took over his post until the magazine's closure. This tradition of male partnership continued in the 1920s when Munīrah Thābit was assisted by 'Abd al-Qādir Ḥamzah in publishing *al-Amal* and when Faṭīmah al-Yūsuf was assisted by Muḥammad al-Tābi'ī in publishing *Rūz al-Yūsuf*.

Only two major magazines were published in Syria and neither was, strictly speaking, a women's publication, because each emphasized literary and national matters, rather than focus exclusively on women's issues. One of these publications was Mary 'Ajamī's[16] *al-'Arūs* (*The Bride*), which was published for an eleven-year period and was at the time the only women's magazine in Syria. This achievement must be assessed in light of the formidable obstacles 'Ajamī encountered while struggling to keep her journal alive, not the least of which were her father's attempts to persuade her to quit (al-Miṣrī and Wa'lānī 1988: 33–34). *Al-'Arūs* was essentially a literary magazine geared to the general public, and most of its contributors were men. The other publication, Nāzik al-'Abid Bayhum's[17] *Nūr al-Fayḥā'* (*Damascus Light*), was the organ of a feminist organization of the same name. This magazine frequently dealt with issues specifically related to women, including education and the role of women in society and in the family, and even supported political rights for women. However, its attention was usually so focused on national independence that feminist concerns became secondary.

In Iraq, women's journals have been impressive enough in number, but none of them has left a lasting legacy in the history of the women's press.[18]

The Salons

Literary salons were the third forum allowing women to contribute to modern Arab letters. Literary salons have a long history in the Arab world; they were initiated by Sukaynah bint al-Ḥusayn (d. 735 or 743) and Wallādah Bint al-Mustakfī (d. 1087 or 1091) hundreds of years before the concept spread to Europe in the sixteenth century.[19] Maryānā Fatḥ Allāh Marrāsh (1848–1919) was the first Arab woman to revive this tradition. She was born in Aleppo to an old and respected family known for its literary interests. Her father was a man of letters who had built up a huge private library, and her brother Francis was a writer and poet who had studied medicine in Paris. Another brother, ʿAbdallāh, was also a writer and had traveled extensively in Europe. In addition to her formal education in missionary schools in Aleppo and Beirut, where she was exposed to both French and Anglo-Saxon cultures, Maryānā Marrāsh was tutored by her father and brothers, especially on the subject of Arabic literature.

Marrāsh began her involvement in the world of letters by contributing articles and poems[20] to journals, especially *Lisān al-Ḥāl* and *al-Jinān* (both of Beirut). In her articles she criticized the condition of Arab women, and urged them to seek education and speak out on matters of concern to them. Like her brothers, she toured several European countries and was impressed and influenced by what she saw of life there. Upon her return to Aleppo, Maryānā Marrāsh turned her house into a gathering place for a group of celebrated writers who met there on a regular basis to cultivate each other's friendship and discuss literature, music, and political and social issues.[21] The members of her circle included the intellectuals Qasṭākī al-Ḥimṣī (1858–1941), Gabriel al-Dallāl (1836–1892), Kāmil al-Ghazzī (1852–1933), and Rizqallāh Hassūn (1825–1880), all of them men, in addition to some politicians and members of the foreign diplomatic corps. Apart from the intellectual discourse in which she was fully engaged, Maryānā Marrāsh used to entertain her salon participants by singing and playing the *canon*.[22]

The most influential salon in modern Arab history was the one established by Princess Nāzlī Fāḍil (d. 1914) in Egypt in the last decade of the nineteenth century, which lasted for almost a quarter of a century. Her father, Muṣṭafā Fāḍil, was known for his comprehensive and varied education and his reluctance to involve himself in politics (though he had given verbal support to the Constitutional Movement that opposed the Ottoman Sultan ʿAbd al-Ḥamīd). His large private library became the core of the *Dār al-Kutub*, the National Egyptian Library. Princess Nāzlī, a niece of the Khedive Ismāʿīl and educated in European schools in Egypt, had lived in London while her husband served as the Ottoman ambassador to Britain and consequently was well-acquainted with Western thought, ideas, and languages (French and English). At her palace in Cairo, Nāzlī gathered about her an intellectual circle that included the most prominent religious, literary, and political figures in Egypt at the time. Among them were al-Afghānī, Muḥammad ʿAbduh, and Saʿd Zaghlūl,[23] Muḥammad al-Muwayliḥī (1868–1930),[24] Qāsim Amīn, Adīb Isḥāq (1856–1885),[25] Fāris Nimr (1856–1951),[26] and Dāwūd Barakāt (1867–1933).[27] The main topic of discussion at their frequent meetings was the social and political predicament of Egypt. The participants kept in touch with Western intellectual trends by reading and discussing books in various European languages, especially books about Egypt (Khalīfah 1973: 27). Nāzlī was convinced that Egypt's plight could be remedied only through education, and she donated some of her land and property to finance the establishment of the first modern Egyptian University in Cairo.

Nāzlī's circle was said to have influenced Qāsim Amīn's book *Taḥrīr al-Mar'ah*. Dāwūd Barakāt, a frequent participant in Nāzlī's salon, revealed to Nāzlī that Qāsim Amīn, in an attack on d'Harcourt, had also spoken out against those Egyptian women who he considered too Westernized, including Nāzlī, who was a liberal and went unveiled. Nāzlī was very displeased about this, and through Qāsim Amīn's friend ʿAbduh she urged him to "correct" his mistake by writing a new book with a more progressive approach. The result, as the story goes, was Amīn's *Taḥrīr al-Mar'ah* (Khalīfah 1973: 27–28).

Like her Syrian counterpart Maryānā Marrāsh, Nāzlī Fāḍil did not overlook the role of music in sustaining her salon. She used to play the piano for her salon's participants (Sufūrī 1928: 686), leaving the singing to the journalist Shaykh ʿAlī Yūsuf and the dancing to her Tunisian maid (Storrs 1937: 100).

At the same time that Nāzlī Fāḍil's salon was attracting the intellectual elite of Cairo, the Lebanese-born Alexandra Avierinoh was busy solidifying her salon in Alexandria. A graduate of missionary schools, she displayed an impressive knowledge of Western thought and languages (English, French, and Italian). A publisher of one of the early women's magazines in Arabic, Avierinoh became a central figure in the intellectual life of her city. One of the most outstanding participants in her salon was the poet Ismā'īl Ṣabrī, who served as the mayor of Alexandria 1896–1899.

Labībah Hāshim, another Lebanese in Egypt, formed a salon centered on her periodical *Fatāt al-Sharq* and composed mainly of journalists, such as Aḥmad Luṭfī al-Sayyid, the editor of *al-Jarīdah*, and 'Alī Yūsuf, the editor of *al-Mu'ayyad*. This circle was almost entirely dedicated to fighting for women's education, for their right to hold public office, and for a strong unified national school system to end dependence on the foreign missionary schools in Egypt (Maḥmūd 1980: 75–76).

Mary 'Ajamī's salon, founded in Damascus in 1922, for three years attracted several young writers, among them Khalīl Mardam (1895–1959), Muḥammad al-Buzum (1887–1955), Aḥmad Shākir al-Karmī, Karam al-Dāghistānī, and Shafīq Jabrī (1897–1980). Although they occasionally discussed some current political issues, the participants restricted themselves mainly to literary affairs and were interested in reviving classical Arabic literature and familiarizing themselves with modern Western thought (al-Kayyālī 1968: 228).

As is true with most of these salons, it is unknown exactly what atmosphere prevailed in Mary 'Ajamī's circle and in which manner topics were discussed and views exchanged. We do know that the salon was enlivened by Mary's sister's piano playing. Mary herself was highly praised for her ability to run the intellectual discourse and was acknowledged as a "skilled talker" ('Ajamī 1969: 11–12).

Ḥabbūbah Ḥaddād's salon in Beirut lasted from 1920 to 1930 and included many leading literary figures, among them Amīn Taqiyy al-Dīn (1884–1937), Shiblī al-Mallāṭ (1867–1961), Rāmiz Sarkīs, Ṭānyūs 'Abduh (1864–1926), Jurjī Niqūlā Bāz, Sa'īd Fāḍil 'Aql (1888–1916), Amīn Nakhlah, and Amīn al-Rīḥānī. Some women writers were also active in this circle, among them Salmā Ṣā'igh (1889–1953), Najlā Abī al-Luma' (1895–1967), Mary Yannī (1864–1933), and Julyā Tu'mah Dimashqiyyah (1883–1954) (Ibrāhīm 1964: 186–187).

A significant, albeit less well-known, salon was founded in Lebanon in 1927 by a Muslim woman, *Ḥājjah* Fāṭimah al-Rifā'ī. Religious, but unveiled, she would convene her salon on three consecutive full-moon nights each month in which the participants (men and women) stayed awake until morning entertaining themselves and discussing literary issues. Among the frequent attendants of this salon were Najlā' Kaffūrī, Salmā Ṣā'igh, and Karam Mulḥim Karam (al-Khaṭīb 1984: 62).

In addition to these major salons, Hudā Sha'rāwī held a salon attended by such celebrated figures as Aḥmad Luṭfī al-Sayyid, Muḥammad Ḥusayn Haykal, Ṭāhā Ḥusayn, Gabriel Taqlā (1890–1943), Anṭūn al-Jumayyil (1887–1948), Khalīl Muṭrān (1871–1948), and Aḥmad Shawqī (1868–1932). Sha'rāwī used to encourage writers by sending them on scholarship to Europe at her own expense and giving a prize for fiction and poetry every year. Despite these impressive aspects, her salon met only sporadically.

Although Nāzlī's salon was influential in the nonliterary fields of politics and religious reform, the one established by Mayy Ziyādah (1886–1941)[28] was, from the strictly literary point of view, no doubt the most remarkably productive salon in the history of Arab letters. Ziyādah was to become the Arab counterpart of Madame de Sévigné (1626–1696), Ninon de Lenclos (1620–1705), and Madame de Staël (1776–1817)[29] through the founding of her salon in 1913 (R. Mūsā n.d.: 55).[30] It was to last for almost three decades,[31] providing a place where Egypt's most celebrated literary figures could meet under one roof and transcend personal animosities or differences of opinion. Every Tuesday a large group, Egyptians as well as non-Egyptians,[32] would meet at Mayy Ziyādah's home to read poetry, listen to music,[33] and discuss literary issues. Her circle included more than thirty intellectuals, the most prominent of whom were Aḥmad Luṭfī al-Sayyid, Shiblī Shumayyil (1853–1917), Sulaymān al-Bustānī (1856–1925), Aḥmad Shawqī, Khalīl Muṭrān, Anṭūn al-Jumayyil, Dāwūd Barakāt, Muṣṭafā 'Abd al-Rāziq (1885–1946), Muṣṭafā Ṣādiq al-Rāfi'ī (1880–1937), Salīm Sarkīs (1867–1926), Ya'qūb Ṣarrūf (1852–1927), Ḥāfiẓ Ibrāhīm, Ismā'īl Ṣabrī (1855–1923),[34] 'Abbās Maḥmūd al-'Aqqād (1889–1964), Manṣūr Fahmī (1886–1959), and Salāmah Mūsā. Women participants included Hudā Sha'rāwī, Malak Ḥifnī Nāṣif, Iḥsān al-Qāṣī, and Amy Khayr (al-'Aqqād 1962: 85). Mayy Ziyādah's salon, unlike Nāzlī's, was open to a large audience drawn from different social classes. It gave young writers a chance to cultivate their talents by mingling with the elite of the Arab intelligentsia and to familiarize themselves with literary trends in the Arab world and in the West. The young Ṭāhā Ḥusayn, for example, joined the salon as a result of a personal invitation from Mayy Ziyādah, who had been impressed by his defense of his doctoral dissertation at the Egyptian University (Ḥasan 1964: 179).

Despite the tremendous reputation of Ziyādah's salon as an institution, one is puzzled by the lack of even basic information about its actual activities, taking place weekly for about three decades. 'Abbās Maḥmūd al-'Aqqād, one of the major participants, laments the fact that those activities remained unknown to the public, claiming that, if the discussions that took place in Mayy's salon were to be collected, they would constitute a modern library equal in literary value to that of Ibn 'Abd Rabbih's *al-'Iqd al-Farīd* and Abū al-Faraj al-Iṣfahānī's *al-Aghāni*. Salāmah Mūsā, on the other hand, accuses Mayy's salon of lacking a program and goal and claims that Mayy instead relied completely upon her beauty, femininity, and charm in keeping the salon intact (S. Mūsā n.d.: 18). Still, one of the significant contributions of Mayy's salon, albeit difficult to measure, was in the sphere of Arabic language. Muṣṭafā 'Abd al-Rāziq points of Mayy's insistence upon using Classical Arabic in all discussions of her salon, thus making this level of Arabic a spoken language even among those participants who did not share her belief as far as Classical Arabic was concerned. Whereas the press, 'Abd al-Rāziq states, was trying to make Classical Arabic a flexible medium in writing, Mayy was doing the same service to Classical Arabic as a living spoken medium (Ḥasan 1964: 159).

Mayy Ziyādah's intellect and personal charm[35] were so overwhelming that many of the writers who attended her salon fell in love with her. Although Mayy Ziyādah did not generally reciprocate this affection, the sentiments she inspired produced some of the most beautiful poetry[36] and prose[37] in Arabic. Her relationships with the men who participated in her salon created a new genre in Arabic literature, one characterized by its intimacy and candidness—the literature of correspondence.[38] Its intimacy stemmed from the fact that these intellectuals were involved in a sentimental relationship with Mayy, whereas its candidness could be attributed to their assumption that this correspondence would remain private.[39] 'Abbās Maḥmūd al-'Aqqād described the correspondence as a private literature (*adab khāṣṣ*), and said: "If the letters that Mayy wrote or that were addressed to her were to be collected . . . a unique treasure would be added to our Arabic literature" (al-'Aqqād 1962: 84).

The tradition of Mayy Ziyādah's salon was carried on, but with much less success, by one of her enthusiastic fans, Jamīlah al-'Alāyilī. Born into a very conservative family in al-Manṣūrah, Egypt, Jamīlah al-'Alāyilī refrained from having her literary production published under her real name, for fear of tarnishing the family's reputation.[40] Her ordeal was greatly eased when she moved to Cairo, where she got married and, together with her husband, established a literary salon in the early 1950s.

Invoking the name of an Arab woman who ran a salon in the eighth century, Thurayyā al-Ḥāfiẓ founded a salon in her house in Damascus in 1953 called *Muntadā Sukaynah* (Sukaynah's Salon). Among the early participants were women from aristocratic families, such as Zāhidah Ḥamīd Pasha, Ramziyyah al-Quwatlī, and Amal al-Jazā'irī, as well as some well-known writers, such as 'Azīzah Hārūn (b. 1923) and Ilfah al-Idlibī (b. 1912). Although the salon's activities were open to men as well as women, the administrative body consisted only of women. This salon, which lasted until 1963, when its founder departed for Egypt, was somewhat ambitious in its declared objectives, which included raising literary and artistic standards, creating strong bonds and cooperation among its members, publishing their works, translating Western literary works into Arabic, and translating Arabic literature into foreign languages (al-Miṣrī and Wa'lānī 1988: 35–36).

The intellectual interaction of women with the Arab mainstream culture started to come about in the 1960s in avenues other than women-run salons. Higher educational institutes, political parties, and mixed cultural platforms were some of these avenues. In Egypt, for example, only one marginal women-run salon was founded in the 1960s which attracted a number of Egyptian writers and artists, that of Khadījah al-Saqqāf.

Women As Poets

Lebanon

The real contribution of women to Arabic belles lettres started in the second half of the nineteenth century. Just as men had done at the beginning of the literary renaissance, women tried their hand at poetry. In 1867 Wardah al-Yāzijī's (1838–1924) small collection of poems entitled *Ḥadīqat al-Ward* (*The Rose Garden*) was published.[41] Wardah al-Yāzijī's educational background and intellectual preoccupations were typical of most of the pioneering generation of Arab women writers. She received her primary education in an American missionary school in Beirut. When she was twelve years old her father, Nāṣīf al-Yāzijī (1800–1871), a towering figure in the world of Arab literature, supplemented her formal education with private tutoring in Arabic language and prosody. As part of her training, she was often asked to correspond in poetry with other literary figures on her father's behalf.

The content of Wardah al-Yāzijī's poetry can be divided into two main fields: eulogy and elegy. Her panegyrics were mainly addressed to high-ranking Ottomans, among them the sister of Sultan ʿAbd al-Ḥamīd who visited Lebanon. The tragic succession of deaths in her family (her brothers died in 1866, 1870, 1874, 1889, and 1906; her sister died in 1876; her father in 1872; and her daughter and son in 1892) gave her ample choice of subjects for elegies. In them, Wardah al-Yāzijī refused to abandon the traditional technique of trying to draw lessons from the phenomenon of death. As a result of confining herself to the rigid æsthetic rules laid down by male poets in the sphere of elegy, her poetry lacks, to a great extent, genuine individuality and personal sentiment. In her love poetry, al-Yāzijī, like some of her contemporaries, resorted to clever devices to express her own intimate inner world. When she set out to write a *muʿāraḍah* (a "remake" of a classical poem using the same meter and theme as the original, but with different imagery) of a love poem by the Abbasid poet Ibn Zurayq al-Baghdādī, she was careful to make it clear that she was doing so by request rather than by choice, even though in this case she was able to use this traditional form to express her own personal feelings. The other device used by Wardah al-Yāzijī to express her personal sentiments was to pretend that she was addressing another woman, as in the following lines dedicated, despite the use of a male pronoun, to a "female friend": "The beloved departed and with him my patience. When will he return to his first dwelling-sites? Then a world which has been darkened since his departure will light up and I will be delighted with reunion before death" (Ziyādah 1975f: 35). Yet, in another poem addressed to ʿĀ'ishah Taymūr, the Egyptian female author, al-Yāzijī used this technique more aggressively by evoking the famous love story between Jamīl (ibn Mu'ammar) and Buthaynah from the seventeeth century:

You are unique among women. So how could I but
love a peerless lover?
You taught me
to compose love poetry and evoked
in me what Buthaynah's love evoked in Jamīl. (Fahmī 1955: 49)

Elsewhere, Wardah al-Yāzijī used the traditional diction of Arabic love poetry to congratulate another friend after her return from a trip: "O moon in the darkness! I thought our reunion took place in a dream while we were asleep. My patience in your love was waning while my yearning was increasing and morning seemed dark to me" (Maskūnī 1947: 139). Wardah al-Yāzijī remained faithful to her literary environment, which was dominated by the endeavors of her father and brother to revive Arabic classical literature. Thus, Mayy Ziyādah concluded, Wardah al-Yāzijī's work lacked both originality and personal warmth. Mayy Ziyādah said of her: "We do not know anything about her [Wardah's] personal life or whether she was happy or not. There are no clues to her private life in her poetry, which draws only an outline and deals with familiar events such as marriage, birth and death" (Ziyādah 1975f: 17–18). Wardah al-Yāzijī's achievements in the area of prose were less impressive than her contribution to poetry. A few articles were published mostly in *saj'* (rhymed prose) in her father's periodical *al-Ḍiyā'*, in which she dealt with some issues related to "the Eastern woman." In one of these articles, Wardah al-Yāzijī criticized the tendency of "the Eastern woman" to imitate blindly her Western counterpart, even to the extent of adopting the latter's language and customs and thus alienating herself from her own society. Wardah al-Yāzijī said that the women of the East, rather than concentrating on such trivia, should involve themselves in science and the arts and other humanist activities (Maskūnī 1947: 56–57).

Syria and Iraq

Wardah al-Yāzijī's counterpart in Syria was Maryānā Marrāsh. In her *dīwān* (collection), *Bint Fikr* (*An Idea*, 1893), Maryānā Marrāsh devoted much space to panegyrics. In these she exalted, among others, Sultan ʿAbd al-Ḥamīd and the Ottoman governors of her native Aleppo, Midḥat Pasha and Amīn Pasha. Her best elegy was composed to lament the death of her brother Francis, in which she followed the traditional patterns of the elegiac genre, identifying herself with al-Khansāʾ. Maryānā Marrāsh's love poetry was more lively and less conservative than that of Wardah al-Yāzijī and showed the influence of the poet ʿUmar ibn Abī Rabīʿah's poetry as well as of the French romantics, especially Lamartine and Musset (al-Kayyālī 1957b: 556).

In Iraq, the pioneering women writers were exclusively poets. Sulaymah al-Malāʾikah (1908–1953), later known under the pen name Umm Nizār, was an autodidact. She familiarized herself with pre-Islamic literature, Umayyad and Andalusian poetry, Arabic history, and primary Islamic sources (Ṭabbānah 1974: 53). When she began to write poetry, she did it so secretively that even some of her closest relatives were unaware of her talent. None of her works was published until 1936, upon the death of the poet and noted advocate of women's rights Jamīl Ṣidqī al-Zahāwī, when an elegy of hers expressing the gratitude of women to al-Zahāwī for his advocacy of their cause was published. The elegy was received enthusiastically by the literary circles of Baghdad, which were surprised that an unknown poet could produce a work of such maturity and artistic value.

Umm Nizār's poetry was collected after her death by her husband and her daughter, the highly gifted poet Nāzik al-Malāʾikah, under the title *Unshūdat al-Majd* (*The Song of Glory*, 1965). Umm Nizār was preoccupied with two main topics in her poetry: patriotism and the cause of Arab women. She glorified the role played by Arab women through history of show that women were worthy of playing a major role in the modern Arab world. She also emphasized the predicament of the women of modern Iraq, victims of ignorance, stagnation, and narrowmindedness; and she urged them to strive to overcome their difficulties. In the sphere of patriotism, Umm Nizār wrote about Iraq's struggle for independence, the Palestinian issue, and other liberation movements in the Arab world. Her poetry was shaped by her exclusively Arabic education, since she did not know any European language (Ṭabbānah 1974: 53).[42]

Egypt

'Ā'ishah Taymūr's Poetry and Fiction. Perhaps the most outstanding female Arab writer to emerge in the second half of the nineteenth century was 'Ā'ishah Taymūr (1840–1902). She was born to an aristocratic and influential family of mixed ethnic background—her father Ismā'īl was Kurdish and her mother was Turkish. Ismā'īl Taymūr was a scholar who had written a family history in two volumes, one of them in Turkish.[43] In addition to his scholarly activities, Taymūr held several official positions under the khedives 'Abbās I, Sa'īd, and Ismā'īl, eventually becoming president of the Foreign Bureau at Khedive Ismā'īl's palace.

Because girls' schools were nonexistent in Egypt during Taymūr's childhood, her father hired two tutors for her. From one she learned the Qur'ān, handwriting, and *fiqh* (religious knowledge); from the other, Arabic and Turkish. At an early age Taymūr showed a great interest in letters, an interest that led to a clash between her parents. Although her father sought to educate her, her mother thought that 'Ā'ishah's inclination toward this learning was a serious deviation from the prescribed role of women in life. She tried, therefore, to keep her daughter away from books and instead taught her needlework, advising her that "the loom is the only tool and instructor of women" (Ziyādah 1975a: 60). Taymūr was torn between her desire for formal learning and her wish to please her mother. As she later recalled: "I used to go to the hall of our house and pass by the writers assembled together, to listen to their delightful voices. But my mother was hurt by my doing this and used to respond with rebukes, threats, warnings, and intimidation. Sometimes she resorted to pleasant promises [by] tempting me with jewelery and exquisite clothes" (Ziyādah 1975a: 61). Taymūr's father was more accepting than her mother, whom he asked "not to break the girl's heart . . . and not to prevent her from fulfilling her wish" (61). Her father soon discovered her literary talent and set out to cultivate it. Between the ages of seven and thirteen, Taymūr stated, she went into seclusion, "devoting myself to my studies, working much harder than my father expected. My father, however, did not allow me to attend men's literary gatherings, but instead undertook teaching me works of Persian literature such as Firdawsi's *Shahnama* and Rumi's *Mathnawi*. He devoted two hours a night to teaching me" (64). The first two lines of verse that

Taymūr wrote were in Persian. Her father encouraged her to write poetry in Arabic and Turkish as well. He planned to engage tutors to perfect her prosody, but at the age of fifteen she married, and to a great extent, the responsibilities of marriage distracted her from her literary career. (In general, we will see that, as with Western women writers, marital and family situations had much to do with the literary activity of Arab women writers.) Nonetheless, she was determined to persevere in the world of letters. After the death of her father (1882) and her husband (1885), she turned the responsibility of running the household over to her oldest daughter. She then hired two female instructors, Fāṭimah al-Azhariyyah and Sutaytah al-Ṭablāwiyyah, to tutor her in Arabic grammar and prosody (Fawwāz 1894–1995: 303). This period of Taymūr's life, in which she was relatively free to concentrate on polishing her literary skills, proved to be very productive. She wrote three collections of poetry, each in a different language: Arabic, Turkish, and Persian.

While she was preparing these works for publication, a tragedy befell 'Ā'ishah Taymūr's family: her oldest daughter Tawḥīdah died at the age of eighteen, a few months before her wedding. 'Ā'ishah Taymūr mourned her daughter's death for seven years, during which she stopped writing and developed ophthalmia. Her daughter's death took its toll on Taymūr's literary career as well as on her emotional well-being; in the depths of her sorrow, she burned much of her poetry, including her Persian *dīwān* (Ziyādah 1975a: 83).

After a prolonged period of mourning Taymūr recovered, and the spark of creativity was rekindled. She authorized her son to prepare her poetry for publication. The result was two collections: an Arabic *dīwān* entitled *Ḥilyat al-Ṭirāz* (*The Garment Ornament*) and another collection of Turkish and Persian poetry, called *Shakūfah* (Istanbul, 1894). Tawḥīdah's premature death had also deepened Taymūr's obsession with metaphysics and led her to concentrate on exegeses of the Qur'ān and *ḥadīth* (Ziyādah 1975: 83). The metaphysical dimension of these works gave some of her poetry a universal appeal.

Most of Taymūr's poetry was written for social and political occasions. Her aristocratic background and strong links with the royal family led her to devote a large proportion of her poetry (at least sixteen poems) to subjects related to Egypt's khedives (Taymūr 1952: 153–161, 175–178, 182). She took a hostile view of 'Urābī's rebellion in 1882 (which was directed against both the British and the khedive Tawfīq), and accused the rebels of being heretical, insane, and ungrateful (155–156).

Elegy was a common genre in Taymūr's poetry. Since most of her elegies are dedicated to immediate relatives (such as her father, mother, sister, and daughter Tawḥīdah), one can detect a strong personal element in them, especially in the elegy to her daughter, where the maternal sentiment is clear and genuine (209–211, 215–218).

'Ā'ishah Taymūr's accomplishment in the sphere of love poetry was remarkable, especially considering the circumstances of her cultural environment and family background.[44] Although she generally remained a traditionalist in her approach to love poetry, she was able to show some originality and individuality, especially in those poems that were published posthumously.[45] To safeguard her "reputation," she would sometimes begin her love poems by stating that what she was saying was only said for the sake of training in the writing of poetry and that she was not addressing any particular man: "*Wa-qālat mutaghazzilah fī ghayr insān, wa-al-qaṣd tamrīn al-lisān*" (233).

In addition to writing poetry in Classical Arabic, 'Ā'ishah Taymūr also took the daring step of including in her *dīwān* love poems in colloquial Arabic, breaking away from the puritanical approach to the Arabic language taken by the mainstream writers of her era. These poems followed the patterns of popular genres such as the *zajal*, *mawāliyyā*, and *adwār* (255–257). In an attempt to hide her true identity, she sometimes resorted in her love poetry to the use of a male persona, writing as a man would write and even using the feminine grammatical forms to address the person who was the subject of her poem. As Mayy Ziyādah noted, two factors were responsible for this; one was that such public expressions of emotion from women were not socially accepted, and the other was that 'Ā'ishah Taymūr tended to imitate male literature (Ziyādah 1975a: 168). She boasted about the veil in her poetry, referring to it as a symbol of virtue (Taymūr 1952: 26), having been born at a time when wearing the veil was not even questioned. However, in her prose she complained that because of the veil she could not attend gatherings of male writers.[46] She therefore apologized for the lack of perfection in what she wrote, saying that it was related to this inability to meet with men and exchange ideas with them (Taymūr 1887–1888: 3–4). In her short treatise *Mir'āt al-Ta'ammul fī al-Umūr* (*The Reflecting Mirror Regarding States of Affairs*, c. 1892), Taymūr attacked men for abandoning their role as guardians of women. By doing this, she complained, they violated one of the principles of Islam according to which men were superior to women in "mental capacity and religious belief."[47] As a result of men's neglect of their family duties, Taymūr said, women were becoming more daring and less obedient (Ziyādah 1975a: 211). But despite her conservative views on the rightful status of women in the family, 'Ā'ishah Taymūr wrote an article in 1888 in which she called for the education of women.[48] She accused men of belittling women in order to assert their own personalities, in contrast to the prevalent practice in the West (Fawwāz 1894–1895: 203).[49]

'Ā'ishah Taymūr's main contribution to Arabic fiction was her book *Natā'ij al-Aḥwāl fi al-Aqwāl wa-al-Af'āl* (*Consequences of Matters Regarding Speech and Actions*, 1887–1888). In the introduction, she claims that her main motive for writing the book was to ease her alienation and loneliness by relating episodes from ancient times (Taymūr 1887–1888: 3). Moreover, she intended to write an instructive and entertaining story that would illustrate the existence both of fortune and of misfortune throughout history (3).

'Ā'ishah Taymūr confessed that her narrative was heavily indebted to tales she had heard from old women when she was young[50] and to her reading of popular stories (*asāṭīr*) and historical works while growing up (2). The historical significance of the book lies not only in the fact that it was the first published work of fiction by an Arab woman, but also in that it was a pioneering experiment in the history of Arabic fiction as a genre (although it has been ignored by the large majority of Arab critics and literary historians as well as Arabists).[51] For content, 'Ā'ishah Taymūr drew the book's themes from popular literature, especially from the *Arabian Nights*. For its style she revived an established classical literary genre, the *Maqāmah* (pl. *Maqāmāt*); however, she adjusted the *Maqāmah* style to fit her own artistic needs. The classical *Maqāmah* consisted of a series of discrete units, each with its own separate episode. Taymūr's narrative, however, is characterized by unity and continuity and by the development of the same plot throughout the whole book, which is divided into four chapters (*faṣl*, pl. *fuṣūl*). Her chief objective was not to display linguistic virtuosity nor to embark on social criticism as the classical *Maqāmah* had done, but to attract the reader's attention to the events in her story as they took place. In addition to being influenced by the the old Arab narrative genres, Taymūr benefited from the first experiments of introducing Western fiction into Arabic through translation and adaptation. The earliest experiment was done by Rifā'ah Rāfi' al-Ṭahṭāwī, when he rendered Fénelon's *Les Adventures de Télémaque* into Arabic as *Mawāqi' al-Aflāk fī waqā'i' Tilīmāk*, which came out in Beirut in 1867.[52] Other translating projects were undertaken by some Syro-Lebanese writers in Egypt, notably those of Salīm al-Bustānī in the 1870s. Muḥammad R. Ḥasan implies that Taymūr had the opportunity to read those translations and alludes to their influence on her work. Taymūr's indebtedness to Fénelon is to be found not only in the subject matter of her story (the moral training of a crown prince by means of example and anecdotes), but is also discerned in her portryal of some characters such as Mālik and 'Aqīl, the king's vazir and confidant, respectively, who fulfill a similar role of the mentor in *Télémaque* (Ḥasan 1974: 138–139).

As in popular tales, the protagonists are of royal origin or high-ranking officials. The heir is the target of conspiracies and intrigues, which he finally overcomes by restoring his authority. Good defeats evil in the end. Taymūr included other elements characteristic of popular tales; for example, arranged marriages between a prince and a princess who then fall in love with each other, dizzying shifts of scene from country to country, and stress on plot rather than on characterization or psychological motives—so much so that the reader feels awash in the sea of dramatic events and must struggle to follow the main thread of the narrative.

The significance of *Natā'ij al-Aḥwāl* lies in the fact that it was a pioneering experiment in modern Arabic literature in general. Not until the second decade of the twentieth century did Arabic novels of real artistic value begin to appear from either men or women.[53]

Other Important Creative Writers

Alice al-Bustānī

Another writer of this generation, Alice Buṭrus al-Bustānī, daughter of the renowned scholar Buṭrus al-Bustānī, also used the struggle between good and evil as the central theme of her novel *Ṣā'ibah* (1891); however, the struggle was a commentary on the issue of marriage, a dominant theme of nineteenth-century Arabic literature. Ṣā'ibah, the protagonist of the story, marries a young officer named Luṭfī instead of marrying her cousin Farīd, who is ill-tempered and pursues pleasure extravagantly. Farīd decides to take revenge on her by ruining her marriage, using her maid Murjān and his Greek friend Būlus in his scheme to do so. Luṭfī becomes aware of the plot and it fails. However, al-Bustānī refrained from giving her story the traditional happy ending. Instead, Ṣā'ibah is shot by Farīd while she is in the midst of intimate conversation with her husband under a tree in their garden.

Al-Bustānī used a more lively and flexible prose in this story than Taymūr had used in hers, and demonstrated a better grasp of the art of narration than had Taymūr. Nevertheless, *Ṣā'ibah* suffers greatly from the inclusion of sermons and digressive episodes that interrupt the natural flow of the story (see Najm 1961: 72–73).

Zaynab Fawwāz

Zaynab Fawwāz (1860–1914)[54] represents a unique phenomenon among the pioneering women writers. Unlike Wardah al-Yāzijī, 'Ā'ishah Taymūr, or Alice al-Bustānī, Zaynab Fawwāz was not from an elite, city family; rather, she was born to a poor, obscure, and illiterate Shiite family[55] in the village of Tabnīn in southern Lebanon. Details of her early childhood are sketchy and sometimes contradictory. Most sources agree that when she was quite young, Fawwāz served as a maid at the palace of 'Alī Bey al-As'ad al-Ṣaghīr, who controlled southern Lebanon during the second half of the nineteenth century.[56] Her work at the palace proved to be of great benefit to her; it gave her the chance to associate with Fāṭimah al-Khalīl, the prince's wife, who was a poet. Fāṭimah al-Khalīl recognized Zaynab Fawwāz's intellectual potential and began to tutor her.[57]

Fawwāz moved to Egypt, where she continued her training in

letters.[58] Ḥasan Ḥusnī al-Ṭūwayrānī encouraged her to allow him to publish her writings in the periodical *al-Nīl*, of which he was founder. Fawwāz became a very prolific writer and was published in most periodicals in Egypt.[59]

Although Zaynab always wore the veil, she vehemently defended the rights of women in her articles. She constantly referred to the advanced status of women in the West. In her article "Taqaddum al-Mar'ah" ("The Women's Advancement"), she said: "How often we have heard that in the European countries and in America there are many women who have taken part in the spread of scientific and industrial progress through periodicals which they edited. On many occasions we were told about some of them [Western women] who toured countries, traversed deserts, and went across rivers while dressed like men, enduring enormous hardships in pursuit of scientific knowledge to report to their newspapers, or out of a desire to explore the conditions prevailing in those countries and to inquire into the customs and beliefs of the inhabitants" (Muḥammad n.d.: vol. 1, 131). Zaynab Fawwāz fought against the idea that women should restrict themselves to domestic affairs. In her article "al-Inṣāf" ("Justice"), she launched a fierce attack upon the Lebanese woman writer Hanā Kasbānī Kūrānī (1870–1898),[60] who had written that women were created to raise children and look after the household. Kūrānī had criticized the attempts of British women to involve themselves in politics; she considered this a deviation from the main function of women as ordained by God.[61] The basis for Zaynab Fawwāz's rebuttal was that women were intellectually equal to men and therefore had the absolute right to take part in all human endeavors, including politics if they so wished.[62]

Zaynab Fawwāz repeated these views in her response to ʿĀrif al-Zayn, the founder of the Beirut magazine *al-ʿIrfān*, who was critical of her attack on Kūrānī. Fawwāz wrote: "As far as your criticism of my demand for granting women their rights is concerned, I have made it [the demand] general rather than specific to Eastern women. I did not violate the legal claims of Islamic jurisprudence (*Sharīʿah*). . . . Your idea that women cannot perform the functions of men is wrong, because Western women have exceeded men by far. As for us, the veil does not prevent us from doing men's jobs" (Ibrāhīm 1964: 34). In addition to her journalistic activities, Zaynab Fawwāz wrote poetry, some of which has been gathered in a collection.[63] Her greatest work, however, was her voluminous *Kitāb al-Durr al-Manthūr fī Ṭabaqāt Rabbāt al-Khudūr* (*The Book of Scattered Pearls Regarding Categories of Women*, 1894–1895),[64] which contains biographies of 456 celebrated female figures, Arab and non-Arab. Among them are some of her contemporaries: 'Ā'ishah Taymūr, Maryam Makāriyūs, Maryam Naḥḥās, and Fāṭimah al-Khalīl. The appearance of this volume was a sign, as we will see later, that the pioneering generation of Arab women writers was developing a sense of solidarity and an awareness of a female literary tradition. In her introduction to the book, Fawwāz made clear her reasons for writing it. She declared that even though history gave a great many examples of talented women who could compete with the greatest male scholars and the best poets, she could not find even one Arabic book dedicated to them. Thus she had embarked upon the writing of her book for the sake of her sex (Fawwāz 1894–1895: 5–6).

In the realm of fiction, Zaynab Fawwāz wrote two novels and one play. Her first novel was *Ḥusn al-'Awāqib aw Ghādah al-Zāhirah* (*The Happy Ending*, 1899),[65] which is set in Jabal 'Āmil, Fawwāz's birthplace. The most interesting feature of this novel is the inclusion of "autobiographical" elements—a first in Arab fiction. The central theme of Fawwāz's story, like those of 'Ā'ishah Taymūr and Alice al-Bustānī, was the fundamental conflict between good and evil that must end with the defeat of the latter. Therefore the characters are never given the opportunity to grow and develop in the course of the story. Like 'Ā'ishah Taymūr, Zaynab Fawwāz relied excessively upon her linguistic virtuosity. The novel consists almost entirely of rhymed prose garnished with verses of her own composition. The influence on Zaynab Fawwāz of Arab popular fiction is shown in the nature of the plot, in her habit of interrupting the flow of events to make a note or an observation, in her use of poetry to comment on some situations, and in the lack of cause and effect in the sequence of events (Badr 1968: 150–151).[66]

Zaynab Fawwāz's view of the function of storytelling was similar to 'Ā'ishah's. The purpose of fiction (*al-Riwāyāt al-Adabiyyah*), as Fawwāz stated in her introduction to *Ḥusn al-'Awāqib*, was to entertain and to instruct (Fawwāz 1984: 37). This statement makes it easy to see why both of these writers, as well as Alice al-Bustānī, were fascinated by the struggle between good and evil and were determined to give good the upper hand in their works.

Zaynab Fawwāz was the first Arab woman to try her hand at playwriting.[67] The result was *al-Hawā wa-al-Wafā'* (*Love and Faithfulness*, 1893). The play is set in Iraq, and its central theme is the obstacles relatives place in the path of true love. The protagonist, Kāmil, falls in love with a relative named Bahiyyah and asks to marry her. Bahiyyah's grandmother opposes the match, wishing instead to marry the girl to her nephew, and Bahiyyah's father yields to his mother's will. In the meantime, Kāmil is force by his brother to marry another girl to salvage the family honor, which has been besmirched by Kāmil's asking to marry Bahiyyah and being turned down. Predictably, death intervenes to snatch away Bahiyyah's father and grandmother, as well as Kāmil's brother, so as to facilitate the union of the two lovers. The play follows an already established tradition by mixing both poetry and prose (often rhymed prose) frequently in the dialogue of the same character.

Zaynab Fawwāz's artistic shortcomings are more easily revealed by her play than by her novels. The characters are flat and static, and therefore less convincing, and inadequate to a dramatic work of this nature. Fawwāz had little success in creating a lively dialogue, partly because she insisted upon forcing her characters to recite a great deal of poetry. She often interrupted the flow of the story with indigestible chunks of declamatory preaching to drive home the moral lesson (Najm 1967: 399–402).

Labībah Hāshim, Labībah Ṣawāyā, and Farīdah 'Aṭiyyah

Like Zaynab Fawwāz, Labībah Hāshim (1882–1952) sought material for her stories in both modern times and ancient history. Born in Beirut,[68] Hāshim received her primary education in French, English, and American missionary schools. In 1990, she and her family moved to Egypt where she continued her study of Arabic with Ibrāhīm al-Yāzijī.

In her novel *Qalb al-Rajul* (*The Heart of Man*, 1904), Labībah Hāshim used the Christian-Druze factional strife in Lebanon in 1870 as a background. The focus of the story is the love affair between Ḥabīb, a Christian, and Fāṭimah, a Druze. Fāṭimah's father, who is a prince, reacts with hostility to this love so that Ḥabīb has to abduct his beloved to marry her.

Labībah Hāshim's true reason for writing this book is disputed. 'Abd al-Muḥsin Ṭāhā Badr alleges that she intended to win sympathy for the Lebanese Christians and defame the Druze (Badr 1968: 58), whereas Muḥammad Yūsuf Najm asserts that the whole story is an outcry for women's rights (Najm 1961: 115).

In its level of characterization and style, *Qalb al-Rajul* represents a remarkable step forward in women's fiction. Labībah Hāshim explores the inner world of her characters and relates their actions to psychological motives. This tendency clearly shows itself, for example, in the way she handles the love affair between two secondary characters, Rūzah and 'Azīz. As far as style is concerned, Labībah Hāshim refrains from using rhymed prose and from ornamenting her story with poetry. Instead, she uses a flexible style more similar to that of journalism. Unlike 'Ā'ishah Taymūr and Zaynab Fawwāz, Labībah Hāshim does not use her fiction as a platform for moral preaching (Najm 1961: 115). Also unlike her predecessors, Labībah Hāshim was exposed to Western fiction through her mastery of English and French. She once translated a French novel into Arabic as *al-Fatāh al-Inkilīziyyah* (*The English Lady*) (Ramaḍān 1976: 122). Although *Qalb al-Rajul* represents a major literary achievement, one can still see in it some of the defects typical of early Arabic novels: melodramatic interferences in the course of events by the author, an abrupt ending (Najm 1961: 115), and the overextension of the scene of events (Lebanon, Egypt, and Europe).

The plot of Labībah Hāshim's second novella, *Shīrīn* (1907) is derived from ancient Persian history as recorded in al-Firdawsi's *Shahnama*. The Persian king Kisrā ibn Hurmuz falls in love with Shīrīn, an Armenian princess, and entertains hopes of marrying her. The king's singer Barbadh and his sister Āzarmīdukht conspire to shatter the king's dream, but they later pay dearly for their act of deceit. The moral of Labībah Hāshim's story is quite clear: destiny never fails to punish criminals for their crimes. Although the story lacks vivid characters, it benefits from the author's use of a simple and lively style (Najm 1961: 218). This style shows to what extent journalism and the exposure to Western discourse had now become incorporated into the language of Arabic fiction.

The political turmoil in Turkey in the first decade of the twentieth century also inspired Labībah Mīkhā'īl Ṣawāyā (1876–1916).[69] Her novel, *Ḥasnā' Salūnīk* (*The Fair Lady of Salonika*,

1909), is based partly on news reports from Istanbul and partly on Waliyy al-Dīn Yakan's book *Khawāṭir Niyāzī* (Najm 1961: 201). It revolves around a liberal Turkish family in Istanbul, consisting of the father Kāmil, the mother Naẓīmah, and their daughter Wasīmah, who is in love with her cousin Zakī. Due to political persecution, the family decides to leave Istanbul for Salonika (Salūnīk) in Greece. Wasīmah is sent to Europe to continue her studies, while her beloved Zakī keeps up the struggle against 'Abd al-Ḥamīd's despotism. When Zakī is killed, Wasīmah vows to take up her lover's cause by nursing the victims in the battle for liberty. In the end, however, her sorrow over Zakī's death overcomes her will to live. She commits suicide, which leads Murjānah, the loyal family maid, to do the same.

Labībah Ṣawāyā seems to be more interested in historical events than in literature *per se*. Her novel even includes the entire list of demands which the Committee of Union and Progress presented to the European countries at Istanbul (203). Like most of the writers previously discussed, Labībah Ṣawāyā relies upon a succession of "epiclike" adventures, coincidences, exaggerations, and tragic deaths, as well as poetry, to maintain reader interest.

Like Labībah Ṣawāyā, Farīdah Yūsuf 'Aṭiyyah (1867–1917)[70] took the political upheaval in the Ottoman Empire as the subject for a novel. In her story *Bayna 'Arshayn* (*Between Two Thrones*, 1912) she deals with the events leading to the 1908 Young Turk *coup d'état* that forced 'Abd al-Ḥamīd to implement the 1876 constitution. She portrays the historical and social atmosphere in which the coup took place, including 'Abd al-Ḥamīd's attempts to stir up trouble in Greater Syria and thus revive the factional strife of 1860. Against this background, 'Aṭiyyah relates the story of a young man from Tripoli named Kāmil and his lover Nabīhah. This love story ends with their marriage in North America after the pair meets by coincidence on a French ship during their escape from Lebanon. 'Aṭiyyah also creats a parallel love story between Armenians in the midst of the Armenian massacres perpetrated by the Turks in 1915 and 1916; however, the second love story overshadows the first and creates a lack of balance in the novel.

The weaknesses of Farīdah's novel are almost identical to those found in the works of Labībah Hāshim and Labībah Ṣawāyā, especially in her overemphasis of the historical context. A large part of the novel is mere historical narration, which is not integrated into the story. Farīdah's language is a combination of rhymed prose and prolonged rhetorical speeches, with numerous citations from poetry thrown in for good measure (208–209).

'Afīfah Karam

These early attempts to establish a fiction tradition by Arab women in Egypt and Syria were echoed and solidified by those of 'Afīfah Karam (1883–1924), a Lebanese immigrant to America. Born in 'Amshīt, a small village in Lebanon, Karam was educated at missionary schools. In 1897 she emigrated with her husband to the United States and settled in Shreveport, Louisiana. Karam's initial intellectual involvement was in the field of journalism when she began contributing articles to the Arabic press, mainly to the daily *al-Hudā* in New York.[71] Her engagement in journalism proved to be beneficial; she had the opportunity to become acquainted with Na''ūm Mukarzil (d. 1932), the editor of *al-Hudā*, who encouraged her to pursue her literary career by providing her with much needed Arabic reading material and editorial assistance, in addition to publishing all her works at his press.[72]

Karam's first novel, *Badī'ah wa-Fu'ād* (*Badī'ah and Fu'ād*, 1906)[73] sets the tone, in many ways, for the rest of her works. The central character is a woman victimized by the rules of society laid down by men or women who have internalized patriarchal values. Badī'ah is introduced as an orphan who was raised at a monastery. Her ordeal starts when she leaves the monastery to work as a maid for a wealthy family, where she meets their only son, Fu'ād; the two fall in love at first sight. The huge gap in their social status prevents the two lovers from crowning their love with marriage. A series of intriguing plots woven by Fu'ād's mother and cousin sends Badī'ah to America to be followed in due time by Fu'ād. The two are united in matrimony only when the truth about her background is revealed and the social gap is narrowed. Badī'ah is not a poor maid; she was born to an aristocratic family that opposed her mother's marriage to a poor French man. Badī'ah, the baby, was put in the monastery only when her mother returned to her family after the death of her husband.

The structure of *Badī'*ah *wa-Fu'ād* betrays the sources that influenced Karam the novelist. The frequent citations of poetry (e.g., pp. 20, 136, 137, 144, 262, 302, 320, 329), the intervention of the author by interrupting narration to comment on the events and highlight the moral lesson that needs to be learned (e.g., pp. 54, 58, 83, 105), the haphazard occurrence of events (e.g., pp. 176, 217, 303), and the constant shifting of the stage of events by directly addressing the reader (e.g., pp. 120, 137) all suggest the impact of popular narrative as well as of the early (post 1870) works of Arabic fiction (both men's and women's) that she probably read in the United States.

The issue of the novel's structure appeared to be of secondary importance to 'Afīfah Karam. From the outset she warns the reader that she did not care much about "arranging and narrating events"; rather, her principal objective was to "propagate ideas of education and reform" (Karam 1906: 4). This tendency suits Karam's approach to fiction as an efficient platform for didactic purposes (Karam 1906: 1). Karam uses this novel, for instance, to train women in the social etiquette, such as for receiving and entertaining guests, to which she devotes a whole chapter (Chapter 3). She sometimes thinly through her flat characters criticizes some modern trends imported from the West, such as dancing and gambling (40). There is also criticism of some bad habits prevailing within the Syrian [Lebanese] community in America, such as the return of young men to Syria for quick marriages (147), jealousy (164), abandonment of modesty by women (170–171), slander and gossip (203), and the abuse of dowry (237).

The apologetic tone of the introduction reminds the reader of a common phenomenon shared by most of the pioneering Arab women writers. Reminding the readers that this is her first novel and that it has been written by a Syrian [Lebanese] woman [in America] in only six months, as if to lower their expectations, Karam admits that she hopes for a "satisfactory" evaluation that will overlook the novel's flaws (Karam 1906: 5).[74] Later, Karam attributed the favorable reviews written about this novel in South America, Egypt, and Syria to the fact that her work was the first novel written by a Syrian [Lebanese] woman emigrant, despite her recognition that "women's weakness in the craft of writing and composition is a known fact since it is still in its infancy" (Karam n.d.: 2). The author is also aware that she is perhaps stepping through a mine field because she is a woman writing about such intimate topics as "love and marriage" (4). The reader, however, cannot miss Karam's defiant attitude and her attempt to justify tackling these matters. In fact, she states from the very beginning that she is writing a women's literary novel that deals with love (*riwāyah nisā'i yyah adabiyyah ghrāmiyyah*), and that it is intended to be read, first and foremost, by women, since they are fond of reading novels (Karam 1906: 1).

The whole novel revolves around Badī'ah, the female protagonist. It is interesting to note that, contrary to the tradition of popular love stories, her name precedes that of her partner, Fu'ād in the novel's title. Perhaps it is the first time in the history of Arabic fiction that we meet a woman advocating, in strong terms, the necessity of a general solidarity among women. When Badī'ah sees a sailor trying to abuse a woman on the ship on her way to America, she intervenes and rebukes the woman for not standing up to the man. "If a noble woman sees another woman humiliated," Badī'ah thinks, "she would let her know that every woman has been humiliated, not just one" (Karam 1906: 124). In another incident, Badī'ah succeeds in preventing a female passenger from committing suicide, and when she is told that the reason for the suicide attempt is an unfaithful man, Badī'ah tells her, "I am a woman like you, my sister. My concern for fellow women makes me say that the woman who suffers when she is capable of being happy, and the woman who harms herself instead of benefitting herself for the sake of a dishonest man, is weak, cowardly and a disgrace to her sex" (132–133). According to Badī'ah, friendship should exist among women themselves because they belong to the same sex (268) and "woman should grant friendship to another woman as she grants it to a man, and in certain circumstances she must give it to a woman rather than to a man" (267).

This solidarity among women exhibits itself in a more intensive manner in 'Afīfah Karam's second novel *Fāṭimah al-Badawiyyah* (*Fāṭimah the Bedouin*, n.d.).[75] This is a love story in which the two main female characters remain faithful to their lovers until the end. Fāṭimah, a Muslim bedouin from Lebanon, falls in love with Salīm, an urban Christian. In a sectarian society, this religious difference proves to be formidable, and the couple decides to go to America without a marriage document. Eventually Salīm secretly returns to his family in Lebanon, abandoning Fāṭimah and their baby because he thinks that the marriage was not legitimate. Only five years later, Salīm casually returns, finding Fāṭimah seriously ill but willing to forgive him.[76] At Fāṭimah's wish, and shortly before her death, the priest is brought to perform the marriage ceremony. When Salīm dies he is buried next to his wife's grave.

The targets for Karam's criticism are expanded in this work to include the clergy in Lebanon,[77] who are portrayed as fanatic and ignorant. The priest in Lebanon objects to Salīm and Fāṭimah's initial attempt at marriage because they belong to two different faiths, although she is willing to convert. This priest's refusal is the reason for the collapse of the couple's relationship. Regarding the priesthood's ignorance, Salīm comments, "The problem of most of our Lebanese villages is that the priest is usually a worthless person who is ordained because he is incapable of doing anything else" (149).

This criticism of the clergy and the government in Lebanon, in addition to the custom of imposing marriage on very young girls, is at the heart of 'Afīfah Karam's third novel, *Ghādat 'Amshīt* (*The Girl of 'Amshīt*, 1914). She emphasizes in the introduction that "although she is a woman and her ideas are feeble, she still has the right to speak up against the oppression of women" (1914: 2).

In this novel, fourteen-year-old Farīdah, who is in love with Farīd, is forced by her father to marry Ḥabīb, a rich man who is about fifty years old. Farīdah, who was educated by nuns, is incapable of rebelling against her father's authority.[78] After the death of her husband, Farīdah chooses to join a monastery, together with her best female friend Sawsan,[79] and dies after a short while. As in the previous novel, the lovers are united only by death.

Karam's language in these three novels[80] is greatly influenced by the Arabic translation of the Bible, which provided the backbone of Arabic studies at missionary schools in Lebanon. An additional influence was the language of journalism, characterized by its practicality and simplicity, to which she was exposed while working at *al-Hudā* and other periodicals, in addition to her own women's magazine *al-'Ālam al-Jadīd*, which she founded in 1912. Her use of Arabic colloquial became bolder with each novel, culminating in *Ghādat 'Amshīt*, in which she not only incorporates some expressions and proverbs in colloquial as she had done in her previous novels, but also employs colloquial in the dialogue, especially in the case of Farīda's father (e.g., pp. 161, 202), Ḥabīb (e.g., p. 208) and Ẓarīfah, Ḥabīb's sister (e.g., pp. 166, 196).

Mayy Ziyādah: A New Dimension

Against this background, women's literature took on a new and rich dimension of writing in the first decade of the twentieth century with the appearance on the scene of Mayy Ziyādah. Mayy Ziyādah's contribution to Arab letters went far beyond her prestigious literary salon. Her talent as a writer began to manifest itself while she was still a student in the 'Aynṭūrah missionary school in Lebanon. During her stay at this boarding school, far from her family, she was able to familiarize herself with Western romantic poetry, which had a great influence on her, especially the poetry of Byron and Lamartine. The outcome of this period was a collection of poems in French called *Fleurs de Rêve* (Cairo, 1911),[81] which was published under the pseudonym of Isis Copia.[82]

Mayy Ziyādah might have continued to write in French had she not met Aḥmad Luṭfī al-Sayyid in Beirut in 1911, shortly after the publication of *Fleurs de Rêve.* He was impressed by Mayy Ziyādah's personality and her defense of the rights of Arab women. He felt that she had a role to play in Arabic literature, rather than French. After their return to Cairo, he advised her to read the Qur'ān to familiarize herself with the best usage of written Arabic. He also gave her as presents Malak Ḥifnī Nāṣif's *al-Nisā'iyyāt,* Qāsim Amīn's *Taḥrīr al-Mar'ah,* and the *dīwān* of Maḥmūd Sāmī al-Bārūdī.[83]

Not only al-Sayyid, but also Mayy Ziyādah's mother and Shiblī Shumayyil encouraged her to write in Arabic. Mayy Ziyādah's background in the Arabic language and literature was enriched when she attended the Egyptian University during World War I. There she studied Islamic philosophy and the history of Arabic literature. Ziyādah's Arabic benefited a great deal, not only from her regular studies, but also from her father's newspaper *al-Maḥrūsah,* to which some renowned writers contributed. Later, in her salon, she became acquainted with writers, especially Ismā'īl Ṣabrī, who used to discuss literary topics in Classical Arabic (al-Ṭanāḥī 1974: 11).

Despite Mayy Ziyādah's genuine enthusiasm for Arabic, she never lost her interest in other cultures. As she said: "Perhaps my knowledge of nine languages has enlarged the borders of my nationality and led me to look at the whole world as my greater homeland. Perhaps my travels in Europe have increased this tendency (*'aqliyyah*) within me" (S. 1928: 660).[84] Her interest in foreign literature led Mayy Ziyādah to translate three European novels into Arabic.[85] Her late acquaintance with the heritage of Classical Arabic literature and her early exposure to Western literature left its mark on her Arabic style, which some, including her friend Ya'qūb Ṣarrūf, criticized as a deviation from the "norms" of Arabic composition. Mayy Ziyādah responded to this criticism by saying:

> My knowledge of other languages leads me to compare our friends [her critics] with a women who spent all her life in a village of no more than seven houses. This woman used to say that it [the village] was the most beautiful city in the world and the mother of the universe. This knowledge [of foreign languages] made me ask myself questions when I read the writings of some who are considered the best writers and the most outstanding poets. How much of their own personalities did these writers put into what they wrote? Where is the individuality, of which I see not a trace?...I hate imitation, which distorts the thing imitated and falsifies the imitator. I like to be myself in my writings. (Sakākīnī 1969: 47)

Mayy Ziyādah's insistence that it was necessary to create a personal style instead of adopting one from earlier Arabic literature could be attributed not only to her deep familiarity with the European Romanticists, but also to the influence on her of the *Mahjar* school, led by Jubrān Khalīl Jubrān and Mīkhā'īl Nu'aymah. Mayy Ziyādah's views as expressed in the preceding quotation, remind us of the call of Jubrān Khalīl Jubrān to Arab poets: "Let your private intents prevent you from following the tracks of the ancients. It is better for you and for the Arabic language that you build a modest hut from your own selves rather than building a lofty edifice from your imitative selves" (Riḍā 1924: 75). Although Mayy Ziyādah was more a woman of letters than a social reformer, she was nonetheless involved in the women's emancipation movement in Egypt.[86] In 1914 she introduced herself to Hudā Sha'rāwī, telling her, "Do not think that my young age prevents me from doing my duty, or deters me from rallying under our banner to serve the cause of women" (M. 'A. Ḥasan 1964: 115). In one of her lectures Mayy Ziyādah surveyed the history of women, describing it as "a long and painful martyrdom" (Ziyādah 1975c: 33). Mayy Ziyādah maintained that the exclusion of women from the mainstream of historical events had crippled ancient civilization by forcing it to rely on men alone, whereas modern civilization was more humanistic because women were allowed to take part in shaping it (37). In the same lecture, Mayy Ziyādah rebutted the theory that women were created only to look after domestic matters, and that they were not entitled to education since it would ruin their beauty, modesty, and grace (38–39). At the end of her lecture, Mayy Ziyādah addressed men on behalf of women throughout history, saying: "O man! You have humiliated me, and therefore you have become humiliated. Free me in order to free yourself. Free me in order to free humanity" (41).

Nonetheless, Mayy Ziyādah retained a fairly conservative view regarding women's duties. The most important responsibilities of a wife and mother, she believed, were to her family. She rebuked women whose activities took them away from their families: "Come home from your long excursions and your many visits and your trivial chats. Come home and kneel in front of [your] baby and apologize to him! You were created a woman before you became beautiful, and nature shaped you as a mother before socialization made you a visitor" (Ziyādah 1963: 31–32). Echoing what some male intellectuals had said about the wife's role in a happy marital life, Mayy Ziyādah listed the woman's "qualifications" for such a role:

> Firstly, satisfying the husband, and by this I do not mean only satisfying him sexually, for the Eastern woman is the most skilled of all women in the world at this art. I mean satisfying him practically and spiritually, that is, she must look to his comfort at home and must raise her intellect to his level, so that he may find companionship with her and not abandon her [to go to] bars and cafés. Secondly, she must be taught home economics and the raising of children. Thirdly, the rich or middle-class woman must be taught how to become woman, articulate and affable. I hate the masculine woman and believe that the real role of the woman is to be a mother and wife.[87]

This apparent contradiction in her views is all the more interesting, considering that she herself never married nor had children.

Mayy Ziyādah's most lasting contribution to the cause of women was undoubtedly to be found in the literary sphere. Her active participation in Arab literary life inspired other women to break the social barriers that discouraged them from trying their hands at letters.[88] Mayy Ziyādah was the first Arab woman in modern times to be recognized as an established writer in her own lifetime. Her contribution to women's literature was best illustrated by three book-length studies she wrote about three of her female contemporaries: 'Ā'ishah Taymūr, Wardah al-Yāzijī, and Malak Ḥifnī Nāṣif.[89] Ziyādah grew famous as an essayist, lecturer, literary critic, translator, and writer of biographies, but never as a writer of fiction. Her contribution in this field was limited to a few short stories and two short plays.[90] In her short story *"al-Sham'ah Taḥtariq"* (*"The Candle Is Burning"*), Mayy Ziyādah plunged into the agonizing world of Yūlindā, a nun working as a nurse, who is torn between her devotion to God and her affection for a wounded soldier (Ziyādah 1934b).[91] Shajiyyah, the protagonist of *"al-Ḥubb fī al-Madrasah"* (*"Love in School"*), is a student at a missionary boarding school (Ziyādah 1934a).[92] There she suffers from loneliness and alienation until an older student is assigned to her as a "caretaker." This older student fills the roles of friend, sister, and mother for Shajiyyah. The special relationship between the two girls is shattered when the school administration decides to separate them, having accused them of having an intimate love relationship. When Shajiyyah's "caretaker" quits school to look after her sick father, Shajiyyah is once again locked away in her lonely private world, deprived of any relationship. Her story, *"al-Sirr al-Muwazza'"* (*"The Uncovered Secret"*) is only two pages long, scarcely more than a character sketch, without dialogue (Ziyādah 1935).[93] Its protagonist, a modern version of Don Juan, uses his "secret"—personal charm and alluring glances—to entrap a young lady who thinks his intentions are honorable and sincere. This story, like Mayy Ziyādah's other two stories, involves a minimal number of characters and emphasizes their psychological motives as the most important part of the tale.

The Generation between World Wars

Between the World Wars there emerged a group of Arab women writers who had had the opportunity to receive higher education. Now women's writings came to include scholarly studies in various disciplines, along with fiction and poetry, though these newer writers did not neglect fiction altogether.

Suhayr al-Qalamāwī (1911–••) was one of the first female students in the Arab world to receive a doctorate in the humanities. She was born in Cairo to a well-to-do family known for its interest in educating its female mambers. After her graduation from the American College in Cairo, al-Qalamāwī intended to follow her father's example and study medicine. When Cairo University rejected her application to study medicine, her father encouraged her to specialize in Arabic literature. During her Arabic studies al-Qalamāwī received guidance and moral support from Ṭāhā Ḥusayn, who was the chairperson of the Arabic Department at Cairo University. After earning her M.A. in Arabic literature, Suhayr al-Qalamāwī was sent to Paris on a scholarship to do research for her Ph.D. dissertation on the *Arabian Nights* under Ṭāhā Ḥusayn's supervision. Upon her graduation she received an appointment as a lecturer at Cairo University and became one of the first women to hold such a post. Within a relatively short time she had become the chairperson of the Arabic Department.

Suhayr al-Qalamāwī contributed to the cause of women not only through her literary activities, but also through her participation in Arab women's conferences, where she vehemently advocated equality between the sexes. She served as president both of the Arab Feminist Union and of the League of Arab Women University Graduates. She later entered the political arena to become a member of the Egyptian parliament, the Majlis al-Sha'b. She also served as the director of the government-affiliated Egyptian Organization for Publishing and Distribution (al-Hay'ah al-Miṣriyyah li-al-Ta'līf wa-al-Nashr), where she labored to encourage young writers, to promote the book industry, and to broaden the audience of readers. In 1978, in recognition of her services to modern Arab intellectual life, al-Qalamāwī was awarded the State Appreciation Prize for Literature—the highest literary prize in Egypt (al-Qalamāwī 1978: 66–67).[94]

Suhayr al-Qalamāwī's contribution to Arabic fiction was

limited to two works: *Aḥādīth Jaddatī* (*My Grandmother's Tales*), a short novel with an introduction by Ṭāhā Ḥusayn, and *al-Shayāṭīn Talhū* (*The Devils Are Dallying*, 1964), a collection of short stories. *Aḥādīth Jaddatī* consists of a series of tales told by a grandmother to her granddaughter, describing manners and customs in Cairo before the British occupation in 1882. Since that time Egypt has undergone enormous changes in every facet of life, and the granddaughter is fascinated by the pre-1882 perspective of her grandmother's stories. Thus, the book has a dual focus—the tales themselves and the granddaughter's reaction to them. However, the author seems to be more interested in the comparison of old and new than in the structure of the tales—so that the book is best regarded as a series of disassociated episodes having no internal cohesion. Although Ṭāhā Ḥusayn had predicted that the book would be of great siginificance (al-Qalamāwī n.d.: 1), his praise is better understood as a mentor's encouragement to his protegée. Nonetheless, al-Qalamāwī was successful in the field of language, using different layers of Arabic to create a lively dialogue. The language of the author was strictly Classical Arabic; the old woman's narration is infused with Egyptian colloquialisms, especially in the dialogue between a child and a maid in one of the tales (see, for example, al-Qalamāwī n.d.: 23, 28–29).

Bint al-Shāṭi' (a pseudonym of 'Ā'ishah 'Abd al-Raḥmān) wanted from the first to major in Arabic studies. She was born in 1913 in the northern Egyptian town of Dumyāṭ. Her father was an instructor in the Dumyāṭ Religious Institute and her mother was illiterate. Nonetheless, she owed her education to her mother, who took advantage of a prolonged absence of Bint al-Shāṭi''s father to enroll her in a school at the age of ten. Later, overriding her husband's objections, her mother sent her to al-Manṣūrah to continue her studies. Bint al-Shāṭi' was then admitted to Cairo University, where she obtained her first degree in Arabic in 1939 and was later appointed a teaching assistant. In 1941 she received her M.A., followed in 1950 by a doctorate with distinction. Thereafter she held various university posts in Egypt and Morocco.[95]

In addition to her numerous scholarly studies, Bint al-Shāṭi' was interested in writing biographies of early Muslim women. These included the mother, wives and daughters of the Prophet, as well as women of letters such as Sukaynah bint al-Ḥusayn and al-Khansā'. Her literary career really began in the late 1930s, when she wrote two books criticizing the social condition of the Egyptian peasantry: *al-Rīf al-Miṣrī* (*The Egyptian Countryside*, 1936) and *Qaḍiyyat al-Fallāḥ* (*The Problem of the Peasant*, 1938).

Although Bint al-Shāṭi' was not known as an active feminist, she often took up the issue of women, bitterly attacking society's attitudes toward them. The inferior status of women in Arab society was a recurring theme in her fiction. In the short story collection *Sirr al-Shāṭi'* (*Secret of the Beach*, 1942), she dealt with some of the social problems that faced women, such as the family's frustrated reaction at the birth of a girl instead of a boy, holding the mother responsible for this "disaster."

Destiny and Demons: Conventional Devices

Bint al-Shāṭi''s novel *Sayyid al-'Izbah: Qiṣṣat Imra'ah Khāṭi'ah* (*Master of the Estate: The Story of a Sinful Woman*, 1942) tells the story of Samīrah, who is the victim of a cruel father and a vicious landowner. Young Samīrah is led to believe that her mother ran away with a lover, leaving her with her father and his new wife. Both the father and the stepmother mistreat her. To get rid of her, her father forces her to work as a maid at the landowner's mansion, ordering her to do anything necessary to please her employer. Her master maneuveres her into having sexual relations with him, which result in her becoming pregnant. This illegitimate pregnancy almost drives Samīrah to commit suicide, but, as she says in the novel, "I refused to do so and chose to live, because I am a mother and it was my obligation to pay the penalty of life" ('Abd al-Raḥmān 1942: 87). To avoid a scandal, Samīrah is forced to marry a shepherd who works for the landowner. When her husband dies and the landowner goes bankrupt, Samīrah returns to her native village, only to face total ostracism. The villagers will have nothing to do with her and will not let her live among them, because they consider her a sinful woman. In the end, only death frees Samīrah from her ordeal, a method of escape that became more and more common in the fiction of women who were critical of patriarchal society and its implications for women. But death also leads to a problem in narration for the author. Samīrah herself is the narrator of the story, and defends herself against the attitudes of the villagers. But after Samīrah's death in the story, a new narrator close to the author herself narrates the story, telling of the rumors surrounding Samīrah's behavior and death.

Sayyid al-ʿIzbah is representative of Arab women's fiction written between the world wars: the emphasis in her writing shifted from historical themes to social topics, dramatizing the predicament of women in a hostile environment, especially in the countryside. The heroine is usually on the edge of an abyss, and any mishap could topple her into it. Such a mishap might result from a mistake on her own part or from something done by male members of society. The tragic fall would automatically lead to her premature death.

Destiny (*al-qadar*)[97] is a always the prime mover behind the heroine's fate. Even when other characters seem to precipitate her fate, they are explained as mere instruments in the hand of destiny, the hidden force that controls all events. Consider Bint al-Shāṭi''s description of Samīrah's first encounter with the landlord: "It was one of those unique and strange coincidences which destiny throws in the path of a human being, to divert the course of his life into a new channel and to determine his fate" (80). Magic and superstition are agents of destiny, because they also operate outside and above human comprehension. The stepmother uses magic to torture Samīrah's mother and force her to flee (16). The village women are amazed at how bravely Samīrah stands up to her enemies and declare that, with the help of magicians, she was communicating with the king of demons (*jinn*) who had: "provided her with an amulet (*taʿwīdhah*) which protected her from the villagers, so that their arrows would not reach her and they could not harm her" (99). Magic and evil spirits also play a role in Suhayr al-Qalamāwī's story. When the grandmother wants to discover the fate of her son Ra'fat, who is participating in the Egyptian campaign to put down the Mahdist rebellion in the Sudan, she turns to a *shaykh* (al-Qalamāwī n.d.: 56–57). On another occasion, she speaks of the bathhouse next to the family's home as being haunted (73–74). The demons living in the bathhouse, the grandmother says, "did not know their way to our house until after the candle of the house was extinguished" (that is, after her husband died) (80).

Social Handicaps

The pioneering generation of Arab women writers worked under serious handicaps insofar as the male-dominated society was not ready for their endeavors. The social and intellectual restrictions imposed on women were so rigid that one wonders how they were able to express themselves at all. 'Ā'ishah Taymūr and Zaynab Fawwāz, for example, wore the veil, and they were fully aware that this made it very hard for them to interact with the outside world. Zaynab Fawwāz adapted to this limitation better than 'Ā'ishah Taymūr, managing to involve herself peripherally in male intellectual life despite segregation by sex. During her stay in Damascus, while married to the Syrian writer Adīb Naẓmī, Fawwāz founded a literary salon in which she took part without being physically present. The male participants assembled in one room while she stayed in another, with her husband acting as a messenger between her and the men (Ibrāhīm 1964: 38).

Even Mayy Ziyādah, who lived in an entirely different environment, made this complaint to Amīn al-Rīḥānī when he was in the United States: "If I were a man I would have devoted at least four months of each year to travelling. But since I am a girl I must satisfy myself with Egypt and Syria" (Sa'd 1973: 86). It was quite common for these pioneering women writers to use pseudonyms in the hopes of avoiding negative reactions from their families and from society in general.[98] Malak Ḥifnī Nāṣif used the pseudonym Bāḥithat al-Bādiyah (Scholar of the Desert); Zaynab Fawwāz signed her polemical articles with the name Durrat al-Sharq (Pearl of the East) (al-Jundī n.d.: 76) or Ḥāmilat Liwā' al-'Adl (Holder of the Banner of Justice).[99] Munīrah Thābit wrote a column in the daily *al-Ahrām*, but she signed it only with her initials. Sulaymah al-Malā'ikah used the name Umm Nizār (Mother of Nizār, Nizār being her oldest son); following her example, the Syrian writer Khadījah al-Nashwātī used the name Umm 'Iṣām.[100] Mary 'Ajamī called herself Laylā (al-Daqqāq 1971: 87). Salmā Ṣā'igh used a number of fictitious names, such as Salwā, Jullunār, and Aphrodite (Nuwayhiḍ 1986: 168). 'Ā'ishan 'Abd al-Raḥmān used the pen name Bint al-Shāṭi' (Daughter of the Beach, referring to her birthplace Dumyāṭ on the Mediterranean).[101] In addition to her pen name of Isis Copia, Mayy Ziyādah hid behind a male persona (Khālid Ra'fat) when she wrote a number of articles in her father's daily *al-Maḥrūsah* in the 1910s and when she wrote an article in the English-language Cairo daily *The Egyptian Mail* about the role of Cairo's Arabic Language Academy in the revival of the Arabic language (Ziyādah 1975b: 42 n).

Most of the pioneering generation experienced difficulties in their personal lives as a result of their attempts to deviate from the prescribed role of women and their involvement in intellectual activities. Mayy Ziyādah, Mary 'Ajamī, and Nabawiyyah Mūsā never married—not necessarily a disaster in itself, but for Arab women, being unmarried also meant being social outcasts and having very limited access to public life, because women needed men for protection and status. No doubt some of these writers saw single life as the lesser of two evils; but even had a woman writer wanted to marry, she would have been found unacceptable by most potential husbands due to her nonconformity to traditional sex roles. Not surprisingly, those who did marry found it extremely hard to conform to the traditional norms of married life. Some, among them Hanā Kasbānī Kūrānī, Salmā Ṣā'igh,[102] and Ḥabbūbah Ḥaddād (Ibrāhīm 1964: 53, 184), ended up divorced at a time when divorce was not socially acceptable and that, for Christians like these three writers, was almost impossible. In fact, the story of Sīzā Nabarāwī's marriage[103] is a good illustration of the dilemma faced by this generation. When Nabarāwī completed her studies in France and returned to Egypt, the well-known Egyptian artist Muṣṭafā Najīb made a proposal of marriage to her. Al-Nabarāwī explained to him that she could not commit herself to a partnership in which the man alone had the right of divorce whenever he pleased. She agreed to marry him, however, after he agreed to give her the right of divorce as well. The marriage lasted four years, at the end of which she vowed never to marry again (al-Jawharī and Khayyāl 1980: 258–259). Malak Ḥifnī Nāṣif and Zaynab Fawwāz[104] ended up even worse off; they suffered what was to them the devastation of polygamy.

Most of the pioneering writers who were really able to devote themselves to their intellectual work were those who were free of marital responsibilities, because the traditional duties of a wife could leave a woman with little time or privacy for her art.[105] Some cases involved the death of the husband, as with 'Ā'ishah Taymūr, Wardah al-Yāzijī, and Hudā Sha'rāwī. Nāzlī Fāḍil was able to retain her salon and pursue intellectual activities with less difficulty by what Ronald Storrs called "marrying, for general convenience" a Tunisian, the mayor of La Marse in Tunis, who chose to continue residing in his home country (Storrs 1937: 97). Other writers never married to begin with, realizing that marital life could jeopardize their creative activities. Zaynab Fawwāz wittily summed up the predicament of women in general by outlining the life of an "average" woman:

> The first fifteen years of her life are spent in the thoughtlessness of childhood. When she reaches the age of forty, she sinks into the troubles of aging. Thus she has no more than twenty-five years in her prime. If we assume that she is a wife and gives birth only twelve times and that only six of her children survive, then her life will be as follows: Nine years of pregnancy, a year and six months of confinement in childbed, six years of breast-feeding, and four years and twenty days of various diseases. So the total of continuous troubles for body and soul is twenty years, six months, and twenty days. What is left to her of days of strength and health amounts to four years, five months, and ten days. And this is true only if health and physical and mental rest are always available to her, which is impossible. (Fā'ūr 1980: 68).

Attempts to leave the domain of the household and enter the world of men had other formidable consequences (Ibrāhīm 1966: 55).[106] For example, Fāṭimah (Rūz) al-Yūsuf, the founder of the first publishing house in the Arab world operated by women, described the problems she faced in her journalistic enterprise: "The greatest difficulty was not the meager financial resources, nor the exhausting effort, nor the limited market for journalism. Rather, it was the fact that I was a woman; this, in fact, was the most important problem. I had to undergo rough experiences and learn rough lessons" (Ḥannā 1979: 34). Suhayr al-Qalamāwī, the first Egyptian woman to teach at Cairo University, recalled her experience there: "I faced many difficulties at the beginning of my work because I was the first Egyptian woman to join the University teaching staff. Many [male] students from other faculties used to come to my lectures to see the woman who was teaching the students. They used to disturb me during my lectures. I, however, used to go on speaking without [showing] irritation until the students had all calmed down" (al-Qalamāwī 1978: 66–67).[107]

Development of a Female Literary Culture

Mayy Ziyādah traces the emergence of a female literary identity in the Arab world back to Bāḥithat al-Bādiyah (Malak Ḥifnī Nāṣif):[108]

> The female literary personality which manifested itself in part of 'Ā'ishah Taymūr's poetry became more clear in some of its features in Bāḥithat al-Bādiyah's writings. With Bāḥithat al-Bādiyah, the tone became different, and the woman's personality tended to achieve independence from the man, her mentor. In literature, we started to recognize the female voice with its warmth and sorrow, its munificence and sweetness, its criticism, irony and pain, its call for reform and progress with a mixture of excitement and poise. No just historian can ignore this curious event because it draws a new face, pours forth new writings and radiates a female personality which did not exist previously in public life. (Ziyādah 1934c: 400)

The road had not been adequately paved to enable these pioneering women to engage in creative writing. Mayy Ziyādah was able to identify the problems they faced. They were at a disadvantage because of much needed female literary culture, yet they were, like their male literary counterparts, struggling to create a modern innovative literature after generations of literary imitation and stagnation.

> In the recent and distant past, the woman used to imitate man in that which she created. Her personality did not differ from his except sometimes in elegy and in some other motifs imposed on her as a woman. Therefore, we are unable to find the female personality from which we can seek inspiration, and that is why it is necessary that we create the female mood, the female rhetoric, the female spirit in modern Arabic literature. It is a tough issue, to the extent that man cannot comprehend it, despite the fact that he himself is creating a new literature which he is adding to the old one. It is a difficulty that strikes us if we write in a foreign language where we find the road thriving with hundreds of past and present female writers. (Ziyādah 1934c: 400)

Yet, from the very beginning of modern Arab women's literature, women showed an awareness of the existence of a women's literary tradition, no matter how marginal it was, within the world of Arab letters. 'Ā'ishah Taymūr, in the introduction to her *dīwān, Ḥilyat al-Ṭirāz,* justified her involvement in letters by referring to "those veiled women who preceded me": Laylā al-Akhyaliyyah, Wallādah bint al-Mustakfī, and 'Ā'ishah al-Ba'ūniyyah (d. c. 1519) (Taymūr 1952: 152). She also mentioned her contemporary Wardah al-Yāzijī (152). In one of her poems, she added al-Khansā' and 'Ulayyah bint al-Mahdī to the list (265).

Another characteristic of this female literary culture was women's interest in writing biographies and historical or literary studies dealing with their female predecessors. As early as 1873 the Lebanese Maryam Naḥḥās began writing her book *Ma'riḍ al-Ḥasnā'fī Tarājim Mashāhīr al-Nisā'* (*The Fair Lady's Exhibition Regarding Biographies of Famous Women*),[109] which included biographies of famous women of ancient and modern times. Naḥḥās's example was followed by Zaynab Fawwāz in *Kitāb al-Durr al-Manthūr fī Ṭabaqāt Rabbāt al-Khudūr,* Widād Sakākīnī and Tamāḍir Tawfīq in their *Nisā' Shahīrāt min al-Sharq wa-al-Gharb* (*Famous Women from the East and the West,* 1959), and Salmā al-Ḥaffār al-Kuzbarī in *Nisā' Mutafawwiqāt* (*Women Who Excelled,* 1961). Other women chose to write biographies of single individuals. Mayy Ziyādah devoted one study each to Wardah al-Yāzijī, 'Ā'ishah Taymūr and Malak Ḥifnī Nāṣif. Bint al-Shāṭi' wrote about the Prophet's mother, wives, and daughters, in addition to her works on Sukaynah bint al-Ḥusayn and al-Khansā' and *al-Shā'irah al-'Arabiyyah al-Mu'āṣirah* (*Contemporary Arab Women Poets,* 1963). Widād Sakākīnī (b. 1913) wrote a book about Mayy Ziyādah, *Mayy Ziyādah fī Ḥayātihā wa-Āthārihā* (*Mayy Ziyādah in Her Life and Works,* 1969). Salmā al-Ḥaffār al-Kuzbarī, the Syrian writer, devoted much of her energy to do justice to Mayy Ziyādah by editing her complete works in two volumes (which includes some works never anthologized before), by presenting Mayy Ziyādah's correspondence with her contemporaries (al-Kuzbarī 1982) and Jubrān Khalīl Jubrān's letters to her (al-Kuzbarī and Bishrū'ī 1984), and by writing an extensive biography of Ziyādah in two volumes (al-Kuzbarī 1982). Among the recent manifestations of this trend are Nādiyā al-Jirdī Nuwayhiḍ's *Nisā' min Bilādī* (*Women from My Country,* 1986) and Emily Naṣrallāh's *Nisā' Rā 'idāt min al-Sharq wa-al-Gharb* (*Pioneering Women from East and West*, 1986).

In addition to the women writers' interest in writing about each other, they were united by special bonds of friendship. In fact, they were in great need of mutual encouragement, especially in the face of the hostility shown by men. Therefore, the early women writers 'Ā'ishah Taymūr, Wardah al-Yāzijī, and Zaynab Fawwāz were close friends and constantly exchanged letters. The same phenomenon existed in the following generation among Mayy Ziyādah, Malak Ḥifnī Nāṣif,[110] and Hudā Sha'rāwī.

The actual volume of literary output of the pioneering generation was modest. In the realm of fiction, four women writers—'Ā'ishah Taymūr, Alice al-Bustānī, Labībah Ṣawāyā, and Farīdah 'Aṭiyyah—produced only one novel each. Furthermore, the works of many members of the pioneering generation either went unpublished or were lost altogether. For example, 'Ā'ishah Taymūr left behind her a number of unpublished plays among which is *al-Liqā' ba'da al-Shatāt* (*Reunion After Separation*), and another unfinished play (Taymūr 1952: 19). The following works by Zaynab Fawwāz remained unpublished: a collection of biographies of renowned men entitled *Madārik al-Kamāl fī Tarājim al-Rijāl* (*Stages of Perfection in Men's Biographies*), a manuscript about Sultan 'Abd al-Ḥamīd entitled *al-Durr al-Naḍīḍ fī Ma'āthir al-Malik al-Ḥamīd* (*The Arranged Pearls in the Glorious Deeds of the Praiseworthy King*), and a large collection of her poetry (Dāghir: vol. 2, part 1, 683). Ḥabbūbah Ḥaddād left two unpublished works: *Nafathāt al-Afkār* (*Outpouring Thoughts*) and *Dumū' al-Fajr* (*Tears of the Dawn*) (Dāghir: vol. 3, part 1, 296). The works of poetry of the Lebanese Wardah al-Turk (c. 1797–1874) and the Egyptian Amīnah Najīb (1887–1927) were never collected (Kaḥḥālah 1979: vol. 2, 314). Alexandra Avierinoh's collection of poetry was never published.[111] The manuscripts of Hanā Kasbānī Kūrānī, including two works in English, were burned by her family after her death (Ibrāhīm 1964: 48; F. Muḥammad n.d.: vol. 2, 111), and the manuscript of one of Mayy Ziyādah's last works, *Layālī al-'Aṣfūriyyah* (*Madhouse Nights*), is still to be located (al-Kuzbrī 1987: vol. 1, 215).[112]

Conclusion

From the very beginning, the pioneering generation was apologetic and hesitant, aware that they were entering a male-dominated arena. To gain acceptance they had to avoid raising the controversial issues of veiling and equality between the sexes. Those who did raise them tended to be far more conservative even than the men, as Malak Ḥifnī Nāṣif was regarding the question of the veil. Paradoxically, they could assert themselves in the literary world only by conforming to male literary tradition and suppressing their own individuality. They generally limited themselves to traditionally feminine genres of poetry, notably to elegy, fully aware that they were addressing a male audience. Mayy Ziyādah confessed to the submission of women writers to the masculine traditions when she said: "Men are our mentors, our teachers and our molders, from whom we take our lessons, and from whose books and writings we acquire knowledge. Their intelligence helps us to polish and develop our own acumen, and from them we are inspired with every great thought and sublime sentiment. Men have monopolized all forms of aptitude, creativity and excellence. As soon as we open our eyes, we see that they symbolize every aspect of power, authority and influence" (Ziyādah 1975a: 168). Poetry, the first literary genre to which modern Arab women contributed, was dominated by men both in its classical and modern subdivisions. Hence, they established the rules of literary æsthetics in both fields. This epoch in the history of Arabic poetry (roughly the last quarter of the nineteenth century through the first quarter of the twentieth century) was generally characterized by vigorous attempts to revive the classical tradition of Arabic poetry, especially that of the Abbasid period, by means of imitation. Women's poetry in this epoch understandably failed to reflect a genuine personal originality, and the female psyche was distorted in their works not only by imitation but also by social constraint. In fact, the imitation was so convincing that, in some cases, critics charged that Wardah al-Yāzijī's poetry, for example, was, in fact, composed by either her father or her two brothers (al-Jundī n.d.: 19).[113]

In fiction, too, women writers found themselves participating in a tradition created by men in the last quarter of the nineteenth century and was still dominated by them. 'Ā'ishah Taymūr's innovative experiment in *Natā'ij al-Aḥwāl fī al-Aqwāl wa-al-Af'āl,* in which she blends for the first time in modern Arabic fiction (not without success) the art of *the Maqāmah* with other popular narrative genres, has remained to be explored. The fictions of Alice al-Bustānī, Zaynab Fawwāz, Labībah Hāshim, and Labībah Ṣawāyā were greatly influenced by the romantic trend initiated by Salīm al-Bustānī (1847–1884) (Najm 1961: 120; Badr 1968: 148–149). Similarly, the treatments by Labībah Ṣawāyā and Farīdah ʿAṭiyyah of the political turmoil in the early twentieth-century Ottoman Empire was a continuation of the original interest in the subject shown by Jūrjī Zaydān (1861–1914), whose novel *al-Inqilāb al-ʿUthmānī* (*The Ottoman Coup*, 1911) was the first Arabic work of fiction to deal with this turmoil.

Women's attempts to make contributions to Arabic literature led to a heated controversy. Unfortunately, some prominent Arab men of letters used their influence to cast doubt not only on women as a gender, but also on some spheres of literary creativity of their female counterparts rather than encouraging them. This was especially true at the delicate moment when women were first breaking into the field of writing. Typical of these male writers were ʿAbbās Maḥmūd al-ʿAqqād and Tawfīq al-Ḥakīm (1898?–1987). Al-ʿAqqād used his three main books dealing with women—*Hādhihi al-Shajarah* (*This Tree*), *Al-Insān al-Thānī* (*The Second Human Person*), and *Al-Mar'ah fī al-Qur'ān* (*Woman in the Our'ān*)—to express his belief that women were dependent and weak by nature and that they therefore needed the guidance and supervision of men. He also claimed that the tendency of women to disobey and rebel was related to their resentment of the way men had been their masters throughout history and that now they had enough and wanted revenge (al-ʿAqqād 1969: 133–138). The strongest weapon women had, he said, was their ability to seduce men—which illustrated their essential passivity and dependence (97–103).[114] These "ideas" influenced al-ʿAqqād's perception of how well women could do at writing poetry: "Among the fine arts women may be able to write fiction or to act or to dance, but they cannot write poetry. The history of the world does not yet include event a single great poetess, because femininity by nature does not express its sentiments and lacks the power to dominate another's opposite personality. It tends rather to suppress and conceal sentiment, or to give it up to someone who can seize it such as a husband or a lover. When a personality lacks sincere expression and sincere desire to extend itself, to expand, and embrace all creatures, then what is left for it in terms of great poetic talent is very little" (n.d.: 144–145). Tawfīq al-Ḥakīm had a negative attitude toward women from the beginning of his literary career. In his play *Al-Mar'ah al-Jadīdah* (*The New Woman*, 1923), he defended the veil and spoke out against the movement to liberate women.[115] Furthermore, al-Ḥakīm raised an issue that was also controversial in the West;[116] namely, the question of why women were not able to assert themselves in certain fields of art (theater, music and architecture, for example) even while they excelled at fiction writing. "Feeling and analysis," proclaimed al-Ḥakīm, "were the cornerstone on which women built all glorious work. . . . Analysis is an indispensable faculty for every writer who concerns himself with writing novels" (al-Ḥakīm 1939b: 7). In other areas of art, al-Ḥakīm believed, two other faculties were necessary. These were thinking and concentration, which he maintained that women lacked. To justify his attitude, al-Ḥakīm said: "In the field of creativity and art, everything divides me from women. I like philosophy, drama, architecture and symphonic music. To these four intellectual bases, on which every great artistic field is founded, women have not contributed" (8).[117] Not all male writers were so hostile to women or critical of their intrinsic artistic qualifications. Al-ʿAqqād's close friend, Ībrāhīm ʿAbd al-Qādir al-Māzinī, in an article published in 1924,[118] states his belief that women did not excel like men in literature, not because of gender, but rather because of the kind of life they have been forced to lead throughout history. This life-style, he maintained, resulted in narrowing their scope, limiting their range of experiences, and depriving them of their freedom. It is difficult, al-Māzinī states, for anyone to express oneself if he or she is not free (al-Māzinī 1992: 47). Al-Māzinī argues that, because the weak imitates the strong, women's literature will continue to be an imitation of men's until women are able to "rid themselves of every trace on their souls and minds of men's domination" (47).

The most important contribution of the pioneering generation was their revival of a women's literary culture in the Arab world, first in poetry and later in other genres. However, as we shall see in the following chapter, not until the 1950s did there emerge women novelists who not only contributed to women's literature, but who also revolted against the whole superstructure of norms set up by men. An emphasis on femaleness and a quest for personal identity characterized the works of these later writers, in contrast to the conformity of the pioneering generation.

3. The Quest for Personal Identity

By the end of World War II, most Arab countries outside of North Africa had achieved political independence. In general, this new condition enabled them to have a more relaxed relationship with the West, especially in intellectual fields. The drive of the newly independent states for national identity and the construction of a modern, and to a great extent secular, society led to a gradual improvement in the social and educational conditions of Arab women. The development of women's education, whether in the home or in foreign institutions, played a significant role in the emergence of a philosophy of individualism and the consciousness of a female identity. Furthermore, by the 1950s, with the relative rise of literacy, the novel had emerged as an established literary genre and as a vehicle of self-expression and social criticism largely at the expense of poetry, which had previously served these purposes.

Amīnah al-Sa'īd: New Beginnings

The publication of Amīnah al-Sa'īd's *al-Jāmiḥah* (*The Defiant*, 1950) was a new departure in the development of women's novel . Born in Cairo in 1914 and a graduate of the Cairo University English Department in 1935, she recalled her experience as the only female student in a class of seven male students: "It was only natural that my male classmates were so self-conscious about their manhood that they refused to consider me fully one of them, and so they called our class 'the class of seven-and-a-half'" (Muṣṭafā 1978: 59). Amīnah al-Sa'īd had been an active feminist ever since her school days. After graduation she joined Hudā Sha'rāwī's Egyptian Feminist Union, and for a time she was the editor of its Arabic-language paper *al-Miṣriyyah*. She was the editor of *Ḥawwā'*, the Egyptian weekly women's magazine, beginning at its foundation in 1954. Her interest in journalism led her to be the first woman to be elected to the Egyptian Press Syndicate executive board; and she served on the executive board of the Dār al-Hilāl publishing house and as a member of the Supreme Board of Journalism in Egypt. Her writings dealt with a variety of subjects important to Arab women. For example, she attacked the veil as an obstacle to the progress of Arab women and as an instrument of their subordination to men.

Al-Jāmiḥah was Amīnah al-Sa'īd's first novel. Unlike previous female novelists who had written about historical themes or tackled social problems outside their own societies, described in Chapter Two, al-Sa'īd chose to look at her own society. Her novel focused on the emotional growth and self-realization of Amīrah, a female artist. Another new element in *al-Jāmiḥah* was the fact that the whole story is told from the point of view of a female character, articulate and conscious of her identity.[1]

The protagonist Amīrah is a woman whose life has been dominated by her father, who has raised her alone because her mother died when she was born. He wants her to be strong and to be guided by intellect alone, never letting "weak emotion" play any role in her life. When she is still small, her father explains his philosophy in these words: "The world does not grant recognition to the weak, and survival in it is for the strong. If you cannot be strong, then at least pretend that you are strong. Do not accept an insult from anyone, even if he is the closest person to you. If a girl strikes you, strike her back; and if she curses you, curse her a hundredfold. No matter how much you suffer from this, you will have satisfied your pride" (al-Sa'īd 1950: 21). As a child Amīrah is obsessed with destructiveness, and a doll is her first victim. When she destroys this doll she discovers her talent as an artist, because the first picture she draws is of this broken toy (only after breaking it does she realize how much it meant to her). Amīrah carries her aggressiveness with her to school, treating her friends much as she has treated her doll. She chooses Fāṭimah, an ugly student her own age who is rejected by the others, as her friend and embraces her as "she had embraced her toy a few years before, and bestowing upon her all the love and faithfulness that she had in her heart" (43). However, she ends up abandoning Fāṭimah, destroying her as she destroyed the doll she loved.

Later, Amīrah decides to cultivate her artistic talent by going to an art institute. There she forms sentimental relationships with a fellow student, Maḥmūd, and with her teacher. She cannot see Maḥmūd as a possible husband since he is poor, and one of "those whom her father described as members of an obscure human herd who work only in order to live, without any great goal to attain" (151). She therefore chooses to marry her teacher. After her marriage Amīrah falls prey to boredom and aimlessness, which leads her to search for meaning in art. Maḥmūd shows up in her life once again, after a long absence, and creates a storm in her heart. Only her fear of remorse stops Amīrah from betraying her husband.

Al-Jāmiḥah contains many themes that are used and further developed by later women's novels of the 1950s and 1960s. One such theme is the role of the family, especially of its male members, in shaping the world of women—not surprising, because women's activities and range of mobility were limited mostly to the private sphere. Amīrah's upbringing renders her unable to develop any meaningful relationships with other people. Her whole life is a series of clashes between the rationality her father overemphasized, and her emotions. Amīrah has no ability to love or maintain emotional relationships. Her only real "friends" are inanimate objects—a doll, and later, after her marriage, a star that she identifies with her husband. Although she feels that both could penetrate her inner world and explore her heart, she is relaxed and intoxicated in the presence of the star, but bothered and scared by her husband.

Another device that recurs frequently in later women's novels is that of the protagonist as artist. This is largely intended to dramatize the search for personal identity by exploring the innermost psyche and the interaction between the psyche and the outside world. Amīrah's artistic skilll reveals itself after she is overcome by the sorrow of having broken her doll; she expresses her feeling by painting a picture of it. She stops drawing for a while after her marriage, but begins again when she cannot find satisfaction in her married life.

As with protagonists in later women's novels, the inability to find fulfillment within marriage leads Amīrah to think about returning to the traditional role of motherhood: "She longed for a little baby who would keep her busy with his smiling face and his sweet tone of voice, and keep her from dwelling on her private thoughts. This longing sometimes brought her to the point of seeing motherhood as the only blessing of marriage" (161).

Laylā Ba'labakkī's Rebellion: Two Novels

Another major Arab woman author, Laylā Ba'labakkī, was born in 1936 in southern Lebanon to a traditionalist Shiite Muslim family. She had to struggle hard to persuade her family to let her have an education. As she later said: "I came from a conservative family which considered women's education a crime. When I finished my primary studies I had to go on a hunger strike for three months so my father would let me go on with my education."[2] She interrupted her studies at the Jesuit University in Beirut to work as a secretary in the Lebanese parliament. At the young age of fourteen her articles and short stories began being published in periodicals, under a pseudonym.[3] In 1960 she went to Paris on a one-year scholarship from the French government.

The protagonist of al-Ba'labakkī's first novel, *Anā Aḥyā* (*I Am Alive* 1958), is a young woman named Līnā. The novel tells the story of Līnā's pursuit of personal freedom and self-fulfillment in a hostile conservative environment both within the home and outside it. Līnā faces a more complex web of family relationships than Amīnah al-Sa'īd's Amīrah; in addition to her father, she has her mother, a brother, and two sisters with whom to deal.

The frequent clashes marking Līnā's attempts to free herself take place in two arenas: family and society. Her first rebellion is against her father, a figure of both male authority and moral corruption. He exerts his authority upon all the members of the family, especially Līnā. He is an opportunist and a war profiteer and has abandoned his studies for commerce. His opportunism also leads him to collaborate with the French mandate and the ruling circles. This treason against his country is paralleled by unfaithfulness to his wife: Līnā once catches him sneaking looks at his neighbor while the latter is undressing and also knows that he once went to Cairo to have an affair when he claimed he was going on business. Līnā hates her father for these traits and for his wealth: "I despise my father and despise his millions. . . . Does he not know that if I had been able to choose my father, he would not have been my father?" (Baʿlabakkī 1964a: 15).

Līnā is disgusted by her mother's surrender to her father's egotism and arrogance. The mother has given up completely her own personality and become a mere appendage of the father, praising him for his accomplishments in life. This character is the stereotypical traditional Arab mother often found in Arab women's novels during this period, seeking, only to please her husband and raise their children. "Poor mother," Līnā reflects at one point in the story, "She knows nothing of life except sharing a man's bed, cooking his food, and raising his children" (112–113). Līnā clashes with her mother because the mother seems intent on remaking Līnā in her own image. Līnā's family situation produces a negative image of marriage in her mind and prejudices her against it. To her, "marriage" means that "I am the slave and he is the absolute master. He asks and I must give. Hunger is mine, satiety is his. I wait and he determines the time of performance" (195). She revolts against femininity as well as against marriage. Her mother's fate frightens her. "The sight of flesh, of my mother's flesh, arouses my disgust towards her. She is a female, the source of giving. She is a gushing river which needs many wide, deep streams to pour into it" (113). Consequently, Līnā comes to see sex as a mechanical and dehumanizing thing, intended not for self-fulfillment but only for the satisfaction of the man's lust and the bearing of children. For this reason she turns down a proposal of marriage from one of her coworkers: "Would I marry [my] colleague? That means: A machine will rub against another machine, and as a result of this friction small machines will be born, machines which will rattle like mice in a box of old books in the corner of an old library" (216–217). Realizing that she cannot be free at home, Līnā leaves to seek her fortune. Her first independent act is to get a job at a company without asking her parents for permission. Unfortunately, the president of the company is her father all over again; he cannot understand why a wealthy young lady would want to work. Līnā becomes fed up with her job and her boss with his "disguised mean face" (58) and quits.

Looking for another path to self-fulfillment, Līnā begins a

love affair with an Iraqi fellow student named Bahā'. Unlike the apolitical Līnā, Bahā' is a committed communist. However, he has come from a conservative environment in which the female body is a taboo shrouded in mystery. However, their relationship is doomed to failure. His attitude toward women is fundamentally no different from that of the other men she has known. He lacks the ability to have a healthy and emotional relationship with a woman, for he is still a captive of the reactionary ideas he has brought from his country.

Līnā finds that every avenue she tries in the world of men comes to a dead end. She has no choice but to return home: "And I returned home as though I were compelled to return home. I must always return home, to sleep in this home, to eat in this home, to bathe in this home, and to have my fate determined in this home" (340). There, Līnā's parents try to "tame" her and train her for the traditional Arab female role of wife and mother. This completes the vicious circle: from home to outside world and back to home.

Anā Aḥyā was the first novel to depict this "vicious circle" theme, which was central to the majority of women's novels in the 1960s and will be discussed later at greater length. In the outside world Līnā cannot find salvation because everyone looks upon her as a female and not a person to be taken seriously. As a result, Līnā's attitude toward men is not totally consistent. Although she keeps complaining about those who seemed set to prey on her, she does not hide her disappointment when a male coworker in the company pays her no attention (Ba'labakkī 1964a: 56). Her ideas about personal freedom are rather confused because she is not sure what she wants to do with her freedom, and as a result she acts in contradictory ways. On the one hand, she wants to be taken seriously, and so wants to break with the traditional stereotype of women. She thus tries to get rid of the physical marks of femininity—for example, by cutting her hair because a young man complimented her on it. On the other hand, when Līnā is unable to deal with Bahā' on an intellectual level, she finds herself forced to use her femininity to salvage their relationship.

Ironically, it is with a man that Līnā finds refuge from men. Her loneliness and the constant male pestering that interrupts it drives her into Bahā''s arms. She ruminates while sitting in a café: "I am lonely. . . . I felt anew my insignificance, and realized that I needed a [male] friend, a man who would occupy my mind with things to which it was not accustomed" (110). Furthermore, Līnā feels that only a man can help her find herself: "He will help me discover my characteristics: Eastern or Western? Beautiful or ugly? Can I express a worthwhile opinion on politics or not? Am I a student or a visitor?" (114). She is even willing to sacrifice all her ideals to save her relationship with Bahā'. As she confesses, "I fear that Bahā' will become angry and abandon me forever, and then I will return to loneliness, anxiety, and emptiness" (309). Her failure at work and study and her inability to assert herself as a "free" woman leads her to return to the norms of society and to try to fulfill herself within them by having children: "I want to exercise my right. I want to have a baby now that I have failed at work and study. But I need a man to have a baby" (317).

Although Līnā's father holds the real power, her mother is assigned to supervise and indoctrinate her. Līnā comes full circle in that she accepts the role her mother has given her. This willingness to play the traditional role of wife and mother is the anticlimax to Līnā's pursuit of uniqueness. From the beginning of the story, Līnā sets her sights on being different from other women, and she even resents her sisters for their willingness to conform to prescribed social roles (272, 290). At the university she is also convinced that she is different from her fellow students and superior to them, although her academic accomplishments are unimpressive: "All these students piled up on stones in the courtyard . . . are stupid" (102). Her superiority complex reaches the point that she does not want her body to be touched by other students as they are leaving the classrooms (69). She even leaves herself set apart by her father's wealth, which she supposedly despises: "I was overwhelmed by a feeling of distinction, importance and superiority over everybody who does not count money (*līrāt*) and into whose hands no salesman puts packages" (315).

Anā Aḥyā marks the first use of first-person narration in Arabic women's fiction, a device that is not insignifigant in the context of this stage of literary development. It is also a striking example of the constant use of the pronoun *I* (*anā*) for emphasis. The idea is to stress the identity and individuality of the protagonist. Indeed, the character of Līnā is the only thing that holds the novel together, because every event, scene, and feeling is presented through her. To see Līnā as a total representation of the author would be going too far, but the novel (which Laylā Ba'labakkī wrote at the age of eighteen) does contain many autobiographical elements, as Laylā Ba'labakkī herself admitted (Ba'labakkī 1965: 6).[4]

Her second novel, *al-Ālihah al-Mamsūkhah* (*The Disfigured Gods*, 1960), differs greatly from *Anā Aḥyā*. The story is told from a number of points of view instead of only one, and its theme is also different: "In *Anā Aḥyā* the issue was how women achieve their social freedom, whereas in *al-Ālihah al-Mamsūkhah* I wanted to show how Easterners worship the woman's body and glorify the past and death."[5] In *al-Ālihah al-Mamsūkhah* the most important part of the female body is the hymen. Ba'labakkī stressed this to shed light on the Arab obsession with female chastity before marriage. The protagonist of the story, 'Āyidah, is a lonely and alienated Lebanese student in London. Her troubles begin when she faints in the university library after hearing the news of her mother's death. She awakens to find herself in the room of a male Indian student, and realizes that he raped her while she was unconscious. 'Āyidah suffers greatly from this event when she marries later on in the story. Her husband Nadīm, who has not known about her experience in London, discovers on the night of their marriage that she is not a virgin and finds this discovery unbearable: "O God. Forgive me, God. The wall is collapsed, O God. You are an infidel. Criminal. You are evil and accursed. How could you dare? How could you dare?" (Ba'labakkī 1960: 21). Nadīm was in the habit of referring to the hymen as "the sacred wall" and "the door of the sublime temple" (21). By convention, Nadīm would be expected to leave her even though he is a well-educated man (a professor of history). The only thing that makes Nadīm stay with her is her money. Nevertheless he is determined to punish her for not being a virgin, and he does so by totally ignoring her and refusing to sleep with her. The curse of her lost virginity follows 'Āyidah like a shadow until her death, even though it was lost due to events beyond her control. She is deprived of her right to have children—a severe loss, because she has much leisure time and no other responsibilities in life. 'Āyidah pours her motherly emotions out upon her doll, Nānā. She treats this doll like a real baby, putting it to bed, taking it to cafés, even breast-feeding it. Eventually Nadīm impregnates her while he is drunk and fantasizing about another woman, and it seems that she might be able to have a real child at last. However, her hopes are dashed again: she has her baby prematurely, and it dies.

In 1954, when she was only eighteen, Laylā Ba'labakkī spoke of the negative impact of parents upon their children: "A constant anxiety has undoubtedly surrounded our childhood, for all of us live in this East and all of us are victims of our forefathers and parents, who cling to everything that has been passed on to them, without adapting their own lives or ours to the conditions and requirements of the age. Some of us are bodies crawling upon the Earth, carelessly heading for our graves, while the others are courageously engaged in a fierce struggle between the old and the new" (Ba'labakkī 1954: 693). The alienation of the new generation was a central theme in Laylā Ba'labakkī's 1959 lecture *Naḥnu bi-lā Aqni'ah* (We Without Masks) in which she summed up the situation of her generation as follows: "We bent our shoulders out of fatigue. We proceeded, while anxiety tore at us, to take a look at the laws which our [masters] created for us, the rules which they imposed on us, and the destinies which they chose for us. And here we cast our eyes away from the earth with frustration: nothing on earth represents or satisfies us, because it was designed by someone other than us. We sent our desperate appeal up to the sky and clung to the blue curtain, seeking an explanation from the Owner of the Sole Truth about ourselves and Him. And all of a sudden we are aliens" (8). The new generation of women was alienated not only spiritually but also physically. Any attempt by women to gain control of their own bodies was doomed to end in tragedy. The overprotection of women's chastity, especially before marriage, by the social norms led them to feel that they did not own their own bodies. Ba'labakkī criticized the sexual segregation practiced in Arab society because it led to repression and anxiety among both sexes. This is evident in the endings of the two novels just discussed. *Anā Aḥyā* ends with Līnā desiring to have a baby. She fails to find a partner because Bahā' detests children, calling them "leeches that suck the parents' blood" (Ba'labakkī 1964a: 320). In *al-Ālihah al-Mamsūkhah* the character Mīrā (in some senses an extension of Līnā) finds a prospective husband in Rajā. She believes that he will free her from her preoccupation with death and rescue her from total boredom, but she is not absolutely sure of him.

The narrative technique used in *Anā Aḥyā* is simple, conventional, and straightforward. It leads the reader to see all the events and look into the worlds of all the characters through the eyes of the heroine Līnā. In an attempt to intensify the individualistic aspect of Līnā's experience, the author frequently resorts to interior monologue. This technique is narrow in scope and leaves the reader in the dark as far as the psychological makeup of the other characters is concerned. Though it is hard to believe Laylā Ba'labakkī's claim that she had never read any novel before writing *Anā Aḥyā*,[6] it is obvious that she was still refining her artistic talents when she wrote it.[7] She shows a more mature understanding of the novel, especially of characterization and narrative viewpoint, in *al-Ālihah al-Mamsūkhah*. She explained the differences between the two books by saying that *Anā Aḥyā* was a loose, spontaneous novel whose structure was largely hidden, a revolt against the traditional techniques of novel writing. It deals with the problems of its protagonists in a simple and clear manner. *Al-Ālihah al-Mamsūkhah*, on the other hand, is a complex novel with a clearly visible structure (Ba'labakkī 1965: 5). In it, Laylā Ba'labakkī uses a variety of literary techniques to present her characters: the epistolary method, the conventional omniscient narrative viewpoint and the stream-of-consciousness technique. In addition, the language in *al-Ālihah al-Mamsūkhah* is more tense, condensed, and emotionally charged, which gives *al-Ālihah al-Mamsūkhah* a poetic quality. This led one critic to label the whole book a poem in prose (al-Dayrī 1960: 4), and evaluation with which Laylā Ba'labakkī agreed: "In it [*al-Ālihah al-Mamsūkha*] I was like a poet who composes a poem. It is close to poetry, based on image, symbol, and concise allusion" (Ba'labakḳī 1960: 7).

Not all reviews of her work were positive, however. Her use of language in fiction was innovative and daring, especially in the second book. She allowed herself to use a great many colloquial words and phrases, something that upset many critics and led them to charge her with chasing after the peculiar and unusual at the expense of the essential eloquence of the Arabic language (see, for example, Idrīs 1961: 60). In addition, Laylā Ba'labakkī's young female characters provoked bitter controversy among Arab critics, including female critics. For example, the Egyptian writer Bint al-Shāṭi' made the following comment to a male interviewer: "The problem with Laylā [Ba'labakkī] and others [i.e., women writers] is that they do not represent the reality of our situation. I am the daughter of a *shaykh* and my husband is a *shaykh*, yet despite that,

I sit with you here in liberty and freedom. Where are those shackles and repression and anxiety about which Laylā and others talk?" ('Abd al-Raḥmān 1962: 168).

Ba'labakkī's troubles with her critics reached their peak with the publication of her next book, *Safīnat Ḥanān ilā al-Qamar* (*Spaceship of Tenderness to the Moon*, 1964),[8] a collection of twelve short stories. In this work Ba'labakkī was more vehement than ever in her advocacy of total freedom of behavior for women, unrestricted by socially imposed codes of ethics. This stance, combined with daring (for the time) descriptions of sexuality in some of the stories, so offended some readers that the chief of the Beirut vice squad summoned Ba'labakkī to an interrogation in his office, and she was ultimately put on trial for the book.[9] The problem arose mainly from two sentences in the short story entitled "Ḥīna Tasāqaṭ al-Thalj" ("When the Snow Fell"):

> He lay on his back and his hand went under the sheets taking my hand and putting it on his chest, and then his hand travelled over my stomach.
>
> He licked my ears, then my lips, and he roamed over me. He lay on top of me and whispered that he was in ecstasy and that I was fresh, soft, dangerous, and that he had missed me.[10]

The reaction began with a review of the book in the Cairo weekly *Ṣabāḥ al-Khayr*. The review, signed by a woman writer named Nādiyah, quoted the sentence in which Laylā Ba'labakkī used the word *licked* (which was to play a major role in the trial later). At the end of the review, Nādiyah said: "I shuddered with disgust and said angrily to myself: O lady Laylā Ba'labakkī, what does "licked" mean? What does "roamed" mean? What does "soft" mean? What kind of literature is this? This is a damned literature, O lady!" (*Difā'an 'an al-Ḥurriyyah* 1964: 176). Another woman writer, Thurayyā Malḥas, used the book to attack male critics. She claimed that the man was always the cause of the woman's downfall because he persuaded her to deviate and then killed her and cut her to pieces when she did. Arab men had not changed, Thurayyā Malḥas went on, but their methods had; now they encouraged women to deviate from norms in the name of literature and art, and women went along because they believed that this was the way to achieve fame. Now that Laylā Ba'labakkī had done this, some male reviewers were publicizing the fact that she was more daring than other women in talking about sexuality. They patted her on the shoulder, forgetting or pretending to forget that there were other men who were ready to entrap her or even kill her for "moral" reasons (*Difā'an 'an al-Ḥurriyyah* 1964: 179–180). Despite these critical reactions, the revolt of women against the rigid social and "moral" norms that prevented them from asserting their own identities continued to be an important theme for women writers. Colette Suhayl al-Khūrī took up the cause in her 1959 novel *Ayyām Ma'ahu* (*Days with Him*).

Colette al-Khūrī: Unconvincing Developments

Colette al-Khūrī was born in Damascus into a Christian family of some prominence (her grandfather Fāris al-Khūrī once served as prime minister of Syria) and was educated there as well, getting an early exposure to French literature. Later she worked as a teaching assistant in the French department of Damascus University, where she was preparing her doctoral dissertation on French literature. Her literary career began with the publication of a collection of poems in French entitled *Vingt Ans* (Beirut, 1958).[11] In it al-Khūrī expressed her discontent with social constraints and the emptiness and aimlessness of her life and described her attempts to find salvation in love.

The protagonist and narrator of *Ayyām Ma'ahu* is named Rīm. Like the protagonists of the other novels, Rīm has to struggle against society in general and her family in particular as she develops her personal identity. There is, however, a difference in that Rīm's parents died when she was young and thus they cannot dominate her adult life. Nevertheless, her father has influenced the development of her character. She is haunted by his sober words: "I will not praise you if you have done something good, for I assume that you should do good—but I will blame you for your mistakes" (al-Khūrī 1967: 99). Also, when Rīm completes her secondary studies her father stops her from enrolling at the university on the grounds, as he puts it, that "women in my country are not in need of advanced degrees" (22).

Since her parents' death, Rīm's uncle and grandmother have taken care of her. When she takes to composing poetry and seeing it published (symbolizing her desire to express herself as an individual), her uncle is indignant: "This girl is not balanced! Why does she publish her poems in magazines? What benefit does she derive from writing poetry? She is an eccentric. I do not like her conduct at all. She is creating problems for us" (23). Even worse, Rīm's grandmother is always preaching to her about the necessity of sexual segregation. "I have confidence in your manners," the grandmother would say, "but you are still young and men in our country are untrustworthy" (116).

Forbidden either to go on with her studies or to seek a job, Rīm sits idle at home. She finds an escape from this dull existence in her relationship with Ziyād, a man of the world. From the very beginning, Rīm is sure that her relationship with Ziyād will come to a bad end. Her friend Najwā agrees: "There are huge differences: religion, background, and age. Yes, Rīm, you are right; any relationship between the two of you will be impossible" (89). It is probable that Rīm's realization that her romance with Ziyād cannot lead to marriage is the very thing that makes the romance possible. Like Līnā in *Anā Aḥyā*, Rīm is repelled by the institution of marriage in its traditional form.[12] She expresses this in forceful terms: "No! I was not born only to learn cooking and then to marry, bear children, and die! If this is the rule in my country, I will be the exception. I do not want to marry!" (22; see also p. 357). Ziyād has a similar attitude toward marriage, but in other ways he is very different from Rīm. He has had extensive contact with the opposite sex, having spent seven years in Europe, and is able to describe the greater sexual freedom there: "In Europe, I would invite a woman to dinner and she would agree. At the end of the evening she would follow me back to my apartment in a very natural way, even though she knew I might never see her again after that night" (56). Unlike Rīm, Ziyād is very materialistic and skeptical concerning love. In fact, he does not even admit that there is such a thing: "Love is a short-lived and silly sentiment. Love is an illusion. I do not love" (73; see also pp. 57, 81, 89, 96).

Ziyād also rejects marriage because he is a musician and fears that the monotony of married life will kill his artistic creativity (72–73, 186). Later, he even comes to feel that even Rīm's jealousy is an infringement on his personal freedom and on his life as an artist. He tells her "You are terrible. Why do you not allow freedom in my demeanor? You are drawing circles around me, trying to set boundaries for my life.... You do not realize that I am an artist. You are destroying my art by placing barriers around me" (275–276).

Rīm sees him both as a father and as a lover, saying of him "I was madly attached to Ziyād. I found in him the father I missed and the lover I was looking for" (152). Part of what leads Rīm to see him as a father figure is his age (about forty, whereas Rīm is nineteen), and his age is one of the things she likes best about him (115–116).[13]

The characters undergo a dramatic but unconvincing change in the course of the novel. At the beginning, Ziyād is assertive, defiant and emotionally independent—exactly the kind of man Rīm wants: "I wished he would remain like that: big, serious and strong, sensing my weaknesses and protecting me. I wanted his arms to stay around my shoulders, lifting from them the responsibilities of life" (109).

She is always ready to fade into his shadow (238). But after they separate for twenty days due to a quarrel, Ziyād returns a different man, even making her a proposal of marriage. Rīm, too, undergoes a complete change in her psychological makeup and turns his proposal down. Ironically, as they "find themselves," each one takes up the philosophy of the other. Now Ziyād is quite ready to give up his hostility to marriage altogether. He is even willing to condemn his whole past as a "black history" (348). Far from being the protector, he now needs Rīm's protection. And who now becomes mad with jealousy? Not Rīm. "I love you [said Ziyād]. I can't stand anymore the thought of your evening parties with friends. Who are these friends? Rīm, I am jealous. I am jealous" (374). And who now finds it impossible to tolerate jealousy? Not Ziyād. Rīm begins to attack Ziyād's jealousy using imagery that is very close to the imagery he earlier used to condemn her jealousy: "Today his jealousy infuriates and irritates me. This jealousy is a barrier which draws circles around my life... and suffocates me" (375). Now she is the one who holds art and marriage to be incompatible: "Should I marry Ziyād? Should I sacrifice everything for his sake? Should I sacrifice my art, my poetry, to become a machine producing children or a piece of furniture in Ziyād's house, for him to use whenever he wants?" (377). Rim first meets Ziyād when he has just come back from Europe to live in his hometown Damascus, which he feels will provide him with the right atmosphere for artistic creativity. However, he is bored and frustrated by the city's rigid social life and provincial character. "I am in need of a new country," he said, "new skies, and new faces. I am bored. I am bored. Boredom is almost killing me" (191). After the change, Rīm complains about the narrowness of life in Syria, which holds her back from cultivating and developing her literary talents. "I want to write, and my art needs new experiences, new scenes and new faces" (408).

In several ways Rīm is similar to Līnā of *Anā Aḥyā*. First, Rīm has problems with men who look upon her as a sex object and treats her as such. During one trip to a café with Ziyād, she feels men's gazes as though they are arrows piercing her body: "[Sexual] hunger shouts from the eyes. The fact that I am a female, whether or not I am beautiful, whether or not I am young, made them forget everything and stop talking, playing backgammon, and drinking their coffee" (132; see also pp. 44, 51, 107). Second, Rīm decides to get a job, which leads to a confrontation with her family and gives her the opportunity to assert herself. Her uncle does not approve of this and advises her to get married as a way of solving all her problems (33). The grandmother considers Rīm's getting a job to be a catastrophe, especially because she is not in financial need (33–34). However, even though Rīm is able to stand up to them and argue her case, her decision to work is actually no more than an act of defiance and a way of relieving boredom in a way reminiscent of Līnā's, rather than a well-though-out act intended to clarify her self-identity. Third, both characters retreat at a certain point. Līnā finds herself forced to go back home after failing to make it in the outside world. Rīm also has to withdraw from the struggle, but does so in a less concrete way. She decides to devote all her energy to verbal self-expression because, as she puts it, "art is the only thing that deserves sacrifice" (334). Art replaces the two men (Ziyād and Alfred) through whom she has tried to fathom her own mind and crystallize her own personal identity.

The two novels also deserve comparison on the level of narrative technique. As Laylā Ba'labakkī had done in *Anā Aḥyā*, Colette al-Khūrī wrote *Ayyām Ma'ahu* as a first-person narrative of the personal experience of its protagonist and made constant use of the pronoun *anā*, "I." This is artistically justified by the fact that the whole story deals with Rīm's emotional and intellectual growth. As in *Anā Aḥyā*, the aim is to emphasize the uniqueness and individuality of the main character. In *Ayyām Ma'ahu* many paragraphs begin with the pronoun, and it is often repeated within the same paragraph: "I want to live my life. . . . I want to obtain high degrees. I want to study music. I want to study singing. I want to write poetry. I want to draw. I want to work. I want to travel. I want. I want. I want" (22). Sometimes it is simply repeated within a single line: "And I. I. Oh, I, I am a woman" (220).

Al-Khūrī's next novel, *Laylah Wāḥidah* (*One Night*, 1961), is more controversial due to the element of adultery as an aspect of self-discovery. Its married heroine, Rashā, tries to find herself and regain control of her life through an extramarital relationship. At the age of fifteen her parents marry her to a thirty-three-year-old man named Salīm. She has almost no say in this and goes along with it only to placate her parents, although she is obviously less than happy with the situation: "Isn't it so that, in my country, if girls pass the age of twenty without being married they will be sentenced to death? . . . Isn't it so that parents will harass a daughter who has held back from getting married, because they are afraid that she will never get married?" (al-Khūrī 1961: 92). During her engagement Rashā is not allowed to be alone with her fiance or even to meet him. Whenever he comes to visit her parents, Rashā peeks at him through the keyhole of the door separating them and is never able to form a clear impression of what he looks like. Once they are married, she confesses to him: "I was shocked when I saw you for the first time because I had been dreaming, like most girls do, of a prince from the *Arabian Nights* . . . who would carry me away and fly" (29). Salīm, who is a businessman, approaches marriage as a commercial transaction lacking any spiritual or emotional dimensions. He treats her as an object, as just a female body instead of as a whole human being, and fails to share with her any of his intimate thoughts or feelings. She later writes to him: "Did you consider even for one day that this woman whom you had brought to supplement the furniture of your house was a human being? That she was a human being, who would a thousand times prefer your sharing of one idea of yours over your offering her the most delicious food" (39).

Because her marriage cannot provide her with a meaningful life, Rashā comes to feel that only having a baby can fulfill her: "I had to give in order to feel that I was alive, and to prove to myself that I was alive" (36). With time, however, it becomes clear that this wish is not going to be fulfilled either; the couple cannot have children. Rashā goes to France to get treatment for her supposed sterility. On the train from Marseilles to Paris she meets Kamīl, a man who is in every respect the opposite of Salīm: he is compassionate, sensitive, and romantic. These traits, as well as his sentimental pride in his Syrian ancestry (his father was Syrian and his mother French), endear him to Rashā. Their short-term acquaintance blossoms into a love affair that is deep and profound, although it lasts only one night, during which they make love. The intensity and richness of that night enables Rashā to discover the intimate link between her body and herself. Her body ceases to be a separate entity outside her control: "For the first time in my life I understood the value of my body. For the first time I understood that it is not just a tool. It is not just a cool stream from which the thirsty one may drink to quench his desire and lust, taking from it temporary pleasure" (191). Rashā sees that her body is rightfully her own property, not her husband's (197).

In *Ayyām Maʿahu*, Rīm feels compelled to deny her femininity (for example, by cutting off her long hair, as Līnā did in *Anā Aḥyā*) to assert her humanity because Ziyād puts so much emphasis on female physical characteristics (157). Rashā, on the other hand, suffers from her husband's failure to acknowledge her femininity (*unūthah*). She complains to him: "Salīm, do you remember that dress? I put it on only once, in Damascus. It was new and I wanted to surprise you with it.... This dress was the last thing my womanhood drove me to do in order to get your attention. But you didn't notice it the first time because all your life you have been unable to see me as a woman" (160). Rashā feels that her femininity, which has been stagnant in her married life, has been revived by Kamīl's romantic nature. When he walks behind her (a bold image perhaps utilized by the author to indicate a reversal of traditional male-female roles) and carries her suitcase for her, she is overcome by a new feeling: "In my unconscious, my rich Oriental imagination let me feel that I was a weak female being spoiled by her strong man" (71–72). This is interesting, given that Rashā is taking such pleasure in the 'advantages" of femininity while she is actually assuming a traditionally masculine position by walking ahead of Kamīl. She seems not to take notice of this contradiction, however.

In this novel, plot and character development leave much to be desired, especially in the case of Rashā. The heroine's imposed marriage is an ordeal for her and should logically lead to a conflict between her and her family. But this conflict is minimized or overlooked altogether. And although her father bears the greatest responsibility for forcing her to marry Salīm, she is portrayed as thinking highly of him: "My father was an amiable and good believer who loved his daughters and strove to give them a life of plenty and opulence" (23). Al-Khūrī also fails to depict in a convincing way the gulf between Rashā and her husband. It is not that Salīm is intentionally cruel to her; the problem is his total immersion in business and her lack of an aim in life. She expects him to show interest in her world, but she shows no interest in his. There is a lack of real conflict between the two. This takes the drama out of Rashā's extramarital affair and thus weakens the whole novel.

The extramarital affair itself is equally unconvincing. The author forces it into the novel without making it fit into the development of Rashā's character. Rashā has shown no ability to assert herself or to rise to challenges earlier in the story, so the reader is left baffled at her daring plunge into an affair with a stranger she has met only hours before. To compound the unlikelihood of this scenario, it is Rashā, not Kamīl, who makes the first move: after Kamīl escorts her to her hotel and says goodbye, Rashā invites him in. This sudden burst of initiative makes the whole episode hard to believe. Therefore the author is forced to resort to supernatural forces in an attempt to lessen the incongruity. The morning after the affair, Rashā contradicts her earlier self-assertiveness and places the responsibility for her act on destiny (*qadar*) (218).

Finally, the novel's ending is weak. Colette al-Khūrī simply kills off her protagonist in an auto accident. Apparently, she has written herself into a corner and is unable to produce an ending that will follow logically from the rest of the story. Even though Rashā is not tied down by children, she lacks the nerve to walk out on her husband and begin a new life as Nora does in Ibsen's *A Doll's House*, and al-Khūrī most likely does not want to have to deal with the possibility of Rashā becoming pregnant as a result of her sexual encounter with Kamīl. The framework of the plot also makes it impossible for Rashā to develop a more lasting relationship with Kamīl because he is married with a daughter, and has no intention of breaking away from the life he is already leading. Having no alternatives, the author gets rid of her wayward protagonist. There is no attempt even to make the accident happen for a believable reason; it occurs because Rashā is careless crossing the street while rushing to the railway station, eager to return to her husband.

The form in which *Laylah Wāḥidah* is written is also inappropriate and lacks verisimilitude. Most of the novel consists of a letter by Rashā that she intends to send to her husband, which tells the story of her life including her marriage and her adventure with Kamīl. The sequence of events in the story suggests that she has writen this "letter" of 186 pages in less than five hours, beginning immediately after her intensive sexual experience and just before her death. It describes dialogues, gestures, tones of voice, and other events (over a very long span of time) in such minute detail as to make the reader suspect Rashā of having carried a sound-equipped movie camera around with her everywhere she went. The fact that Rashā is still thinking of going back to her husband anyway while she is writing this letter makes it even less believable.

Given all these weaknesses, *Laylah Wāḥidah* represents a decline when compared with *Ayyām Ma'ahu.* The Egyptian critic Fu'ād Duwārah aptly noted that it lacks complexity, depth of experience, and diversity of feelings and events, because of the lack of coordination among the characters' inner drives, their actual behavior and the circumstances in which they find themseves (Duwārah 1968: 145–146).

Laylā 'Usayrān: More Experiments

The next Arab woman to emerge as a major writer was Laylā 'Usayrān. She was born in Baghdad in 1934 to a Lebanese family. She received her primary and secondary education at the American College in Cairo, then returned in 1949 to Beirut where she earned a B.A. in political science at the American University in 1954. After graduating she worked as a journalist in Lebanon, serving as a correspondent for the Cairo magazines *Rūz al-Yūsuf* and *Sabāḥ al-Khayr.* In 1958 she married Dr. Amīn al-Ḥāfiẓ, a professor of economics at the Lebanese University. He was also a member of parliament and a chairman of the Foreign Affairs Committee. In the late 1970s he became prime minister of Lebanon.

Laylā 'Usayrān's first novel was *Lan Namūt Ghadan* (*We Will*

Not Die Tomorrow, 1962). Its protagonist, ʿĀ'ishah, resembles Rīm of *Ayyām Maʿahu* in that she decides that creative writing alone will make her existence meaningful. Like the heroines of all the novels discussed so far, she belongs to a wealthy family. The family lives in a great mansion and can afford a maid, a gardener, and many other luxuries. ʿĀ'ishah has a private car, and her money and free time enable her to follow the latest fashions in clothes and cosmetics (ʿUsayrān 1962: 9, 12, 42).

Unlike Līnā of *Anā Aḥyā,* ʿĀ'ishah lacks the courage to challenge her father or his absolute authority over the household. The depiction of the father is sketchy and sometimes contradictory, and ʿĀ'ishah's feelings toward him are also inconsistent. She sees him as a wise and open-minded man who had liberated his wife from the veil and given his son and daughter a chance at a university education (23), but she also admits that "he is the only person whom I dread, and it would be impossible for me to imagine myself marrying a main like him" (23). She realizes how vulnerable to him she is: "I fear his might. He is almighty. I frankly admit to feeling that if I had an important request to make, resulting from some real problem of youth, I would not be able to oppose his will if he turned me down" (23). In her father's presence ʿĀ'ishah feels as helpless as a small child, losing her self-confidence and even her ability to speak (24). Like Līnā's father, he wishes his daughter had been a son (56). When the possibility arises that ʿĀ'ishah, a Muslim, might marry Nabīh, a Christian, her father prohibits it absolutely.

The character of ʿĀ'ishah's mother also contains contradictions, but basically she is liberal and progressive, especially in her attitude toward marriage—a glaring exception to the rule regarding living mothers in women's novels of this period. She advises ʿĀ'ishah to ignore her father's insistence that she marry as soon as possible, saying instead that she should wait until she finds a husband who meets her expectations. Because she has such a poor relationship with her father, ʿĀ'ishah turns to her mother when she has problems: "How marvelous is my mother. I find no comfort except in her presence. Her ability to keep my anxiety under control is remarkable, and therein lies the secret of her skill as a mother. Nature has given her a magic power able to eliminate whatever causes her children pain. All my strength, vigilance and self-sufficiency collapse in the face of her motherly wisdom, and I feel whenever I turn to her, crying like a baby, I can enter the world of her compassion with no difficulty" (65). In terms of their values, ʿĀ'ishah's parents live in two different worlds. This sets the scene for a clash between them, but amazingly enough the author does not supply one. On the contrary, ʿĀ'ishah describes the relationship between her parents as excellent, full of frankness and mutual agreement (55–59). Thus, there is a lack of correspondence between the reader's view and the character's view concerning the relation between ʿĀ'ishah's parents. In the case of Līnā's parents in *Anā Aḥyā* the lack of parental coflict is logical, because both of them had the same views on Līnā's sexuality and role in society. In *Lan Namūt Ghadan* the philosophical differences between the parents make their harmonious relationship seem artificial, especially when it is not even important to the plot. This lack of conflict between the parents (as well as between them and ʿĀ'ishah) deprives the novel of much of the intensity that might otherwise have made ʿĀ'ishah's story richer.

ʿUsayrān chooses to have ʿĀ'ishah begin her struggle for personal identity in that outside world rather than at home. ʿĀ'ishah's first close encounter with a man is with Nabīh al-Khūrī, a friend of her brother. She is attracted to him because of his creativity and skill at conversation, not because of his looks. His charm lies in his honesty; his behavior truly reflects his inner character (18). ʿĀ'ishah has always had a low general opinion of men: "How tired I have become of men's lascivious glances. Why do they single me out as a target for this nonsense when there are dozens of other girls whose gestures and way of dressing show that they are interested in demonstrating the sexual side of their femininity?" (53). In Nabīh, ʿĀ'ishah feels that she has found an exception, a man who will not be like other men. However, she quickly grows disenchanted with him as she discovers that he is not really very different. When she asks him what it is about her that most draws his attention, he does not hesitate to say: "Your eyes and lips" (77). When he asks that she kiss him she flies off the handle, calling him "savage, savage, savage!" Obviously, Nabīh alone is not responsible for the sad end of his relationship with ʿĀ'ishah. She is deeply prejudiced against men, a bias that she discloses to her closest friend Nādiyah, telling her that men behave like adolescents and usually pay attention to her physical appearance and ignore her intellect (81). Thus when Nabīh tries to make their relationship a physical one, he triggers this prejudice, and their friendship comes to an end.

The death of 'Ā'ishah's father is a turning point in her struggle to realize herself. At first it comes as a severe shock to her, but in the end she is able to get rid of her father's power over her, which has held her back from having healthy emotional relationships with men. Here we are reminded that the Mīrā of *al-Ālihah al-Mamsūkhah* also fails to establish a real love relationship until she revolts against the control of her dead father by breaking his photograph. After spending a week alone at the family estate recovering from her father's death, 'Ā'ishah realizes that "her intellectual deviation from the society and environment to which she belonged did not have to prevent her from conforming, in a natural manner, to the prevailing customs" (111). However, her attempt to come to terms with her society is short lived. She can find no route to self-fulfillment in her upper-class environment, and the problem of just where she belongs becomes more acute: as she puts it, "I found that all that connected me to my acquaintances was a superficial, feeble link" (130). Her alienation from her social class becomes the major crisis in her life, forcing her to see that "I no longer belong to this class of people" (131).

'Ā'ishah's break with her class allows 'Usayrān to widen the scope and setting of *Lan Namūt Ghadan*, for the protagonist now goes to Cairo. At first she encounters nothing but people of her own social background there, and when an Egyptian journalist named Sharīf 'Āmir points out that she does not fit in very well in such circles, she answers by saying, "It may appear that I am not different from them at all, because I live the same empty routine. But the difference between me and them is the fact that I am not satisfied with my life, whereas they consider their way of life the ideal to which everyone aspires" (175). The most important change in 'Ā'ishah's psyche comes about when she is introduced to the editorial staff of the Egyptian magazine *al-Nahḍah* (significantly, this means "The Awakening"). There she meets men who are committed to their work and who do not look upon her, as members of her own class have done, as a sex object. Her involvement with this group deeply affects her values and even her appearance. She stops wearing high-heeled shoes and fancy clothes and begins to dress simply. Only in this atmosphere is she finally able to find a healthy relationship with a man, a journalist named Aḥmad. This relationship involves both body and spirit and inspires her to make her first committed efforts at creative writing. When she has her first article published in *al-Nahḍah* she feels at last that she is on the road to the kind of life she wants (235). It is worth noting that, as the story line proceeds, from the beginning of 'Ā'ishah's involvement with the staff of *al-Nahḍah*, the "Cinderella Complex" does not play a part in the formation of 'Ā'ishah's self-esteem. The root of her fulfillment is her commitment to her work, and its rewards—one of which is the ability to have a healthy romantic relationship.

The novel ends with two births: one literal, the other figurative. 'Ā'ishah's friend Nādiyah has a baby, and at the same time 'Ā'ishah begins writing a novel. Laylā 'Usayrān's attempt to link the two events was rather artificial and also artistically inappropriate. Nādiyah is unhappily married to a man named Ṣalāḥ and is also having a sexual affair with 'Ā'ishah's brother Kamāl, and her baby is presented as the fruit of this unhappy situation. The novel 'Ā'ishah is writing symbolizes just the opposite: her success at finding a meaningful role in life.

Alienation and the search for commitment in life and in emotion are at the core of Laylā 'Usayrān's second novel, *al-Ḥiwār al-Akhras* (*The Mute Dialogue*, 1963). Its protagonist is a woman named Jacqueline who, unlike 'Ā'ishah, begins her search for personal identity after she is already married. At the age of eighteen she marries a forty-year-old man who is the Lebanese ambassador to France. The novel sheds little light on her life before her marriage; only once in the story does she refer to her past, and that is when she realizes that she does not even have any memories of her childhood because she spent it as a slave to regulations at a strict boarding school ('Usayrān 1963: 34). Her marriage is not happy either: "To my husband I was only a beautiful painting with which he decorated his coarse, boring life. He did not talk to me; I was the one who used to talk to him. He did not argue with me to learn what I was thinking. Suddenly I came to realize that he had robbed me of my youth" (112). When the couple returns to Beirut, Jacqueline's sense of loneliness and uprootedness grows worse. In Paris, she had been able to compensate for her husband's indifference by attending concerts, going to theaters or museums, or even just reading books. In Beirut her alienation takes on both personal and political dimensions. She cannot identify with the elitist circles in which she has to move. At the same time, her frustration with this class reinforces her sense of uprootedness from her nation.

Jacqueline's salvation comes about through Kamāl, a rising political leader. When she meets him she becomes interested in his political work, and this interest gradually develops into emotional involvement. "He had been there forever to show me the path, the path of belonging to myself and thus to my homeland" (117). Jacqueline's relationship with Kamāl enables her to explore her own mind and to open true communication with other people. It also changes her perception of her self. In the earlier stage of her life she is disgusted with her femininity and wants to give it up. But after she comes to know Kamāl she feels that she has matured and become fulfilled as a woman (157). Ironically, though, this fulfillment is achieved through self-denial rather than assertion. Her life becomes an extension of Kamāl's, so much so that she is ready to "dissolve" herself in his personality (125). She derives satisfaction from Kamāl's accomplishments instead of trying to accomplish anything for herself.

This subtle barrenness in Jacqueline's life is symbolized in the novel by the fact that the couple cannot have children, although 'Usayrān does not give any biological grounds for this inability. Jacqueline once refers to her baby who "would never be born" (33). Although she is unable to carry and give birth to a baby, Jacqueline goes through an experience that is a symbolic substitute. When Kamāl reaches the peak of his political success (partly through Jacqueline's constant encouragement), she feels that she has in a sense delivered a baby. However, she realizes that this "baby" is not, in the final analysis, her own: "When I came back to my senses I felt that I had given birth to a dead fetus, because it was not my own . . . but rather that of others, for it was the outcome of Kamāl's interaction with others. I realized that I had no connection with this 'newborn baby' since its blood, sentiment, and soul would never be mine" (175). Realizing that she has still not really fulfilled herself, Jacqueline decides to leave. Her sexual involvement with Kamāl goes on, but he has never been able to make a true emotional commitment. As he says, "I am a man without a heart. How can I love and give?" (107) Jacqueline goes on feeling alienated from her nation, and feels it necessary to go to Paris to get away from her husband and start a new life.

As far as the development of her literary technique was concerned, Laylā 'Usayrān was following a pattern similar to that of Laylā Ba'labakkī. Her earlier *Lan Namūt Ghadan* is spontaneous and loose, narrated from an omniscient point of view, while using 'Ā'ishah as a focus. In *al-Ḥiwār al-Akhras* her technique became more sophisticated, and the story is told from two different perspectives by the two main characters (Jacqueline and Kamāl). Laylā 'Usayrān said that she intended this dualism to show the chasm separating the minds of the two, by dramatizing their different attitudes toward life. The very nature of the two characters also made such a double focus necessary, because both of them are introverts: Kamāl is very much locked into his own private world and unwilling to expose his inner self or even his political plans to others, whereas Jacqueline has no time for anything but her own personal ordeal.[14]

Laylā 'Usayrān's third novel, *al-Madīnah al-Fārighah* (*The Empty City*, 1966), is the story of a group of aimless young men and women trapped in an impersonal and merciless city. This city, with its dehumanizing values and lifelessness, holds no hope of salvation for them. As Walīd (one member of the group) says, "The city's head is made of stone and its womb is made of stone. The city is pregnant but it will deliver nothing but stones" ('Usayrān 1966: 90).

Each of the narrator's friends has some personal predicament. The narrator (who stays nameless throughout the novel) is an orphan and a victim of poverty and is seeking companionship in the group after a failure in her love life. Another woman, 'Ā'idah, has a crippled father and is ashamed of being poor. Another, Ḥanān, is unemployed and is not trying to find a job because she considers herself lacking in any useful skill. The male members of the group are no better off. One, 'Ādil, is a newspaper editor who is unable to assert himself in the world of journalism or write about issues that interest him. Walīd is a government clerk fed up with the monotony, corruption, and emptiness of his work. Akram dreads the prospect of one day having to take over running his father's store, which he finds boring. Ghassān, an interior decorator, feels frustrated because he can never make his personal mark upon his work.

As individuals, the members of the group have little in common with each other. In the words of one of them, "We were a contradictory grouping, motivated by mysterious feelings. We began to gather like fugitives from a great jail without bars or guards" (20). What holds them together is their resentment of the city and of what it represents—as well as their search for new values in life, because they are disillusioned with the values of the older generation (54).

In spite of their rebelliousness, all the members of the group are lacking in vision and thus remain either passive or confused. 'Ā'idah, for example, is upset about how poor her family is, and she becomes obsessed with money. However, she is unwilling to look for any practical way of realizing her wish to escape poverty. 'Ādil holds that the natural obtuseness of the city should not hold the individual back from self-fulfillment, but he is himself hesitant about taking any concrete step toward his own goals.

The inability of the group's members to reach beyond their confused selves also prevents them from having sound romantic relationships. 'Ā'idah's inferiority complex about her poverty ruins her relationships with two wealthy men, 'Ādil and Akram, because she is unable to handle any such relationship without money coming to dominate it.

The artistic value of *al-Madīnah al-Fārighah* is undermined by a combination of weaknesses. These include a lack of action, an overabundance of characters, and a tendency to philosophize about various aspects of life having no real connection with the story. The characters do whatever the author wants them to do, without the credibility of cause and effect. The ending is a mere summing up of the destinies of the various characters: 'Ādil joins a leftist political party, 'Ā'idah marries a foreigner, Ghassān marries Ḥanān and abandons his interior-decorating business to become a farmer in the mountains, Akram is left friendless, and Walīd reluctantly sticks to his government job. The narrator leaves her own fate vague: "God, why did I find my tranquility and belonging in some illogical thing that I knew did not exist?" (167).

Unlike Laylā Ba'labakkī and Colette al-Khūrī, Laylā 'Usayrān fails to create a lively style of her own. To a great extent her language remains prosaic, lacking warmth and originality. She denies that she had been influenced by Ba'labakkī, saying, "Laylā (Ba'labakkī) has style but she does not have a subject matter. Her style is readable but she does not say anything."[15] Also unlike the other two, 'Usayrān was already married with a child when she began her literary career and her rebelliousness may have been already suppressed. It may be that her conventional style and weak plots were due to this.

Emily Naṣrallāh: Village Novelist

Another important writer in this group of writers is Emily Naṣrallāh. She was born in the small village of al-Kfayr at the western foot of Mount Hermon in southern Lebanon. After her graduation from the Beirut Girls' College she went to the American University of Beirut, where she majored in education and literature. While she was still a student she began contributing to the Lebanese periodicals *Ṣawt al-Mar'ah* and *al-Ṣayyād*, sometimes using a pen name. Her husband, Philip Naṣrallāh, encouraged her literary career, and all her books were published after their marriage (Jammūl 1973: 52). A mother of four, she denied that motherhood was necessarily a hindrance to women writers: "As far as the woman writer or artist is concerned, I believe that children are a source of inspiration. The writer who is a mother sees in her children the history of humanity" (53).

Unlike Laylā 'Usayrān's characters, who are trapped in the city and trying to escape from it, Emily Naṣrallāh's characters yearn to abandon their village existence and move to the city in search of a better life. Her first novel *Ṭuyūr Aylūl* (*September Birds*, 1962) uses three tragic love stories to dramatize village life. The tragedies develop out of the conflicts between the lovers and the rigid village tradition that denies women the right to shape their own destinies, even in a sphere of life as personal as love.

The first love story is between Fawwāz, a bereaved young man whose mother died a few hours after his birth, and his sweetheart Miriam. Fawwāz finds life miserable and looks upon marriage to Miriam as his only hope of ever being happy. Her father considers him unworthy of her, saying, "Who is that dog that I should give him my daughter?" (Naṣrallāh 1962: 35) Fawwāz is so traumatized by this contemptuous rejection that he shoots Miriam and runs off to become a hermit in a cave. The whole village is shaken by Miriam's death, and takes a long time to recover from it.

The second love story of Najlā and Kamāl explores a different dimension: the two belong to different religious sects. This proves to be a formidable problem, and Najlā feels that even her mother will never understand her dilemma: "Even my mother will not hear my voice, my mother who carried me for nine months while my heart lay beside hers. My mother will not be able to hear my voice because she began to close her ears to me the moment my first cries broke the silence of her existence and I was separated from her to form a new generation" (178). Najlā does not have the courage to defy the village code of behavior; she "stifled her feelings and went along with the herd" (167). The "herd" decrees that Najlā has to marry another man named Salīm. She feels that she has no choice but to give in.

The most important of the three love stories in *Ṭuyūr Aylūl* is that of Mirsāl and Rājī. Through it the author develops her main theme, the discontent of the younger generation with the narrowness and meagerness of village life and their desire to explore other ways of life outside the village.[16] Rājī becomes so unhappy with the heavy and unrewarding work in the fields that he decides to emigrate to the United States, even though it means leaving his aged father and his sweetheart Mirsāl behind. For a while Mirsāl remains loyal to Rājī and writes poetry to express her secret love for him. However, with the passage of time she comes to realize that she has lost him forever. She decides to marry a rich Lebanese-American instead, even though she feels no love for him.

The character who ties the three otherwise diconnected stories together is Munā, with whom the author herself identifies: "I was Munā in the story. I was born and grew up in a small village where the sun burned my skin as I picked fruit with my friends. . . . I can still feel the heat of the sun on my back, the rich red soil under my feet, the ripe fruit in my hands" (al-Qalamāwī 1965: 150). Munā is the female counterpart of Rājī, but her character is much richer than his and she is a more pervasive figure in the novel. Munā is the only female character who revolts against the mentality and customs of the village. At first her revolt is directed at the deep-rooted tradition of valuing males more than females[17] (e.g., Munā becomes outraged when she is forbidden to leave the village to continue her studies in the city as her brother had done: "Why did they let him fly off like that without question? Why should I stay here within these narrow walls, crushing my hopes and ambition into the dust?" [Naṣrallāh 1962: 20]. Munā's life is dominated by her father, whose views on the relationship between the sexes are summed up in the words: "A decent girl does not mix with men" (30). Under these conditions Munā comes to see romantic love as an inner refuge from the depressing outer world. Because of her romantic dreams and her love of nature, her personality comes to be controlled by escapist desires and dreams, and so it remains, even after she leaves the village. Like Līnā in *Anā Aḥyā*, Munā is repelled by the relegation of women to the status of mere breeding machines. She grows frightened at the very thought of meeting this fate, the fate of most village women. However, she cannot solve her problems in the city either; she merely replaces one alienation with another. Indeed, she is so disillusioned with the city that she uses rape as a metaphor to describe her encounter with it (188–189). Her feelings of isolation drive her to nostalgia for the village she left, and so she goes back. However, she realizes that there is no longer a place for her there either; the village has erased her from its memory. She is too different now to be able to take up her old life. As she concludes, "The village was as I had left it; it was I who had changed so much" (201). Munā remains torn between two worlds, unable to identify with either.

Ṭuyūr Aylūl lets the reader look at the unique world of the village, with all its contradictions. Although it shows women suffering from discrimination, it also shows them playing major roles in decision making about various private matters; for example, it is Salīm's mother who asked another woman, Ḥannah, to find a bride for her son (153). After the wedding night of another character, the mother makes sure that the blood-spotted sheets are put on display as proof that her daughter was a virgin. Women even set up and defend the village standards of honor. Ḥannah denounces Najlā's love for Kamāl as "shameful" (112) and declares that "girls cannot be given freedom" (127). She complains that "today girls are uncontrollable. We [Ḥannah's generation] never dared to talk about love. Nowadays they [girls] are shameless" (114). Another influential woman, Salmā, holds the position that marriage is the only way to safeguard the honor of girls, and therefore it has to be imposed upon them regardless of their own desires. Ironically, Salmā's husband is more open-minded than she is when the subject of their daughter's marriage comes up. He thinks it appropriate to ask for the daughter's opinion, but Salmā dismisses this idea out of hand, saying, "You are emboldening the children too much. Since when does a girl have an opinion? When we were girls our families arranged our marriages for us. The universe was only ruined when women began to have a say" (159). However, such power and influence is reserved only for women who follow traditional gender role prescriptions.

The character of Munā holds the novel together in spite of its many disconnected episodes. Naṣrallāh uses Munā's flashbacks to tell the story. These flashbacks are made up of Munā's nostalgic recollections of her village life while she was in the city, and they suffuse the whole novel with a romantic tone and imagery. This romanticism is reinforced by the fact that Mirsāl, a major character, is a poet who writes verse to express her private feelings and thoughts. In addition to flashbacks, Emily Naṣrallāh's other main storytelling device is the use of letters to shed light upon things that cannot be recaptured by mere memory (177–180, 192–198). One problem disrupts the story, though. The language in the dialogue is rather inconsistent and confused. Some characters such as Mirsāl and Rājī speak in Classical Arabic, whereas others such as Salmā and Ḥannah are restricted to dialect. In some cases, the confusion is even more pronounced, as when Abū Rājī suddenly switches from dialect to eloquent Classical in midstatement with no artistic justification (68–69). The discrepancy between the supposed low educational level of the characters and their sophisticated speech is often striking.

Emily Naṣrallāh's second novel *Shajarat al-Diflā* (*The Oleander Tree*, 1968) deals with another heroine. Rayyā, who rebels against village morality. Unlike Munā in *Ṭuyūr Aylūl*, Rayyā pays for her rebelliousness with her life. Rayyā is a victim of the strict village code of behavior, which suppresses all signs of individuality and thus prevents people, especially women, from fulfilling themselves.

Rayyā has been unwanted since her very arrival in the world. After Rayyā's birth, her mother felt frustrated at having had a mere girl, which made the father lose status. (In keeping with Arab custom, the villagers call the father "Bū Sa'd" even though he has no son called Sa'd, on the assumption that his firstborn will be a son by that name. Since the firstborn is a daughter, the title "Bū Sa'd" has taken on a hollow ring.) Even after his death, the father continues to dominate the family through his picture hanging on the wall, like the photograph of Mīrā's father in *al-Ālihah al-*

Mamsūkhah. Whenever differences arise between Rayyā and her mother, her mother "consults" this picture.

Rayyā's life is a series of difficulties. In her early childhood she undergoes a devastating experience that leaves its mark on her psyche for much of her life: she is sexually assaulted by a shopkeeper named ʿImrān. She cannot erase this event from her memory: "A dirty man. His smell still sticks in her nose, a smell of rice dust, hemp ropes, home-made soap, and fertilizers. He had big, disgustingly yellow teeth" (Naṣrallāh 1968: 125). Later, Rayyā is unable to conform to the social rules of the village, and she is always obsessed with the thought of fleeing. Sometimes she dreams of a remote island where she would be safe from people (48), and sometimes of a more concrete and realizable refuge—the city (320). Finally, Rayyā marries a man named Makhkhūl. In this marriage she has a great deal of freedom, but she also discovers that she has problems adjusting: "The freedom which I had demanded became a collar around my neck" (147). In the end she turns against Makhkhūl, taking out all her pent-up frustrations on him.

In *Ṭuyūr Aylūl* the female characters represent traditional moral values, but in *Shajarat al-Diflā* a male character—Bū Daʿʿās, the guardian of Rayyā's mother—does so. He bases his views on the idea that a woman's honor (*sharaf*) is like a sheet of glass; once broken, it can never be mended. Like Salmā in the earlier book, Bū Daʿʿās is very alarmed by the younger generation's deviance from the old social order and describes them as "a bunch of oddities, a herd of strange animals" (9). When Rayyā dares to disobey her husband, Bū Daʿʿās has a straightforward recipe for how to deal with her: the only way for a man to handle his wife, so he believes, is to treat her harshly and mercilessly. Otherwise she will control him (179–180; see also p. 169).

Shajarat al-Diflā had little to say that *Ṭuyūr Aylūl* had not already said; the two novels are variations on the same theme. This may be because of the overwhelmingly favorable public response to the first novel,[18] which Emily Naṣrallāh believed was due to her ability to portray the long-ignored village society. Most Arab novelists, both male and female, had concentrated upon the city society because its dramatic social, economic, and cultural changes made it more interesting. Trying to duplicate her early success, Emily Naṣrallāh not only set her second novel in a village but also made the situation so similar that the two villages might have been one. Again she emphasized the villagers' conception of marriage as a public matter rather than something for the individual to decide privately.

Like some earlier women novelists, Emily Naṣrallāh uses fatalism as a device to avoid having to deal with the motivations of her characters. In doing this she is, in a sense, reflecting the very "village mentality" she is attacking. In *Ṭuyūr Aylūl*, Najlā cannot find any sensible reason for her love of Kamāl and decides that destiny (*qadar*) is responsible, saying at one point, "Why did destiny choose us, Kamāl, to undergo all this suffering together?" (Naṣrallāh 1962: 129).[19] Destiny is depicted as a frightening beast holding Najlā in its claws (129). To some extent this interferes with the message of the novel, because this means that it is not Najlā herself who has decided to break the village code of behavior by having an affair with someone of a different religion. In the same way, the author deprives the rebellious Rayyā in *Shajarat al-Diflā* of truly human motivations by depicting her as a spindle in the hand of destiny: "I do not have the ability to object. It was not up to me to raise objections about my birth. . . . I am a puff of air. No, I am a drop of water which tried to flow against the current" (Naṣrallāh 1968: 18). When she decides to go with Makhkhūl she attributes her decision to destiny, because she sees destiny as stronger than herself (114). By presenting her heroines as mere puppets in the hands of fate, Emily Naṣrallāh undermines the message that their struggles for independence were intended to convey. Ostensibly, these struggles fail, not because of social conservatism (which was the real author's target), but because the heroines are fighting an invincible power.

All the dialogue in *Shajarat al-Diflā* is in Lebanese dialect, a great improvement over the chaotic mixture of dialect and Classical Arabic that marred *Ṭuyūr Aylūl*. However, the dialogue is still unsatisfactory in other ways. Emily Naṣrallāh is unable to write dialogue that reflects convincing inner worlds for her characters, and the fact that the dialogues are written and not actual conversation remains painfully obvious.

Nawāl al-Sa'dāwī: Militant Fiction

Nawāl al-Sa'dāwī whom Fedwa Malti-Douglas refers to as "the most articulate activist for women's causes in the Arab

World" (Malti-Douglas 1991: 112) represented a new phenomenon in Arab women's literature, both because of her background as a physician and her militant writings on the struggle for women's liberation. She was born in the village of Kafr Ṭaḥlah by the Nile, was graduated in 1955, and became a doctor. For a time she served as Egypt's director of public health, but was fired as a result of the storm of controversy surrounding her first nonfiction book *al-Mar'ah wa-al-Jins* (*Women and Sex*, 1972).

In this book she puts forth a whole series of explosive ideas. At the dawn of history, she says, women did not have a lower social status than men. On the contrary, they had had a very high status as shown by the emergence of matrilineal culture. Later on, mainly because of economic factors, men had been able to subjugate women and deprive them of their rights (al-Sa'dāwī 1972: 127–130).[20] Al-Sa'dāwī goes on to claim that women are mentally and biologically superior to men, quoting some Western scholars to support her view (67–82). Other issues the book examines are discrimination between the sexes, the virginity of women before marriage and the moral corruption of Arab society.[21]

As time passed, writing and political activism began to overshadow al-Sa'dāwī's career in medicine. In 1981, she was, together with hundreds of Egyptian intellectuals, imprisoned because they were critical of President Sadat's domestic and foreign policy. In 1983, she founded and led the Arab Women's Solidarity Association, which was so threatening to the dominant system that it was dissolved by the Egyptian government in 1991 and its newsletter was discontinued. But it is mainly Nawāl al-Sa'dāwī's fiction rather than her nonfiction that concerns us here. Her first novel, *Mudhakkirāt Ṭabībah* (1965),[22] deals with many of the same issues previously discussed in relation to other women writers. Although this work cannot be considered strictly autobiographical, it does contain many elements from al-Sa'dāwī's own life.

The heroine of *Memoirs of a Woman Doctor* is a woman whose name remains unknown throughout the book. The novel, written in the first person, describes the narrator's painful life story from childhood to adulthood, emphasizing the devastating impact of family and society upon her female psyche. From her earliest childhood, this narrator understands her predicament as a female in a prejudiced society.[23] She senses the difference between the way her parents treat her and the way they treat her brother, to whom the family refers as a "god": "My brother woke up in the morning and left his bed just as it was, while I had to make my bed and his as well. My brother went out into the street to play without asking my parent's permission and came back whenever he liked, while I could only go out if and when they let me. My brother took a bigger piece of meat than me, gobbled it up and drank his soup noisily and my mother never said a word." (9–10). Under these conditions the narrator begins to resent her femininity: "I felt sorry for myself and locked myself in my room and cried. The first real tears I shed in my life weren't because I'd done badly at school or broken something valuable but because I was a girl. I wept over my femininity even before I knew what it was" (10). She comes to see her body as a deficiency (*'awrah*). Like Līnā in *Anā Aḥyā*, she hates her long hair, an obvious symbol of femaleness. Adolescence only makes matters worse, as she is forced to face the development of her body into one which is distinctly and obviously female. She especially detests her breasts, "these two lumps of flesh which were determining my future! How I wished I could cut them off with a sharp knife!" (16). The onset of menstruation convinces her that God himself is biased against women, otherwise he would not have chosen blood as the mark of their maturity (12). Another discouraging aspect of her femaleness is the fact that the heroine's mother constantly reminds her of her prescribed role in life, telling her, "Marriage is your destiny. You must learn how to cook" (14). This is the mother's favorite piece of advice, and its effect is to strengthen the heroine's hostility toward marriage. She comes to associate her hypothetical future husband with food and to detest both (14). She feels no solidarity with women, even as she struggles against male domination, and feels like a social misfit among others who seem to accept freely their prescribed gender roles.

It is revealing that the heroine's first physical contact with a male is with a dead body in the course of her medical studies. This impresses upon her how far from godhood the male really is, regardless of what her mother thinks: "Here was just such a body spread out before me naked, ugly and in pieces" (26). The heroine takes an almost sadistic satisfaction in avenging herself upon male tyranny by dissecting the corpse. As Malti-Douglas points out, the heroine's medical training exposes her to the physical similarity between men's and women's bodies: "The body as physical entity is the great equalizer" (Malti-Douglas 1991: 123). In fact, the training itself is an equalizer, as female physicians may assume positions of power generally reserved for males. In addition, al-Sa'dāwī takes medicine a step ahead further as an "equalizer": not only does she "develop[ ] the sexual politics of medicine" by "using it as a vehicle for women to regain their lost power, " but also by "making it the focus of her own call for integration of traditionally male and female qualities" (134).

After finishing her medical studies, and after revelling for awhile in the power and magic that medicine at first represents to her, the heroine undergoes a crisis. When she is unable to save the life of a woman who dies in childbirth, she begins to question her belief that medicine is all-powerful, and becomes convinced that her career is nothing more than a series of depressing exposures to the failures of the human body. She is so disillusioned that she retreats to a village to consider her options.

There she finds new meaning in her work, as well as a new relationship with herself and with life in general. She immerses herself in nature and reclaims her own humanity, which enables her to recognize that her patients are also human beings with feelings and not mere bodies to be handled and labeled. She experiences the revelation that her body is not shameful, that being a women is not a tragedy, that her society has taught her to hate herself. Her values change drastically as she begins to understand the need for balance between professional success and human contact and as she realizes that the conventional opposition of scientific reasoning and feelings is false and misleading. "There was a new language to my heartbeats which neither science nor medicine could have explained, a language I understood with my newly awakened feelings but which would have been incomprehensible to my old experienced mind. I felt that emotion was sharper-witted than reason. It was more deeply rooted in the human heart, more firmly bound to the distant history of the human race, truer and more reponsive to its nature and thoroughly proven by its existence" (42). She returns to her life in the city with a new vision of her role and her value and is anxious to find someone with whom she can share her life.

Her marriage, however, is a rude awakening. In making a housecall late one night to the house of a dying women, she meets a man (the patient's son) who is grateful and touched by her willingness to help. This man visits her the next day to express his gratitude and admiration, and he is so gentle and even childlike in his behavior toward her that, when he asks to see her again, she agrees. She has finally met a seemingly agreeable man who does not treat her like an object or an inferior being. Although he slowly begins to treat her more as a mother figure than a romantic partner as their relationship progresses, she accepts his proposal of marriage because he tells her that he wants "a partner" and is "proud" of her intellect (56). Given the other men she has known, the heroine decides to marry him even though he does not arouse her sexually; after all, was she likely to meet another man whom she liked and who respected her as an equal, who did not require her to submit to him in any way?

The ordeal of getting married foreshadows events to come. She is horrified when she realizes that she practically signs away her human rights on the marriage contract, but accepts her husband's reassurance that this is "just a formality" (62). Soon after, however, he becomes corrupted by the power granted him as her husband and insists that she close down her medical practice and focus on meeting his needs. The heroine agonizes about her responsibility to the marriage and finally decides that the mistake of marrying this man would be a small one compared to the mistake of remaining with him under these conditions. She divorces him despite the inevitable social stigma, which is far less demeaning to her than her marriage was. Although she is at first glad to be free once more, it is not long before she feels lonely enough to try again to find a life partner.

She decides to search everywhere she can think of, but she is not immediately successful. She meets a man who engages in a power struggle with her and who cannot take her seriously as an equal. She becomes so discouraged by this and also by the fact that her friends, family, and community at large all attack her for living without a man that she decides to give up looking for a man altogether and derive satisfaction from other sources, such as her career. She becomes more and more successful in medicine, but also more and more lonely and unfulfilled at the same time. In trying to fight society's mandate that a woman live with a man, she has forgotten that personal relationships are necessary for her happiness.

Just as she finally concludes that material success is no substitute for love, she is invited to a party where she meets a musician who is different from the other men she has known. They begin to see each other socially and soon fall in love. The fact that this man is an artist is no coincidence. As an artist, he is extremely observant and sensitive and more likely than most other men to recognize social constructions. He is therefore less invested in rigid gender roles and is able to treat the heroine with respect without assuming the position of a child, something her husband had been unable to do. He also serves another purpose, that of further calling into question the separation of science and art:

> He smiled gently and said, "Your house is beautiful—the house of an artist."
> "I love art," I said, "but medicine takes up all my time."
> "Medicine is an art in itself," he said, and looked at me. (93)

Later, as the man is playing music which he composed, the subject comes up again:

> "How beautiful art is. If only I'd studied music so I could write tunes like that!"
> "If only I'd studied medicine so that I could heal people!"
> "Medicine only heals. Art heals and creates."
> "You could be creative in medicine. There are illnesses which no one's found a cure for yet." (96)

This collapse of the art-science division in al-Saʿdāwī's works does not go unnoticed by Malti-Douglas, who writes: "Medicine becomes a space of purification, the locus where the raw social power of science is transmuted into the acceptable sociall power of art. As such, it is the ultimate women's trick, but a modern one this time: linking individual with collective emancipation" (Malti-Douglas 1991: 143). Not only is medicine linked to art, then, but also to "collective emancipation" as well. An excellent example of this is the heroine's decision to perform an abortion for a young unmarried woman who would certainly be killed by her family if they were to discover her pregnancy. In making this decision, she thinks, "How could I punish her alone when I knew that society as a whole had participated in the act . . . ?" As for herself, she is convinced that she is doing no wrong, even though she knows that she would be attacked, even killed, if those in power were to find out about this: "I'd accept my fate and meet death with a satisfied soul and an easy conscience" (El Saadawi 1988: 81). Only a few pages later in the novel, just as she is becoming acquainted with the artist, he complains about the agony of pleasing his public versus pleasing himself, and his words describe the heroine's recent resolution as exactly as they do his own: "An artist isn't content unless he himself is satisfied with what he's done" (89). In her medical act, which contributes to the collective emancipation of women, then, the heroine has indeed behaved as an artist should. Medicine, art, social power, and political solidarity all converge in this novel as they have in al-Sa'dāwī's own life.

Near the end of *Memoirs of a Woman Doctor*, the artist accompanies the heroine on an emergency call, during which she experiences the most powerful revelation of her career. As an extremely sick and obviously poor young man tries to give her money, she comes to the conclusion that her monetary success is not only unfulfilling, but to a certain degree unethical as well. She realizes suddenly that the purpose of medicine is not to grow rich from the illnesses of others, but to heal the sick. Giving, not taking, should be the essence of her practice. At last she has found meaning in her work: "Thirty years of my life had gone by without my realizing the truth, without my understanding what life was about or realizing my own potential. How could I have done, when I'd only thought about taking and taking?—although I couldn't have given something which I didn't have to give" (100). She has discovered the destructiveness of living only for herself, in part because she had also found a partner who defies cultural attitudes toward women, who can understand and accept her for who she is, and who is capable of truly loving her. Finally, she has found someone whom she can trust with her vulnerability: "For the first time in my life I felt that I needed someone else, something I hadn't felt even about my mother. I buried my head in his chest and wept tears of relief" (100–101).

Memoirs of a Woman Doctor is remarkable because it deals with important social issues from a feminist point of view, unapologetically and directly. The way in which these are examined, however, constitutes the novel's most noticeable artistic shortcoming. Al-Sa'dāwī's strong commitment to the cause of women's liberation tends to overshadow many of her stories to such a degree that, at certain points, the thoughts and statements of her characters seem forced and inappropriate. (Al-Saʿdāwī's novel *Imra'atān fī Imra'ah,* "Two Women in One," which is discussed at length in Chapter Four, suffers from the same deficiencies.) *Memoirs of a Woman Doctor,* in certain places, thus functions more as a soapbox from which al-Saʿdāwī preaches her views in a declamatory manner unsuited to a novel: "The weak spot that a man focuses on in his attempt to gain control over a woman: her need to be protected from other men. The male's jealousy over his female: he claims to be frightened for her when he's really frightened for himself, claims to be protecting her in order to take possession of her and put four walls around her" (63). This causes character development to suffer, as does the fact that al-Saʿdāwī is somewhat obsessed with the mental problems of women caused by the patriarchal Arab society and, in an effort to show the effects of oppression on her heroines, sometimes uses her characters as mere vehicles for the depiction of these complexes, rather than allowing them to develop naturally within the literary settings she had created. Male characters are portrayed with even less depth and are occasionally compared to animals. The heroine, as her husband tries to convince her to quit her practice, recalls, "I could see right up close to me his teeth and his big flat rabbit's ears" (65); and while avoiding the sexual advances of a doctor she has begun to despise, she asks: "Why did a man crumble in the face of his desire? Why did his willpower vanish the minute he was shut in with a woman so that he turned into a wild animal on four legs? Where was his power? Where was his strength? . . . How weak men were!" (76). These are not only unflattering in terms of the images al-Saʿdāwī creates, but even more so in the context of Arab culture where comparison of people to animals is one of the worst possible insults.

Al-Saʿdāwī's novel *al-Ghā'ib* (*Searching,* 1970),[24] the heroine of which is more well-developed psychologically, is a great improvement over the aforementioned works. Although *Searching* is a more cynical novel than *Memoirs of a Woman Doctor* in that there is no "happy ending," the reader is given a more detailed tour of this heroine's psyche than of the heroines of *Memoirs of a Woman Doctor* and *Two Women in One,* and political and social messages are more artfully embedded in this narrative.

Searching takes place over a short period of time in the life of Fouada, the heroine, just after her lover, Farid, turns up missing.

Fouada, a chemist who aspires to make a great scientific discovery, is aptly named. She believes that she is exceptional and uncommon, having been told this by several people close to her; and although Fouad (Fu'ād), which in Arabic means "heart," is a popular name for males in Arabic, the feminine form Fouada (Fu'ādah) is extremely rare, if not completely unique. Fouada wants to be "special," thinking she can accomplish things that most cannot.

Like the heroine of *Memoirs of a Woman Doctor*, she sacrifices any feeling of solidarity with others (women, for example) for this uniqueness and is quite traumatized by the results of puberty; but, unlike that other heroine, she never comes to terms with her body or her political identity as a woman, and her uniqueness translates into loneliness and identity crises for the most part. Partly because of this image of herself, Fouada is very depressed and becomes increasingly devoid of hope about her future as she realizes that Farid is missing, her job is meaningless, and she might never find a way to make the scientific contribution she so desperately wants to make—in short, that her life and her problems are ordinary. She makes every effort to correct the situation: she dials Farid's number many times and even goes to his apartment; she attempts to quit her job at the Ministry; and she opens her own chemical analysis laboratory with money she convinces her mother to loan her.

None of these solutions bears fruit for her, however. Farid never reappears, she cannot manage to give up the security of her Ministry job, despite her hatred for it, and her laboratory does not draw the business she needs to stay afloat financially. During all this, though, as Fouada is searching for Farid and for meaning in her own life, she muddles through her daily life in a sort of fog, asking questions about existence and marveling at the ways in which her mind works and the ways in which those around her behave. As in *Memoirs of a Woman Doctor*, the separation of emotion and science is examined:

> She looked around, confused. Were feelings true or false? Why, when she looked into Farid's eyes, did she feel that he was familiar and when she looked into Saati's eyes, feel that he was a thief? Was that illusion or knowledge? Was it a random in the optic nerve or a conscious movement in the

> brain cells? How could she distinguish the mistaken vibration of a pressed nerve from the healthy idea emanating from a brain cell? And how did a brain cell think? How could a small mass of protoplasma think? Where did an idea come from and how did it pass through her cellular tissue? Electronically? A chemical reaction? (El Saadawi 1991: 94).

It is through this stream-of-consciousness style that political and social issues are examined, and al-Saʿdāwī again uses science as a vehicle for examining them. This time, however, the characters seem to be speaking their own words, rather than force-feeding the reader with uncharacteristic and unmotivated sermons, as they do in some of al-Saʿdāwī's other works.

> What else could there be? That illusion which beckoned through the mist? Test tubes from whose mouths a new gas danced? What could a new gas do? A new hydrogen bomb? A rocket with a new nuclear head? What did the world lack? A new means of killing?
>
> Why the killing? Was there nothing else of use? Something to eliminate hunger? Disease? Suffering? Oppression? Exploitation? (88)

The portrayals of men in the heroine's life are not much different than in *Memoirs of a Woman Doctor* and *Two Women in One*, however. With the exception of Fouada's lover, Farid, the men with whom she comes into contact are portrayed negatively in the extreme. Here father "threw his dirty clothes everywhere, raised his gruff voice from time to time, coughed and spat a lot, and blew his nose loudly" (14). And, as in *Memoirs of a Woman Doctor*, men are compared with animals. Here only male customer at the laboratory beats his wife "like a wild beast" (78). One man, Saati, who rents Fouada the space for the laboratory at a reduced rate and then pursues her romantically, is represented as the worst sort of man. "She glanced at Saati. His portly body was leaning against the window supported by legs that were thin, like those of a large bird. His eyes—now like a frog's, she thought—darted behind the thick glasses. It seemed to her that before her was a strange type of unknown terrestrial reptile—that might be dangerous" (82). Later, when Saati is pursuing Fouada romantically, the description is of a man attempting to wield male privilege over her:

> He was carrying a small packet in his cushiony hand. His upper lip lifted, revealing the large, yellow teeth, and his prominent eyes quivered behind the thick glasses.
>
> "A small present," he said, putting the package on the table and sitting down.
>
> She remained standing, staring at the thin green ribbon tied around the packet.
>
> "Open it," she heard him say hoarsely.
>
> He was giving her an order, had taken upon himself the right to give her orders, had paid the price of this right and had the right to use it. She looked at his eyes. They were quieter, as if he had begun to gather confidence in himself. He was giving her something, having paid a price for her, and was now able to buy something from her, anything, even the right to order her to open the packet. She remained on her feet, unmoving. (96)

Although Fouada has found a man who makes her happy, it is clear that he is very unusual (in fact, *farīd* means "unique" in Arabic). One twist here is that the only exposure we have to Farid is filtered through Fouada's memory. This complicates his character, because we not only have to take into account Fouada's partial knowledge of him (she knows very little about him, actually), but her desire for him to be ideal as well. For example, there are no physical descriptions of Farid anywhere in the story, because these would, depending on their content, necessarily either detract from Fouada's projection of him as being unlike any other person or diminish the credibility of the story. Such perfection in a man as Fouada clearly sees in Farid, and such a perfect relationship as they have, could not exist in reality. "But between her and Farid, there were no 'others,' or any such thing as her self against his self. They shared everything in love, even their selves—she became him and he became her. He protected her rights and she his. Something strange, something extraordinary happened between them, but it happened effortlessly, spontaneously—as naturally as breathing" (16). In fact, Fouada's memories of Farid and their relationship have such fantasylike qualities that we must wonder if Fouada's imagination has perhaps embellished her actual experiences. In any case, some level of cynicism is evident about positive, balanced relationships between women and men: either they are possible only in a fantasy world[25] or they are unable to survive because there is no social-political space for them (we find out at the end of the novel, through a letter that Fouada receives from him, that Farid has been abducted for political reasons). And, of course, only the most unusual sort of individuals can even hope to achieve them.

Malti-Douglas is not alone in her assessment of al-Saʿdāwī as a leading feminist in the Arab world. As an author and an activist, al-Saʿdāwī has drawn remarkable attention worldwide. Not surprisingly, more and more of her novels are being translated into English and other languages, more than those of other Arab women novelists, and the body of criticism of her work is growing as well. The first critic to devote an entire book to al-Saʿdāwī's work was George Ṭarābīshī; and although this undoubtedly marks a milestone in al-Saʿdāwī's literary career, this particular study is also somewhat disturbing. The title, *Unthā ḍidda al-Unūthah: Dirāsah fī Adab Nawāl al-Saʿdāwī ʿalā Ḍawʾ al-Taḥlīl al-Nafsī*,[26] leaves the reader with little doubt as to Ṭarābīshī's views of al-Saʿdāwī's work and the author herself, views that al-Saʿdāwī found so objectionable that her reply to the study has been included in its English edition.

In *Woman Against Her Sex* Ṭarābīshī closely analyzes several of al-Saʿdāwī's works, drawing largely on psychoanalytic theory. He draws fine and sophisticated connections between various elements in the novels he examines, demonstrating (perhaps unwittingly) that al-Saʿdāwī's narratives are impressively complex. However, these observations notwithstanding, Ṭarābīshī makes the case that al-Saʿdāwī, although purporting to be a feminist author, actually works against women in her work. His reasons are problematic and, as al-Saʿdāwī vehemently argues, suggest a lack of distinction between the author and her characters and between the characters' own conscious beliefs and the messages the novels are meant to convey. For example, in his discussion of *Memoirs of a Woman Doctor*, Ṭarābīshī offers many examples of alleged misogyny on the part of the heroine, one of which is the heroine's observations of the freedom enjoyed by her brother but denied to her and her subsequent statements of loathing toward women. "By brutally severing her solidarity with members of her own sex, the heroine has . . . established the framework of her struggle against her femininity. It is not a struggle against the social injustice which hierarchically legalizes and standardizes anatomical differences between the sexes: it is a struggle against . . . femininity as a physiological concept, against the natural law which deems that a human being is born, or behaves, as half-man and half-woman. In a word, it is a struggle that is against nature and not against society" (Tarabishi 1988: 37). This is followed by a passage from *Memoirs of a Woman Doctor* in which the heroine recalls weeping "over her femininity before I even knew what it was" (38), apparently meant to underscore Ṭarābīshī's point here. However, just because the character says that she cried before she knew what femininity was does not mean that we are supposed to believe that she did not, on some level, understand it. Actually, given her statements (which Ṭarābīshī cites) about her brother's freedom from housework and from long hair and his being allowed to play actively and without express permission, it is clear that her primary consideration is the sex-based life-style differences between her and her brother. It seems rather unlikely, then, that she is not indeed rebelling against "society" and "social injustice."

One must assume, from the title of his book, that Ṭarābīshī takes the heroine's statements to be examples of al-Sa'dāwī's own hatred of women or at least of her failure to write a truly feminist story. But the first-person narration of *Memoirs of a Woman Doctor* is an artistic device, and its importance must not be underestimated. The preceding remarks are made by a girl–young woman who has been socialized to internalize sexism, something that happens to many women, especially if they decide at an early age that the "rewards" of feminine behavior are insufficient compensation for the corresponding lack of power it entails. But this does not mean that al-Sa'dāwī is recommending that girls and women everywhere disassociate themselves from other women; rather, *Memoirs of a Woman Doctor* comments on the tragedy of women's internalized sexism in patriarchal societies. Ṭarābīshī's remark that "feelings of hostility" toward women "positively ooze from all three novels" (148) (referring to *Searching, Memoirs of a Woman Doctor,* and *Two Women in One*), further illustrates his confusion of the characters with the overall meanings of the novels and thus with al-Sa'dāwī herself.

One of Ṭarābīshī's more problematic interpretations along

these lines is outlined in his discussion, however brief, of *Ughniyat al-Aṭfāl al-Dā'iriyyah*.[27] In a departure from the style of other novels discussed here, al-Sa'dāwī creates what could be termed a "mythical" or "dream" novel. The two main characters are "identical" twins, although they are a brother (Hamido) and a sister (Hamida). Their bodies are the same, exhibiting female physical characteristics, but the boy sometimes carries a stick which causes him to behave like a boy-man. Their lives, although different in significant ways due to their perceived sexual identities, are similar in more mundane ways, underscoring the message that the major aspects of our lives are dependent on how others define us in sexual terms. A striking feature of *The Circling Song* is that, in discussions of sex differences, it is taken for granted that the female genitalia are considered the norm, the original form, and that male genitalia are difficult to define and are a deviation from the female, rather than vice versa. There is even a reference to a myth of the origin of sexuality, which Hamido recalls hearing from his mother. According to her, people had had no sex organs prior to Adam's commission of "The Great Crime," after which he grew a penis. Before this, love had been "pure" and people "honorable" (El Saadawi 1989: 41). No mention is even made of the original female sex organs—the focus is on the male and his crime.

This is a clever way to comment on the nature-versus-nurture debate regarding sex and sexuality, but it also simultaneously confronts the Judeo-Christian myth of (Eve's) Original sin and the classical Freudian theory of penis envy. Hamida views Hamido's stick as evil and knows to avoid him when he is carrying it—hardly a sign of envy: "Whenever Hamida heard her brother speak with his rough intonation she knew that the stick was in his possession. She couldn't see it, of course, but knowing he had it hidden somewhere beneath his *gallabiyya*, she would take flight, Hamido following at a run" (24). Reading this part perhaps too literally, Ṭarābīshī asserts that this "reverses" Freudian theories and "insists" on "the uniformity of sex and its origins" (because Hamido and Hamida were conceived as a single embryo) (166–167). To call this a "startling new theory of infantile sexuality" is to miss al-Sa'dāwī's point here. *The Circling Song* is not a detailed, carefully argued case against traditional psychoanalytic theory and in favor of a new one that privileges women as the norm; rather, it challenges those traditional myths and theories by reexposing them as such, reminding us not to view them uncritically. Al-Sa'dāwī is not trying to replace them; rather, she is attempting to displace them.[28]

Al-Sa'dāwī, although she begins her reply to Ṭarābīshī by expressing respect for his hard work in his study, makes it clear that she sees his use of psychoanalytic theory to brand her characters as neurotic and sick as a "subjective personal attack," because these conclusions are then applied to her as if her novels were autobiographical—something that would never have happened, she claims, were she a male author of the same kinds of texts (189). Al-Sa'dāwī makes a point of insisting that her novels are in no way autobiographical, but rather that they merely use certain elements from her life as backdrops for the stories. Al-Sa'dāwī takes Tarābīshī to task with respect to his uncritical acceptance of Freudian theories, despite more modern feminist (and other) challenges and revisions to them. She does this to call his expertise into question more than to defend her stories, as she continues to demand that her stories be read as novels only.

It appears that al-Sa'dāwī feels cornered; surely her novels contain more scenes, feelings, and experiences from her own life than she will admit in her reply to Ṭarābīshī. Ironically, though, although this line of defense does expose important weaknesses and omissions in Ṭarābīshī's analyses, al-Sa'dāwī ends up cornered from a different angle by another critic. The Egyptian critic Sabry Hafez regrets al-Sa'dāwī's strict classification of her work. As political statements, as autobiography, he argues, her stories work despite their artistic weaknesses; however, Hafez finds them greatly lacking as novels in the traditional sense (for many of the same reasons outlined earlier in this discussion). He does join in defending al-Sa'dāwī's work from Ṭarābīshī, pointing out that "in certain works Saadawi's critical portrayal of her female characters, which ostensibly appears to be anti-feminist, succeeds, on a deeper level, in demonstrating the scars of oppression on these characters" (Hafez 1989: 197). But perhaps Hafez's most compelling remarks are about al-Sa'dāwī's popularity in the West. Since there are many Arab women novelists who not only share al-Sa'dāwī's political views and write about them, but who are "more competent novelists" (188), and there is a significant gap between her standing in the West and her position in her own culture, Hafez wonders, "[Is there] something in her writing that makes it appeal more to the Western reader than to the Arab? Do her views tell the Western reader what he or she wants to hear about the nature of the treatment of women in a Muslim culture? Has she attained her fame because she vindicates the main tenets of the traditional orientalist discourse on the position of women in Arab society, and confirms many of the prevalent stereotypes about Arab women and men?" (189).

As an example, Hafez cites the scene in *Memoirs of a Woman Doctor* in which the heroine reluctantly changes her name to that of her husband—a popular issue in Western feminism, but a nonissue in the context of the novel because "in Egypt, women do not change their maiden names after marriage" (189). And, interestingly, the published title of the English translation of *al-Ghā'ib* (literally "the absent one") is *Searching*, which would seem to confirm Hafez's suspicions. The title *Searching* shifts the focus from the missing male lover to the heroine herself, which might appeal more to Western feminists. Although some might argue that *Searching* is more descriptive of the novel's content and gives the heroine her due as the main character, the fact remains that the original title means, literally, "the absent one." Unless al-Sa'dāwī truly consented, this borders on literary vandalism; however, if al-Sa'dāwī did expressly approve the change, one must still ask what the reasons were, if not to appeal to Western readers even at the expense of her artistic integrity.[29]

Discussion: Themes, Patterns, and Problems

The generation of Arab women novelists who began their literary careers in the late 1950s not only were able to keep the female literary culture alive but also worked tirelessly and successfully to enrich it. They set out to explore the feminine psyche that had been *terra incognita* throughout the history of Arabic literature, because that literature had been almost exclusively the product of male writers. Laylā Ba'labakkī and those who followed her brought the discourse of a female point of view into the mainstream of Arab writing. Until then, the majority of the literature was written from distinctly male points of view.

When Arab women set out to discover or establish their own identities, the first thing they had to do was to confront the fact of their femaleness in a male-dominated culture. This confrontation often took the form of a rejection of the female body. Although this body was the incarnation of womanhood, it was also a sex object for men. It therefore came to be seen as an obstacle to the woman's self-fulfillment. For example, Najlā', the heroine of 'Ināyāt al-Zayyāt's[30] *al-Ḥubb wa-al-Ṣamt* (*Love and Silence*, 1967), rebels against her body: "How I hate this beautiful body and feel embarrassed by it! Its femininity announces itself whether I want it to or not. In the street I hear lustful calls all around me, and I wish the earth would open and swallow me up. These obscene expressions frighten me and make me feel like the sheep which are hung up by their tails and make people feel hungry" (al-Zayyāt 1967: 53–54). Similarly, the heroine of Mājidah al-'Aṭṭār's *Murāhiqah* (*Adolescent*, 1966) cannot escape from this problem even at the university. Her male fellow students treat her not as a person but as a collection of female physical attributes, seeing in her only "hair, lips, breasts and legs" (al-'Aṭṭār 1966: 155).[31]

Consequently, Līnā (*Anā Aḥyā*) and Rīm (*Ayyām Ma'ahu*) cut their hair; Rashā (*Laylah Wāḥidah*) walks in front of Salīm; 'Ā'ishah (*Lan Namūt Ghadan*) stops wearing high-heeled shoes; and the heroine of *Mudhakkirāt Ṭabībah* wants to cut off her breasts. This rejection is also manifested in the way various heroines' mothers are portrayed, and the heroines' attitudes toward them—a phenomenon labeled *the bad mother* by Nina Baym (1987), who has observed it in many Western feminist novels. In many of these novels, as we have seen, mothers are obstacles to their daughters' self-actualization, discouraging their daughters from nontraditional life-styles and condemning their independence, and the heroines often feel disgust or pity toward them for their conformity to old ways. This is partly due to the fact that women have been given a small but seductive stake in patriarchy (in Arab society, a mother might have the responsibility of proving that her daughter's virginity is preserved until the wedding night, for example, or for teaching her how to conform properly to traditional gender roles). But "the bad mother" is also part of the psychological process of declaring independence in this "feminist" stage of Arab women's literature, because mothers represent the daughter's own connections to traditional ways, as well as the threatening possibility that the daughters might take the mothers' places in the existing order eventually. Elaine Showalter calls this reaction *matrophobia*, or "the fear of becoming one's mother," which, she argues, is actually a metaphor for self-hatred (Showalter 1985: 135). Based on Nancy Chodorow's school of theory regarding mothers and daughters, if mothers are the primary parent, we can expect girls to learn to see themselves relationally, as connected to others, and especially as continuous with their mothers. If, in addition to this, daughters also rebel against traditional gender roles and values, they see both themselves and those traditional ways in their mothers—an intolerable combination that produces the "matrophobia" Showalter describes and results in the "bad mother" pattern identified by Baym.

Fathers and male relatives, however, are not immune in the novels. The vast majority of heroines in women's novels hold men responsible for their ordeals on the grounds that men have tried to remold women to fit their tastes. In many cases the heroine directs her hostility toward her father, the first male encountered in a woman's life and the embodiment of male authority and oppression. For example, as mentioned earlier, the heroine of al-Saʿdāwī's *Searching* finds her father disgusting. Al-Khūrī (in whose case the uncle assumed the father's role) and Baʿlabakkī developed this theme in detail in their fiction, as we have seen. Another good example is Sulaymā Qumayrah's *Qabla al-Awān* (*Before Its Time*), in which the heroine, Munā, hates her father for his tyranny (Qumayrah n.d.: 89–90) and indeed comes to hate all men after her marriage (78, 87, 157). In Rajāʾ Niʿmah's *Ṭaraf al-Khayṭ* (*The End of the Thread*, 1973), the protagonist Nadā refers to men as dogs (Niʿmah 1973: 24) and says that her father's voice resembles "the barking of a hoarse dog" (6). In Munā Jabbūr's *Fatāh Tāfihah* (*Insignificant Woman*), the protagonist (also called Nadā) is utterly contemptuous of her father's attempts to indoctrinate her into traditional womanhood: "He thinks that I will marry and bear children, and spend all night with the crying of babies, and lie at my husband's feet when he stares at me with his cruel look. He thinks I will wear perfume for some repulsive hyena like himself who will share my bed and fill my nights with his snoring and with the smell of his stinking mouth" (Jabbūr n.d.: 47). These characters' negative images of their own bodies and their rebellion against men leads most of them to look upon pregnancy with horror. Laylā Baʿlabakkī was probably the first woman novelist to show disgust for pregnancy, but the motif recurred frequently in later novels. In the aforementioned *Fatāh Tāfihah*, Nadā includes reproduction among the manifestations of femininity of which she is trying to cleanse herself (6). Laylā, the married heroine of Hind Salāmah's *al-Dumā al-Ḥayyah* (*Living Dolls*, 1968), resorts to abortion several times because she is nauseated at the thought of carrying a fetus in her body (Salāmah 1968: 96). This is not surprising, given that, to these women who are rebelling against patriarchal constraints, pregnancy most likely has come to symbolize lack of control over the body, traditional (male-dominated) family structure, and increased dependence on men.

Al-Sa'dāwī makes this association explicit in *Memoirs of a Woman Doctor*, when the heroine decides to perform an abortion for a young girl whom she sees as a victim of their patriarchal society. Nevertheless, positive images of motherhood and maternal sentiments are not entirely absent from women's fiction. At one point in *Anā aḥyā*, Līnā is ready to have a child by any man who will give her one. In *Murāhiqah*, Lamyā' is obsessed with the idea of having a baby: "There is only one thing I really know that I want out of life. I want a child" (al-'Aṭṭār 1966: 214). In other novels, the heroines shower motherly feelings on their lovers, as Munā does with her lover Samīr in *Qabla al-Awān*. The heroine Salmā in Umayyah Ḥamdān's *Wa-Antaẓir* (*And I Wait*) also wishes several times in the story that she were the mother of her lover 'Āmir (Ḥamdān n.d.: 208–209).

To understand the internal conflicts of these heroines regarding the traditional roles of wife and mother, one must recall the kind of experiences that typify their lives as females from birth. Nawāl al-Sa'dāwī summed up the ordeal which these experiences constituted: "From the moment she is born and even before she learns to pronounce words, the way people look at her and their glances and the expression in their eyes somehow indicate that she was born 'incomplete' or 'with something missing.' From the day of her birth to the moment of her death a question will haunt her: Why? Why is her brother preferred over her, despite the fact that they are the same, or that she may even be superior to him in many ways or at least in some ways?" (1980: 12). On one hand, there is some awareness of, and resentment toward, being discriminated against by a sexist society; on the other, given the limited means of acquiring and exercising power for women in patriarchy, it is no surprise that these heroines sometimes pay the price of conformity and enforcement of the status quo to gain the diluted but certain power that this buys them.

As we have seen, this "curse" of having been born female haunts most of the heroines in the fiction of (for example) Ba'labakkī and Naṣrallāh and drives them to try to assert themselves as human beings first and foremost. This theme recurs constantly in al-Sa'dāwī's novels, starting with her first one. *Searching* also contains a scene in which a man refuses to kiss his wife after the birth of their child because the baby is a girl (El Saadawi 1991: 59). In *al-Ḥubb wa-al-Ṣamt* the heroine Najlā' wonders why her parents keep ignoring her; she later learns that when she was born her parents had been expecting a boy (al-Zayyāt 1967: 53). Laylā in *al-Dumā al-Ḥayyah* finds herself in the same predicament; her psychiatrist decides that her mental problems are related to a lack of love from her parents, who are disappointed that she was born a female (Salāmah 1968: 109). Being deprived of her parents' love for this reason has made her suppress her femininity and behave like a man (110). In *Fatāh Tāfihah*, Nadā's tragedy begins when her mother gives birth to a dead male fetus and afterward becomes sterile. The father cannot bear the disaster of having only one child, and of that child being a female. Reflecting on the father's attitude. Nadā thinks: "I am a girl. I am a weakness, incomplete (*uqnūm*), a shame, and a disaster in the eyes of my father" (Jabbūr n.d.: 46).

Much of the hostility of Arab parents toward female offspring was due to the Arab cultural obsession with a peculiar notion of honor—that is, that the family's honor depended upon its women's virginity before marriage and chastity after marriage. 'Āyidah in *al-Ālihah al-Mamsūkhah* is made to suffer heavily for the loss of her hymen (though it was involuntary) and her marital life is shattered. Sihām, the heroine of Ibrīzā al-Ma'ūshī's *Hal Aghfir lahu?* (*Should I Forgive Him?* 1962), considers committing suicide after losing her virginity. She cannot make herself do it, but decides never to marry (al-Ma'ūshī 1962: 96, 102, 106). In Hālah al-Ḥifnāwī's book *Hal Akhla' Thawbī?* (*Should I Take My Dress Off?* 1969), the heroine Thurayyā is told by her mother that the hymen is a garden that should be preserved for the wedding night: "Keep your garden, my daughter. Its walls must be kept intact untill the promised night. A great number of your relatives will be behind the door listening. Let me see your red banner in their eyes. Are you going to let me down in their presence?" (al-Ḥifnāwī 1969a: 6).[32]

With this obsession so strong, it is perhaps not surprising that Arab parents generally saw daughters as a burden. The birth of a girl meant that, from that moment until she was married, the parents would have to worry about the risk of their daughter besmirching the family honor by losing her virginity. These complexes about women's sexual behavior led the parents (especially mothers) to do all they could to keep their daughters ignorant of sex-related bodily functions in the hope this would discourage sexual activity. When Lamyā' in *Murāhiqah* reaches the age of her first menstruation she is completely confused, yet her mother's explanation is not of much help: "You didn't do anything, but you are not a little girl anymore. Now you have become just like me" (al-'Aṭṭār 1966: 15). Nawāl al-Sa'dāwī, many of whose heroines react violently to the onset of menstruation, described the terror that struck her when she first began to menstruate:

> It would be difficult for anyone to imagine the panic that seized hold of me one morning when I woke to find blood trickling down between my thighs. I can still remember the deathly pallor of my face in the mirror. My arms and legs were trembling violently, and it seemed to me as thought the disaster I had been dreading for so long had finally happened: that somehow, in the dark of night, a man had crept into my room while I was sleeping and succeeded in causing me harm. This possibility had never left my thoughts, so that each night before going to bed I used to close the window overlooking the street as tightly as possible.[33]

Situations like this one may seem to help justify the common "bad mother" character, but it is important to understand these mothers' behavior in the context of the culture in which they found themselves. Like women in many patriarchal societies they are sometimes in the very difficult position of having to negotiate power for themselves at the expense of other women's power and of wanting to find validation for their own lives, based on old ways, in the lives of daughters who want to destroy the old order. The threat of invalidation of life experience, combined with the intense pressure on women and mothers to protect the family honor even from things beyond their control is more than enough to create a "bad mother" from a daughter's point of view—especially if the daughter is rebelling against tradition. A mother may be "portrayed" by the daughter as an evil and willing tool of patriarchy, but such a mother is entangled in a complex web of power struggles and is not simply "the enemy."

Another frequent theme in these novels is that the home is not the right place for a woman to reach her full psychological and intellectual potential, so that the heroines have no choice but to leave home and try their luck in the outside world. One common response is to take a job, either to break the monotony of home life or (more important) to achieve economic independence; for example, Nadā of *Fatāh Tāfihah* is determined to go to work so that she will be able to live without need of men or of marriage (Jabbūr n.d.: 44). The families of most of the heroines find this latter objective intolerable and fight against it.[34] But as a rule, these attempts to escape oppressive homes by going to work ended in failure. At work their bosses simply take over the oppressive roles formerly played by their fathers, and at home the pressure to give up working is intense. When Līnā in *Anā Aḥyā* takes a job in defiance of her family's wishes, her father is extremely upset; and when she quits (to please her boyfriend), he rewards her by buying her a new dress (Ba'labakkī 1964a: 235). Rīm of *Ayyām Ma'ahu* takes a job to free herself from the loneliness, emptiness, and boredom of her life (al-Khūrī 1967: 30), but her grandmother and uncle collaborate to try to stop her on the grounds that she comes from a rich family and therefore does not need a job (33–34). Najlā' of *al-Ḥubb wa-al-Ṣamt* believes that work will enrich her personality and free her from boredom, but can find no argument to convince her father that she should be allowed to take a job. He fears that letting his daughter work will harm the reputation of his family (which is also rich) ('I. al-Zayyāt 1967: 29).

Notably, none of these heroines is forced to work for financial need, which would be an acceptable reason for a woman in their society to take a job. This not only weakens the credibility of the stories, but renders the heroines' resolve to work rather unstable when combined with family pressures. They always know that they can quit and return home, be welcomed by their rich families and take up again the traditional roles created for them by society. Most of them end up doing just that, so that the vicious circle is complete and they find themselves in the same circumstances in which they began. For these characters, the price of economic security is sexual inequality—not surprising, because wealth is usually in the possession of men and accompanied by an investment in conservatism. Al-Sa'dāwī's work is an exception to this: many of her main characters (like those of *Memoirs of a Woman Doctor* and *Searching,* as well as *Two Women in One* and *God Dies by the Nile,* both addressed in Chapter Four) escape from their original circumstances, but they pay for change or independence with loneliness, alienation, and frustration, some for the rest of their lives.

These novels that deal with the search for personal female identity draw heavily upon the lives of their authors, being filled with autobiographical or semi-autobiographical material. This may explain why the novelists' first books were usually their best, because they tended to exhaust their material in the first books so that later ones were repetitions or expansions of themes that the earlier works had already covered. Laylā Ba'labakkī, Colette al-Khūrī, Laylā 'Usayrān, Emily Naṣrallāh, and Nawāl al-Sa'dāwī all followed this pattern. The shortage of material was partly due to the cramped lives of the novelists themselves (who, after all, were limited by having to live in the restrictive society they were depicting).[35] In some cases, a novelist was able to write only one novel: examples already mentioned included 'Ināyāt al-Zayyāt, Mājidah al-'Aṭṭār, and Sulaymā Qumayrah. Two others, who wrote one novel each, were Laylā al-Yāfī, who wrote *Thulūj Taḥta al-Shams* (*Snow Under the Sun*), and Balqīs Ḥūmānī, who wrote *Ḥayy al-Lujā* (*The Lujā Quarter,* 1969).

Related to this is the fact that, especially for those with limited mobility and experience, autobiography provides a topic about which an author can claim expertise without the risk of being accused of "arrogance" or "authoritarianism" (Roller 1986: 37)—qualities especially despised in women by patriarchal society. But Susan Gubar makes the point that external pressure is not the only factor in women's decisions to write about their own lives. She argues that, because "women have had to experience cultural scripts in their lives by suffering them in their bodies," and the woman artist's "sense that she is herself the text means that there is little distance between her life and her art," the "attraction . . . to personal forms of expression like letters, autobiographies, confessional poetry, diaries, and journals points up the effect of a life experienced as art or an art experienced as a kind of life, as does women's traditional interests in cosmetics, fashion, and interior decorating" (Gubar 1985: 299). Also, given the association of women and femininity with "personal" matters and "subjective" thinking, writing autobiographically may have allowed women to gain access to the literary world more quickly than if they had continued to write like male authors.[36]

Another aspect of autobiographical (or semi-autobiographical) writing is that it is especially conducive to the theme of fragmentation, which, Judi M. Roller argues, is extremely common in feminist novels in the West (Roller 1986: 68). Most of the reasons she cites for the theme apply to Arab women as well and are evident in their novels, such as "the schizophrenia of modern culture's views of women and the battle in women themselves between the old ways and the revolutionary spirit" and a nonlinear life structure (relative to men) (68). Roller discusses several manifestations of the theme of fragmentation, ones found in the novels discussed in this chapter. An obvious examples is the characters' own divided lives and experiences of a divided world, or "the division of modern culture represesented by the persistence of the old ways and of a restrictive social structure and the simutaneous emergence of the revolutionary spirit in women's ambitions and desires" (77). This struggle between old and new is central to most of the novels discussed here, embodied in mother-daughter relationships, family and social pressures on "rebellious" women to conform, and heroines' disappointment in the sexism of the "real world," to mention a few examples. Another method of incorporating the fragmentation theme is the multiple-point-of-view style, which "frequently reflects the fragmentation of an individual female character or of woman generally into many characters" and illustrates the cultural "schizophrenia" and inner "battle" mentioned previously (68). Examples of this style include Laylā Ba'labakkī's *al-Ālihah al-Mamsūkhah* and Laylā 'Usayrān's *al-Ḥiwār al-Akhras*. The theme of fragmentation can also come into play in a novel via its pattern, specifically in the separation of a novel "into sections focused on different characters or . . . different stories" (68). 'Usayrān's *al-Madīnah al-Fārighah* and Naṣrallāh's *Ṭuyūr Aylūl* are fragmented in these ways, through characters and through stories, respectively. According to Roller, in cases like these, "the pattern of the novel, not its progression, is essential to its meaning; giving such a shape to a novel allows the female author to dispense with the necessity of writing and conversing linearly" (68).

In fact, any of these methods allow an author to avoid linear structure, which itself is an important topic in feminist literary theory. Many Western feminist critics have tried to show a direct connection between the nonlinear patterns they observed in women's writing and women's own life structures, experiences, and physical makeup. Roller sees this connection in the fact that women's lives tend to adhere to patterns like those in their novels: in the words of Suzanne Juhasz, "repetitive, cumulative, cyclical" (68). After all, women historically have been confined to less physical space than men; and, in addition, "female development is so fragmented and discontinuous" that, in novels written by women, female characters very often return to their origins. For them, "origin and destination are identical" (Hirsch 1983: 44–45).

This can be seen in novels by Arab women, too, especially in the "vicious circle" theme that appears so often in them. According to Roller, many twentieth century Western feminist novels "end in flight and escape or death, literal or symbolic," reflecting cynicism about the possibilities of improvement in social conditions (14). In a number of Arab women's novels, the heroine attempts escape. Some, like ʿĀ'ishah in *Lan Namūt Ghadan* and Jacqueline in *al-Ḥiwār al-Akhras*, succeed well. Others succeed in escaping, but at the price of alienation (like Munā in *Ṭuyūr Aylūl* and Fouada in *Searching*), or literal death (like Rashā in *Laylah Wāḥidah* and ʿĀ'ishah in *al-Ālihah al-Mamsūkhah*). These characters effectively refuse to occupy the place that society tries to force them into as women; but many fail to escape and end up living the life they tried to avoid, thus getting caught in the "vicious circle" mentioned earlier. Līnā, in *Anā Aḥyā*, for example, attempts to commit suicide (seeking death as an escape) but fails and is doomed to live out her life in the conventional role she had always resisted.[37] Josephine Donovan points out the more concrete fact that women are expected to do domestic work, which is "nonprogressive, repetitive, and static" (Donovan 1987: 101). In addition, Donovan argues, women's physical processes (like menstruation for most and, at least for many women, childbirth and breast-feeding) "contribute to a sense of being bound to physical events beyond the self, and in the case of menstruation to a consciousness of repetition and of interruptibility of one's projects" (104–105).

Although it would be difficult to prove these theories as "true" in any absolute sense, it seems reasonable at least to relate women's nonlinear writing patterns to the ways in which social contexts affect *perceptions* of women's lives, work, and bodies as cyclical, repetitive, and interruptive. Elaine Showalter advocates reading women's works with a "model of women's culture" as frame of reference, because how "women conceptualize their bodies and their sexual and reproductive functions are intricately linked to their cultural environment" (1985a: 259). By extension, this also applies to how women see their work and general life structures.

Feminist psychoanalytic theorists, most notably Nancy Chodorow, provide even more substantiation for these explanations of women's writing styles. In a society where women do almost all the work of "mothering," girls develop to see themselves as "more continuous with and related to the external object world" (Donovan 1987: 104). This sets the stage for writing novels structured on something other than the traditional linear, progressive, unidirectional plot. A great deal of fiction by women went largely unnoticed or unacclaimed until recently, when feminist theorists and critics suggested that absence of traditional structure does not necessarily indicate lack of structure (101–102). Because their theories are based on psychoanalytic theory, French feminists (such as Hélène Cixous and Luce Irigaray), too, have contributed to this discussion by developing concepts to explain women's language use (which both reflects their psyches and informs their writing) and to theorize a (written) female language that, according to some, has yet to be written but that will prove revolutionary for women when it is finally used. As one might expect, it is described with words like *fluid, open, nonlinear,* and *fragmented* (Baym 1987: 49).[38] Although it is important to remember that these theories are based on Western perspectives, and Chodorow's ideas are reflective mainly of white, middle-class American experience, there are enough similarities between Western patriarchy and Arab patriarchy to suggest that these theories can at least be considered as potentially useful (to some degree, anyway) for reading Arab women's texts. The similarities between the techniques, styles, and themes evident in the writings of both Arab and Western women (such as mother-daughter confict, nonlinear plot structure, and first-person narration, to name a few) seem to indicate that the theories in question may be less limited in their applicability than many critics might argue.[39]

Even some artistic shortcomings in Arab women's novels bear a great resemblance to those obseved by critics in Western feminist novels. For example, a major weakness in these novels is the presence of unconvincing male characters. The men in the stories tend to fit into one or the other of two basic categories. One is the member of the older generation (usually the heroine's father, but sometimes also a boss or a religious figure) who is undisguisedly a male chauvinist. The other type is the member of the younger generation, a man who claims to represent a new and more liberal order in society but who deep down is just as prejudiced as his elders and thus cannot have healthy relationships with the female protagonists. Bahā' of *Anā Aḥyā* is a good example. Both types of men are portrayed in an oversimplified way and are thus unconvincing. Muḥyī al-Dīn Ṣubḥī, noting that Ba'labakkī's depiction of male characters is both troublesome and unconvincing, attributes this phenomenon to Ba'labakkī's advocacy of women's liberation, which led her to believe that she was more mature than men. As a result of this belief, Ba'labakkī, Ṣubḥī argues, tends to depict men in a comical manner (1974: 107–108). Aḥmad M. Zayn al-Dīn, on the other hand, sees this inadequency rooted either in her "subjective" outlook or her hostility toward men (1979: 79, 83). One reason for this problem was probably the seclusion of women in Arab society to some degree, which prevented them from having contact with men (even with their own fathers, because the mother tended to function as a messenger between father and daughter). These writers thus had no direct experience of what men were really like or how they really lived. This is similar to the problem faced by women writers in Victorian England. Charlotte Brontë wrote, "In delineating male characters, I labour under disadvantages; intuition and theory will not adequately supply the place of observation and experience. When I write about women, I am sure of my ground—in the other case I am not so sure" (Showalter 1977: 133). Margaret Oliphant also pointed out this problem, describing even George Eliot as "feeble in her men" (that is, in her ability to depict male characters) (Showalter 1977: 135).

This shortcoming in Victorian women's writing was not

always due to inability or lack of experience and knowledge, however. Rather, Showalter argues, it was "frequently the result of prudence or self-censorship" (1977: 135). As Margaret Oliphant added to the preceding comment: "Sometimes we don't know sufficiently to make the outline sharp and clear; sometimes we know well enough, but dare not betray our knowledge one way or other: the result is that men in a woman's book are always washed in secondary colours" (Showalter 1977: 135). And, although the types of male characters Showalter discusses in Victorian women's novels differ greatly from the ones discussed here, the same argument may serve as one of the reasons the authors discussed in this chapter were unable to create convincing male characters. Lack of exposure to men, combined with some awareness of the danger in creating too-realistic characters (because, as proper young women, they were supposed to be largely ignorant of men) would be enough to keep their male characters "washed in." But one other reason suggests itself here, one perhaps not shared by Victorian woman novelists in general, which may be more central than the others: an intense, conscious feminist anger and determination to criticize patriarchy explicitly, which are arguably most pronounced in al-Saʿdāwī's work. Showalter discusses "model heroes" and "brute heroes" in Victorian women's novels (1977: 140), but here there is no equivalent pattern; rather, there are chauvinistic men with few redeeming qualities. They are brutes but not heroes, and there are very few "model" counterparts.

Another pervasive problem for these writers not shown by their Western counterparts was their inability to master the art of writing dialogue, indicated by their failure to use the level of Arabic appropriate to the educational status and the emotional and mental makeup of their characters. In Arabic novels, either literary Arabic or dialect may be used for dialogue, provided the author sticks to one or the other. The well-known fiction writer Yūsuf Idrīs, for example, used Egyptian dialect, whereas Nobel Prize winner Najīb Maḥfūẓ stuck to literary. Within each of the two main types of Arabic there are several levels of sophistication, so that an author can use different registers within the type of Arabic used to create an appropriate style of speaking for each character. The novelists discussed in this chapter failed to do this. Instead, they tended to use unvarying Classical Arabic (as did Amīnah al-Saʿīd) or various mixtures of Classical and colloquial Arabic (as did

Laylā 'Usayrān). This makes the dialogue very unconvincing. They also failed to make their characters speak in a natural or convincing way, making the dialogue lifeless and impersonal. Of course, this was not due to lack of talent or ability. These failures resulted from the fact that most of the women novelists were very young (Laylā Ba'labakkī was only fourteen when she was first published, for example) and were partly educated in foreign (non-Arabic) schools. This means that they did not have the exposure to Arabic literature necessary to develop an understanding of how to write dialogue, because they lacked reading time and access to education in Arabic letters—things that their male counterparts as a whole did not lack. The irony here is that foreign-educated girls and women were more likely to become writers in the first place, because they were exposed to Western ideas and role models and could more easily entertain the idea of becoming writers themselves. (Both Mayy Ziyādah and Collette al-Khūrī, for example, were foreign educated, and their first books—poetry collections—even were published in French.) Likewise, it was easier for a very young woman to begin a writing career than for one who might be married, have children, or at least be experiencing familial and social pressures to take on these responsibilities.

In other kinds of language use though, these authors accomplished a great deal. They incorporated many colloquialisms and foreign words into their writing—a radical and daring feat, considering the cultural beliefs in the sacredness of the Arabic language as it appears in the Qur'ān. As a group, Arab women writers of this period were far less puritanical in their language use than their male counterparts. They had much to gain, after all, in subverting the dominant discourse, which was created by and for a patriarchal culture and which relegates women to the margin.

Another feature of these novels is the way the authors used colors in their communication. Although technically not a linguistic device like colloquialisms and foreign words, this use of color is another way in which the dominant discourse is subverted in the novels. For example, one of the most striking features of Laylā Ba'labakkī's fiction is her use of color, not only for normal description, but also to illustrate the psychological or emotional moods of her characters, or to represent other aspects of them. In *Anā Aḥyā*, colors carry important associations. Līnā identifies Bahā' with the color black in a negative context. He comes from a country in which women wear black veils, so he has not had the chance to see women's real faces. Bahā' sees a parallel between the situation of the actual veil and the hidden world of women in general, and tells Līnā, "I will tear off the black silk which covers the face of every woman" (Ba'labakkī 1958: 251). Līnā is an anticommunist, and in her eyes the newspaper of the Communist party to which Bahā' belongs is nothing but black lines (239, 318–319). Red is another color connected with Bahā'; it is associated both with his ideological commitment and with his plans to kill his enemies in Iraq (295, 300, 320).

Color is used even more frequently in *al-Ālihah al-Mamsū khah*, and hardly a place in the novel lacks a reference to it. Mīrā, obsessed with death, refers to it throughout the novel as "the violet cloud." Sometimes Ba'labakkī uses colors to replace direct description of sexual experience, such as when the Indian student was having sexual intercourse with 'Āyidah: "I was lost in waves of red, yellow, green, gray, and white lights" (1960: 21). Mīrā uses some of the same colors (green, yellow, and red, as well as blue, in reference to her sexual encounter with Rajā (83). Laylā Ba'labakkī also uses color to dramatize the loss of personal identity by both Līnā and 'Āyidah. Līnā cannot even be sure whether she is pale or dark; whereas 'Āyidah suffers from similar uncertainties about what she is really like, and when she is suffering she feels as though she has lost all her traits and become colorless (81–82).

Colette al-Khūrī uses colors in a more sophisticated and subtle way in *Ayyām Ma'ahu* than Ba'labakkī had done in *Anā Aḥyā*. This may be related to the fact that the two main characters, Rīm and Ziyād, are artists. Rīm is prone to associate colors, especially those of her clothes, with her various moods. At one point in the novel she exclaims: "What should I put on? The wide gray dress? Or the narrow violet one? The choice tormented me. Finally I made my mind up to put the black dress on, because to me this color suggests sublimeness and lightness" (al-Khūrī 1967: 77). At another point in the book Rīm suggests a color for each letter of the Arabic alphabet (335).[40]

This keen sense of colors and their connotations had never before manifested itself so strongly in Arabic fiction. The whole subject of how women approach and conceive of color, especially in literature, is still new and merits further investigation. Robin Lakoff's attempt to explain it in her book *Language and Woman's*

Place, is based on a solid but limited analysis; she links women's sense of color to their powerlessness in the world of men, leaving out some important contextual factors:

> We might ask why fine discrimination of color is relevant for women, but not for men. A clue is contained in the way many men in our society view other "unworthy" topics, such as high culture and the church, as outside the world of men's work, relegated to women and men whose masculinity is not unquestionable. Men tend to relegate to women things that are not of concern to them, or do not involve their egos. Among these are problems of fine color discrimination. We might rephrase this point by saying that since women are not expected to make decisions on important matters, such as what kind of job to hold, they are relegated to noncrucial decisions as a sop. Deciding whether to name a color "lavender" or "mauve" is one such sop. (Lakoff 1975: 9)

But to gain a fuller understanding of women's cultivation of their sense of color, we must look at their historical experience as well. For hundreds of years, women have been largely restricted to the household and put in charge of decorating the home. This suggests that they may have had to develop their awareness of colors more than men did. In addition, most societies have placed strong emphasis on women's value as sex objects for men, and have thus required them to pay great attention to self-beautification, including the harmonious use of colors in their clothes. From this angle, we can argue that women are not as passive in their focus on color as Lakoff's statements suggest; and an examination of the ways in which Arab women use color in their novels puts into question the idea that women's "preoccupation" with color is necessarily degrading or pitiable. In fact, in some of these novels, the use of color proves to be a creative and, I would argue, subversive stylistic device. Given the language's design to mute women's voices, and its emphasis on the Self-Other dichotomy (where women are the eternal Other), one would expect women writers to experiment with unorthodox ways to communicate meaning. Using colors to convey moods, for example, makes use of very visual symbolism in a literary medium and blurs the line between verbal and nonverbal communication. In addition, the authors are also taking an area not coincidentally deemed both unimportant and "feminine" and creating a high symbolic value for it. Clothes and home decor, for example, become symbols of feelings and association within the novels, rather than mindless or coquettish preoccupations. This challenges the devaluation of the feminine and makes color use more of an active choice for the authors, rather than a manifestation of passive acceptance of patriarchal assignments. To borrow from feminist rhetoric surrounding the issue of violence against women (violence that, one can argue, also happens in patriarchal language), this renders the authors survivors rather than the mere victims that Lakoff's analysis seems to portray.

Not surprising, in this context of having created a place for and an image of female speaking subjects in a culture that works to deny them both, all the novels discussed in this chapter strongly emphasize autonomy. One means of expressing this is by the already-mentioned use of the pronoun *anā*, a device that originated with Laylā Ba'labakkī's *Anā Aḥyā* and the majority of these writers adopted. Another is the use of the stream-of-consciousness style of narration (especially in Rajā' Ni'mah's *Ṭaraf al-Khayṭ*) (Ni'mah 1973). Yet another way of stressing individuality is an emphasis on subjective time as opposed to objective time. Līnā makes this explicit in *Anā Aḥyā* when she says, "I am time. I am its characteristics, because I am the only one who can give it the quality of slowness or lingeringness or delicacy or tragedy or mercy" (Ba'labakkī 1964a: 223).

Anā Aḥyā stands out as the most original of all these novels. It raised issues that came to make up the "agenda" of the later novels, and it has been widely imitated. Through her authorship of this book, Laylā Ba'labakkī can take credit for having begun a whole new era in women's fiction. Līnā's quest for personal identity in *Anā Aḥyā* is, of course, an intensely individual matter. It would be wrong to say that she has no interest in the wider concerns of her homeland, but the nationalist element is definitely less emphasized than the personal. The next chapter will look at those novels in which the quest for national identity and its connection with the quest for individual identity are given more emphasis.

4. The Quest for National Identity

We have seen that Arab women novelists throughout the 1950s and 1960s were preoccupied with the search for self-fulfillment. They directed the full strength of their wrath against the society in which they lived, a society whose norms and values were set by men. Their frustration with this culture, and their resulting sense of alienation, were the main reasons that women's fiction of that generation for the most part showed little or no interest in national issues.

In Ba'labakkī's *Anā Aḥyā*, for example, Līnā is totally preoccupied with her determination to achieve personal freedom. She regards any distraction from this pursuit as irrelevant: "I have not listened to the news for two days. I have not read a single newspaper. He [Bahā'] does not know that I was in front of my mirror, that for the last two days I have been listening to a more important and valuable news broadcast by my own body which is striving to attain its freedom" (Ba'labakkī 1964a: 170). This insistance on individual freedom for women makes Līnā look upon the Arab's struggle for political independence from a special perspective. She takes into account the predicament of Arab women, who are often either forgotten or persecuted: "I know that [freedom] is for the young man whose leg was blown off by guns of the French. It is for the orphan whose father the Ottomans hanged in the Martyrs' Square [in Beirut]. It is [also] for my ill-treated grandmother who was forbidden to go out in the street" (191).

From this perspective, politics appears as an exclusively male sphere of activity. It is thus pervaded by men's complexes and hypocrisies and especially by their sexual depravity. When Līnā tries to express her opinions to a group of male university students from various Arab countries, all she can see is "shining heads moving in the blazing sun: red, black, yellow, old, new, and dark." But despite the diversity of these heads (referred to in a rather impersonal way) they have something in common: "The eyes were fixed on my rebellious and daring breast. I examined the eyes carefully and found them all hungry, ready to plunge through seas of the blood of all nations, not to propagate socialism, not to unite the Arab countries under the ceiling of one parliament, not to regain Palestine, and not to liberate Algeria as they had proposed a moment before. Now they were completely ready to drink each others' blood to get a kiss from a rebellious lip, or to touch a breast" (103). Despite Līnā's obsession with her quest for personal identity, *Anā Aḥyā* does make some reference to the heroine's dilemma of national identity. Līnā's resentment of her father is in part a reaction to his collaboration with the French authorities in Lebanon, a collaboration seen as part of the general moral decay.[1] Līnā makes only one brief reference to her national identity, however. She expresses her irritation at her family's adoption of French cuisine: "I am not French. My picture in the mirror testifies that I have descended from the first man who lived on our shores thousands of years ago, deeply rooted in the radiant [Arabian] Peninisula. . . . I am not French. I am not French" (77).

Al-Sa'dāwī: A Link between Personal and National Identity

Whereas Ba'labakkī, for example, remained locked in a paradoxical attempt to realize herself outside of any social or political context, Nawāl al-Sa'dāwī, in some of her work, went a step further by exploring the interaction between personal and national identities. In fact, Bahiah, the heroine of al-Sa'dāwī's *Imra'atān fī*

Imra'ah (1975),[2] ends up by denying her individuality to dissolve it in a collective identity. At the outset of the novel, Bahiah is obsessed by the feeling that she is utterly unique and distinct from the common herd of both women and men, a feeling that shows itself in her rejection of conventional behavior. As early as the first page of the novel, she is shown adopting a stance considered totally inappropriate: "She stood with her right foot on the edge of the marble table and her left foot on the floor, a posture unbecoming for a woman" (El Saadawi 1986: 7).

Bahiah's dilemma cannot be fully appreciated without an understanding of her parents' role in depriving her of any sexual identity. Deep down, her father wishes that she had been a boy, and her constant denial of her femininity pleases him (73).[3] Her mother, for her part, wants Bahiah to remain female but ignorant of her sexuality. Bahiah is unable to rid herself of the memory of an incident that took place when she was three years old, the discovery of her sex for the first time: she took off her clothes to show her mother her femaleness, but her mother punished her and told her never to do it again (12). Bahiah cannot identify with either sex. She considers all women essentially the same: fat thighs tightened together as if fearing that something (the hymen?) might drop out (El Saadawi 1986: 7).[4] In spite of this impersonality (or because of it) she sees men as a sexual threat: "But since she was a woman, it was legitimate to stare. Her body was the victim of hungry, deprived eyes" (120). Later, she has traumatic experiences with her husband and a university professor. On her wedding night she refuses to respond sexually to her husband, despite the fact that the bedroom has been stocked with all manner of "tools" meant for sexual enhancement. The passage describing her discovery of these, although it constitutes an example of al-Saʿdāwī's tendency to sermonize in her novels (discussed in Chapter Three), suggests that Bahiah's situation is meant to represent that of women in general:

> She found nightdresses with cut-away fronts, backs and bellies, kinky underwear, perfumes, red, white and green bottles of make-up, eye brushes, slippers with red roses on them, hand towels, toilet soap, hair-removing cream, deodorants, and massage and body oils. Women's tools in their married life are all sexual. A girl moves from her father's

> house to husband's and suddenly changes from a non-sexual being with no sexual organs to a sexual creature who sleeps, wakes, eats and drinks sex. With amazing stupidity, they think that those parts that have been cut away can somehow return, and that murdered, dead, and satiated desire can be revived. (101)

When her husband makes advances, she kicks him until he gives up. The next day she meets her professor and explains that she has run away from her husband. This professor offers to protect her, but instead makes sexual advances toward her himself. Again, to stop unwanted sexual intrusion, she kicks him (knocks him down, in fact) and leaves.

As the title of the novel, *Two Women in One*, suggests, two quite different personalities dwell within Bahiah, which is not uncommon among girls and women who are not content with conventional women's roles. Her surface personality, the one seen by the outside world, is a quiet and diligent student of medicine whose reputation and conduct are praiseworthy (36–37). This personality is, however, really only a mask for the real Bahiah who knows very well that she wants to avoid conventional life: "All she knew was that she did not want to be Bahiah Shaheen, nor be her mother's or father's daughter; she did not want to go home or to college, and she did not want to be a doctor. She was not interested in money, nor did she long for a respectable husband, children, a house, a palace or anything like that" (60). Bahiah's first attempt to resolve the conflict between these two coexisting personalities is to seclude herself, pick up a pencil, and draw her real, hidden self. As she draws, the two personalities, drawer and drawn, somehow resolve themselves in a kind of unity. It is only in the company of others that Bahiah agonizes over the dichotomy between her two selves. This is because female socialization has been unsuccessful in her case. She knows what is expected of her by those around her and can behave in ways that please them; but because her parents have discouraged her from developing a sexual identity as a woman and her father has actually, encouraged "masculine" behavior in her, these expected feminine traits seem particularly foreign to her. Even her name, she feels, belongs to someone else, because that name is what others call her and is associated with her public persona. When others look at her, she believes that they are seeing another person.

However, this dichotomy is entirely eliminated when Bahiah meets Salim, another unique individual amidst the "herd" of impersonal creatures. He is Bahiah's other self, resembling her even in some physical respects: "They stood before the painting, shoulder to shoulder. He was the same height as she. They stood side by side. His leg was just like hers" (39). Furthermore, Salim is a painter, which jibes with Bahiah's attempts to explore her other real self through drawing. She sees her "real" self, hidden until now, reflected in his eyes, which allows her inner and outer selves to mesh for the first time. Although being with Salim does not create a sexual identity for herself in her mind, she is at least finally able to see herself as one unified person.

But Salim is also the gateway through which she is able to interact with the national struggle of her people. The occasion which leads Bahiah to feel part of a whole rather than being in a locked-away separate world of her own is a university student demonstration which gives vent to Egyptian patriotic slogans. When she sees the participants, she realizes that they have individual features and are no longer merely parts of the "herd" which she had previously found threatening:

> She saw faces different from those she knew from the dissecting room, bodies different from those she had seen forcing their way into the lecture hall. Their features were as sharp as swords, their complexions muddy, their backs straight and unbending, their eyes raised and their legs firm and rippling with muscles, as their feet strode over the earth, shaking sky and trees. (82)

When she joins a university student demonstration, shouting "freedom for Egypt," she had a new sensation, a "strange sensation of blending into the larger world, of becoming part of the infinite extended body of humanity" (82). Her body stops being a burden and becomes a means to achieve unity with the world. Bahiah feels that love, true love, is the single factor responsible for this drastic change (84). Thus it is no surprise to her to find that Salim is also taking part in the demonstration.

Meeting Salim and taking part in the demonstration do not, however, lead to Bahiah's salvation. In the end, contrary to what one might expect, they do not greatly alter her hostility toward society and its sexes. She does not develop a feeling of solidarity with women nor does she truly commit to the national struggle. Her reaction to the demonstrations is not based on political beliefs, but merely on the pleasure of belonging and forgetting the loneliness resulting from her "uniqueness." "Her body felt a hidden desire since childhood, since she developed a body of her own separate from the world. It was a persistent desire to return to the world, to dissolve to the last atom so that she would be liberated and disembodied and weightless, like a free spirit hovering without constraints of time or place and with no chains to tie her to earth" (83).[5] In the end, she turns herself in to authorities not to make a political statement or rebel against repressive rule, but rather because she wants to be with Salim, who is in prison. Her ostensible search for a collective political identity thus seems artificial and imposed by the author, and it constitutes another example of the weak character development typical of al-Saʻdāwī's earlier works (mentioned in Chapter Three).

However, we must not overlook the positive contribution al-Saʻdāwī makes with *Two Women in One*. Again, as in earlier works, she addresses women's situations fearlessly and challenges the framework upon which sexist oppression is based. Bahiah's sexual development, arrested though it may be in most respects, is approached with uncommon sensitivity and in detail. Her first sexual experience with a man is a joyful one, described in positive terms. The way in which her mother terrifies her at young age into giving up the exploration of her own body is portrayed as a tragedy in Bahiah's life.

> She could not stand to look at her naked body in the mirror. When her fingers approached her genitals while washing, she would jerk them away, as if her hand had touched an electrified or prohibited area. She still remembered the rap her mother gave her as a child. The traces of her mother's big fingers were engraved in her memory and stuck to her skin like a tattoo. Her mother's voice still rang in her ears: "Don't do that. Say 'I won't do it again!'" She did not say it. What could there be in that forbidden area? She would examine

> her body with trembling hands. She felt that something dangerous was concealed in that forbidden place.... It must be dangerous and frightening. (El Saadawi 1986: 74)

Al-Saʿdāwī questions the definition of "woman" in this novel, once again exposing the flaws in patriarchal logic suggesting that gender is strictly a natural (not cultural) phenomenon. This time, however, she does so in the context of national struggle. Even though this struggle does not succeed as a motivating political factor for Bahiah, al-Saʿdāwī does raise the topic in relation to her heroine's search for an identity, helping to pave the way for other authors to do the same.

In her 1976 novel, *Mawt al-Rajul al-Waḥīd ʿalā al-Arḍ*,[6] al-Saʿdāwī continues to challenge the social structure in her culture, doing so in a much more subtle manner as she examines rural life for women. The result is a more artistically accomplished novel that investigates relationships between religion and sexuality and between the struggles for sexual and national freedom. The story takes place in a small village, ruled by a corrupt mayor and his small circle of collaborators. With the help of these cohorts, the mayor uses his position to manipulate the peasants. He is able to coerce the family of two young, attractive sisters to allow them to become his personal servants and proceeds to become sexually involved with each one while she is working for him.

The mayor represents two forms of tyranny: sexual and imperialistics. His mother is British, and references to his appearance suggest that his English inheritance is not only genetic:

> He was tall with big, hefty shoulders and a broad, almost square face. Its upper half had come to him from his mother: smooth silky hair, and deep blue eyes which stared out from under a prominent, high forehead. The lower half came from the upper reaches of the country in the south, and had been handed down to him by his father: thick, jet black whiskers overhung by a coarse nose, below which the lips were soft and fleshy, suggesting lust rather than sensuality. His eyes had a haughty, almost arrogant quality, like those of an English gentleman accustomed to command. When he spoke his voice was hoarse, and unrefined, like that of an Upper Egyptian peasant. But its hoarseness was endowed with a mellow,

> humble quality that belied any hint of the aggression often found in the voices of men cowed by years of oppression in former colonies like Egypt and India. (El Saadawi 1985: 8)

The connections between struggles for national and sexual freedom, mentioned previously, are drawn via the mayor's character, because interests in both intersect most clearly at the position he holds. He acts on the village as Britain acted on Egypt; and he represents patriarchal rule in a very literal way, as his inside circle is made up of men only and they govern in their own best interests as men and as political leaders. Anyone who challenges the mayor or in any way interferes in his plans is eventually sent away or taken away to prison on some pretense. The first of the two sisters, Nefissa, he sends away because she is pregnant, which he must keep hidden from the villagers. The second young girl, Zeinab, resists working for him for a long time. The mayor frames her father, Kafrawi, as a murderer, convinced that he has been influencing his daughters to resist the mayor. When this still does not bring Zeinab to his household, he resorts to an elaborate scheme involving the local clergyman, and finally Zeinab comes to work for him.[7]

Al-Saʻdāwī is commenting on the hypocrisy and corruption among religious power figures here, as the clergyman in this story knows full well that the mayor wants Zeinab for sexual reasons. The mayor is no innocent bystander with respect to religious corruption either. He uses religious rhetoric only when doing so is to his advantage. He encourages Zeinab's belief that God wants her to work for him, but treats a foundling that his own wife has taken in as if it were the devil because it was "born in fornication" (114)—even though he has recently sent away Nefissa after impregnating her. This baby is eventually treated as a scapegoat by some of the villagers because of its supposed sinfulness, and the mayor's wife and the baby are killed one night by a group of them, following a fire they believe was caused by the baby's presence. This is all done in the name of religion, despite the child's helplessness, because this baby is a painful reminder to some of the adults of their own sins.

After all of the mayor's efforts to secure Zeinab's services, she later leaves his household to get married. Unable to persuade her to continue working for him after her wedding (because she is convinced that her husband needs her at home), he frames the husband as a thief so that this obstacle can be "legally" removed. In the end, though, the mayor's plans backfire: Zeinab leaves the village to find her husband, and shortly thereafter the aunt of the two girls, Zakeya, who has now lost her entire family because of the mayor's greed and corruption, beats him to death with her hoe. The mayor has forgotten an important fact: if poeple are abused to a point where they have nothing left to lose, they become dangerous.

LAṬĪFAH AL-ZAYYĀT: *THE OPEN DOOR*

Another novelist who defined her heroine within a plitical context is Laṭīfah al-Zayyāt, born in 1925 Dumyāt, Egypt. She received her Ph.D. in English literature from 'Ayn Shams University in Cairo. Her years of study at Cairo University (1942–1946) were marked by her extensive political activities. Faced by the two major political forces, the Muslim Brotherhood and the Communist party, which were then active on campus, she did not hesitate to affiliate herself with the latter. Justifying this ideological choice, al-Zayyāt states, "I was a woman with special temperament who was moved and inspired by the values of equality among the two sexes and all human beings regardless of color, sex or creed" (Laṭīfah al-Zayyāt 1993: 55). She became one of the prominent leaders of the Student's and Workers' Committee (Lajnat al-Ṭalabah wa-al-'Ummāl), which was a formidable political force in the later 1940s in Egypt. In 1949 her political activism brought her to jail twice. Reflecting on the profound impact of this stage in her intellectual life, al-Zayyāt says, "My work in this phase... took on a double meaning, because it was a collective act in which the personal self dissolved only to be enriched by the collective one, and because it was an act against the authority which charges all the psychological and mental faculties of the human being" ("Ḥawla al-Iltizām al-Siyāsī" 1990: 138). After graduation, she held a position as a professor of English at the Girls' College of 'Ayn Shams University, and after a few years became chairperson of the English Department. Laṭīfah al-Zayyāt also served as a director of the Egyptian Academy of the Arts and often represented Egypt at international conferences. During Sadat's regime, al-Zayyāt found out later, her house was under constant surveillance, and in 1981 she was imprisoned for her political activities (al-Zayyāt 1992: 232).

Laṭīfah al-Zayyāt's first novel was *al-Bāb al-Maftūḥ*[8] (*The Open Door*, 1960). It is the story of the emotional, psychological, and political growth of Laylā, the daughter of a conservative family. The backdrop for her story is a turbulent period of modern Egyptian history that began on February 21, 1946, when the Egyptian people held massive demonstrations against the British military presence in Egypt. The turbulence extended through the period of Egyptians' attacks on British troops in the Suez Canal Zone, the Cairo fire, and the 1952 revolution, and ended with the Battle of Port Said in the 1956 war between Egypt and an Israeli-French-British alliance.

Laylā's ordeal, like those of al-Sa'dāwī's heroines, begins when she first reaches the age of menstruation. The beginning of this age is marked by a bloodstain that appears on Laylā's skirt and is removed with a knife by her cousin in the school's bathroom (not surprisingly, symbols of violence are associated with the process of sexual maturity). Recalling the happiness of her father when her brother Maḥmūd came of age, she expects the same reaction from him when she tells him her news. He reacts with alarm, however, and Laylā hears him weeping in his room and praying to God to provide him with enough strength to withstand this critical development in the life of his daughter, to whom he refers to as *wiliyyah*, "helpless girl." He acts quickly to protect the family "honor" by telling her, "You have to realize that you have already grown up. From now on you cannot go out or pay visits alone" (al-Zayyāt 1960: 21). To further protect Laylā, he orders his son not to bring home "immoral" novels or magazines but rather to read them elsewhere and to meet his friends in a club or café instead of bringing them home (22). Laylā begins to feel that her home has become a jail and her father and brother, the jailers. This feeling of imprisonment is intensified by the absence of any meaningful communication with her father: "A huge wall always stood between him and her as if they did not speak the same language" (279). The next phase of life for Laylā, controlled as she is by the rigid rules of a conservative family, is marriage. Without her knowledge, her father promises her in marriage to Ramzī, her professor at the university. This marriage is enthusiastically blessed by Laylā's mother, who insists on celebrating it ostentatiously to impress her friends and relatives.

Laylā represents the younger generation that has achieved, mainly through education, a certain degree of self-awareness, but that remains confused about how to apply it in practice. Laylā's friend Sanā' sums up the dilemma: "Our mothers knew their situation, whereas we are lost. We do not know if we are in a harem or not, or whether love is forbidden or allowed. Our parents say it is forbidden, yet the government-run radio sings day and night about love. Books tell women they are free, and yet if a woman really believes that, a catastrophe will happen and her reputation will be blackened" (71). Al-Zayyāt tries to link Laylā's personal struggle for fulfillment with Egypt's fight for political independence. This gives Laylā's struggle a much wider scope than it would have otherwise. Laylā is somewhat active politically: in secondary school she takes part in anti-British demonstrations. In the first demonstration, Laylā, like Bahiah in al-Sa'dāwī's *Two Women in One*, experiences a feeling of transcending her individual self and becoming part of a larger one: "She was fused in a whole, pushing her forward, embracing her and protecting her. She shouted anew in a voice different that hers, a voice which unified her being with a collective one" (45). Even Laylā's perception of her body undergoes a significant change. When she first joins the demonstration, she is shy and self-conscious about her "full body" and feels that she is a sex object. When she blends into the crowd at the demonstration, she is overwhelmed by a state of exultation and feels that she is "strong and light as a bird" (44–45). This uplifting experience is later marred, however: her father beats her after seeing her in the demonstration, which devastates her and leads her to wonder whether she is a human being or merely a "floor mop" (47). The turning point in her life is the eruption, in 1956, of the Suez War. By then, she is working as a schoolteacher in Port Said and has the opportunity to experience firsthand a popular fight against the invading enemies. There she meets Ḥusayn, a patriot and engineer who has participated in designing the Aswān High Dam and whom she first met when he was visiting her brother. Laylā's experience of the war, highlighted by the renewal of her relationship with Ḥusayn, is so intense that she changes drastically. She comes to recognize the essential ties linking personal and national identities: the goal of freeing Egypt from foreign powers is similar to her determination to free herself from backward social customs. When Egypt wins the war, Laylā wins herself. She decides to break up with her fiancé, who represents the past[9] and opens herself to Ḥusayn's love.

Laylā believes that the end of the Suez War means that her struggle is over: the national goal (the defeat of the invaders) and her personal goal (the abandonment of the past and the anticipation of a fulfilling emotional relationship with her new lover) have both been achieved. Ḥusayn, however, has a wider vision. He sees the political triumph as only the beginning, not the end, of a new era even on the personal level. He asks her not to submerge herself in a lover relationship, but rather to widen her love to embrace the aspirations of the nation: "Set out, my beloved, to link your being with the rest of the millions, with our good land and with our good people" (210). This optimism stems from Ḥusayn's constant attempts to identify Laylā with Egypt. In a letter to her he writes, "My love for my country blended with my love for you until you became a symbol for everything that I love in the homeland" (276).

Although the national struggle has the greatest impact on Laylā's life, changing its course significantly, it also plays a role in the lives and attitudes of other characters. For example, Maḥmūd, Laylā's brother, decides against his father's will to withdraw from the university to participate in the struggle against the British. This experience provides Maḥmūd with enough self-confidence to rebel against his father's authority in such crucial matters as his own marriage. He does not seek his father's counsel but, rather, simply breaks the news to the family at the dinner table that he is getting married (276). Even Laylā's aloof father is emotionally moved almost to embrace his daughter while listening to Nasser's historic speech in which he nationalizes the Suez Canal Company (306). These changes in the characters' outlooks and values, however, remain to a great extent superficial and contradictory. Maḥmūd is portrayed as a progressive and committed person, politically and socially, but his attitude vis-à-vis the role of women is obviously reactionary. When he volunteers to go to the Suez Canal to fight the British, and Laylā wishes to join him on his mission, Maḥmūd replies, "It is pretty early. Only when we run out of men will you ladies be able to emerge" (87). Furthermore, when the war erupts, Maḥmūd orders the women to leave Port Said City immediately not to be in the way of "fighting men" (324).[10]

Al-Zayyāt demonstrates in this novel a great deal of artistic maturity and sophistication atypical of a first work.[11] Although she employs Classical Arabic in narration and Egyptian colloquial in dialogue,[12] al-Zayyāt knows how to effectively manipulate the different layers of the Arabic language, depending on the educational background of the characters and the nature of the subject discussed, without falling into the trap of artificiality. The language used by Professor Ramzī, for example, differs from the language of Laylā's father, not only in vocabulary, but also in terms of syntax and relationship to Classical Arabic. The language of women, on the other hand, is peppered with foreign words and expressions, especially if the subject is fabric or fashion (see 105–107, 255–256).[13]

Al-Zayyāt also resorts to the technique of foreshadowing events in the text with symbols. For example, the marriage of Jamīlah, Laylā's cousin, is clearly failing. She is married to a rich man whom she does not love and has become unfaithful to him. While Jamīlah's wedding party is in progress, the great fire of Cairo erupts and all the participants go up to the roof to see the event. Now Laylā describes Jamīlah as if describing a wedding photo: "She was standing still in her white dress while clouds of thick ugly smoke surrounded her like a frame" (150).[14] This image is evoked in Laylā's mind while she is preparing for her engagement to Ramzī, whom she does not really love. The suggestion that Laylā's fate will be identical to Jamīlah's is enhanced by the fact that Jamīlah has planned the whole event (Laylā's engagement party) down to the last detail to be identical to her own wedding party (262–263). Only the political turmoil saves Laylā from a fate similar to Jamīlah's.[15]

Al-Bāb al-Maftūḥ remained al-Zayyāt's only creative work in the field of fiction for over a quarter of a century when her collection of short stories, *al-Shaykhūkhah wa-Qiṣaṣ Ukhrā* (*Old Age and Other Stories*, 1986) was published. The reason given by al-Zayyāt for this interruption will enable us to understand to what extent politics has shaped the intellectual makeup of some women Arab writers. After the Arab defeat of 1967, al-Zayyāt reveals, she detested words and hence she detested literature, and her reading was confined to history and economics. She argued that "one shot against the [Israeli] enemy is more precious than all the words" (Ḥawla al-Iltizām al-Siyāsī 1990: 146). One of the victims of her negative attitude toward the usefulness of literature in the face of a total political and military collapse was a play of three acts dealing with the difference between love and possessiveness that al-Zayyāt had started writing in 1966 but discarded after the war (146).[16]

The Palestinian Question and the Novel

Of all the political problems that have come up in the twentieth century, none has so preoccupied the minds and hearts of the Arab people as has the Palestinian question. This concern was at first reflected in poetry, especially after the June 1967 War, but later it found its way into all fields of literature, including the novel.[17] Novels written on this subject by Arab women, especially by Palestinian women, are particularly significant in that, over time, the search for personal identity became absorbed in the search for national identity, even to the extent of sacrificing the former for the sake of the latter. To the authors, the present matters only insofar as it is the outcome of the past. Therefore they push aside the immediate problems of women struggling for individual freedom in a conservative society, and emphasize instead the heroines' childhoods in their homeland before they had been uprooted from it.

In Hiyām Ramzī al-Durdunjī's novel *Ilā al-Liqā' fī Yāfā* (*Till We Meet in Jaffa*, 1970), the main character, 'Ablah Amīr is sentenced to death by an Israeli military court for planting a bomb in a wastebasket next to a Jerusalem theater. While in jail she recalls the story of her life, going back to her birth in Jaffa.

In 1948 she was forced to leave her country and ended up living in a refugee camp in Gaza, where she witnessed the 1956 Israeli attack on Sinai. In 1956 she moved to Jordan and became engaged to an officer of the Palestine Liberation Army. Their marriage was delayed while her fiancé went to China for training. When he came back, he took part in the battle against the Israeli army at al-Karāmah and was killed. After his death 'Ablah decided to join the Palestinian guerillas. 'Ablah's political awareness was brought to the surface by meeting a man, in this case her fiancé. This use of the male as a catalyst is a common device in women's novels that deal with national concerns. The implication is that the world is still a man's world, and the task of women is to adjust themselves to it, always living through others.

Al-Durdunjī's fondness for historical events interferes both with the development of the heroine's character and the plot of the novel, because it led the author to insert irrelevant historical digression. These include discussions of the Suez War, the U.N. resolution to partition Palestine in 1948, and the relationship between Britain and Zionism. She also persisted in including the full texts of declaration and announcements by al-Fatḥ, without any artistic justification (al-Durdunjī 1970: e.g., p. 171).

The battle of al-Karāmah was also used as a dramatic setting by Salwā al-Bannā in her novel *'Arūs khalfa al-Nahr* (*A Bride Beyond the River*, 1972). The most striking feature of this work is its use of a very few characters. The whole story is built around the character of Ibrāhīm, the fiancé of the heroine who, like the author, is named Salwā. Yet this Ibrāhīm is more a symbol than a credible human being. He is the perfect freedom fighter, devoting his whole life to his homeland and seeing Salwā's love as only a small part of this greater love of country. He refuses to take even a brief vacation from the military struggle to spend time with his fiancée. Amazingly, Salwā does not complain about this but rather reveres Ibrāhīm all the more for it: "Your silence and calmness attracted me to you and made you a legend in my eyes, an eternal symbol and a sacred secret" (al-Bannā 1972: 20).

Ibrāhīm not only remains a secret in Salwā's eyes but also becomes a puzzle in the eyes of the reader, who finds his activities and godlike image difficult to fathom. Like the pre-Islamic hero of popular fiction 'Antarah, Ibrāhīm moves from place to place with superhuman ease. For example, after the battle at al-Karāmah, he goes to Jerusalem to see what impact the battle has had on the people there. How he manages to cross the Jordan River and get past the Israeli army remains a mystery. It seems to be part of al-Bannā's portrayal of Ibrāhīm as an almighty hero unrestricted by time and space.

Al-Bannā's style is basically journalistic (the heroine is a journalist) and remains prosaic despite some rather unsuccessful ventures into a stream-of-consciousness style. The nature of the relationship between Salwā and Ibrāhīm rules out psychological tension from the very beginning; the Palestinian struggle is the center of both of their lives, and the main difference is that Ibrāhīm is ready to give his own life for it, whereas Salwā is prepared only to talk about it.

Salwā ends up merely a passive follower of Ibrāhīm, but other writers were willing to give their heroines more active roles. In

Imtithāl Juwaydī's novel *Shajarat al-Ṣubbayr* (*The Cactus Tree*, 1972), the heroine Widād is the focus of the action. Widād's life story matches the history of the Palestinian problem so well that the novel is best taken as an allegory of that history.

Juwaydī divides her novel into three chapters, each of which deals with one period in Widād's life. The first chapter, "al-Raḥīl" ("The Exodus"), takes place when Widād is eight years old (or six—the novel is inconsistent regarding her age at this time) and tells of her departure with her family from Jaffa in 1948. The second chapter, "al-Mukhayyam" ("The Camp"), describes the miserable lives of the Palestinian refugees in their camps. It carries Widād's story through the early 1960s. The final chapter, "al-Jarīmah wa-al-'Iqāb" ("Crime and Punishment"), deals with the emergence of the Palestinian resistance movement after the 1967 war and ends with the death of Gamal Abdel Nasser, the president of Egypt, in 1970.

Widād directs much of her anger and frustration at her father, a representative of those men who have brought their families out of Palestine to protect their women's "honor" (*'irḍ*) (Juwaydī 1972).[18] To her, these men were wrong to do this because their women's honor was also in danger in the refugee camps. A Lebanese intelligence man, for example, threatens Widād with rape as soon as she grows up. As she reflects: "Did not these men flee to protect their honor? Why did they leave, since their honor then became the target of bad men in the [Lebanese] authority here? Had the men stayed in their homeland they would not have starved as they have and alienation would not have sucked the last drop of their masculinity out.... The diaspora-land has devoured men's vigor and injured women's honor" (75). Widād is totally dedicated to the national cause, suppressing her own emotional needs. Indeed, at the age of nineteen she is still insisting that time stopped for her when she left her homeland at six (169). She can hardly bear the expressions of sexual admiration that the men of the camp heap on her. They make her want to throw up (104). Her heart has no room for anything except love of the homeland: "The key to my heart is my [national] cause and my cause is the key to my heart, and whoever adopts my cause as his, defends it, and adheres to it sincerely, will receive the key without argument or discussion" (170). As if to underscore this theme, characters in *Shajarat al-Ṣubbayr* represent actual historical figures involved in the Palestine problem. Aysar (sometimes called Ayman) is a leader whom Widād sees as responsible for the loss of Palestine. He stands for al-Ḥājj Amīn al-Ḥusaynī. Jāsir Bey, a rich and powerful man who offers to pay for an operation to restore the sight of Widād's brother, represents Gamal Abdel Nasser of Egypt.

Jāsir Bey attributes his own readiness to help to his good humane nature, but Widād notices that he is also sexually interested in her (147). He allows Widād and her family to live in a building he owns, and their relationship culminates with a proposal of marriage. She accepts on the condition that they remain engaged for one year, during which he is not to ask her for anything. During this year she intends to go with her family to their refugee camp. The dowry Widād wants from him is not personal, but national: "My dowry is you, Jāsir Bey. I want your blood, soul, wealth, prestige, though and power to flow in the spring of my cause" (306).

When Widād comes back from the refugee camp she discovers that one of Jāsir's brothers (a reference to King Hussein of Jordan) has killed two of her brothers and wounded three. (This symbolizes the "Black September" massacres of Palestinians in Jordan in 1970.) When Jāsir Bey dies of a heart attack, Widād is blamed for his death, and she has to defend herself in public against the charge. The allegory becomes literal and transparent when she identifies herself with the cactus tree (a distinctively Palestinian fruit-bearing plant): "Ladies and gentlemen, I am the tough and defiant cactus tree, the friend of deserts and the lover of valleys. My fruit is delicious and tasty, but it is surrounded by harsh pointed thorns" (301–302). Wāṣif K. Abū al-Shabāb has claimed that Juwaydī resorted to symbolism in her novel in an attempt to ease the gravity of the political events therein and avoid the monotony of straightforward historical exposition: however, she was still much too explicit about the political and national purposes of her novels, which are usually dealt with more subtly.[19] As Abū al-Shabāb correctly points out, she failed in her attempt to both write an artistically sound novel and to get her political message across (1977: 173).

Laylā 'Usayrān's career as a writer was also profoundly affected by the 1967 war, which proved to be a turning point in the thematic development of her fiction. Before the war she had concentrated on the dilemma of the individual who had to fight against the group to assert personal freedom and individuality; after the war she became more interested in the role of women in crystallizing the Palestinian national identity.

Her novel *'Aṣāfīr al-Fajr* (*The Birds of Dawn*, 1968) tells the story of a woman named Miriam whose views and values change drastically after the war. Before the war she is paralyzed by her fear of death; however, the Arab defeat in the war rids her of this personal fear, and her sense of national identity becomes a burning issue. She is uprooted from her homeland and has to live in the diaspora. She pours her anger out upon her parents who have abandoned their native land and chosen to become homeless. On the sixth day of the war, when the guns fall silent and the Arab armies have been defeated, Miriam rejects the silence and commits herself to the Palestinian cause. She realizes that her past, which her parents want her to forget, lies in the future. The emergence of the Palestinian resistance movement restores her pride in her political identity: "I used to be ashamed of my identification card, and avoided belonging to my people. Being a refugee was a mental complex which only the days of war solved. This news which I read [about the Palestinian guerrillas] began to bring me back my honor which I had lost by myself" ('Usayrān 1968: 111). This resurgence of national feeling damages Miriam's relationship with her boyfriend 'Iṣām, who has become politically indifferent since the war. She feels that his face has become "remote and mysterious" (86) and that she can no longer identify with him; she comes to identify with a cause rather than with a man.

Suhayr, the other female character in *'Aṣāfīr al-Fajr*, was born and raised in eastern Jerusalem in a conservative and patriotic family. They let her continue her education and become a teacher, and she compensates for the narrowness of her experience of life by reading books voraciously. The knowledge gained thereby helps to liberate her mind, but she is incapable of breaking through the social barriers of everyday life, and so her rebellion remains internal rather than taking the form of action. The immediate impact of the June 1967 war on Suhayr is to shatter her religious faith. After she rejects God, Suhayr finds it much easier to revolt against all the inherited values and traditions that are responsible for the Arab defeat. She joins a political party, which gives her a feeling of rebirth. Her most intense experience, however, comes when she joins the Palestinian fighters: "I feel that a pure new blood has entered through the pores of my body, and a great love which cannot be measured by other human feelings, which gives and gives to me" (92).

The publisher's notes on the back over of *'Aṣāfir al-Fijr* might be considered a valid, if superficial, comment on the book: "The writer lived in the environment of the guerrillas (*al-fidā'iyyīn*), in their places of work and activity, and her writing narrates real events which took place and which she put into the form of a novel in order not to have to maintain the sequence of time or to mention names." To this, we should perhaps add that 'Usayrān's experience with the guerrillas was external and distant, and that she overlooked the inner psychological worlds of her characters. An example of this shortcoming was the way the characters suddenly change the course of their lives right after the 1967 war, without the author showing the inner conflict which they would have to undergo. Miriam easily abandons 'Iṣām and joins the resistance forces. Her brother Salmān, earlier shown to be a playful and self-centered person, decides to stop his studies in Germany to join the Palestinian fighting group al-'Āṣifah. Aḥmad, a member of a political party that opposes the military struggle, makes up his mind to join the resistance movement after treating a wounded man who was expelled from Palestine. The ambiguity of the characters as a result of unresolved conflict is best illustrated by lapses in Suhayr's religious faith. Once Jerusalem has fallen into Israeli hands, she says, "The injustice of God, which I cannot understand, means that God does not exist" (57). Nevertheless Suhayr continues to speak of Jerusalem throughout the rest of the novel as a holy city and a seat of God, rich in churches and mosques, and desecrated by infidels.

Laylā 'Usayrān's novel *Khaṭṭ al-Af'ā* (*The Line of the Snake*, 1972) also features a heroine named Miriam. This Miriam is obsessed by a desire to cross the Jordan, free Palestine, and avenge the deaths of her parents at the hands of the Israelis in 1948. These strong feelings lead her to join a Palestinian guerrilla group in Jordan, becoming its only female member. There are contradictions in the characterization of these fighters, of which the author seems unaware. The fighters are portrayed as progressive and idealistic people, able to transcend their egoism for the sake of the national cause. Their social backgrounds are interestingly diverse; the group includes a rich man, an illiterate peasant, a university graduate, and a youngster who is learning to read and write. Their views of women, however, remain as backward and reactionary as those prevailing in the Palestinian Arab society around them. For example, shortly after Miriam joins the group Abū al-Layl, as one of its commanders calls himself, asks her to go to the kitchen and prepare the meal. She does not like this: "I felt that he wanted to humiliate me a little, to remind me that I do not fit except as a girl" ('Usayrān 1972: 116). When she wants to join a reconnaissance patrol, another commander tells her that "only when men perish can our women take part in a patrol" (271). Some members of the group even think they are treating Miriam as a "lady" by making her eat alone so that she will not be bothered by their presence (199).

One of 'Usayrān's major failures in *Khaṭṭ al-Af'ā* is her confused use of symbolism. For example, Abū al-Layl, despite his aforementioned reactionary mentality as far as women are concerned, is symbolically associated with the Jordan River or with the lost homeland (themselves symbols of progressiveness) or with both: "During my last night with them [the fighters] I lay on the ground with my headdress under my head and the vision of the river in my eyes, and I asked myself which I love more, him [Abū al-Layl] or the homeland?" (139). Abū al-Layl, as a symbol, is flat and one-dimensional. For example, Miriam says of him, "Abū al-Layl is my land before being my life. He is the flowers, birds, and rocks. He is 'Aylabūn, Gaza, Hebron, and al-Karāmah. He is the victim whom the world buried in its conscience, and his blood will awaken the conscience of everyone" (242). Another character whom Miriam comes to associate with Palestine is Umm Yūsuf, whose son was killed by the Israelis. "Umm Yūsuf came to us like lightning with her bag and the pants she wore underneath her khaki dress [khaki was the color of the guerrillas' uniforms], Umm Yūsuf with her overflowing compassion for each one of us, like the fertile land of the [Jordan] river" (121). And yet this Umm Yūsuf who is being so admiringly described has once boasted that, in her role as a midwife, she brought only male babies into the world (28)—hardly the epitome of a progressive character. Of course, the implication here is that Umm Yūsuf has brought many fighters into the world to help liberate Palestine; but this uncovers one of the major problems in women's novels concerning the issues of national identity and liberation, which is that these are often dealt with at the expense of feminist concerns. Miriam herself, after all, is a fighter, and the contradiction between this and the belief that boys must be born so that fighters may be gained is never addressed. In such cases internalized patriarchal values seem to go unnoticed and unchallenged (because they are less guarded against), and end up hurting the cause of women in the long run.

ʿUsayrān unintentionally reduces Miriam's character to a mere caricature. Miriam keeps asking everyone she meets what color the Jordan River is, so that the reader comes to wonder why she does not simply go to the nearby Jordanian bank of the river and see for herself. She gets different answers, sometimes green (133) and sometimes khaki (154), because ʿUsayrān is also using the river (rather ineptly) as a symbol. When Miriam joins the guerrillas she faces an embarrassing situation when she has to go to the bathroom, and the others tell her that they do not have one and she will have to go in the open when it is dark. In this situation she is scared to death, but later insists on taking part in a dangerous operation on the West Bank and shows great courage there (indeed, it makes her feel like a "real man") (258). After her participation in this raid she rushes to get rid of a yo-yo she has always taken to bed with her as a sort of security blanket. (This yo-yo, mentioned only twice in the whole novel, never worked well as a symbol.) Even more ridiculous is the fact that ʿUsayrān does not mention until the end of the novel that Miriam is a poet (258). There is no sensible reason for the author to have hidden this important detail until the end. In any case, even being a poet cannot add any depth to Miriam's shaky and unbelievable character.

Laylā ʿUsayrān seemed to insist on depriving her characters of natural human motivations, a problem already been discussed in Chapter Three in connection with both Laylā ʿUsayrān and Emily Naṣrallāh. The characters in *Khaṭṭ al-Afʿā* are mere puppets in the hands of a destiny that controls their lives. Miriam describes how she joined the guerrilla fighters: "Ibrāhīm [Abū al-Layl's real name] knocked on the door of my room and I walked with him as if I were walking in the broad daylight on the road of the stars, heading toward my destiny" (40–41). The end of Miriam's relationship with Abū al-Layl is also planned by destiny: "Destiny gripped me and Abū al-Layl and separated us" (237). Even when she crosses the Jordan on a raid against the Israelis (a raid in which she feels she has finally realized herself), she describes her experience by saying: "and my feet moved from the river to the land. Then I knew the pleasure of life as if by the miracle of destiny" (281). Emphasizing the role of destiny still further, Laylā 'Usayrān uses as a refrain throughout the novel the Palestinian proverb *Illī inkatab 'al-Jibīn lāzim Tshūfuh il-'Ayn*, meaning literally, "What is written on the forehead the eve must see [carried out]." The saying refers to the folk belief that the destiny of an individual is written on that person's forehead (that is, where he or she cannot see it) and that one has no other role in life except to watch one's fate as it unfolds. This leaves the impression that all the human characters are really controlled by supernatural forces, depriving them of that free will which is basic to human beings and fictional characters depicted with depth. This lack of free will naturally leads to a lack of real conflict in the hearts and souls of the characters and undermines the communication of a substantive political message through the novel.

The Achievement of Saḥar Khalīfah

Like laylā 'Usayrān, the Palestinian novelist Saḥar Khalīfah (b. 1941) began her literary career by dealing with the personal freedom of Arab women.[20] This issue was at the core of her first novel *Lam Na'ud Jawārī Lakum* (*We Are No Longer Your Slaves*, 1974), which dwells on the tragic clash between defiant female individualists and rigid patriarchal social values on the West Bank in the 1960s. This work was only a modest artistic achievement, partly because the unrestrained anger and frustration it expresses are imposed artificially by the author rather than being rooted in the novel's fictional world.[21] Another problem is that the author constantly tries to impress her readers by showing off her wideranging knowledge of Western art, literature, and philosophy through a superabundance of references that have no real relevance for the novel, at the expense of dramatization and plot development. Thus she reduces her book to a gallery of abstract ideas having little to do with the real problems of the characters.

In the Palestinian society of the West Bank under Israeli occupation, Khalīfah finds a real experience with which to make her abstract ideas concrete. In *al-Ṣubbār* (1976)[22] she portrays the drastic change in the fabric of the society, emphasizing the conflict between generations. *Wild Thorns* is the story of the al-Karmi family, a microcosm of Palestinian culture. The head of the family is an old sick notable who represents oppressive patriarchal authority. Lacking any real national feelings, he is ready to acquiesce to the foreign occupation to maintain his social and economic prestige. The elder son Adil, who does not rebel, represents the in-between generation that tries (if somewhat reluctantly) to come to terms with the older generation. Significantly, the only family member who rebels against the authoritative father and the helpless, ineffectual mother is Basil, the younger son, showing that the hope for social change will be realized by the new generation. Basil is the embodiment of both personal and national rebelliousness. (The use of a male character in this role was itself a new departure in women's fiction.) His father sees Basil as a threat, and rages against him: "This whole generation is rotten. God curse all who planted their seed!" (Khalifeh 1991: 196). Basil resents the family's scheme to force his sister Nuwar into an arranged marriage with a man she does not love, because he knows that she is secretly in love with another man, named Salih al-Safadi, who is in jail for resisting the occupation. Basil eventually grows impatient with Nuwar's silence and submission, so he decides to reveal her secret even though it will shock the family (199). Toward the end of the novel, his constant efforts to get her to stand up for herself bear fruit as she declares: "I will never marry anyone except Salih, even if I had to wait a hundred years. I'll only marry Salih" (200).

In this novel, Khalīfah portrays in detail life for Palestinians under Israeli occupation, without reducing the Israelis to unfeeling monsters in the process. This is not to say that Khalīfah is equally sympathetic to both Palestinians and Israelis: the novel illustrates in many places the kinds of humiliation to which the Israelis subject Palestinians under occupation, such as intense interrogation, general verbal abuse and market control, not to mention torture and murder. However, many scenes in the novel humanize the "enemy." One of the most effective of these is a scene in which Nidal, the five-year-old son of an imprisoned resistance activist, comes to prison to visit his father, whose face he has not seen before. At first he mistakes another prisoner for his father, and then is finally reunited with Abu Nidal. As this is taking place, not only are the boy, his father, and other prisoners crying, but the Israeli guards also shed tears as they watch (147–148).

Even the characters in the novel feel compelled at times to acknowledge the humanity and suffering of the Israelis with whom they come into contact. When one woman, Um Sabir, is at the market, she becomes enraged at an Israeli officer and his wife and daughter who are able to afford foods that she cannot. She curses them vehemently; but when the officer is stabbed (by Usama, Adil's militant cousin) a moment later, Um Sabir's remark, "You're a hero! You've done well!" is followed shortly by feelings of sympathy (158–159). She says to the officer's wife, "God have mercy on you!" and then to his daughter, "I'm so sorry for you my daughter" (159). As she speaks to the little girl, she is covering up her legs, which have been left exposed in the confusion and which remind Um Sabir of the honor of her own daughters and of girls everywhere (159). Khalīfah captures many complexities of the Palestinian-Israeli opposition here: just as the Israelis are not dehumanized in the novel, neither are the Palestinian characters portrayed as blind to the humanity of the "enemy."

Kahlīfah digs even deeper to expose some of the issues involved in the divisions among Palestinians themselves, particularly the one between those Palestinians who have taken jobs in Israel and those who believe that to do so is to betray Palestine. Class issues come into focus here, as many of the characters who have taken jobs "inside" have done so because they feel their families would not survive otherwise. The occupation has lowered wages in the West Bank and has left some workers without work permits. They believe they must choose between starvation and Israeli jobs. Palestinian businessmen, eager to take advantage of the situation for their own individual benefit, are implicated. For example, Abu Sabir recalls that his last Palestinian boss would not pay him his preoccupation wage, and said to him, "[T]here are plenty of workers looking for jobs. If you don't like the wages, you can leave" (46). The view that inside jobs should be avoided if possible is not renounced in the novel, however; one character, Shahada, has draped himself in status symbols which his job in Israel has made possible. Usama is disgusted by what he sees: "Shahada wore a leather jacket with a fur collar. His curly hair stood out around his head like a giant halo in an Afro at least four inches high. Thick sideburns sprouted like miniature hedges on both sides of his face. In his hand, adorned with an expensive gold ring, he held a pipe, and he spoke out of the corner of his mouth, like some big foreign film star" (90–91). Shahada is condescending to the people around him, and continually throws his money around for all to see. Greed is not only the domain of the business owners: for some workers, too, the desire to move up in class rank overshadows feelings of national solidarity.

Apparent lines of division continue to blur and change in the novel, depending on circumstances, which calls into question the rigid dichotomies formed to define the opposing factions. It is unclear which side Shahada would choose if caught in an outright war zone, but for Zuhdi, a Palestinian who has reluctantly taken an inside job, the choice is clear. Earlier in the novel, Zuhdi violently attacks his Israeli supervisor for saying "dirty Arabs," even though it will mean going to jail. Later, when he finds himself in the midst of an armed attack on the buses taking him and other Palestinian workers to their jobs in Israel, his loyalty is nevertheless with the attackers. Usama is one of the guerrillas and has fired on friends and fellow Palestinians on the buses, perhaps even killing some of them, which has been his plan since returning to the West Bank from an "oil" country. He has justified his plan by convincing himself that it would be for the good of the homeland, failing to comprehend the complexity of the situation. As the Israelis retaliate and the skirmish becomes more violent, Zuhdi, whom Usama has considered an enemy of sorts, runs to Usama, who has been shot by return fire, and ends up killing Israeli soldiers while trying to protect him. In a tragedy of errors, Zuhdi, the very one whom Usama has almost killed in the initial attack is in the end killed by Israeli bullets at Usama's side.

Lines of division between men and women are also examined in the novel. Palestinian society is changing rapidly in the face of the occupation, and women's position is not keeping pace with those changes. Sons are still favored greatly over daughters, and women are still perceived by men and many women themselves as keepers of the home and of family honor. Most of the activists in the novel are men, but the trend of women's increasing involvement is addressed. Lina is one example of a woman active in the resistance; in fact, contradictions between old and new perceptions of gender come to light when her role is brought up. Usama is giving Basil advice on how to survive as an activist: "Be careful, Basil," he warned. "This is a serious business. You know the consequences. I won't repeat the advice I gave you earlier. But don't make any decisions without consulting Lina. That's crucial. She's a very solid girl. And she's had lots of experience. Now, let me kiss you goodbye. I may not see you again. *Be a man, Basil.* Don't trust anyone. Especially the people in this house" (162, italices mine). Contrasted with this is the situation of Nuwar, Lina's close friend. They are friends despite the vast differences in their positions, which serves to illustrate the continuing problem of the oppression of women. Nuwar is expected by her family and tradition to marry whomever her father chooses, even though she has fallen in love with Salih. She is understandably afraid to speak up, as she knows her sick father will object and possibly die from the stress of her announcement. But Basil is able to see that it is necessary to stand up for her rights, even if her father does die as a result. Basil's actions support the notion that men must participate in the break with oppressive traditions, because they are in power where these issues are concerned and it is men's reactions to such a challenge that, understandably, many women fear. This is addressed as a factor in the general struggle to be free, suggesting that it is in Palestine's best interests to fight for the freedom of all of its citizens. Indeed, *al-Ṣubbār*, hardly leaves a stone unturned in this examination of life in the West Bank under Israeli occupation.

Khalīfah goes on with the saga of the al-Karmī family in her next novel *'Abbād al-Shams* (*The Sunflower*, 1980), in which she expands the range of characters and events. 'Ādil's girlfriend Rafīf and the next-door neighbor Sa'diyyah become central figures, and the family's prosperity is shattered after the Israelis blow up their home in retaliation for Bāsil's joining the resistance. From the very beginning, Khalīfah portrays Rafīf, a poet and the editor of a women's column in a magazine, as a radical feminist, while 'Ādil remains a "rational" conformist. Rafīf's rebelliousness is shown by such symbolic acts as crossing the street when the light is red. When 'Ādil scolds her for this, she turns on him fiercely: "I intended to say that the street was designed for pedestrians before car riders. I wanted to say that the lights are a trick and a conspiracy. Who put the light signals there and determined how they work? Only stupid people obey them. I do not obey and therefore I cross the street whenever I want. I am a free person. I cross the street whenever I want and do not wait for the light signals. I create light by myself" (Khalīfah 1980: 10). Muhammad Siddiq also sees this as a manifestation of Rafīf's feminist commitment;

the traffic lights, he argues, represent today's "rational order" (patriarchal rule and linear thinking). "By seeking to enforce the law of this civilization, 'Ādil inadvertently (and symbolically) becomes an 'accomplice' in perpetuating the male supremacy inherent in it" (Siddiq 1986: 156).

Rafīf holds the cause of women to be inseparable from that of the homeland (17). However, if the Palestinian people as a whole are oppressed, it is the women who are worse off because they suffer personally and socially, as well as politically. Men, she feels, have for centuries treated women as slaves and tools with which to pursue their egotistical goals (213). But the views Rafīf expresses when she is demanding equality for women are inconsistent and contradictory, partly because she is reacting to the attitudes of her fellow editors (including 'Ādil) instead of stating her own convictions. At first, she demands that the magazine get rid of its special women's column because it perpetuates sexist notions about women. But later on, Rafīf seems to forget her point and tries to persuade the editors to enlarge the women's column to occupy half of the magazine.

Rafīf's relationship with 'Ādil reflects her personal growth and struggle to attain independence. In the first stage of the relationship she remains tied to him despite sporadic episodes of rebelliousness. As Rafīf herself becomes more and more independent, her relationship with 'Ādil takes a different turn. He stops being the center of her life, especially after a massive uprising by West Bank Palestinians against the Israelis who are confiscating their land. 'Ādil himself is the first to realize the change: "He looked attentively at Rafīf's profile as she sat next to him. Nostalgia came back to his heart and he remembered the days which had gone by. Once she had never taken her eyes off of him, and had never missed an opportunity to hold his hand or come close to him. And now here she was, sitting next to him, and what was preoccupying her was watching the people" (250). Revealingly, Rafīf finds herself when she becomes able to reach out and identify with others. When 'Ādil becomes alarmed at this deep change and tells her "You've grown up, Rafīf," she can well understand the root of his fears: "Is it because of this that they [men] find it hard to put their principles into action when women are concerned? They fear that (women) might become stronger . . . and get used to life without their protection" (251). The novel has another major subplot that revolves around Saʻdiyyah. Unlike Rafīf, she is an uneducated and practical-minded woman. After the Israelis kill her husband Zuhdī, her neighbors treat her kindly out of sympathy. But as time goes by she faces greater difficulty: "When Zuhdī disappeared and she went out into the wide world she discovered how hard a man's life was. It was even harder for a woman to live that life. . . . A young, beautiful widow. . . . A widow, meaning that she was without a man who was ready to break the neck of anybody that might attack her. [She was] like a land without a guard. . . . [Men] taught her to suspect all intentions, no matter how true they were" (30). Saʻdiyyah ends up having to work for an Israeli textile company to support her family. This job rouses the suspicion of the neighbors, who accuse her of collaborating with the occupiers. Saʻdiyyah's dream becomes to move out of her present residence, where she is always reminded of her humble origin, by buying land on the mountain slopes around Nablus where well-to-do families live. To realize this dream she works very hard and sternly warns her children (especially Rashād, her eldest son) not to get involved in the resistance movement.

Saʻdiyyah devotes herself entirely to the enterprise of building her new home and comes to see everything else as insignificant. When she is mistakenly jailed in Tel Aviv with another woman, she refuses to escape when the chance presents itself. Her husband died for what he saw as a just cause, but was soon forgotten by his friends, so she does not want to get involved in politics. However, this reluctance does not last. When the Israelis confiscate the area in which Saʻdiyyah has bought land—an unbearable blow—and the people of Nablus rise up against this injustice, she and Rashād join their protest. When a policeman hits her she does not hesitate to kick him in the groin, and when the protesters begin throwing rocks at the police she realizes that Rashād is continuing his father's struggle and urges him on: "Attack them, Rashād! Attack them, my son! Attack them, my dear Zuhdī!" (279).

Despite this seemingly radical move, traditional (patriarchal) values creep into the text elsewhere. Like other writers before her, for example, Khalīfah tended to describe her heroine as "feeling like a man" whenever she accomplished something. When Saʻdiyyah begins earning money and shopping for the family, she feels "that she has become a man, or half a man" (35). As we have seen, Miriam has the same experience in ʻUsayrān's *Khaṭṭ al-Afʻā* when she is finally able to cross the river and take part in a guerrilla attack. Like Abū al-Layl in *Khaṭṭ-al-Af'ā*, the Zuhdī of *Al-Ṣubbār* is, to a great extent, a male chauvinist. He "falls in love" with Sa'diyyah when he sees her spilling water on herself while filling a container with water from the neighborhood spring, causing her dress to cling to her and revealing the shape of her body. Two days later, on the strength of this essentially physical attraction, he becomes engaged to her. Thereafter he forbids her to go out and fetch water any more, telling her that she thenceforth belongs to him alone (65). The fact that this is not a negative portrayal undermines other progressive messages in the novel concerning the relations between the sexes.

Khalīfah's literary skills, especially language, reach maturity in *'Abbād al-Shams*. Although she uses mainly the omniscient point of view, she sometimes resorts to other techniques especially internal monologue. Her language is very expressive and effective in portraying both external events and the inner worlds of her characters. Sometimes (especially in narration) the author lets her sentences become very long and relaxed, while elsewhere (in emotionally charged scenes or sketchy reconstructions of the past through flashbacks) she makes them short and terse. Sometimes a certain word evokes a series of associations in a character's mind, associations that seem unrelated on the surface but that eventually become related through the consciousness and experience of the character. At the beginning of the third chapter, for example, Rafīf is riding in a taxi from Jerusalem to her hometown Nablus: "From Jerusalem to Nablus. Do not feel sad, my heart. The windows are closed and one of them [the passengers] is smoking and a woman with a cold is sneezing. Achoo! May God have mercy on you, on you and on us. He does not have mercy on us. May he not have mercy on the Horn of Africa or the Egyptian Alliance. May he have mercy on America and the oil and the Keren Kayemet. Their actions are a noose around the city's neck. June [of 1967] brought us the bulldozers with their infernal jaws devouring land, rocks, trees, and people. Their settlements spread like mushroom fields" (20). The word that evokes all these associations in Rafīf's mind is *yarḥam*, "to have mercy," which comes into her consciousness simply as a result of the woman's sneeze and the normal response of the passengers ("May God have mercy on you"). This reference to God's mercy, which Rafīf considers to be absent from politics, leads her mind to some then-contemporary political events: the struggle in the Horn of Africa between the two superpowers, the emergence of a new political party in Egypt that opposes Sadat's policy (his visit to Jerusalem, also mentioned in the novel), the American policy in the Middle East (upon which she sarcastically calls down God's mercy), Arab oil, the role of the Zionist Keren Kayemet in seizing Palestinian land, and finally the June 1967 war that resulted in Jewish settlements being built on the West Bank.

In some cases, Khalīfah makes special use of words having more than one meaning, in such a way that saying or hearing the word with one of its meanings brings the other meaning to a character's mind. An example is Khalīfah's use of the word *'ayn*, which means both "eye" and "water spring": "The hand which is not used to the knife will get hurt. The hand, the heart, and the eye (*'ayn*) were hurt and it [the knife] hurt me. Even the spring (*'ayn*), from which I had filled containers so that people could drink, dried up [a reference to the Israelis' taking over sources of water in the West Bank for their own settlements]" (231).

LIYĀNAH BADR: A COMPASS FOR THE SUNFLOWER

Liyānah Badr also drew directly from her own life experiences to write *Būṣlah min ajl 'Abbād al-Shams* (*A Compass for the Sunflower*, 1979),[23] another novel dealing with the Palestinian-Israeli conflict. Badr, however, did not live on the West Bank during occupation; she has lived in the diaspora since she was a girl. Badr's family was forced to flee their home many times, and Badr ended up living in Syria, Egypt, and Jericho, among other places, never knowing how long she would stay. Her family was often separated as well, because her father was a political activist and occasionally was imprisoned or forced into exile. She even spent a few years in an orphanage in Jerusalem,[24] which, as tragic as this might seem to others, gave her the means (through books and instruction in the arts) to begin to develop her literary interests and skills.

Many of the events of Badr's childhood, as described in her interview with Bouthaina Shaaban (Shaaban 1991), are virtually replicated in *A Compass for the Sunflower*, and others are more loosely represented in the novel.[25] This autobiographical quality translates into a narrative that is detailed and believable. It also means, in this case, that the story does not adhere to a classical novel formula, but instead is fragmented in terms of both textual format and chronology. Although the story "takes place" in the early 1970s, when Jinan (the main character) is living in Beirut, the novel follows her thought processes in a stream-of-consciousness style that takes the story back in time to Jinan's earlier life in Jericho and in the camps at Amman. In fact, probably the majority of the novel consists of Jinan's memories of earlier times, not surprising, since she lives in a kind of limbo in Beirut, away from her beloved Jericho and many of her family and friends. Events and images in the present trigger memories of these places and the people there, so that time and place change quickly in the novel, sometimes without warning. For example, the novel opens with Jinan waiting for a taxi. She sees a pool of blood on the sidewalk, and is suddenly transported back to the first aid station at a camp in Amman during Black September of 1970 in Jordan:

> Blood! I turned in sudden surprise to look for the source of the red puddle and saw a butcher hanging up the animal he had just slaughtered. I averted my eyes. Blood mingling with the grey and blue and white, and springing up through the cracks of memory. You forget, then suddenly you glance behind.
>
> A man came towards me, supporting a woman. Tenderness welled up from his arms, and the woman was like a plant growing from his body, branching outwards but hesitant to break away from the cramped pot. Her young, tired face, already lined by the years, sent a violent wave of emotion surging through me, triggered off by some memory I couldn't locate.
>
> The service taxi had drawn up. I took my seat and was engulfed by a powerful smell of antiseptic coming from the woman as she stepped into the taxi. I found myself looking involuntarily at the pool of blood mixed with mud and water. That feeling of heaviness descended on me, and I expected to hear the long-drawn-out cry of the little girl as she rolled on the cold tiles: I'd grabbed hold of her to stop her moving while the nurse went on stitching up her hands, which were full of tiny fragments of shell. (Badr 1989: 1–2)

The suddenness of these changes, along with the novel's division into short, choppy chapters, both results from and captures the instability and fragmentation of the author's own life that, she points out to Shaaban, still involves sometimes having to leave her home and all of her possessions suddenly and start over again "from scratch" (Shaaban 1991: 162).

Badr's life experiences also contribute directly to the fact that, in *Compass*, the main "events" are mostly Jinan's memories of earlier events. As is the case with many of the novels discussed in this book, *Compass* does not have a "plot" in the conventional sense. After the fighting began and Jinan had to flee her original home in Jericho, her day-to-day survival has precluded the kind of major life events which are usually associated with a novel plot. Badr comments on life as a refugee: "If I were living in Palestine, even an Israeli-occupied Palestine, things would be much clearer. I would at least be living in a Palestinian world the features of which I know and am sure of. But living here I feel lost, because I have to live out all the crises of the Arab citizen, and in addition suffer the huge problem of having no home, no land, no job and no rights" (Shaaban 1991: 160). Living without the organized and familiar social structure in which she grew up makes it impossible, in Badr's view, to live the kind of life that has room for a "plot" of any recognizable sort.[26] Jinan just seems to exist day to day: there is no mention of future events to which she might look forward. Even her relationship with Shaher, which seems to be somewhat long-standing and of a romantic nature, is never clearly defined. We know that they feel a commitment to each other, but we do not know if they are married or planning to marry. This is significant in that, because institutions like marriage are parts of a social structure and Jinan and Shaher are currently living outside the system in which they grew up, the definitions belonging to that system would have little meaning for them now—especially in such volatile times (Shaher barely survives breaking through an Israeli roadblock near the end of the novel).

The "Palestinian question" is the driving force behind the events in the novel; however, like some of her contemporaries, Badr has not left the "woman question" out of the picture. In an interview, Badr brings up her belief that Palestinian women cannot carry on an effective struggle against sexism until Palestinians live in an independent state (Shaaban 1991: 157), because it is impossible to build a base of operations (literally or figuratively) in such an unstable environment.[27] However, although she argues that she cannot give women's rights "priority in a society which is rife with social and political problems and whose very identity and existence are in question" (160), she nonetheless considers feminism an important movement,[28] and sexist oppression is alluded to directly several times in the novel. Amer, who Jinan has known since childhood and who throughout the course of the novel is attempting to hijack an airplane in order to negotiate the release of prisoners, once told Jinan of his plans for marriage: "Nonchalantly he passed me photo after photo of pretty girls who looked like film stars, and told me proudly, 'They're all faithful to me, but I'm not faithful to a single one of them. When I come back for good I'll marry a girl who knows how to make sage tea and cook chicken in the oven with olive oil and onions'" (Badr 1989: 21). The supposed epitome of a progressive man, Amer has clearly not progressed in terms of sex relations.

In another remembered scene, this time from the 1967 war, the enormous importance placed on women's virginity is addressed.[29] Amer's young niece has been wounded in an attack and her thighs are badly cut. The girl's grandmother cries, not for the girl's pain, but because she is sure that no "nice man" would ever "believe that one of the casualties of the attack had been her granddaughter's virginity" (Badr 1989: 28). Jinan herself remembers being aware at a young age of her value as a woman in her society, and recalls wishing she could be a boy and enjoy the freedom denied to girls: "As it was I had the strong sensation that I was like a chicken, raised for an obvious, clearly defined economic purpose. From home to school and back again I went, acquiring the features of the most superior type of education and upbringing in the eyes of the world. In time my progress would be reversed and marriage would be my lot, as they say; then for a change I would move from my husband's room to the kitchen, and from the kitchen to the children's rooms and the guest rooms" (Badr 1989: 50).

Jinan's close friend Shahad not only understands the problem of sexism, but realizes that traditional Arab women's roles have unfortunately become one of the few ways available for maintaining her national identity in the face of the threats to the Arab world and particularly to Palestinians: "Where can I find myself if I don't stay connected with what remains of traditional femininity, when it's been reinforced in us over the past thousand years?" (117). This is a serious problem for Palestinian women, given the fact that their society's "identity and existence are in question," as Badr points out; however, the author still manages to introduce the subject of sexist oppression from a feminist angle in the novel enough times to make a statement.

Badr speaks of her fervent belief that oppression can be eliminated only through collective struggle (Shaaban 1991: 157). In the novel, Jinan is saddened as Amer's hijacking operation unfolds; she loves Amer and understands that his ultimate goals are hers as well, but believes that his handful of men are more likely to be killed than to have their demands met as a result of their attempt. She imagines speaking to Amer: "Your existence is my existence in the largest sense, so why are you trying to die like this? Our principles are the same, and there are many different routes to take, so why should this square be more firmly sealed than your eyes or my eyes can perceive? Why don't you answer me?" (Badr 1989: 91). At the novel's end (as we might expect, given Badr's position), it is implied that Amer and his comrades will indeed meet with failure on their mission. Badr's prescription is for collective action and peaceful struggle as much as possible. Underscoring this is the constant stream of memories that constitute most of the narrative. Because there is no collective without collective identity and because this identity is all the more fragile to Palestinians scattered over so much foreign land, memory is absolutely crucial The topic is introduced early in the novel, when Jinan is recalling a conversation with Shaher:

> Now it was my turn to sound perplexed: "Why do the tanks always come and eat up periods of our history? The only dates we remember are the Balfour Declaration, the Rogers visit and the carnage of Black September."
>
> He reached for a match and struck it, then said in a low voice, before he lit his cigarette, "Because the exile has left firm, clear footprints. We mustn't forget them or, as Salima Al-Hajja says, we'll become gypsies roaming the earth in permanent exile." (Badr 1989: 5)

Badr herself has experienced the dangers of memory loss, and realizes the harmful effects it could have on a national struggle.

She recalls what happened after yet another sudden move in 1982, when she again had to leave her possessions behind: "I suffered a sudden loss of memory, and to a certain extent, loss of identity. I had to forget that I spent most of my life trying to forget things dearest to me: colourful Ariha [Jericho], the old Jerusalem, my books in Amman and in Beirut; I had to forget the records and the beautiful music I used to write about. It is this urge to forget which turns Palestinians into people with no memory and no past. I try to keep these memories and this past very much alive in my writings. This has become my most urgent task" (Shaaban 1991: 163). Badr remains faithful to this task in *A Compass for the Sunflower*. While describing life in exile as a result of the Israeli invasion of Palestine, an angle not often found in novels by Arab women, Badr brings memory to the forefront as both a political strategy and a means of storytelling.

THE LEBANESE DIMENSION: GHĀDAH AL-SAMMĀN

The eruption of the civil war in Lebanon in 1975, and its tragic results for the Arab world in general and the Lebanese people in particular, provided the raw material for a score of novels. The endless day-to-day human suffering, the civil strife that took on religious and political dimensions, and the interference of outside forces all became themes that writers of fiction tried to capture and dramatize. The volume of the women's contributions to fiction on the Lebanese civil war is impressive.

Ghādah al-Sammān, a Syrian fiction writer who had lived in Beirut since 1964, actually foresaw the civil war. Born in Damascus in 1942, Ghādah al-Sammān had been tutored in French by her parents before going to school. Her mother, who used to teach her the Qur'ān, died when she was five. Her father continued to tutor her, and their relationship became very close. Her father, a self-made man, had been a professor and later a rector at Damascus University and eventually held a ministerial post. Al-Sammān earned a degree in English literature from Damascus University in 1961 and went on to work as a civil servant, journalist, and university instructor. In 1964 she enrolled in the American University of Beirut, where she earned her M.A. degree in English literature. After graduating, she spent three years traveling extensively in Europe. Her father died during this period, which threw her onto her own resources financially and emotionally. While in Europe she got a taste both of spiritual alienation and personal independence:

> I traveled to London and settled down there and wandered around the various European capitals, and was lonely as never before. My father, who had provided me with spiritual and economic protection and who was a great psychological support for me, died. I also lost my job during that period. Then I was sentenced to jail in Syria because I had left my job there as an employee and lecturer at the university. . . . I suddenly found myself lonely and without income. I found myself forced to rise to the challenge. I could not go back to Syria and take up the role of an heiress and fall under the authority of family and society. For the first time I became aware of the cruelties and responsibilities of life, but despite the price I paid I did not retreat. (al-Sammān 1980: 33)

Nor had al-Sammān retreated from a previous clash in which she was involved in the early 1960s over a controversial article she wrote, entitled "Let Us Pray for the Slave Who Is Flogged." This article criticized the women of Ḥamāh in Syria who refused to vote in elections. It angered religious conservatives, who issued a harsh rebuttal. Al-Sammān stuck to her guns, and wrote another article with the provocative title: "Let Us Demand Emancipation for Men Too" (see Fattūḥ 1964: 53). Al-Sammān's conviction that both sexes in the Third World were in need of liberation, rather than believing in women's emancipation as a separate issue,[30] always remained a cornerstone of her philosophy: "To demand women's rights is both a strategic and a tactical mistake at the same time. We should demand rights for women and men together—that is, demand rights for that repressed human race of which women form such a large part. In other words, it is wrong for women to present their demands to men. The man is not the woman's enemy. He is her partner in suffering" (1980: 170).[31] As with previously mentioned authors, Ghādah al-Sammān emphasizes in these stories the quest for individual freedom. This emphasis is quite clear throughout *'Aynāka Qadarī* (*Your Eyes Are My Destiny*, 1962), which was her first collection of short stories. For example, the story "Rajul fī al-Zuqāq" ("Man in the Alley") is of a young woman whose father tries to make her abandon her university studies and marry a rich man she does not love (al-Sammān 1962: 115–129). She rebels and finally gets her own way, realizing in the process that she can control her life if she asserts herself.

Even when one of Ghādah al-Sammān's heroines achieves independence and material success, however, she remains plagued by inner turmoil and doubt. She still yearns for a man with whom she can share married life. This yearning becomes especially intense when the heroine goes to visit her brother in London. There the emotional dilemma of the heroine takes on national overtones. The heroine of "al-Muwā'" ("The Meow") feels alienated by, among other things, the supposed lack of masculinity of European men: "This new generation of London frightens me. Its men have long hair and an unbearably effeminate appearance. Men in my country are still solid" (al-Sammān 1966: 22–39). She consoles herself by thinking back on her Palestinian lover. This is problematic in terms of women's status; if she must have a man to be complete, and he must be traditionally masculine (meaning very different from women, not "effeminate"), the implication is that she should be dependent on a man and be "feminine." Because dependence and the other elements of traditional femininity are what keep men in power to begin with, this heroine's comment about European men—although understandable and perhaps not unusual—reveals issues of women's internalized sexism, which are one of the major themes in al-Sammān's fiction.

Al-Sammān's later collection *Raḥīl al-Marāfi' al-Qadīmah* (*The Departure of Old Harbors,* 1973) marks a turning point in her choice of subject matter. She switches from an emphasis on personal freedom to an emphasis on the disastrous 1967 war and the dramatic reconsideration of values which it caused. The stories cover the issues of sex, social inequality, the need for radical changes, and the Palestinian resistance movement. The heroine of the story "al-Dānūb al-Ramādī" ("*The Grey Danube*"), is plagued with guilt because she has helped cause the deaths of her brother and several other fighters by reading false military information over the radio during the war (she works as a broadcaster, and the radio station is deliberately transmitting false information as propaganda). Rather than go on helping to spread lies to the people, she rebels against her boss Ḥāzim (who is also her lover) and quits her job. She ends up pursuing a life of promiscuity in an attempt to forget her guilt, but this, too, proves to be an empty way of living. The theme of alienation as the logical outcome of escape is a recurring one in al-Sammān's fiction. Nūf, the heroine of "Ḥarīq Dhālika al-Ṣayf" ("The Fire of That Summer"), flees her village in southern Lebanon after the Israelis destroy it. In Beirut, her whole life becomes devoted to trying to forget her past existence, to the extent that she has fantasies about returning to the womb.

After seeing four short story collections published, al-Sammān finally wrote her first novel, *Bayrūt 75* (*Beirut 75*, 1975). The shift from one form to another was not, in fact, a clean break, since each of her short story collections has a common theme that binds its individual stories together. (Indeed, when the Egyptian critic Maḥmūd A. al-'Ālim reviewed her collection *Layl al-Ghurabā'*, he treated it as a novel rather a collection of short stories (Ṣubḥī 1978: 154). Jalāl al-'Ashrī did the same when he approached the stories of this book as a series of variations on the same theme (in this case alienation) (al-'Ashrī 1967: 54–63).

Ghādah al-Sammān confessed that the subject matter itself made her decide to shift from the short story format to the novel. When she sat down one day in the fall of 1974 to write *Bayrūt 75*, she had no definite idea about the final form the book would take. She later recalled: "I set out to write, and since it is the ideas that determine the form, they chose at that moment a novel as the body in which they would be incarnated" (al-Sammān 1980: 105). However, one could look at *Bayrūt 75* as a collection of five short stories, each able to stand on its own. Yet, the link between their different plots is fine and subtle. One is reminded of Ghādah al-Sammān's answer when she was asked (before writing *Bayrūt 75*) why she had never written a novel: "Perhaps the most important reason could be related to my impetuous nature, which still prevents me from [embarking on] the continuous, slow, geometrical, structural work that a novel generally needs" (Ṣubḥī 1978: 154). The first chapter of *Bayrūt 75* introduces the main characters in a taxi traveling from Damascus to Beirut. Two of them are Syrians fleeing a miserable past and hoping to become rich and famous and realize their dreams in Beirut. Yāsmīnah comes from a family so conservative that her mother still wears the veil, but she herself is completely different from her mother (for example, in the taxi she is wearing a short dress that shows her legs). She has run away from the boredom of her job as a teacher at a convent where "the days passed by as heavy as an anesthetized body on an operating table" (al-Sammān 1975: 9).[32] She has two main reasons for deciding to go to Beirut: she wants the freedom to form relationships that are impossible in Damascus, where women are expected to suppress their romantic feelings; and she wants to exploit Beirut's wealth of publishing houses in search of success as a poet.

The other Syrian passenger is Faraḥ, a handsome young man blessed with a beautiful voice. He, too, is fleeing a boring job (as a clerk) and is traveling to Beirut with a letter of recommendation from his father to a relative named Nīshān. This Nīshān already moved to Beirut some time before, and has become rich, famous and influential there.

Ghādah al-Sammān is careful to foreshadow the tragic fall of Yāsmīnah and Faraḥ from the very beginning of the novel. She does so by using symbols and mental associations and by describing natural objects and events in human terms: "The sun was fierce and glowing. Everything in the Damascus street was bleeding sweat and panting. The buildings and pavements were shaking with fever and trembling behind the hot steam rising from everything . . . and for a moment it seemed to Faraḥ that the whole street would faint; trees, cars, pedestrians, vendors, and the man who stood in front of the gate of the taxi station calling in a slain voice: 'Beirut, Beirut'" (5). This scene, with its references to death, with its expectation of a mass fainting (or death) of objects as well as people, and the unbearable heat as the image of hell, serves to prefigure the tragedy of Yāsmīnah and Faraḥ in Beirut. This foreshadowing is furthered by the taxi itself, which is rich in symbols. It is black like a hearse. Its driver is mute—he neither speaks nor smiles throughout the whole trip—and he is as cold and impersonal as if he were delivering the passengers to a cemetery. Yāsmīnah and Faraḥ are sitting in the front seat; in the back seat sit three veiled women swathed from head to toe in black as though they were going to a funeral. Faraḥ refers to these three women as the sorceresses of fate (*'Arrāfāt al-Qadar*): "I wonder if I am being driven to my death and these sorceresses of fate are escorting me and mourning me" (7). As Ghālī Shukrī noted, these three women are playing the same role as the witches in Shakespeare's *Macbeth*: they prophesy inevitable tragedy (Shukrī 1977: 111). The three women get out of the taxi as soon as it crosses the Lebanese-Syrian border, leaving Yāsmīnah and Faraḥ alone to face what now awaits them in Beirut.

The closer the taxi comes to Beirut, the clearer the evil omens become. People are celebrating the Festival of the Cross ('Īd al-Ṣalīb, a Middle Eastern Christian holiday) and the smell of burning wood makes Faraḥ ill at ease, feeling "as if I were at a ritual where a human sacrifice had been offered to a vicious god" (9). When they look down upon the city at night from the mountains, "Beirut, at the bottom of darkness, looked bright and shining like the finery of a sorceress who had come down to the sea to swim at night, leaving on the shore her pearls and jewels and colorful magic things, her boxes of evil and happiness inlaid with ivory, her sandals and amulets and secrets" (10). The novel picks up Yāsmīnah's story in Beirut as she lies nude on the yacht of her new boyfriend Nimr. It is the first time she has publically taken all her clothes off and she thinks back on her former self: "How could she have carried her body all these years like a burden, a corpse, a mere instrument to move around and to carry pieces of chalk? Now she is discovering it as a world of pleasures" (15). Taking off her clothes on the yacht is the beginning of Yāsmīnah's fall. She still cannot get out of her shell (the rigidity of tradition). Yāsmīnah and Nimr are not alone on the yacht; in one corner is a slow-moving turtle, unable to get out of its shell to enjoy the sun, symbolizing Yāsmīnah's inability to free her body without being doomed to a tragic fate.

The social injustice and political events that led to the civil strife in Lebanon in the mid-1970s serve as a background for Yāsmīnah and Faraḥ as they pursue fame and riches. When Israeli jets scream over Beirut and shatter windows, both Yāsmīnah and the turtle are frightened. Nimr, however, is indifferent, claiming blandly that the planes will not hurt anyone except the Palestinian guerrillas. The Israeli planes show up again when Faraḥ is looking for Nīshān in the luxurious al-Ḥamrā' street in Beirut. He sees a group of Lebanese watching a man making a small monkey dance. Only the monkey seems to respond to the threatening sound of the planes: "It buried its face in the pavement and turned its rear to the audience, and began crying with a sad voice" (18).

In the end, Nimr abandons Yāsmīnah to marry the daughter of a notable, a match more in line with his own selfish interests. Left alone in the cruel city, Yāsmīnah turns for help to her brother, a resident of Beirut. She is desperate, for the only other avenue open to her is prostitution.[33] Yāsmīnah does not become a prostitute, but her fate is nevertheless tragic: her brother kills her, not because she tarnished the family honor as he claims, but because she becomes unable to continue to buy his silence by providing him with money (88–91).

Unlike the majority of women writers, who choose female characters as representatives of their own philosophies, al-Sammān uses a male character named Muṣṭafā: "Muṣṭafā, the fisherman, represents my outlook on life at a certain stage while the personality of the heroine Yāsmīnah has nothing to do with mine. She does not represent me at all, either in the past or in the future. She worships the male, whereas I reject the attitude of worship in matters of love" (1980: 162). Muṣṭafā is the only character in *Bayrūt 75* who manages to find salvation in the urban inferno. His father has worked as a fisherman for thirty years, during which he had been exploited by the powerful families who control the fishing industry. The father grows obsessed with finding the magic lantern that will pull him out of his poverty. When his eldest son dies at sea, he makes Muṣṭafā abandon his studies and come home to help him in the fishing business. Muṣṭafā, who has seen enough of the miserable conditions in which the fishermen live, dedicates himself to helping them organize themselves and fight for their rights.

In *Bayrūt 75*, al-Sammān shows a keen eye for exposing the social, political, and economic failings of Lebanese society. All these weaknesses are obviously an ideal recipe for a civil war, which indeed erupted a month after the book was published.[34] Al-Sammān foreshadows this catastrophe in the book. At one point in the book, Fāḍil Bey al-Salamūnī, a morally corrupt aristocrat and member of parliament, visits Fāyizah the fortune-teller to ask about his prospects for advancing further in Lebanese political life. Fāyizah's forecast is far from rosy: "I see much sadness. I see blood. Plenty of blood" (48).

When the war actually came, Ghādah al-Sammān was one of the first Arab novelists to write about it. She felt not that the war was an outside experience to which she was a mere spectator, but rather that the civil war gave a wider dimension to the personal war that had taken up all of her existence:

> In a way, my whole life was a war. In this first war the weapons were different. I was always subjected to a social

bombardment. Social terror was always practiced against me. There were always new rounds being fired between me and the society. The wartime bullet was no more painful than the peacetime one, and the wartime experience was not the most difficult of my life. Before, I died alone and bled alone. In the [Lebanese] war I died with the group. This war led [me] to a communal awareness of others' suffering, whereas before I was locked away in my own sorrows as if they were a shell. For the first time I feel that my suffering is not individual . . . that the road to salvation passes through others and that it is a communal quest rather than a personal one. (Shukrī 1977: 205–206)

The heroine of al-Sammān's war novel *Kawābīs Bayrūt* (*Beirut Nightmares*, 1976)[35] remains nameless throughout the novel. She is trapped in her apartment in the middle of the civil war, unable to go out safely because the building lies between two opposing armed groups. When the war begins she evacuates all the members of her family (except her brother Shādī) and sends them to relatives outside the war zone. Soon afterward, the police jail her brother when he is out getting food, because they catch him carrying a small pistol. (The author keeps referring to this incident throughout the novel, to express the irony of a society where order has degenerated into war and the police pick on ordinary citizens rather than on the militiamen who are armed to the teeth.) Thus the heroine is left alone in her third-story apartment, having constant contact only with the landlord Fu'ād and his son Amīn.

The heroine is a revolutionary writer and journalist who works for a radical publishing house. All her life she has advocated setting up a new Arab society free from oppression, social injustice, and sectarianism. Her strong sense of identity with her nation has brought her back to her homeland after years of self-imposed exile in Europe. "Life taught me that escape from my real identity was futile. I am the daughter of this land, the daughter of the boilingly turbulent Arab world. I am the daughter of this war. This is my destiny" (al-Sammān 1979: 41). This is in stark contrast with the situation described in Chapter Three, referred to as the *vicious circle*, in which female characters feel trapped in their home towns and gender roles, and where those who leave the traditional life-style for Arab women are scorned or pressured to return to a life of passivity, dependence, and servitude. Growing concern for national unity and identity transformed the image of returning home in fictional works by Arab women.

In fact, this heroine is so actively involved that she feels that she herself helped to start the war, although she is not in favor of the killing it entailed: "I did participate in creating this war.... My writings always carried a cry for change, to remove ugliness from the face of this homeland and wash it with justice, joy, freedom, and equality. All that the fighters are doing is executing that in their own way. They are my letters, coming out of my books, taking the shape of human beings carrying arms and fighting. Did I really want a revolution without blood? Yes, I am—like all artists—contradicting myself" (41). Not only does she feel responsible for the war, she has a definite stake in it. She believes that the revolution is necessary, to expose and rid the society of curruption and injustice. She stands against the economically privileged class, for example, never feeling a need to defend even her own upper-class neighborhood.[36]

During the war, the heroine faces a dilemma: can she condone violence as a means of achieving her revolutionary goals? For some time she has held that her idealistic humanism cannot be reconciled with killing, and that the murder of even one man is a massacre (44). The incompatibility in her mind between the bullet, symbol of violence, and the pen, symbol of intellectual advocacy, gives the civil war an intimate personal dimension, as we see from the heroine's reaction to a stray bullet shot through her apartment that grazes her ear: "I grasped the bullet and put it next to my pen. (Put a bullet next to a pen and you will see that the pen is longer.) But this particular bullet... seemed to me at first sight as long as my pen. Then it grew and became a pillar of fire, while my pen trembled and shrank and became like the feather of a wounded bird in the presence of that inferno" (50). Another bullet scores a direct hit on the heroine's framed university diploma, which hangs on the wall. Nonetheless, toward the end of the novel the heroine finds herself forced to carry the pistol as well as the pen: "It is true that I no longer see it [the pistol] as a mere ugly dark spot, as if I am trying to see it in a new light; still, I cannot hold back a tremor in my limbs when I touch it, as if my relationship with it were some sort of imposed marriage.... I need it, but I still detest it" (316).

It is revealing that the heroine makes this decision to arm herself only after her private library is burned by a missile that explodes in her apartment.[37] From the beginning of the story it is clear that there is an almost physical relationship between the heroine and her library. Both it and her body are alarmingly fragile in the face of war's destructiveness. Furthermore, the library represents the heroine's past inner life and her intellectual growth: "As far as I was concerned, my library was not merely books. It was a dialogue. Every book was a man with whom I had argued. On the margins of all my books I wrote down the yells of approval, anger, exclamation, or argument. Every book that I read, I read as though I am rewriting it or sharing with its author his anxiety and exploration and self-questioning. My books are not mere decorations. Rather, they are minutes of meetings between me and their authors" (247). The library plays a major role in her decision to settle down in her homeland rather than continuing to wander from airport to airport in Europe: "My library alone was able to persuade me to put an end to my wandering, because the library could not live on the wings of airplanes and in transit halls any more than moss can grow on a rolling stone" (196). The library also includes revolutionary books that the heroine has written or translated and whose principles she believes are being put into action by one of the fighting groups in Lebanon.

The heroine of *Kawābīs Bayrūt*, like those of Saḥar Khalīfah (Sa'diyyah) and Laylā 'Usayrān (Miriam), ironically feels like a man when she achieves a sense of fulfillment. She refuses to let the war drive her away from her apartment (thus showing "manly" bravery), while her brother becomes obsessed with the thought of leaving. In fact, throughout her life she has been as independent as a man is expected to be: "Since my adolescence I have worked and supported myself, and lived my life like any 'man' in the family" (36).

In contrast to the heroine, the landlord's son Amīn proves to be less "masculine." This was the main reason for his hatred of her. "Amīn secretly hates me, as the rest of my family does. He feels that I am the 'man of the family,' and he is shocked to realize through me that physical differences are no longer very important. . . . My 'masculinity' is a challenge to his mental laziness" (63). Amīn's father Fu'ād, like his son, is selfish and totally indifferent to the political turmoil afflicting his country. He is eighty-five years old, an ex-statesman who has become wealthy in politics but is now clearly in decline; he is hard of hearing and sometimes falls asleep while he is talking. His attachment to his wealth, however, has not weakened with age. For example, he gathers all his silverware together and sits down to guard it until he dies. His death symbolizes the death of the older generation: "He was wearing his old official Ottoman suit and had his chest covered with medals, as if he was waiting for an important visitor (death) who did not fail to come" (185). When Fu'ād dies, his son refuses to remove him from the building, merely dragging his corpse from one room to another. In the end he grows very frightened of his father's corpse, and they finally have to get rid of it by putting it in the garbage container. With this corpse, the past itself is symbolically thrown away.

In *Kawābīs Bayrūt*, Ghādah al-Sammān was faced with a difficult artistic problem—a lack of action. Her heroine (the focal point of the novel) is externally passive, because she is locked at home all the time, and the two men trapped with her are passive in every sense. To compensate for the lack of external events in the novel, al-Sammān resorts to devices that give the novel its internal unity. First, she makes her fictional world into a fantasy inhabited not only by people but also by abstract ideas such as death and religious holidays, which have roles like real characters. The novel is written as a series of nightmares, a technique al-Sammān has also used at the end of *Bayrūt 75*. *Kawābīs Bayrūt* contains 207 nightmares,[38] followed by 1 optimistic dream, and it ends with projections of future nightmares. These nightmares are by no means only bad breams of the heroine, but all her waking experiences in that atmosphere of war and horror. Nightmares symbolize the highest state of consciousness, and the nightmares become the expression of the heroine's state of mind during the civil war. As Samar R. al-Fayṣal has noted, the division of the novel into nightmares instead of conventional chapters grows out of the fictional situation itself. A normal chapter division will in itself be a conscious, logical act; war, as seen by the heroine, is illogical and irrational (al-Fayṣal 1979: 225–226).

Second, constant references to the heroine's boyfriend Yūsuf are in part another aspect of the nightmarishness of the fictional world. He falls victim to the religious fanaticism that, at least on the surface, characterizes the civil war. He is killed when he runs across a blockade set up by a militia of a religion different from his own. His memory haunts the heroine, who keeps his papers and some of his personal belongings in a safe place in her apartment. His frequent "visits" (in the heroine's mind) after he dies are associated with various natural phenomena and replete with references to sex and death:

> It is sunset. My beloved [Yūsuf] always comes with the sunset, with dawn, with thunder, with rain, and with everything solemn and eternal. My beloved always comes to me with autumn, as if autumn were the trace of his feet on the Earth. He comes down to me from the madness of the symphony of death and explosives, and enters torn with bullets like the last time I saw him. I run to his chest which is covered with broken glass. A piece will penetrate my chest too. I hug him close so that we stick together with death and pain and the splinters of glass become bridges, or rather joint arteries for our bodies—and gradually darkness permeates. (29–30)

Only when the heroine is rescued from the war zone is she able to free herself also from the bloody memory of Yūsuf. She throws his papers and personal belongings into the sea, an act that symbolizes her determination to leave the past and look forward to a better future for herself and for her nation.

Third, Ghādah al-Sammān used what T. S. Eliot called an *objective correlative*[39] to express her thoughts and feelings to avoid being either direct or sentimental. Al-Sammān's objective correlative is a pet shop, which she mentions for the first time in "Tenth Nightmare" (through flashbacks). The heroine remembers her visit to the nearby pet shop with a friend who was going to buy a cat. (This friend stands for the kind of people who often buy pets in Beirut. She is the mistress of a rich married man who does not want to leave his wife and children to marry her. Because this means she cannot hope to have children to whom she can give her affection, she decides to buy a cat.) This pet shop is a figure for Lebanon before and during the civil war. The heroine notices that the shop is divided into two sections. The front, where customers would come, is designed to impress those customers (or "foreigners," as the heroine thinks of them). It is "clean, beautiful, and well-arranged, like a Swiss shop in which one could find all the trappings, of our consumer age—like, for example, al-Ḥamrā' Street, the Airport Street, the Transit Hall, al-Rūshah and the Casino" (14). The symbolism is quite clear. The front section stands for the deceptive showcase of the Lebanon that the tourists see (the Lebanon that has been called the *Switzerland of the Orient*). This false front does not fool the heroine; she sneaks into the back section (representing the Lebanon behind the façade) to get a firsthand look at the real condition of the pets. She describes these animals like human beings: 'Behind the wall, cages of various sizes and shapes were jumbled together and stuck together like coffins in a paupers' cemetery. The sun, wind, dew, and blue sky could not reach them. Inside the cages there were creatures resembling people in their diversity: dogs of various kinds . . . cats . . . rabbits . . . mice . . . animals of different colors, shapes, and temperaments, all of whom had cages, imprisonment and misery in common. They were so worn out that the cats did not exactly meow, and the dogs did not bark very well, and the birds did not sing" (14).

The heroine senses the unhappiness of the caged animals (who stand for the Lebanese people, as is clear from the human qualities she attributes to them and the human terms she uses to describe them): "I could hear the united sad voice of the nation (*sha'b*) of pets inside the cages. It was like the sound of a demonstration of the sick, the wounded, and the tired, but still it was a threatening and fiercely menacing sound. It was clear that the shopkeeper fed them barely enough to keep them alive so that he could seel them" (15). On the second day of her imposed imprisonment at home, the heroine comes to identify herself with the caged animals. In her case, the cage is widened to include and imprison the whole homeland (21). It is interesting to note that the only place the heroine is able to go to, under cover of darkness, is that pet shop. On a later visit there she breaks into the back section through a window, determined to open the cages and free the animals. This proves futile because the animals have grown used to life in captivity, and there is still some food and water in their cages, so they will not leave. Later, however, after the shopkeeper has closed his shop on account of the war and can no longer provide them with food and water, the heroine's attempt to free them succeeds, allowing the hunger-driven animals to attack their owner and tear him to pieces. Significantly, the first animals to attack the shopkeeper are two hunting dogs that the heroine likens to Arabian horses (149–150). The first thing these dogs do, when freed, is destroy the customer's section of the pet shop, the tourists' façade of Lebanon with its European decor.

The series of nightmares in *Kawābīs Bayrūt* ends with an optimistic dream full of nearly transparent symbolism.[40] A woman named Līnā (who stands for Lebanon) is trying to discover the identity of her father (that is, Lebanon's national identity). She goes to King Solomon, who convenes an assembly of sorcerers to decide the issue. This assembly agrees that Līnā's father was one of the fighters of the last battalion of the Crusades (reflecting the Maronite vision of Lebanon as a country closely linked to Europe). Līnā's mother, however, insists that Līnā's family tree has been Arab for more than a thousand years. Līnā meets a stranger (the Palestinian people) whose family (the Arab states) abandoned him in childhood and left him to grow up in the woods (refugee camps). There he has spent much time in contemplation, and there nature has taught him how to defend himself with the strength of his own youthful body (a figure for the Palestinian guerrilla fighters). In contrast to Līnā, this stranger is absolutely sure about the names of his forefathers. In April (a reference to the Palestinian and Lebanese demonstration of April 1975, in which some members of both peoples were killed) Līnā becomes pregnant. This "illegitimate" pregnancy angers King Solomon (the Lebanese authorities), and he forces her to promise that she will not give birth. Līnā rebels against this and decides, along with her husband, to fight. She loses her left hand in the fighting, but the fetus remains safe. This fetus, however, is not born in the ninth month as expected because it is not a normal baby. It might stay in Līnā's womb for as long as nine years, and is not going to be born only once, but rather "more than once and in more than one place" (337).

The use of the nightmare technique not only solves the aforementioned problem created by the dearth of external events in the novel, but also frees the author from the restrictions of chronological time.[41] The whole experience is filtered through the heroine's nightmares that, being dreams, do not have to conform to the fixed rhythm of objective time. In the novel subjective time is real, despite the many references to the outside flow of events. According to Mona Fayad, the highly subjective point of view created in this novel (first person, no external narrator) is a device that lends itself better than any other to "the attempt to articulate a subjective desire" (Fayad 1987: 7).

Ḥanān al-Shaykh and *The Story of Zahra*

Al-Sammān is not alone in this achievement, however. Possibly the most impressive work in the history of Arab women's novels is Ḥanān al-Shaykh's *Ḥikayāt Zahrah* (*The Story of Zahra*, 1980),[42] which is remarkable not only in its portraryal of life during the civil war in Lebanon (presented in the second part of the novel), but also in that it is a milestone in terms of its feminist commentary on Lebanese society in general. For the first time in this literary tradition, nationalist and feminist causes are treated as inseparable and equally critical. Unlike many of her contemporaries, al-Shaykh shows that the strengths developed in the earlier periods must not necessarily be diminished to address ethnic and national issues.

Al-Shaykh was born in 1945 in the town of al-Nabaṭiyyah in southern Lebanon and, like Laylā Ba'labakkī, she had a strict Muslim upbringing. She wrote her first novel, *Intiḥār Rajul Mayyit* (*Suicide of a Dead Man*, 1970) at age twenty-two while attending the American College for Women in Cairo (Accad 1990: 43). Her second novel, *Faras al-Shayṭān* (*The Praying Mantis*, 1976), contains some autobiographical elements; the heroine comes from a conservative family from southern Lebanon, she studies in Cairo and then returns to her country, working in television (al-Rubay'ī 1984: 54). Her third work was a collection of short stories, *Wardat al-Ṣaḥrā'* (*The Rose of the Desert*, 1982).

The crowning achievement of al-Shaykh's literary efforts, however, came in the form of *The Story of Zahra*, an articulate and politically astute novel about a woman looking back on her years of physical, emotional, and sexual abuse while growing up, and dealing with all of these in addition to her own resultant self-abuse and identity crises as an adult, both before and during the war. Throughout her life, she is repeatedly driven to a kind of "madness" by abuse and frustration. As a young girl, Zahra is forced to accompany her mother on adulterous visits to men, who give Zahra toys to distract her while they are there. Zahra wants desperately to be close to her mother and fantasizes about being "closer to her than the navel to the orange" (al-Shaykh 1989: 6). However, she feels emotionally abandoned by her mother on these outings as well as at home—not surprising, because her mother has all she can do to fend off Zahra's abusive and suspicious father. He strikes both of them in unsuccessful attempts to extract an admission of his wife's infidelity and is cruel to them as a general rule. Zahra's feelings for him resemble those of Līnā for her father in Ba'labakkī's *Anā Aḥyā*; both daughters rebel against paternal tyranny (not surprising in works by these authors, both of whom suffered from similarly repressive family lives while growing up). Zahra despises her father and describes her memory of him as an ugly and frightening monster: "My father was always brutal. His appearance seemed to express his character: a frowning face, a Hitler-like moustache above thick full lips, a heavy body. Do I misjudge him? He had a stubborn personality. He saw all life in terms of black or white" (7).

Zahra learns to appreciate at an early age the impact of gender upon the quality of her life. She notes, as have other female literary protagonists, the preferential treatment accorded her brother Ahmad by her parents; she gets little or no meat so that he may enjoy it in abundance, and his education is made a financial priority for the family despite the fact that his performance in school pales in comparison to Zahra's. However, unlike these other heroines, Zahra does not begin to consciously despise her femaleness. Instead, during her youth she interprets the oppression and abuse she suffers as being purely the results of bad luck and of her own individual flaws; thus she internalizes these experiences and feels she must accept abuse from others and even add to it herself. Al-Shaykh shows with great attention to detail the devastating effects of oppressive environments on the psyche, and the enormous effort it takes to overcome them. As she grows into womanhood, Zahra realizes that the men outside her immediate family consider her their sexual property. She is sexually molested by her cousin while she is still very young, and a friend of the family rapes her repeatedly, resulting in her having to undergo two abortions while a teenager. This lack of control over her own body brings on a nervous breakdown and eventually drives Zahra to turn her rage against herself and scar her face by aggravating her acne with her hands.

Zahra decides to escape from her oppressive family and community by going to Africa, where her uncle, Hashem has been living in exile for some time. But her homesick uncle sees Zahra as representative of Lebanon and his family back home and finds himself so drawn to her that she finds no peace there. He wakes her early each morning, is overly attentive to her, and eventually begins to touch her in ways objectionable to her because she associates them with sexual behavior. Frequently, she is forced to seek refuge in the bathroom.[43] It is a bitter disappointment for Zahra, and she is eventually driven to her second nervous breakdown; however, we see the promise of survival for her when she tells her uncle that she detests his behavior and that he has directly caused her illness.

> In an ostrich's voice I replied, as my heart beat wildly, "Whatever happened to me was your fault?"
>
> "My fault?" He stared at me and asked hysterically, "My fault? How can you say such a thing, Zahra?"
>
> Once again, in my ostrich's voice, not knowing how the words escaped, I replied, "Yes. Your fault. Perhaps you didn't intend it, but I never cared for your behaviour towards me."
>
> He yelled back, "What are you saying, girl? What behaviour?"
>
> Again in the ostrich's voice, "At the movies, when you held my hand. In the mornings, when you slept by my side. It troubled me until it made me sick." (33)

She is old enough now to know her feelings and to begin to actively resist the oppressive conditions that cause her so much pain.

Zahra's next plan of escape is to accept the marriage proposal of her uncle's friend Majed; she also "escapes" from the storytelling, because the point of view changes for two chapters. One is narrated by Hashem and the other by Majed. These points of view are essential to the novel not only because the reader is given knowledge not possessed by Zahra (or that she would have no "reason" to relate) about other characters, but also because their stories make it difficult to view Hashem and Majed as stereotypical "bad" men. This makes it possible for al-Shaykh to write a story that demonstrates the complexity of the relationships among war, sexuality, feminism, and nationalism; that holds society at large accountable for the construction of oppressive values; and that also holds the reader accountable as an individual because, in identifying on some level with Hashem and Majed, the reader is discouraged from projecting his or her own participation in oppression onto convenient "villains."[44]

Hashem, we learn, grew up with significant feelings of inferiority that he carried into adulthood. At a young age, he got involved in radical political activism and, after his participation in a failed coup attempt, had to flee from Lebanon. He thought Africa would be an appropriate choice for living in exile, because be had heard of others who had gone there and had lived well. As it turns out however, he has never recovered from having to leave his beloved homeland. He mentions Zahra's letters as having given him something to hold onto, and her impending visit excites him very much. To him, Zahra represents Lebanon, his family, his culture. Her presence causes such turmoil in him that he can hardly contain his enthusiasm and wants to touch her and spend time with her, which translates into some sexual interest of which he seems only dimly aware. He tells himself that, were Zahra not his relative, he would marry her, but he seems to see nothing inappropriate in this or in his behavior. In fact, he is shocked when Zahra tells him that his actions have caused her breakdown. His lack of self-awareness and sometimes misdirected social consciousness, along with his own experience under oppressive conditions, makes it difficult to view him simply as Zahra's harrasser. Al-Shaykh creates a character much too complex for that.

Majed, like Hashem, sees Zahra as representing not only his homeland, but at first as an economic convenience as well—if he marries her, he will not need to travel to Lebanon to find and court a potential wife. In addition, he sees their marriage as an acquisition of property for him: "How I wished, when I first lay on Zahra, that she might scream and pound my chest and cry out, 'Stop! Stop! You're hurting me. Please don't hurt me.' But she only turned away her face, her body still under me. Even so, despite the fact that Zahra is not beautiful, I was so happy on my wedding night that I couldn't describe my joy. Here I was, married at last, the owner of a woman's body that I could make love to whenever I wished" (69). We find out as Majed tells his story that he also has felt inadequate in many ways. His feelings of displacement in Africa are magnified by the fact that he is excluded from the upper-class Lebanese in his African community, something he never expected and something that leaves him feeling like more of an outcast. In response to this feeling, he articulates his desperate desire for more money as a means of becoming more powerful. Added to these feelings is his sexual frustration, both physical and emotional. Growing up, Majed was shamed by his mother (and, indirectly, by the culture in general as well) for masturbating, causing him to believe that this activity was a terrible sin for which he might well someday be punished. Sexually, he is so self-involved and obsessed that he is unable to connect emotionally with a partner, as the previous passage indicates. He does not even consider that Zahra's depressed state during their engagement and later indifference to his sexual advances might mean that she was truly unhappy with him. In fact, it never seems to occur to him that it would be desirable for his wife to enjoy sex with him. Not surprising, when the sheets used on their wedding night are not blood-stained the next day, the idea that she has had sex prior to their marriage enrages him. As far as he is concerned, he has been fooled into accepting secondhand property. In a critical moment, however, Majed concludes that his bride's virginity may not be so important to him after all: "After several days, the intensity of these issues seemed to fade, as if such formidable questions became insignificant here in Africa, where there is no culture, no environment, no family to blow them up out of all proportion; for here every man stands on his own like a lone tree, like someone without a past who has only himself. Perhaps it is because there are no parents here, or because those who happen to be here have integrated into Africa and lack any culture to relate to. Traditions surface from time to time, but remain transplanted and so lose their former authority" (74).[45] Like Hashem, Majed is portrayed in such a way as to make it difficult for the reader to dismiss him as another typical abuser. We are shown the progression of his beliefs as they are influenced by his culture and lack of self-esteem (which are not necessarily separable).

This portrayal notwithstanding, Zahra realizes that this situation is no more tolerable for her than the last. The encounter with Majed over the status of her virginity precipitates another breakdown for her, and she goes back to Beirut with the unrealistic expectation that she will find peace and comfort in her parents' house. Of course, she is disappointed: her parents interrogate her ceaselessly about why she left Majed, and she knows that she can never make them understand her ordeal. She heads back to Africa, determined to make the best of the situation there with Majed. She thinks, "All I need to do is keep my real self hidden" (90), apparently forgetting that it is exactly this sort of existence that has made her life miserable to begin with. Although there is a low period at first, she soon decides to have another marriage ceremony in order to enter the marriage actively, rather than passively as she did the first time. Not only is a description of her first wedding left out of the novel completely, but the wedding night is narrated by her husband in the chapter told from his perspective; both of these literary techniques serve to emphasize her lack of involvement in that arrangement. Zahra's new resolve to force her marriage to work does not last past the reception, however, and she ends up screaming at the guests to leave her house. Shortly after, she leaves Majed for good and returns again to Beirut.

Zahra's only alternative, in her weakened emotional state, is again to retreat to her parents' home and try to erect enough walls around herself to protect her from her family, her community, and the world in general, all of which offer her no viable options for living comfortably and "respectably." In marriage, Zahra is virtually owned by her husband and expected to conform to societal expectations that she finds tedious and meaningless, not to mention threatening to her as an individual woman. So miserable does she find that life that she chooses this retreat that, under normal conditions, would afford her only slightly more freedom and privacy. Zahra's return to her parents' home, however, is not a simple case of the "vicious circle" phenomenon discussed in Chapter Three; the eruption of civil war at home postpones the necessity of yet another escape for Zahra, long enough for her to achieve an awareness of herself and her surroundings far beyond that of the heroines in most of the other novels discussed in this book.

This transformation becomes possible when Zahra finally gives up trying to fit into the conventional spaces reserved for women. Whenever she tries, she loses her already tenuous grasp on her sanity. It must be remembered, however, that her "madness" is not necessarily "unreasonable." In her introduction to *Madness and Sexual Politics in the Feminist Novel*, Barbara Hill Rigney points to a common belief about women's madness held by many feminists and some well-known theorists that madness in women should be interpreted in many (perhaps even most) cases as a reasonable response to living in a patriarchal culture (6). Zahra's life would support this reading, because her breakdowns are always the direct result of the restrictions and expectations placed on her primarily because she is a woman.

The second part of the novel, "The Torrents of War," is devoted to her life back in Beirut during the war. Ironically, although the war is symptomatic of an internally fractured and misguided country, it is exactly what Zahra needs to gain some freedom and a sense of normalcy. As Cooke shows us, we are forced to realize the relativity of her "madness": "[The war] forced others—particularly those beautiful women who had always been so far from her—to act as she had: to withdraw. It made her withdrawal normal. Her home became her world, shutting out others, whatever they desired, whatever they needed. For the first time she felt that she was not marginalized by people like her parents and her brother. Everyone was alone. But where others fought this aloneness she embraced it, since it represented the normalization of her madness, the accomodation of her otherness" (Cooke 1987a: 54). Even when Zahra comes out of her withdrawal to face the war fully, which, ironically, means that she is again marginalized (Cooke 1987a: 55), she is nevertheless an island of sanity among all of those in denial of the war and its meanings. At that time when her community is most out of control, Zahra is most in control of her own life. Her "madness" cannot be defined or determined because the war has made conventional sanity unavailable for comparison. Perhaps more important, because the war changes her family's living arrangements (her parents escape to the village and her brother is usually away fighting or looting), it also disrupts the usually rigid social norms, which include severe restrictions for women. She can move freely, make sense out of the reality the war has become, and make her own decisions without fear of retribution from her parents, brother, or husband (in fact, her family members are so distracted that Zahra hides her birth control pills in Ahmad's sock drawer with complete confidence). These circumstances, and the fact that Zahra's reaction to the war is horror and a willingness to confront it with total awareness, mean that psychologically Zahra is better able to survive now.

Zahra's life improves in many concrete ways during the war. Her face clears up (a sign that she has stopped abusing herself, at least in that regard), and she experiences her first real sexual pleasure with Sami, the sniper she has taken as a lover in an effort to distract him from his killing.[46] Zahra becomes well because she is allowed to live and develop so much more freely than before the war. She is still struggling alone, because those surrounding her have either left Beirut, withdrawn into denial of the war's existence, or joined in the fighting for individual reasons.[47]

By this time, aloneness is not alienating for her. Cooke writes, "From her new perspective—the madness that before has spelt oblivion—Zahra could look back on the anxiety that had been her pre-war condition. She could take another look at that suffering, uncolored by flashback and hallucination, and by naming it, end it. The silent Zahra was finally acquiring a voice" (Cooke 1987a: 56). Only when Zahra forgets that the new reality she has adopted is temporary and dependent on the "logic of the bullets" (Cooke 1987a: 54) does her survival become impossible. Zahra's downfall is precipitated by her unplanned pregnancy, which occurs while she is taking birth control pills. Because she does not believe she could be pregnant, it is not until the fourth month that she discovers it. By then she is unable to find a doctor to perform the abortion she so desperately wants, and she briefly considers suicide as preferable to being single and pregnant. Again, she experiences a kind of temporary madness when caught in the trap set by a male-dominated society. Zahra knows that war has not completely eradicated the cultural mandates for women and that her very survival would be endangered if she had to face her parents pregnant with no impending marriage. Accad sees this incident as underscoring the lack of control Zahra has (always had) over her body and her sexuality (Accad 1990: 92), and I would suggest that it also symbolizes the lack of control women in general have had over these areas.

Zahra begins to hope that Sami is not really a sniper and he has feelings for her that could lead to their marriage and a happy life together. But when she announces the pregnancy, Sami angrily blames her for it and demands that she have an abortion. When Zahra explains the situation to him and becomes almost hysterical with fear, he changes his position suddenly, telling her that he will indeed marry her and that they introduce each other to their families the very next day. He even expresses his hopes for the baby's future: "I hope, God willing, that you will be born a fighter, surrounded by the noise of rockets and bazookas" (179). Sami's sudden change in attitude, coupled with his plea that she stop crying, lends an air of insincerity to his promises, but Zahra takes no notice of this.

They argue briefly after Zahra breaks their unspoken agreement not to mention his occupation by asking him outright if he is a sniper; he angrily denies it and she apologizes, and they part on outwardly friendly terms. As Zahra walks home from that encounter, believing that everything has returned to normal and blissfully planning her future, she is shot several times. She knows that Sami is shooting at her. Enduring terrible pain, she runs through the possible reasons he would have for killing her: "Does he kill me because I'm pregnant? Or is it because I asked him whether he was a sniper?" (183). She thinks about her mother and brother, then succumbs to the darkness that "becomes fear." In her last moments, moments of excruciating cynicism, Zahra begins to recognize that her recent idealism was groundless: "I close my eyes that perhaps were never truly opened. I see rainbows processing towards me across white skies with their promises only of menace" (183–184).

Zahra does not survive the war because the future she plans with Sami and their child is illusory. Because the war has not brought about true revolution, especially with respect to women and sexuality, Lebanon is doomed to remain an oppressive patriarchal state even after the war. "Sexuality is much more fundamental in social and political problems than previously thought, and unless a sexual revolution is incorporated into political revolution, there will be no real transformation of social relations" (Accad 1990: 12). As Cooke concludes, Zahra's mistake is in believing that the power she has over her life during the war can be taken with her when she settles into postwar life. "War had given Zahra the illusion that she could live in peace as a normal person.... Yes, the war had opened up new vistas, but *within* its own logic.... For daring to use the war against itself she had to pay a price, her life" (Cooke 1987a: 58).

The Story of Zahra has been an extremely successful novel. Considered a work of belles lettres in its own right, it was widely read in the Middle East even though it some Arab countries it was officially banned (Accad 1990: 45). It is also one of the growing number of Arab women's novels to have been translated into English. With *The Story of Zahra*, al-Shaykh made such important literary contributions to the tradition of novels written by Arab women that this novel could be deemed a major literary milestone. Not the least of these contributions is the fact that she is the first to have written a novel containing such graphic and sensitive descriptios of sexual experiences. Sexual activity, expecially the nonmarital and autoerotic varieties, were and still are strictly taboo subjects, particularly for women writers, who are not supposed to have the knowledge necessary for such writing, but this descriptiveness makes it possible for al-Shaykh to connect war and sexuality in deeply personal and political ways.

As the title of the first part of the novel, "The Scars of Peace," suggests, prewar life is miserable for Zahra. She spends most of her time trying to escape from confining situations.[48] She escapes into Africa twice and to Beirut after each times; she escapes to the bathroom (itself a very confining space, which highlights how confined she feels outside the bathroom) while living with her uncle and husband; and when all else fails, she escapes into "madness" by having nervous breakdowns.[49] Finally, at the end of the novel, her only escape is death because she cannot live under the conditions that are sure to follow.

Gilbert and Gubar (1979: 64, 82) identify "imagery of confinement" and themes of escape in women's novels as a result of their "anxiety of authorship" (51), combined with the fact that women are usually confined in men's spaces, both literally and figuratively (83). This could be expected in the case of *The Story of Zahra*, because Arab women as a group have endured a high level of such confinement for much longer than their Western counterparts and because this novel in particular—with its groundbreaking language and subject matter—is certain to have produced a great deal of anxiety in its author. In fact, Zahra seems to function in the story as her own "mad double," a phenomenon in women's writing that provides a relatively safe outlet for frustration and rebellion. "For it is, after all, through the violence of the double that the female author enacts her own rageing desire to escape male houses and male texts, while at the same time it is through the double's violence that this anxious author articulates for herself the costly destructiveness of anger repressed until it can no longer be contained" (Gilbert and Gubar 1979: 85). As Gilbert and Gubar point out, a woman writer—unlike men writers—must struggle "not against her (male) precursor's reading of the world but against his reading of her" (49). This struggle is intensified for a woman writing in ways that men have deemed inappropriate for her, as al-Shaykh did with *The Story of Zahra*.

Rigney's book also provides a useful frame of reference for understanding the issue of madness in *The Story of Zahra*, because Zahra's "insanity" is in some ways strikingly similar to that of the feminist protagonists Rigney discusses. Not only do these protagonists share "a sense of victimization by a world made up of male dominators, associated in each novel with the image of the German fascist" (125),[50] but the search for the mother or mother figure by these protagonists, which Rigney explores at length, can be traced quite clearly throughout Zahra's struggle to find peace. The elements of rejection of the father and separation from the mother (Rigney 1980: 11) are unmistakable in *The Story of Zahra*. Zahra is obsessed as a child with her desire to be "closer to her than the navel to the orange" (al-Shaykh 1989: 6) and with the failure of her mother to connect with her. Rigney mentions that the actual mothers in the novels she examines tend to be either dead, impotent, or phsically far away (Rigney 1980: 11); Zahra's mother is ineffective and, for most of the novel, far removed from Zahra. This adds another dimension, then, to the fact that Zahra returns home twice after she is married. These returns are not merely retreats, but manifestations of her continuing search for her mother. Zahra does ultimately find her mother in herself, which all of the protagonists in Rigney's study finally realize they must achieve (Rigney 1980: 11–12), although this is possible only after her own mother is again removed and the war is raging. Unfortunately, this does not lead to permanent salvation for her: the war will eventually come to an end, and her parents (along with society as a whole) will be able once again to exert their authority once more.

Early on in her life, with all of the constraints placed on her, Zahra is unable to know herself or develop fully, especially in terms of her sexuality. She does not experience true sexual pleasure until she is in the midst of a war because the war has removed the authority figures from her life and suspended the usual rules for daily living, and this means Zahra's life and sexual behavior have become more her own than ever before. This cause and effect relationship is further emphasized by the fact that Sami, the man with whom Zahra has this sexual relationship, is none other than the local sniper, the symbol of the war at its most terrifying because the sniper is unpredictable and apparently indiscriminate when it comes to choosing human targets. Furthermore, the description of Zahra's first glimpse of Sami is tinged with sexual imagery. "Then I saw that he was leaning against the water cistern, his feet spread out and a clay pitcher at his side. Binoculars dangled around his neck and his hands rested on the rifle, dormant at his hip. He looked as if he slept" (134). What seems intriguing about this image is that, even though the rifle can be read as a phallic symbol and the position of the sniper's hands on the rifle can be seen as symbolizing male sexual desire or arousal, his relaxed state and the rifle's "dormancy" preclude the one image one might expect from a sniper in this situation—that of sexual potency, aggression, or even danger.

However, this makes sense if we consider Zahra's relationship to him at this moment. She is in the process of trying to attract his attention, walking half-dressed on her aunt's balcony across from the roof where he is standing. After they exchange words, their next encounter follows Zahra's decision to visit him, and then to keep visiting him and having sex with him. Zahra's plans bring about their relationship and she remains in control of it for most of the story after this point. She can choose to see him or not, and he does not appear to have any physical or emotional control over her. The fact that she pursues him makes Zahra the "aggressor" here, in a way, although not in the conventional sense of the word. Zahra and Sami are equals in this relationship, and they are in a war zone; it is no wonder that this would be the only place Zahra develops as a sexual being (in peace her body was to her a war zone in which people waged war on her psyche and physique, likewise in war her body to her is a peace zone which she does try to use to gain peace). It is the only time she has ever been in a position of power over her body and sexual activity.

This changes only with her pregnancy, when Zahra becomes somewhat dependent upon Sami for support and protection from life as an unwed mother. The freedom she has experienced is neither limitless nor permanent, and she has come up against one of the walls. (As if to exacerbate her difficulties, Zahra's parents return just as the symptoms of her pregnancy begin to plague her.) Given the changes in Zahra since returning to Beirut, there is no way she can survive the inevitable power imbalance between her and Sami and the impending loss of control she is beginning to experience over her body and her life.

Ahmad, Zahra's brother, also experiences a kind of sexual freedom during the war, but the result is that he feels free to masturbate in front of Zahra. This is less a positive "freedom" for men than an example of the danger of repressing sexual behavior; it is only because it has been so forbidden that Ahmad finds pleasure in going to the other extreme of masturbating in his sister's presence. His doing so in spite of Zahra's embarrassment and horror makes this as much a sexual power play as an act of resistance. Ahmad feels empowered by the war and its amplification of his masculinity, and he is increasingly less inclined to consider others' feelings (or property, as his stealing demonstrates).

If, as Accad believes, true political revolution requires sexual revolution, *The Story of Zahra* provides us with a demonstration we desperately need. Ahmad's actions are a mix of misguided sexuality and misdirected resistance, both of which are informed by the patriarchal environment. And although Zahra does gain freedom during the war, it is not because of the war's success or direction, and it is clear at the end that her new freedom will not last after the war's end.

Other Novelists and the Civil War

Laylā 'Usayrān was moved by her experiences of the war to write about it in *Qal'at al-Usṭah* (*The Foreman's Fortress*, 1979). Just as *Kawābīs Bayrūt* uses a library to symbolize the heroine's intellectual life, so Laylā 'Usayrān's *Qal'at al-Usṭa*[51] uses a house to represent the very existence of its protagonist Miriam. This house is the "fortress" of the title, and Miriam leaves the reader in no doubt about her attachment to it: "I am Miriam. It never occurred to me to think to live in any place except in my house. I was one of its bricks, and its walls and roof. I felt towards it as anyone would feel toward his house, and I did not consider it a mere roof covering a little museum of my life's memories. . . . My house was like my late father . . . a unique kind of personal attachment grew up between me and the house. . . . I admit that I used to rush to it, running to its wall, kissing its bricks, telling my husband: 'I wish I could embrace it!'" ('Usayrān 1979: 16–17).

Miriam's house, like the apartment in *Kawābīs Bayrūt*, is

located between two opposing groups in the civil war. It is also not far from the Palestinian refugee camp Tall al-Za'tar. When the house was partially destroyed, Miriam talked about it as though it is a human being falling sick: "She would say that cancer had invaded the house's bricks. . . . Or she would say that the house had become crippled or maimed or paralyzed. . . . This house became a human being missing his eyes and forearms and with his legs cut off" (101). Only after the house is completely destroyed does Miriam give in, reluctantly, to her husband's insistence that they leave their homeland. This is a new direction for the house as a symbol for a female character: whereas it formerly was used as an extension of woman's existence in the private sphere—indeed, to emphasize privateness of her life—now it becomes a symbol of her national identity and even of the homeland itself.

Laylā 'Usayrān also uses the symbol of the Arab popular hero, who stands for the Palestinian guerrillas. Miriam (like the Miriam of 'Usayrān's other novel, *Khaṭṭ al-Af'ā*), takes part in the Palestinian military struggle in Jordan. The novel also covers the destruction of Tall al-Za'tar, a Palestinian refugee camp: "In those days Tall al-Za'tar was not a symbol of change or a spring in the oases of revolution. . . . it was merely a huge, neglected refugee camp" (25). When Tall al-Za'tar is sacked by the Phalangists, Miriam feels that 'Antar, too, was murdered in Lebanon before he had a chance to be martyred in Palestine.

Miriam has a complex, almost "split" personality. In the presence of outsiders she tries to project an iron personality capable of adjusting to the war situation and helping the whole neighborhood. She tries to play the role of "man of the house" in the absence of her husband, who by his own choice is staying in the other section of Beirut and with whom she is in frequent contact by phone. Miriam's sixteen-year-old son, who is staying with her, shows signs of discontent with this behavior of his mother and wishes she would not take on too much "masculine" responsibility. For example, when the overhead water storage tank gives way he insists on climbing onto the roof to inspect it instead of letting his mother do so. Surprisingly (and here the other face shows), Miriam is pleased by this. Her feeling is that "he instinctively granted me my right to femininity and realized that a man goes ahead of a woman into danger" (39). Whenever Miriam locks the door of her bedroom she goes back to being her other self: insecure, sentimental, and helpless. Again we see the phenomenon of female characters feeling like men when they develop confidence or when they assume control and responsibility over their lives and households. This is not necessarily a contradiction. The unfamiliarity alone of the image of themselves as confident or ultimately responsible for their families would be enough to cause an identity crisis for those who had not been actively seeking such developments in their lives. In Miriam's case, she is glad to have her son assume some of the responsibility, probably because she cannot reconcile the masculine image of responsibility and strength with her image of herself as a woman. The contradiction lies in the fact that many of the authors in question do not seem at all critical of the reasons that their characters feel "like men," while at the same time their writing contains statements advocating sexual equality. This weakens the feminist or progressive impact of the stories by reinforcing the beliefs that qualities such as strength and independence are "naturally" masculine.

In *Qal'at al-Usṭah* Laylā 'Usayrān carries on the practice, seen in so many of the other novels discussed here, of deemphasizing her characters' human motivations by putting them under the control of the invisible, superhuman force of destiny. Even 'Antar, the central symbol of the novel, is not free from of the power of destiny—another way in which some of the progressive impact of the novels is diminished. When a bullet barely misses the picture of 'Antar and his horse, Miriam reflects: "I looked, and was surprised by the coincidences of destiny. Destiny had chosen to save 'Antar" (51). It seems problematic that these authors promote fighting for the rights of Arabs, and of women in general, and even promote revolution (like 'Usayrān and Naṣrallāh), but place destiny in control of the outcome. It must lead at least some readers to doubt the value of fighting, of violence and bloodshed, if the outcome is unrelated to the efforts of those involved. Again, contradictory values seem to be entering the text unnoticed. As I mentioned in Chapter Three, Arab women have long called upon destiny as an explanation for their oppressed state, as a group or as individuals—an effective way to avoid the trap of blaming themselves for their own oppression. But doing so also entails giving up the hope that people can effect change for themselves by education and fighting for their rights, so that this use of destiny detracts from the "call to action" evident elsewhere in the novel.

Like Miriam, Mahā, the heroine of Emily Naṣrallāh's *Tilka al-Dhikrayāt* (*Those Memories*, 1980) also lives by herself in civil-war Beirut. Her husband has had to take a job in another Arab state after the destruction of his farm. Also, like Miriam, Mahā has to flee overseas with her husband to escape the war.

The Lebanese civil war does not lie at the core of *Tilka al-Dhikrayāt*, but serves as a background against which Mahā and her friend Ḥanān look back on their past, recalling their own personal war against family and society to achieve self-fulfillment. Ḥanān's participation in the political struggle is the manifestation of her yearning for individual freedom: "When Ḥanān marched in the demonstration, she was releasing her anxiety and personal yearning for liberation, making of them a stream which gushed into the general one" (Naṣrallāh 1980: 100). Though Mahā showed some interest in politics while she was a student, the turning point in her political awareness came after the 1967 war: "That week was an important turning point in my life and feelings, and I lost first and foremost the pleasure of enjoying life and the beautiful things which make life colorful, like love and gaiety. Even my love for my husband and children no longer had its former flavor. I became like someone who had caught a severe cold and lost his senses of smell and taste. . . . I realized that a human being cannot live in a secluded cave, and that he is linked to his large and narrow societies with ties of responsibility" (172). Perhaps one of the shortcomings of *Tilka al-Dhikrayāt* is that the writer does not dramatize this drastic change in Mahā's life through action or conflict. Naṣrallāh blurs this point by concentrating on the life story of Mahā's friend Ḥanān. She does so to such an extent that she reduces Mahā, supposedly the protagonist, to a minor character and a mere source of reflection on Ḥanān's past and present existential crisis.

Ḥanān is in Beirut during the war on a visit. She has left her husband in London, where they moved earlier to escape the war. She is moved by the destruction that took place in Beirut while she was away and comes to feel guilty at having abandoned her city during the ordeal. Ḥanān's identification of herself with the wrecked city is related to the disfiguration of her face in a car accident. Though she has recovered from the accident "her face still carried mysterious imprints from that unfortunate event, which looked like words written by fingers of time" (147).

Regarding the style of *Tilka al-Dhikrayāt*, as in her other novels, Naṣrallāh's language is highly poetic and emotionally charged. When she wishes to convey a message for which even poetical prose will not do, she shifts to straightforward poetry (201–233) just as Ghādah al-Sammān does in *Kawābīs Bayrūt* (1979: 161–164).

In her novel, *Al-Iqlā' 'Aks al-Zaman* (*Flight Against Time*, 1981),[52] Naṣrallāh again explores the civil war in Lebanon, although this time from a different angle. The main character, Radwan, and his wife, Raya, are the only members of their immediate families living in Lebanon, and *Flight Against Time* is the story of the generations of their families separated by emigration to the West (mostly the United States and Canada). This novel examines emigration from several angles and explores a wide range of emotions and experiences that accompany and follow the decision of whether or not to emigrate.

Radwan and Raya receive an invitation from their children to visit them for six months in Canada. They are overjoyed to accept, because they have never met their grandchildren and miss their own children very much. Through Radwan's eyes we experience the bewilderment of first-time travel by airplane and visiting a country whose appearance and customs are completely foreign. Throughout the novel, we are exposed to Radwan's great love for his homeland, as he dreams of his early life and muses about his current situation.

Although Radwan is very happy to learn that his friends and family members who live in Canada are prospering, and despite his fascination with the modern conveniences they all enjoy, he is still unable on some level to understand why they do not have definite plans to return to Lebanon. No matter how comfortable their lives are, Radwan is convinced that nothing could take the place of living where he feels he truly belongs, where he is counted, respected and valued in the community, where the language and culture are his own. He sees a widening gulf between him and his family, especially the grandchildren (who do not speak Arabic at all), and is afraid that the national and familial bonds will soon dissolve completely if action is not taken. Reluctant to interfere, he only gently raises these concerns to his children, who take them seriously, but can manage only rather ineffective measures to solve the problem.

As it turns out, Radwan's children have been plannig the entire time to keep their parents in North America because the civil war in Lebanon seems to worsen every day. They, along with Radwan's friends and extended family in Canada, slowly begin hinting at the idea of Radwan and Raya remaining in Canada, at least until the war subsides. Even Raya's siblings in New York, also long lost to her due to their emigration from Lebanon decades earlier, try to convince the two that they should stay.

Raya is willing to consider the offer, but Radwan is unalterably opposed. In fact, as the pressure to stay builds and Radwan becomes more and more homesick, and as he grows more alarmed at reports of the escalating violence at home, he is determined to return to his village immediately, even before the six months are over. It is not that Radwan is hostile toward those who have emigrated, or that he does not realize that there are valid reasons to do so: "Which was better: remain in one's homeland and be subjected to all kinds of humiliation and torture, even death, or emigrate to another country where one suffers from the cold and the constant yearning for one's homeland?" (Naṣrallāh 1987: 127). However, even as he intellectualizes this dilemma, there are never any doubts that he himself will never emigrate. Although he is saddened that so many others have left Lebanon, he is able to accept their decision, especially when he sees that they are happy and doing well in their new home; but he is someone who is so tied to his traditional life and his community that he would never consider leaving his country for good. To him, it would not be simply a matter of leaving a life and situation that is familiar and that he loves; it would be the equivalent of abandoning his own mother in difficult times. His strong ties to Lebanon are illustrated by the handful of soil he brings from home as a gift to his family in Canada, so that they may remember their village and the smell of the earth there.

Radwan works hard during his visit to learn about Canadian ways and view them with fascination instead of judgment. Usually he is successful; however, the one cultural difference between home and Canada that Radwan is unable to accept is that of funeral customs. When his son-in-law's father, Saleem, dies while Radwan and Raya are in Canada, he attends the funeral and is apalled by the silence during the rites. Back home, there is wailing and crying and spontaneous eulogizing, to praise the deceased and help their souls on their journey to the afterlife. Radwan knows that customs are only that, but is forced to realize that some things are so deeply embedded in his understanding of the world that they cannot (and need not) be given up simply because of a change in geographical location.[53] He knows that, even if he were able to acclimate himself to life in Canada, even if he could give up living in his village, the one thing he could not tolerate was the idea that his funeral would resemble Saleem's.

> Yet he did not want to stay and die here, however easy the death trip was. He wanted everybody to say good-bye to him with songs, in laments, with the traditional tunes that helped one approach the places of joy.
>
> He wanted to see around him all those he loved and those who loved him in that warm corner of the earth. He wanted the wailing women to surround him and the female mourner to raise her voice, enumerate his good deeds, to seek everyone's abundant tears, and remember all the dead who preceded, inviting them to accompany him on the paths of his new trip. (194)

Radwan does return to Lebanon early, even without Raya and despite great risk to his life. Ironically, he is soon granted his wish for a traditional funeral in his own village. He is a victim of the war in Lebanon: kidnapped, tortured, and killed by three attackers in disguise—exactly the kind of outcome his family and friends in North America had feared for him. But at his funeral, he is surrounded by many of those who knew him, by mourners crying loudly and praising his character, just as he wanted. This, coupled with the observation by Radwan's son and a local midwife that Radwan is smiling all through the funeral, turns the ending into one that cannot rightly be termed tragic, at least not completely. Radwan dies at home, among friends, as he wished; and even if there is not peace in his country, he is at peace with himself.

Flight Against Time is about different kinds of survival. On one hand, many people have felt forced to emigrate or face certain death or poverty in Lebanon, especially during or following times of war. Others, perhaps because of education or encouragement by emigrated relatives, have felt that there was a better way of life awaiting them and their children in the West. Political and economic reasons drive such people to emigrate. For Radwan, however, cultural survival is more important than material comfort and physical survival. The latter would be insignificant for him if he had to have them in a place where he felt separated from his roots and the community that gave him his identity. It comes down to a choice of the lesser of two evils for the characters in the novel. *Flight Against Time* portrays the lives of Radwan's family members as physically and economically secure, but we can sense throughout the story that they are cut off in many ways from Lebanon. They feel less and less that they belong to Lebanese society, but also realize that they will always feel like outsiders to some degree in Canada. And while they are successful in their businesses, they are also so busy that they are not passing down to their chidren the history and language of their ancestors, which is likely to result in identity problems for them as well. The novel also underscores another basic problem with emigration, especially during times of war, which is that it ultimately decreases the capacity of Lebanon to overcome its problems. There is promise of individual survival and economic improvement in the West for many Lebanese individuals, but at the same time, national survival depends on a community being present and willing to work toward peace. This is the dilemma.

Naṣrallāh takes this dilemma seriously, exposing the complexities of a subject that others have viewed as a simple matter of right and wrong. Although the novel portrays life outside Lebanon as cold (literally, in the case of Canada) and less desirable in many ways than life in Lebanon, Naṣrallāh clearly does not condemn those who choose to leave. Radwan recalls the story of Raya's brother, Raji, who had emigrated to New York decades earlier. He had been drafted into the military during the Ottoman period and eventually escaped because he was so mistreated and sick that he was near death. After being nursed back to health by his parents, he had to flee Lebanon because of his status as a deserter.

Another important aspect of the emigration issue involves women. Although the main character of *Flight Against Time* is a man, the problems of patriarchal rule are not left out of the novel. When Radwan recalls his first meeting with Raya, he remembers what she said about the fact that she was working alongside the men from her village. So many men had felt forced to leave Lebanon that women were beginning to take over traditionally male responsibilities. When Radwan tries to ease Raya's burden, she replies, "Working is not a shameful thing. . . . The women of our village are equal partners with men" (45).

There is also the problem of women, especially ones who were lucky enough to be well-educated, who wanted to be independent or pursue interests other than marriage and motherhood. Many women emigrated to enjoy personal freedom and career opportunities not available to them in Lebanon. Radwan's daughter, Nawal, is one example; she emigrated to Canada and now teaches at a university there, something that would have been more difficult in Lebanon. Raya, exemplifying the women who have not left, has become accustomed to keeping her opinions to herself, even though we are made aware that she is very intelligent and could be of more benefit to Radwan and others if tradition allowed. Radwan is only mildly aware of his own culture's unfair attitudes toward women: at one point, as he considers his female pigeon's ability to lure male pigeons for him to kill, he tries to construct a parallel between the pigeon and women: "He laughed in secret when he thought of Sricca's trick. He could not help comparing her with humans, for women acted much the same. He was about to curse their gender, but then he remembered Um Nabeel [Raya]. She had been beside him all her life, a model of loyalty, love and sacrifice. No, no. Her name was sacred and he did not allow himself to put her on the same level as other women" (33–34). As sensitive as Radwan is and even though he realizes that such attitudes are unfair to his wife, he is unable to reach the conclusion that they are unfair to women in general. He does reconsider what he was raised to believe about women's intellectual abilities, however, when he tries to draw another parallel between the superior cleverness of male pigeons over female pigeons and humans. He immediately thinks of his daughter, a university professor, which "caus[es] him to change many of his earlier theories about women" (35). However, he does not pursue these considerations much further in the novel.

Naṣrallāh gives us the opportunity to reexamine an issue that is far more complex than we may have realized. Although she draws attention to the need for Lebanon to retain its people, she refrains from oversimplifying the problems involved and shows us that there are valid reasons to emigrate which should not be overlooked.

Another novelist who takes an unconventional approach to the civil war is Umayyah Ḥamdān. The heroine of her novel, *al-Azraq al-Qādim Ma'a al-Rīḥ* (*The Blue [Sea] Coming with the Wind*, 1980) withdraws into her own inner world to look for personal answers rather than social or political liberation. This constitutes a throwback to the self-fulfillment novels of the earlier period. "The Arab street is full of oppressed people. The cafés are crowded with oppressed people. Our whole Arab world is oppressed, suffocated by the smell of its oil. We have lost salvation. There is nothing except personal salvation. A room with a bed and a library where I can search for myself underneath the rubble" (Ḥamdān 1980: 20).

Nadā's husband is a poor man named Amīn. Her marriage to him was an act of rebelliousness against her family, who did not want her to marry a poor man. She was attached to him because he was a revolutionary writer who dreamed of changing the existing reality of the Arab world. However, he has become discouraged because he is unable to bring this transformation about. His inactivity angers Nadā and arouses in her the desire to return to the traditional female role, rather than continuing to be the family breadwinner: "Don't you want to do something? Aren't you bored with the walls of this house? I can't bear the burden of life all by myself. I am a female. I am a woman, and you are the man. Home is my kingdom" (69). In addition to being a retreat to individualistic goals, this reversal of the roles of the sexes is an anticlimax to the struggle of women to rebel against their confinement in the home and find their places in the outside world. This is, no doubt, yet another manifestation of the internalized conflict between femininity and autonomy or responsibilty. But just as important is the fact that, when women's roles do change to include more mobility, responsibility, and freedom to work outside the home, often there is insufficient recognition by men of the need for redistribution of energy. Nadā feels that she is expected to do all the work now that she has assumed a role of responsibility and can hardly be blamed for finding the traditional setup more attractive at the moment than being overburdened and underappreciated.

Conclusion

Recent political events in the Arab world, from the loss of Palestine in 1948 to the Lebanese Civil War, have left their mark on the minds of Arab writers, including women writers. When national identity itself was in danger, personal concerns seemed either to diminish or to find expression in the collective struggle for existence. The paradox here lay in the fact that to free oneself one had to escape from self-centeredness and embrace the national "self."

The majority of novels of the later period revolve directly or indirectly around the Palestinian problem, including those novels about the civil war in Lebanon because the Palestinian element was a major factor in the conflict. Novels by Palestinian women show an overwhelming interest in the historical details of the Palestinian issue at the expense of characterization and the inner conflicts of their heroines who lose their individuality and become mere shadows of godlike male characters in the guerrilla movement. This artistic shortcoming could in part be attributed to the fact that these writers lacked experience in "the world of men" and therefore overlooked the complexity of the issues involved. Consequently, they failed to portray characters who could do justice to these issues. Saḥar Khalīfah was an exception to this trend. Her life on the occupied West Bank gave her firsthand experience of the social and political pressures and conflicts. Her novels are able to deal well with the tension between national commitment (in a society seen as antifeminist) and the pursuit of personal freedom.

The work of the Lebanese writer Laylā 'Usayrān represents a change in Arabic thinking that became widespread after the humiliating defeat of June 1967: the view that the only hope for national recovery lay in the Palestinian guerrilla movement. In fact, given their political views (evident in their writing and personal statements), 'Usayrān and al-Sammān could be called *nationalists par excellence.*[54] But here 'Usayrān was venturing into an area of which she knew very little, and the literary results were disappointing. She stripped her characters of their humanity and of credible motivation and described them as being under the control of inexorable destiny, which contradicted the apparent intended message in the novels, that freedom was worth the violent struggle. Her attempt to compensate for this shortcoming by creating symbols was also quite weak.

However, the civil war in Lebanon proved to be a very rich source of raw material for Syro-Lebanese women novelists, who found in it an echo of their own internal personal strife. Their heroines are able to go through intense experiences on their own without being overshadowed by men. The heroine of *Kawābīs*

Bayrūt removes her entire family from the war zone at the beginning of the novel (even sending her brother to jail) and faces the war alone. Other novelists have their married heroines living in the war zone while their husbands are physically (and to some extent spiritually) removed from the picture. *Qal'at al-Usṭah, Tilka al-Dhikrayāt*, and *al-Azraq al-Qādim ma'a al-Rīḥ* are all examples of this. *The Story of Zahra*, in its skillful demonstration of the connections between national issues and women's issues, takes this a step farther. Zahra, who ultimately faces the war alone, succeeds (if only temporarily) *because* she is alone, rather than in spite of this. All their heroines exhibit political consciousness and are able to interact with the ongoing war on both personal and ideological levels. Miriam Cooke goes into great detail in *War's Other Voices: Women Writers on the Lebanese Civil War*, her study of those women writers she calls the *Beirut Decentrists*. Despite some disagreements between the premises of this chapter and her work, I find Cooke's study to be a significant contribution to the fields of Arab and feminist literary theory. She identifies and explores many major themes, images, and ideas in these writers' works, shedding light on what makes these women's perspectives different from those of men (and other women, as well). For example, Cooke shows how these women set a goal of meaningful survival for their characters (and for all members of society, by extension) during a time of chaos and terror (1987a: 119). Leaving Lebanon became a nonoption for "true" citizens (143), partly via this body of literature (specifically in the work of Naṣrallāh), which effectively helped to transform women's waiting (and staying behind when men leave) into a revolutionary, meaningful, necessary act (166). Everyone involved is identified as responsible to and for the war, and non-participation in the struggle is a "crime" (100–101). Cooke also points out other contributions of these writers, such as writing about "the dailiness of war" (and moment-to-moment survival) and developing a feminist consciousness with respect to the national struggle (3).

Al-Shaykh's *The Story of Zahra* clearly fits the profile just described and excels in the accomplishments Cooke describes. "Meaningful survival," "the dailiness of war," and the necessity of facing the war with open eyes are main themes in *The Stoy of Zahra*, and al-Shaykh presents in this novel her vision of the interrelatedness of sexuality and war on both personal and political levels, a vision so well developed and presented that there is no need for the story to include "direct" commentary (e.g., "preaching") on this subject in the text.

The novels discussed in this chapter show certain distinguishing features both in their technique and in their subject matter. Whereas the heroines' concerns in the earlier periods are essentially personal, self-centered, and focused on the effects of patriarchy on the individual, the concerns of the heroines discussed in this chapter are wider in scope and linked to a broader communal existence. The authors tried to make their own experience concrete by giving it a national dimension, even placing feminist concerns within the context of the national identity crisis. As far as technique is concerned, these novelists tried to enhance their own highly personal styles through symbolism. In this, and in their attempts in general to balance the individual and the collective, they did not always succeed. When the balance was achieved, however, it contributed greatly to the success of a novel, as in the case of al-Zayyāt's *al-Bāb al-Maftūḥ*, al-Sammān's *Kawābīs Bayrūt*, and al-Shaykh's *The Story of Zahra*.

5. Conclusions

The novel is a relatively new genre in Arabic literature, one that is to some extent still in its formative years. This is especially true of those novels written by women. The development of the novel in Arabic literature has taken a somewhat different course than in the European and American literature, in part because of the highly political role of literature in Arab culture. Function is at least as important as form, which means that honing the fine art of narrative fiction writing has not been the sole aim of the writers—they have also worked to comment on and change society, and there has been much more pressure on them to accomplish this through writing than Western readers might imagine. In addition, narrative in general was, until recently, a form of literature that received little respect among the literati of the Arab world, although certain types of narrative form (*Alf Laylah wa-Laylah*, for example) enjoyed popularity among the masses but were excluded from the formal literary tradition. Arabic writers first really began producing novels in the second decade of the twentieth century, under the influence of Western literature. The lack of a formal narrative tradition in Arabic led to a lack of definite æsthetic theories, which handicapped the early Arab writers.

To understand the works discussed in this study, one must understand not only the literary tradition with which Arab women had to deal, but also the position of women in that tradition and in the culture as a whole. Arab women's writings were necessarily affected by how their society dealt with womankind as a whole (a situation not unlike that in the West). When one considers the obstacles for women writers, it seems nothing short of amazing that they have developed their own "tradition" in the short time since the Arabic novel became popular. Nawāl al-Sa'dāwī describes her view on the subject: "Because of the patriachal capitalist system which oppresses particularly women, women's physical, intellectual and psychological abilities dwindle from childhood until the end of their lives. Only a few are saved that fate. Women remain wavering between two things: their intellectual faculties and their femaleness, because they have been brought up to believe that their role in life is marriage and bearing children and not intellectual creativity" (al-Sa'dāwī 1988: 79).

Added to the difficulty girls and women have experienced in imagining themselves as writers (the first step in *becoming* writers) is the difficulty others have had believing that women could write well. Literary critics, for example, have increased the burden on women writers to prove themselves. In 1939, the distinguished Egyptian writer Ṭāhā Ḥusayn stated that, in criticizing women writers, he would treat them with far more gentleness and kindness than he would their male counterparts—though, he claimed, this was due not to any weakness in women's literature but rather to his own "care, regard and good patience" (Ḥusayn 1939: 7), as if this did not already imply some weakness. In 1987, Maḥmūd Fawzī made a study of sixty Arab women writers and, despite the late date, entitled it *Adab al-Aẓāfir al-Ṭawīlah* (*The Literature of Long Nails*).[1] Of course, this is not to say that criticism of Arab women writers has not improved over the decades, but there is still a great deal of prejudice, hardship, and restrictions with which women must contend.[2] Even if women do prove their ability, there are still the problems of interpretation of their work and the belief that women should not write at all. Ghādah al-Sammān, for example, complains that her critics confuse her with her fictional characters, "they argue with me about the conduct of the heroines of my stories to the extent that I was once afraid of being jailed because one of my heroines had committed a crime!" (al-Sammān 1980: 162). And Nawāl al-Sa'dāwī was forced by her (second) husband to choose between preserving marriage or asking for divorce if she insisted on pursuing her writing career (Badran and Cooke 1990: 399).[3]

These women writers have not merely entered the field of

literature on men's terms, but have changed it according to their own terms and ideas. To assess the influence of women writers on the portrayal of their own sex in Arabic fiction, for example, we need only to compare their images of women with the images of women created by male writers. The earliest male novelists seldom used Arab heroines—when they needed female characters, they wrote about foreign women or women belonging to ethnic minorities within the Arab world. The reason for this was that Arab women's freedom of action was so restricted by society at that point in history that interesting stories about them would hardly have been possible.[4] The one major exception was in the field of historical novels, which were set at times when social conditions were different and more active female characters could be portrayed. Later men writers, especially Najīb Maḥfūẓ, introduced two main types of female Arab characters—the "angel" (usually a mother), passive, submissive to her husband and devoted to her traditional role within the family; and the prostitute.[5] Prostitutes made good characters for novels because they were freer than other women in their dealings with the world around them. Consequently, Maḥfūẓ's prostitutes were his most convincing women characters (Mahmoud 1976: 22–23).

Women novelists greatly increased the range of female character types, which both reflected and helped bring about greater freedom for women in Arab culture. A large majority of their heroines are writers, artists, journalists, and even fighters. The great number of heroines who are journalists or writers is a result of the semi-autobiographical nature of many of the novels. Several of the novelists have readily and explicitly acknowledged that they identified with their heroines. Not surprising, then, one image that remains largely absent in terms of main characters is the positively portrayed wife and mother, as most women writers were neither of these themselves. Most of their heroines reject marriage and children, and mothers usually appear as marginal and negative characters. As explained in Chapter Three, this was also the logical result of the the writers' realizations that they lived in a culture in which marriage and children greatly restricted women's freedom, as well as a result of their association of their own mothers with traditional, oppressive ways.

Language and stylistics were other areas affected by these women. Although there was initially a lack of understanding of the appropriate use of different levels of Arabic, making convincing dialogue difficult to create, this did improve with time (especially as access to education in Arabic became more available to girls), and other aspects of their writing introduced new ways to use language in the art of fiction writing. As outlined in Chapter Three, these include the use of colloquialisms and foreign words, which was a bold rebellion in the face of the belief in the sacredness of the Arabic language as it has existed for centuries. Because this language is also a cornerstone of the patriarchal structure, such defiance is a positive act in the fight for women's freedom.[6] The stylistic devices developed by these writers are also of some importance, such as the fragmenting of novels into sections, the use of multiple points of view to narrate stories, and the "schizophrenic" presentation of the conflict between traditional and progressive values. These are some of the ways Arab women writers created space for themselves within a tradition that, by design, tended to silence them.

These novels, besides effecting changes in writing itself, also helped change the culture at large for women and for Arab people in general—despite significant problems with the novels' internal credibility. How believable the novels are depends greatly on the authors' choices of subject matter. On the whole the writers discussed in Chapter Three produced more credible novels than those discussed in Chapter Four, because the authors discussed in Chapter Three wrote about problems and issues with which they were personally familiar—although, admittedly, they had more difficulty in creating believable male characters than the following generation, also because of limited experience. Many of the novelists covered in Chapter Four wrote about war, nationalism, and international politics, subjects with which they, like most Arab women, had little direct involvement or firsthand knowledge. They did not understand the complexities of the guerrilla experience, for example, and so ended up writing largely in clichés. Two notable exceptions were Saḥar Khalīfah, who actually lived in Nablus under Israeli occupation and was able to use her firsthand knowledge to write two superior novels about life on the occupied West Bank, and Ghādah al-Sammān, whose *Bayrūt 75* and *Kawābīs Bayrūt* reflect her personal experiences living in Beirut before and during the civil war.

The novels of Arab women writers not only fostered positive

social change, but also reflected it in their text. For example, the location of most of the events in the novels discussed in Chapter Three indoors, in shut-off rooms, or in other enclosed spaces demonstrates the degree to which women's lives were restricted at the time. In *al-Ālihah al-Mamsūkhah,* for example, ʻĀyidah is constantly locked in her room and the other apartments in the apartment building are also described as locked. Most of the events in *Ayyām Maʻahu* take place within Rīm's house. The two main settings in *Laylah Wāḥidah* are a train and a hotel room. When the heroines venture out into less restricted surroundings, such as cafés, they feel uncomfortable with the unabashed stares of the men. In Chapter Four, however, we can see that the settings have changed to reflect greater mobility for women. Of course, this was partly due to necessity (war zones are some of the more "open" spaces used as settings, for example), and by no means were closed rooms a thing of the past in women's novels. But changes were occurring, and it is evident in these later works.

The emergence and development of the Arab women's novel from the middle of the nineteenth century to the present can be divided into three basic, interrelated stages. The first is characterized by the early literary productions of women writers. The difficulties encountered by the authors of these early efforts were related to the low status of women in Arab society before the 1930s. Access to education was still limited for girls, as were social and critical acceptance. Consequently, during the two following decades (1930–1950) there emerged a generation of women novelists whose novels constitute what may be called the *imitative phase.* During this period they showed little originality, and they shared both thematically and æsthetically the norms and values of men Arab novelists of the period. They based their work on the only available models—men's novels—before defining new styles and values of their own.

In the 1950s and 1960s, women novelists began to assert themselves as "beings in society" and at the same time achieved a heightened sense of individuality. Their novels no longer conformed so strictly to male-defined standards and, in fact, often rebelled against them openly. They exposed patriarchy and its effects on women as individuals and declared the right to self-determination for their heroines.

As the world around them continued to change, though, Arab

women writers suffered through agonizing social and cultural changes, a sense of disorientation in a hostile world, and a traumatic political malaise as a result of the catastrophic political events in the Middle East of the time, especially the 1967 Arab-Israeli War. These latter feelings spurred them on to seek a collective national identity as well as individual ones. During this period, Arab women writers were distinguished by the appearance of several creative and original novelists: Ba'labakkī, 'Usayrān, Naṣrallāh, al-Sa'dāwī, Khalīfah, Badr, al-Sammān, and al-Shaykh, who gave modern Arabic literature a new dimension and expressed a unique vision of both their own inner worlds and the world around them.

These stages constitute one of the most important developments in modern Arabic literature: the active contribution of Arab women writers. Although Arabic literature has a rich and extensive tradition, before this century the contributions of women to that tradition were small in number and completely marginalized, the canon consisting almost entirely of works written by men. Now, works by women are no longer unusual or banished to the margin. Women's writing has become a familiar part of Arabic literature in general—a positive reflection on the collective Arab consciousness. Along with the continued improvement in the status of women in Arab culture, I see a promising future in which Arab women writers are everywhere, part of all activities, more aware of women's movements and world politics in general, and expressing themselves through the arts of poetry, fiction, and drama (although women are still much less visible in this last genre than in others). Some (such as Salmā al-Ḥaffār al-Kuzbarī, Samīrah al-Māni', Ḥanān al-Shaykh, and Ḥamīdah Na'na') are already traveling and living outside Arab culture and writing about the conflict between East and West, for example, and this is a direct result of greater acceptance of their work and greater mobility and freedom for themselves. And the fact that novels by Arab women are now being translated into many other languages at a highly encouraging rate means that their influence and visibility will only rise and that their tradition will continue to develop and inspire new generations.

Appendices

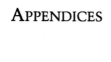

APPENDIX 1
Women's Journals in Egypt[1]

Year Founded	Place	Magazine	Founder
1892–1894	Alexandria	*Al-Fatāh* (monthly)	Hind Nawfal
1896	Cairo	**Mir'āt al-Ḥasnā'* (fortnightly)	Maryam Maẓhar[2]
1896	Cairo	*Al-Firdaws* (weekly)	Louise Ḥabbālīn
1898–1907[3]	Alexandria	*Anīs al-Jalīs*	Alexandra Avierinoh[4]
1898	Cairo	*Al-ʿĀ'ilah* (1898–1904 monthly; 1904–? weekly)	Esther Azharī Moyāl[5]
1901	Cairo	**Al-Mar'ah fī al-Islām* (fortnightly)	Ibrāhīm Ramzī
1901	Alexandria	*Shajarat al-Durr*[6] (monthly)	Saʿdiyyah Saʿd al-Dīn
1901	Cairo	*Al-Mar'ah* (monthly)	Anīsah ʿAṭallāh
1902	Alexandria	*Al-Zahrah*	Maryam Saʿd
1902	Cairo	*Al-Saʿādah* (fortnightly)	Rūjīnah ʿAwwād
1903–1930	Alexandria	*Majallat al-Sayyidāt wa-al-Banāt* (monthly)	Rose Anṭūn (Ḥaddād)
1906–1921 1924–1947	Cairo	*Fatāt al-Sharq* (monthly)	Labībah Hāshim
1907–1908	Cairo	*Al-Rayḥānah* (monthly)	Jamīlah Ḥāfiẓ
1908–1925	Cairo	*Al-Jins al-Laṭīf* (monthly)	Malakah Saʿd
1908	Cairo	*Al-Aʿmāl al-Yadawiyyah* (fortnightly)	Vasila ?
1908	Cairo	*Tarqiyat al-Mar'ah* (monthly)	Fāṭimah Niʿmat Rāshid

APPENDIX 1
Continued[1]

Year Founded	Place	Magazine	Founder
1909	Al-Manṣūrah	*Princess*	Fitnat Hānum
1909	Cairo	*Murshid al-Aṭfāl*	Anjilīnā Abū Sha'r
1912	Cairo	*Al-Jamīlah*	Fāṭimah Tawfīq
1912	Cairo	*Al-Iqdām* (daily)	Alexandra Avierinoh
1913	Cairo	*Fatāt al-Nīl*	Sārah Mīhiyyah
1920–1939	Cairo	*Al-Mar'ah al-Miṣriyyah*	Balsam 'Abd al-Malik
1921	Cairo	*Fatāt Miṣr al-Fatāh*	Emily 'Abd al-Masīḥ
1921–1939	Cairo	*Al-Nahḍah al-Nisā'iyyah* (monthly)	Labībah Aḥmad
1922	Cairo	*Shajarat al-Durr*	Munīrah Muḥammad Manṣūr
1923	Alexandria	*Tarqiyat al-Mar'ah*	Nabawiyyah Mūsā[7]
1924	Cairo	*Fatāt Miṣr*	Amālyā 'Abd al-Masīḥ
1924	Alexandria	*Al-Jihād* (daily)	Zaynab 'Abd al-Ḥamīd
1924–1926	Cairo	**Al-Mar'ah al-Jadīdah* (weekly)	'Abd al-Wahhāb al-Ṣabbāḥ
1925	Cairo	*Al-Ḥayāh al-Dunyā* (weekly)	?
1925	Al-Fayyūm	*Ādāb al-Fatāh*	Victoria Mijallī
1925	Cairo	*Al-Ḥisān* (weekly)	Farīdah Fawzī (with Faraj Sulaymān Fu'ād)
1925–(present)	Cairo	*Rūz al-Yūsuf* (weekly)	Fāṭimah al-Yūsuf[8]
1925	Cairo	*L'Egyptienne* (fortnightly)	*Al-Ittiḥād al-Nisā'i al-Miṣrī* (Sīzā Nabarāwī, editor)

APPENDIX 1
Continued[1]

Year Founded	*Place*	*Magazine*	*Founder*
1926	Cairo	*Al-Nadhīr*	Mufīdah Muḥammad Sulaymān
1925–1967	Cairo	*Al-Amal*[9] (weekly, 1925–1927; monthly, 1952–1967)	Munīrah Thābit[10]
1930 (Feb.–Oct.)	Cairo	*Fatāt Miṣr*	*Hānum Muḥammad al-ʿAsqalānī*
1930–1932		*Ummahāt al-Mustaqbal* (monthly)	Tafīdah ʿAllām
1934–1943	Cairo	*Al-Thurayyā* (weekly)	Thurayyā ʿAbdallāh Ḥassūn
1937–1940	Cairo	*Al-Mahrajān* (fortnightly)	Fāṭimah Niʿmat Rāshid
1937–1943	Cairo	*Al-Fatāh* (weekly)	Nabawiyyah Mūsā
1937	Cairo	*Al-Miṣriyyah* (fortnightly)	Al-Ittiḥād al-Nisā'i al-Miṣrī (Fāṭimah Niʿmat Rāshid, editor)
1939	Cairo	*Anā wa Anta* (monthly)	Fāṭimah Muṣṭafā Maḥmūd
1945–1957	Cairo	*Bint al-Nīl* (monthly)	Durriyyah Shafīq[11]
1945–1947	Cairo	*Fatāt al-Ghad* (monthly; fortnightly, July–Oct, 1945)	Fāṭimah Niʿmat Rāshid
1949	Cairo	*Al-Ahdāf*	Jamīlah al-ʿAlāyilī
1950–1958	Cairo	*Majallat Al-Sayyidāt al-Muslimāt*	Zaynab al-Ghazālī (al-Jubaylī)[12]
1953	Cairo	*Alwān Jadīdah* (monthly)	Saniyyah Qurāʿah

APPENDIX 1
Continued[1]

Year Founded	*Place*	*Magazine*	*Founder*
1955–(present)	Cairo	*Ḥawwā'* (monthly, 1955–1957; weekly, 1957–present)	Amīnah al-Sā'īd, editor
1989–1990	Cairo	*Nūn/Nashrat Taḍāmun al-Mar'ah al-'Arabiyyah* (quarterly)[13]	Jam'iyyat Taḍāmun *al-Mar'ah* al-'Arabiyyah (Nawāl al-Sa'dāwī, editor)

APPENDIX 2
Women's Journals in Lebanon[1]

Year Founded	*Place*	*Magazine*	*Founder*
1909	?	*Al-ʿĀlam al-Jadīd al-Nisā'i*	Ingilīnā Abū Shaqrā
1909–1912	Beirut	**Al-Ḥasnā'* (monthly)	Jurjī Niqūlā Bāz
1914	Beirut	*Fatāt Lubnān* (monthly)	Sulaymā Abī Rāshid
1918	Beirut	**Al-Fatāh*	Muḥammad al-Bāqir
1919	Zaḥlah	*Fatāt al-Waṭan* (monthly)	Mary Zammār (Faraḥ)
1919–1927	Shuwayfāt and ʿĀleh	*Al-Khidr*	ʿAfīfah Ṣaʿb
1920	Beirut	*Al-Fajr*[2] (monthly)	Najlā Abī al-Lumaʿ
1920–1926	Paris; Beirut	*Al-Ḥayāh al-Jadīdah*[4]	Ḥabbūbah Ḥaddād[3]
1921–1928	Beirut	*Al-Mar'ah al-Jadīdah* (monthly)	Jūlyā Ṭuʿmah Dimashqiyyah[5]
1923–1930	Beirut	*Minerva*[6] (monthly)	Mary Yannī (ʿAṭallāh)
1923	Beirut	*Mawrid al-Aḥdāth*	Amīnah al-Khūrī al-Maqdisī
1924	Beirut	**Fukāhāt al-Jins al-Laṭīf*	Anīs al-Khūrī
1925	Beirut	*Samīr al-Ṣighār*	Jūlyā Ṭuʿmah Dimashqiyyah
1926	Beirut	*Al-Nadīm*	Jūlyā Tuʿmah Dimashqiyyah
1932	Beirut	*Al-Jāmiʿah* (daily)	Maryam Zakkā
1938–1943	Tripoli	*Al-Mustaqbal* (weekly, 1938–1943; daily, 1943)	Alfīrā Laṭṭūf
1945–1958	Beirut	*Sawt al-Mar'ah*	Idvīk Shaybūb, editor Jāmiʿat Nisā' Lubnān
1948	Beirut	*Al-Mar'ah wa al-Fann*	Janet Ibrāhīm

APPENDIX 2
Continued

Year Founded	*Place*	*Magazine*	*Founder*
1951–1966	Beirut	**Dunyā al-Mar'ah* (monthly)	Nuwayhiḍ al-Ḥalawānī
1951	Beirut	*Al-Safīr*	Mary Lawūn al-Ḥā'ik
1955	Beirut	*Shahrazād* (weekly)	Lūrīn Shuqayr Rīḥānī
1957	Beirut	*Risālat al-Jāmi'iyyāt* (weekly)	Ittiḥād al-Jāmi'īyyāt fī Lubnān, Zāhiyah Qaddūrah, President
1960	Beirut	**Hiya* (weekly)	Ḥasan Zakariyyā al-Lādhiqī
?	Beirut	*Ṣawt al-Fatāh* (monthly)	Salwā Sa'd
1962	Beirut	*Al-Aswāq* (weekly)	Jacqueline Majdalānī
1963	Beirut	*Shahrazād* (weekly)	Fāṭimah Nā'ūrah al-Sardūk
1964	Beirut	*Dunyā al-Aḥdāth* (weekly)	Lūrīn Rīḥānī
1964	Beirut	*Al-Firdaws* (weekly)	Firdaws al-Ma'mūn
1970–present	Beirut	**Al-Ḥasnā'* (weekly)	George Shāmī
1979–present	Beirut	*Mishwār* (weekly)	Dār al-Mishwār
1981–present	Beirut	*Saḥar* (weekly)	Dār al-Ṣayyād
1981–present	Beirut	*Nisā'*	Dār al-Muthaqqaf al-'Arabī
1981–present	Beirut	*Fayrūz** (weekly)	Dār al-Ṣayyād

APPENDIX 3
Women's Journals in Iraq[1]

Year founded	Place	Magazine	Founder
1923	Baghdad	*Laylā* (monthly)	Būlīnah Ḥassūn (monthly)
1935	Baghdad	*Mulḥaq al-Nās al-Usbūʿī* (weekly)	Victoria Nuʿmān
1936	Baghdad	*Al-Mar'ah al-Ḥadīthah* (weekly)	Ḥamdiyyah al-A'rajī
1936	Baghdad	*Fatāt al-ʿIrāq* (weekly)	Ḥasībah Rājī, publisher; Sukaynah Ībrāhīm, editor
1937	Baghdad	*Fatāt al-ʿArab*	Maryam Nurmah
1946	Baghdad	*Taḥrīr al-Mar'ah* (fortnightly)	Jamʿiyyat al-Rābiṭah al-Nisā'iyyah
1946	Baghdad	*Al-Umm wa al-Ṭifl* (monthly)	Jamʿiyyat Ḥimāyat al-Aṭfāl fī al-ʿIrāq
1946	Baghdad	*Al-Riḥāb*	Aqdas ʿAbd al-Ḥamīd
1948	Baghdad	*Bint al-Rashīd* (fortnightly)	Durrah ʿAbd al-Wahhāb
1950–1954, 1958	Baghdad	*Majallat al-Itiḥād al-Nisā'ī* (monthly)	Āsyā Tawfīq Wahbī,publisher; Suhaylah Mundhir, editor
1958	Baghdad	*14 Tammūz*	Naʿīmah al-Wakīl
1958–1963	Baghdad	*Al-Mar'ah*	Rabiṭāt al-Mar'ah al-ʿIrāqiyyah

APPENDIX 3
Continued[1]

Year founded	Place	Magazine	Founder
			Naẓīrah al-Dulaymī, editor
1960	Baghdad	*Jannat al-Aṭfāl*	Salmā al-Shaykh Muḥammad al-Nā'ib
1963 (Aug.–Nov.)	Baghdad	*Risālat al-Mar'ah*	Munaẓẓamat Nisā' al-Jumhūriyyah Bushrā al-Kanafānī, editor
1968	Baghdad	*Al-Ẓarīf*	Rābiḥah al-Jumaylī
1970–present	Baghdad	*Al-Mar'ah* (monthly)	al-Ittiḥād al-ʿĀmm li-Nisā' al-Irāq Ramziyyah al-Khayrū, editor

APPENDIX 4
Women's Journals in Syria[1]

Year founded	*Place*	*Magazine*	*Founder*
1893	Aleppo	*Al-Mar'ah* (monthly)	Nadīmah al-Ṣābūnī
1910–1918	Damascus	*Al-ʿArūs* (monthly)	Mary ʿAbduh ʿAjamī
1920	Damascus	*Nūr al-Fayḥā'*	Nāẓik al-ʿĀbid
1925	Damascus	*Al-Rabīc*	Mary Ibrāhīm and ʿAbd al-Salām Ṣāliḥ
1926	Ḥimṣ	*Dawḥat al-Maymās*	Mary ʿAbduh Shaqrā
1934	Ḥamah/ Aleppo	*Al-mar'ah*	Nadīmah al-Minqārī
1947	Damascus	*Al-Mar'ah al-Jadīdah*	Nadīmah al-Minqārī and Ḥamdī Ṭarbīn
1962	?	*Al-Aḥādīth*	Daʿd al-Khānī
1968	Damascus	*Al-Mar'ah al-ʿArabiyyah* (monthly)	Al-Ittiḥād al-Nisā'ī

APPENDIX 5
Women's Journals in the Rest of the Arab World and Abroad

Country and Year Founded	*Magazine*	*Place*	*Founder*
Algeria			
1970	*Al-Jazā'riyyah*	Algiers	Al-Ittiḥād al-Waṭanī li-al-Nisā' al-Jazā'iriyyāt
Brazil			
1914	*Al-Karmah*	São Paulo	Salwā Aṭlas (Salāmah)[1]
1955	*Al-Marāḥil*[2]	São Paulo	Maryānā Da'būl Fākhūrī[3]
Chile			
1923	*Al-Sharq wa-al-Gharb*	San Diego	Labībah Ḥāshim (Māḍī) and Milḥim Khayrallāh
France			
1981–present	*Al-Sharqiyyah* (monthly)	Paris	Samīrah Khāshuqjī[4]
Jordan			
1961	*Al-Usrah*	Amman	?
Kuwait			
1965–present	*Usratī* (weekly)	Kuwait	Ghunaymah Fahd al-Marzūq[5]
1993	*Samrah**[6]	Kuwait	Dār al-Waṭan Li-al-Ṣiḥāfah wa-al-Ṭibā'ah wa-al-Nashr
Libya			
1965	*Al-Bayt**[6] (fortnightly)	Tripoli	Al-Mu'assasah al-'Āmmah li-al-Ṣiḥāfah
Morocco			
1965	*Al-Shurūq*	?	Khannāthah Bannūnah[7]
Palestine			
1991	*Shu'ūn al-Mar'ah*	Nablus	Jam'iyyat Shu'ūn al-Mar'ah (Saḥar Khalīfah, editor)

APPENDIX 5
Continued

Country and Year Founded	*Magazine*	*Place*	*Founder*
Qatar			
1978–present	*Al-Jawharah** (monthly)	Doha	Mu'assasat al-ʿAhd li-al-Ṣiḥāfah wa-al-Nashr
Saudi Arabia			
1981–present	*Sayyidatī** (weekly)	Jedda	Al-Sharikah al-Saʿūdiyyah li-al-Abḥāth wa-al-Taswīq
Sudan			
?	*Al-Usrah al-Saʿīdah*	?	Jamʿiyyat Tanẓīm al-Usrah al-Sūdāniyyah
?	*Al-Mar'ah al-jadīdah*	Khartoum	Dār al-Ayyām li-al-Ṭibāʿah wā-al-Nashr
Tunisia			
1954	*Al-Ilhām*	Tunis	Fāṭimah ʿAlī
1960	*Ṣawt al-Mar'ah*	Tunis	Zakiyyah Qāwī
1961	*Al-Mar'ah* (mothly)	Tunis	Al-Ittiḥād al-Qawmī al-Nisā'i bi-Tūnis
United Arab Emirates 1979	*Zahrat al-Khalīj* (weekly)	Abu Dhabi	Mu'assasat al-Ittiḥād li-al-Ṣiḥāfah wa-al-Nashr
1992–present	*Hiya* (monthly)	Abu Dhabi	Mu'assasat al-Waḥdah
USA			
1912	*Al-ʿĀlam al-Jadīd*	New York	ʿAfīah Karam
Yemen			
1941	*Fatāt al-Jazīrah** (weekly)	Aden	Muḥammad ʿAlī Luqmān

APPENDIX 6: NOVELS WRITTEN BY ARAB WOMEN (1887–1993)

'Abbāsī, Nihād Tawfīq. *Dārat Matālūn*. [Damascus?]: Maṭba'at 'Ikrimah, [1987].

———. *Ḥiṣn al-Mawtā*. [Damascus?], [1988].[1]

'Abdallāh, Ibtisām. *Fajr Nahār Waḥshī*. Baghdad: Maṭba'at al-Adīb, 1985.

———. *Mamarr ilā al-Layl*. Baghdad: Dār al-Shu'ūn al-Thaqāfiyyah al-'Āmmah, 1988.

'Abdallāh, Ṣūfī. *La'nat al-Jasad*. Cairo: Mu'assasat Kāmil Mahdī li-al-Nashr, 1958. 2nd ed., Beirut: Al-Maktab al-Tijārī li-al-Tibā'ah wa-al-Nashr, 1958.

———. *Dumū' al-Tawbah*. Beirut: Al-Maktab al-Tijārī li-al-Ṭibā'ah wa-al-Nashr, 1958. 2nd ed., Cairo: Al-Sharikah al-'Arabiyyah li-al-Ṭibā'ah wa-al-Nashr, 1959. 3rd ed., Cairo: Dār al-Hilāl, 1970.

———. *Nifirtītī*. Cairo: Dār al-Hilāl, 1952.

———. *'Āṣifah fī Qalb*. Cairo: Dār al-Hilāl, 1961. 2nd ed., Cairo: Dār al-Ma'ārif, 1973.

———. *Mu'jizat al-Nīl*. Cairo: Al-Hay'ah al-Miṣriyyah al-'Āmmah li-al-Kitāb, 1964.

'Abd al-Dāyim, Kawthar. *Ḥubb wa-Ẓilāl*. Cairo, n.d.

'Abd al-Hādī, Hadiyyah. *Ghāliyah*. Amman: Ibn Rushd, 1988.

'Abd al-Ḥusayn, Laṭīfah. *Māta al-Nahār*. Baghdad, 1966.

'Abd al-Karīm, Sawsan. *Imra'ah fī al-Ẓill*. Cairo: Mu'assasat Rūz al-Yūsuf, 1979.

———. *Al-Jannah al-Mafqūdah*. Cairo: Mu'assasat Rūz al-Yūsuf, 1981.

'Abd al-Majīd, Nādiyah. *Abū al-'Alā' Yaktub min al-Ākhirah*. Cairo: Dār al-Thaqāfah al-Jadīdah, 1979.

'Abd al-Malik, Rajā'. *Lā Kibriyā' fī al-Ḥubb*. Cairo: Dār Nāfi' li-al-Ṭibā'ah, 1980.

'Abd al-Qādir, Laylā. *Nādiyah*, vol. 1. Baghdad: Maṭba'at al-Mutanabbī, 1958.

'Abd al-Qādir, Zakiyyah. *Amīnah*. Tunis: Dār al-Qalam, 1983.

'Abd al-Raḥmān, 'Ā'ishah. *Sayyid al-'Izbah: Qiṣṣat Imra'ah Khāṭi'ah*. Cairo: Maṭba'at al-Ma'ārif, 1944.

———. *Raj'at Fir'awn*. Cairo: Dār al-Ma'ārif, [1949].

———. *Al-A'māl al-Kāmilah: Wuqūd al-Ghaḍab*, vol. 2. Cairo: Al-Hay'ah al-Miṣriyyah al-'Āmmah li-al-Kitāb, 1986. (Consists of two novels: *Sayyid al-'Izbah: Qiṣṣat Imra'ah Khāṭi'ah, Raj'at Fir'awn*).

Abū al-Nūr, 'A'īshah. *Al-Imḍā' Salwā*. Cairo: Maṭbū'āt 'A'īshah Abū al-Nūr, 1985.

———. *Musāfir fī Damī*. Cairo: Dār al-Hanā li-al-Ṭibā'ah, 1981.

Abū Zayd, Laylā. *'Ām al-Fīl*. Rabat: Maṭba'at al-Ma'ārif al-Jadīdah, 1983. 2nd ed., Beirut: Dār al-Āfāq al-Jadīdah, 1987. Translated into English by Barbara Parmenter as *Year of the Elephant: A Moroccan Woman's Journey Toward Independence* (Austin: University of Texas Press). The name of the author was transliterated as Leila Abouzeid.

———. *Rujū' ilā al-Ṭufūlah*. Rabat: Maṭba'at al-Najāḥ al-Jadīdah, 1993.

Aḥmad, 'A'īshah Zāhir. *Basmah min Buḥayrāt al-Dumū'*. Jedda: Al-Nādī al-Adabī al-Thaqāfī, 1980.

Aḥmad, Farīdah. *Akhāf 'Alayka Minnī*. Cairo: Qiṭā' al-Ādāb bi-al-Markaz al-Qawmī li-al-funūn wa-al-Ādāb. 1982.

ʻAkkāwī, Andrée Ṭurbayh. *Ẓam'ānah fī Wāḥah*. Beirut: Maktabat al-Ma'ārif, 1961.

al-ʻAlāyilī, Jamīlah. *Al-Ṭā'ir al-Ḥā'ir*. Mīt Ghamr (Egypt): Maṭbaʻat Wādī al-Nīl, 1935.

———. *Al-Amīrah*. Cairo: Maṭbaʻat Saʻd, 1939.

———. *Al-Rāʻiyah*. Alexandria: Al-Maṭbaʻah al-Malakiyyah al-Fārūqiyyah, 1946.

———. *Bayna Abawayn*. Cairo: Al-Majlis al-Aʻlā li-al-Thaqāfah wa-al-Funūn, 1981.

———. *Al-Nāsik*. Cairo: Al-Hay'ah al-Miṣriyyah al-ʻĀmmah li-al-Kitāb, 1982.

———. *Anā wa-Waladī*. Cairo: Dār al-Ta'līf, 1982.

al-ʻAlī, Fāṭimah. *Wujūh fī al-Ziḥām*. Kuwait: Maṭbaʻat Ḥukūmat al-Kuwayt, [1971].

ʻAlī, Samīḥah. *Riḥlatī*. Beirut, 1981.

ʻĀlim, Rajā' Muḥammad. *4—Ṣifr*. Jedda: Al-Nādī al-Adabī al-Thaqāfī, 1987. 2nd ed., Beirut: Dār al-Ādāb, 1987.

ʻĀmir, Madīḥah. *Ayna Yadhhab al-Ḥubb*. Cairo: Al-Hay'ah al-Miṣriyyah al-ʻĀmmah li-al-Kitāb, 1987.

ʻAnānī, ʻAhd Muḥammad. *Dhikrayāt Imra'ah*. Jedda, 1407 A.H.

al-ʻArūsī, ʻAfāf (al-Muḥāmiyah). *Al-Muḥāwalah al-Ūlā*. Cairo: Al-Dār al-Qawmiyyah li-al-Ṭibāʻah wa-al-Nashr, 1966.

al-Asʻad, Suʻād. *Ghadan Sa-Aʻūd*. Beirut: Al-Mu'assasah al-ʻArabiyyah li-al-Dirāsāt wa-al-Nashr, 1983.

ʻĀshūr, Raḍwā. *Ḥajar Dāfi'*. Cairo: Dār al-Mustaqbal al-ʻArabī, 1985.

———. *Khadījah wa-Sawsan*. Cairo: Dār al-Hilāl, 1989.

———. *Sirāj*. Cairo: Dār al-Hilāl, 1992.

al-ʻAssāl, Najībah. *Al-Ḥā'iṭ al-Rābiʻ*. Cairo: Al-Hay'ah al-Miṣriyyah al-ʻĀmmah li-al-Kitāb, 1990.

ʻAṭiyyah, Farīdah Yūsuf. *Bayna ʻArshayn*. Tripoli (Lebanon): Maṭbaʻat al-Najāḥ, 1912.

al-Aṭrash, Laylā. *Wa-Tushriq Gharban*. Beirut: Al-Mu'assasah al-'Arabiyyah li-al-Dirāsāt wa-al-Nashr, 1988.

———. *Imra'ah li-al-Fuṣūl al-Khamsah*. Beirut: Al-Mu'assasah al-'Arabiyyah li-al-Dirāsāt wa-al-Nashr, 1988.

'Aṭṭār, Mājidah. See Murād, Mājidah 'Aṭṭār.

al-'Aṭṭār, Samar. *Līnā: Lawḥat Fatāh Dimashqiyyah*. Beirut: Dār al-Āfāq al-Jadīdah, 1982.

———. *Al-Bayt fī Sāḥat 'Arnūs*. Merrylands (Australia): Charbel Baini, 1988.

al-'Awf, Mu'minah Bashīr. *Madd bilā Jazr*. Beirut: Dār al-Manār, 1992.

Badr, Liana. See Badr, Liyānah.

Badr, Liyanah. *Shurfah 'alā al-Fākhānī*. Damascus: Dā'irat al-I'lām wa-al-Thaqafah, 1983. 2nd ed., Dā'irat al-Thaqafah al-Jadidah and Dā'irat al-Thaqafah, Munaẓẓamat al-Taḥrīr al-Filasṭīniyyah, 1989. Translated into English by Peter Clark with Christopher Tingley as *A Balcony over the Fakihani: Three Novellas* (New York: Interlink Books, 1993).

———. *'Ayn al-Mir'āh*. Casablanca: Dār Tūqbāl li-al-Nashr, 1991.

———. *Būṣlah min ajl 'Abbād al-Shams*. Beirut: Dār Ibn Rushd, 1979. 2nd ed., Cairo: Dār al-Thaqāfah al-Jadīdah, 1989. 3rd ed., Beirut: Dār al-Ādāb, 1993. Translated into English by Catherine Cobham as *A Compass for the Sunflower* (London: Women's Press, 1989).

al-Badrī, Hālah. *Al-Sibāḥah fī qumqum 'alā Qā' al-Muḥīṭ*. Cairo: Dār al-Ghad li-al-Nashr wa-al-Di'āyah wa-al-I'lān, 1988.

Bāghaffār, Hind Ṣāliḥ. *Al-Barā'ah al-Mafqūdah*. Beirut: Maṭābi' al-Miṣrī, 1972.

———. *Ribāṭ al-Walāyā*. Jedda, 1977.

Baghdādī, Ṣafiyyah. *Al-Ḍiyā' wa-al-Nūr Yabhar*. Jedda: Maṭābi' Samar, 1986.

Bakr, Salwā. *Maqām 'Aṭiyyah*. Cairo; Paris: Dār al-Fikr li-al-Dirāsāt wa-al-Nashr wa-al-Tawzī', 1986.

———. *Al-'Arabah al-Dhahabiyyah Lā Taṣ'ad ilā al-Shams*. Cairo: Sīnā li-al-Nashr, 1991.

———. *Waṣf al-Bulbul*. Cairo: Sīnā li-al-Nashr, 1992.

Ba'labakkī, Laylā. *Anā Aḥyā*. Beirut: Dār Majallat Shi'r, 1958. 2nd ed., 1963. 3rd ed., Beirut: Al-Maktab al-Tijārī li-al-Ṭibā'ah wa-al-Tawzī' wa-al-Nashr, 1964. Translated to French by Michel Barbot as *Je vis!* (Paris: Seuil, 1961).

———. *Al-Ālihah al-Mamsūkhah*. Beirut: Al-Maktab al-Tijāri li-al-Ṭibā'ah wa-al-Nashr, 1960. 2nd ed., 1965.

al-Bannā, Salwā. *'Arūs Khalfa al-Baḥr*. Dār al-Ittiḥād, 1972.

———. *Al-Ātī min al-Masāfāt*. Beirut: Al-Ittiḥād al-'Āmm li-al-Kuttāb wa-al-Ṣuḥufiyyīn al-Filasṭīniyyīn, 1977.

———. *Maṭar fī Ṣabāḥ Dāfi'*. Beirut: Dār al-Ḥaqā'iq, 1979.

Banūnah, Khanāthah. *Al-Ghad wa-al-Ghaḍab*. Casablanca: Dār Al-Nashr al-Maghribiyyah, 1980. 2nd ed., Baghdad: Dār al-Shu'ūn al-Thaqāfiyyah al-'Āmmah, [1987].

Bāqī, 'Āyidah. *Shajarat al-Yāsamīn*. Kuwait: Dhāt al-Salāsil, 1989.

Barakah, Iqbāl. *Wa-li-Naẓall ilā al-Abad Aṣdiqā'*. Cairo: Dār al-'Ilm li-al-Ṭibā'ah, 1971.

———. *Al-Fajr li-Awwal Marrah*. Beirut: Dār al-Quds, 1975.

———. *Al-Ṣayd fī Baḥr al-Awhām*. Cairo: Mu'assasat Rūz al-Yūsif, 1979. 2nd ed., Cairo: Al-Hay'ah al-Miṣriyyah al-'Āmmah li-al-Kitāb, 1984.

———. *Laylā wa-al-Majhūl*. Cairo, 1980. 2nd ed., 1981.

———. *Timsāḥ al-Buḥayrah*. Cairo: Maktabat Gharīb, 1983.

———. *Kullamā 'Āda al-Rabī'*. Cairo: Mu'assasat Akhbār al-Yawm, 1985.

Barakāt, Hudā. *Ḥajar al-Ḍaḥk*. London: Riad El-Rayyes Books, 1990.

———. *Ahl al-Hawā*. Beirut: Dār al-Nahār li-al-Nashr, 1993.

Barakāt, Najwā. *Al-Muḥawwil*. Beirut: Manshūrāt Mukhtārāt, 1986.

al-Baṣṣām, Sājidah. *Al-Ḥayāh al-Bā'isah*. Baghdad: Maṭba'at al-Najāḥ, 1953.

al-Bāti', Fathiyyah Maḥmūd. *Mudhakkirāt Zā'ifah.* Beirut: Dār al-Najāḥ, 1975. 2nd ed., Algiers: Al-Mu'assasah al-Waṭaniyyah li-al-Nashr wa-al-Tawzī', 1984. 3rd ed., Algiers: Al-Mu'assasah al-Waṭaniyyah li-al-Nashr wa-al-Tawzī', 1990.

———. *Wadā' ma'a al-Aṣīl.* Algiers: Al-Mu'assasah al-Waṭaniyyah li-al-Nashr wa-al-Tawzī', 1980.

———. *Nabtah fī al-Ṣaḥrā'.* Algiers: Al-Mu'assasah al-Waṭaniyyah li-al-Nashr wa-al-Tawzī', 1981.

al-Bāz, Nu'm. *Ummat al-Razzāq.* Cairo: Akhbār al-Yawm, 1988.

Bint Baradā. Also see al-Ḥasanī, Amīrah.

Bint al-Hudā. See al-Ṣadr, Āminah Ḥaydar.

Bint al-Shāṭi'. See 'Abd al-Raḥmān, 'Ā'ishah.

al-Būhī, Fawziyyah Labīb. *Al-Shahīd al-'Aẓīm.* Cairo: Al-Majlis al-A'lā li-Ri'āyit al-Funūn wa-al-Ādāb wa-al-'Ulūm al-Ijtimā'iyyah, 1980.

Bulayl, Zaynab. *Al-Ikhtiyār.* N.p., n.d.

al-Bustānī, Alice Buṭrus. *Ṣā'ibah.* Beirut: Al-Maṭba'ah al-Adabiyyah, 1891.

Būẓū, Mājidah. *Sajīnah.* Latakia (Syria): Dār al-Majd, 1991.

Dāghir, Kātrīn Ma'lūf. *Kifāḥ Imra'ah.* Beirut, n.d.

———. *Ghuṣṣah fī al-Qalb.* Beirut: Maktabat al-Ḥayāh, 1965.

Dālātī, 'Alyā' Hūjū. *Khada'atnī al-Mir'āh.* Beirut: Manshūrāt 'Ashtarūt, 1969.

———. *Tā'ihah fī Bayrūt.* Beirut: Mu'assasat al-Ma'ārif, 1973. 2nd ed., 1984.

Dārī, Sanā'. *Ajrās al-Raḥīl al-Bayḍā'.* Beirut: Dār al-Ḥadāthah, 1993.

al-Darrājī, Samīrah. *Risālat Ghufrān.* Mosul (Iraq): Maṭba'at al-Zawrā' al-Ḥadīthah, 1969.

Dhiyāb, Fāṭimah. *Fī Qiṭār al-Māḍī.* Acre (Israel): Dār al-Qabas, 1973.

al-Dulaymī, Luṭfiyyah. *Man Yarith al-Firdwas.* Cairo: Al-Hay'ah al-Miṣriyyah al-'Āmmah li-al-Kitāb, 1987.

al-Durdunjī, Hiyām Ramzī. *Ilā al-Liqā' fī Yāfā.* Tripoli (Libya): Al-Maṭba'ah al-Lībiyyah, 1970. Amman: Dār al-Kitāb al-Dhahabī li-al-Nashr wa-al-Tawzī', n.d.

———. *Wadā'an Yā Ams.* Tripoli (Libya): Dār Maktabat al-Fikr, [1972].

———. *Al-Nakhlah wa-al-I'ṣār.* N.p., 1974.

Fahmī, Sihām. *Ḥubbuka Nār.* Cairo: Idārat al-Kitāb al-'Arabī, 1960.

———. *Lan Abkī Yā Ummī.* Cairo: Idārat al-Kitāb al-'Arabī, 1960.

al-Faqīh, Jamīlah. *'Alā Darb al-Sa'ādah.* Damascus: Maṭba'at al-Ḥijāz, 1977.

Faraj, Sanā' Muḥammad. *Ṣabāh fī al-Mukhayyam.* Cairo: al-Hay'ah al-Miṣriyyah al-'Āmmah li-al-Kitāb, 1991.

Fatḥī, Ḥanīfah. *Al-Rajul al-Ladhī Uḥibbuh.* Cairo: Dār al-Qalam, 1962.

Fawwāz, Zaynab. *Ḥusn al-'Awāqib aw Ghādah al-Zāhirah.* Cairo: Maṭba'at Hindiyyah, 1899. (Republished in Fawwāz, Fawziyyah (ed.) *Ḥusn al-'Awāqib, al-Hawā wa-al-Wafā'.* Beirut: Al-Majlis al-Thaqāfī li-Lubnān al-Janūbī, 1984.)

———. *Al-Malik Qūrūsh aw Malik al-Furs.* Cairo: Maṭba'at Hindiyyah, 1905.

Fu'ād, Munā Aḥmad. *Laylat Ṣarakha fīhā al-'Aql.* Qalyūb (Egypt): Maṭābi' al-Ahrām al-Tijāriyyah, 1990.

Fu'ād, Sakīnah. See Fu'ād, Sukaynah.

Fu'ād, Sukaynah. *Tarwīḍ al-Rajul.* Cairo: Akhbār al-Yawm, 1986.

Ghurayyib, Rose. *Al-Mu'annā al-Kabīr.* Beirut: Al-Ḥikmah, 1971.

———. *Riwāq al-Lablāb.* Beirut: Dār al-Fikr al-Lubnānī, 1971.

al-Ghurayyib, Terese. *Mā Warā' al-Ladhdhah.* Beirut: Maṭba'at al-Ghurayyib, [1970].

———. *Liqā' fī al-Jāmi'ah.* Beirut, 1982.

Hādī, Laylā. *Abī wa-'Iṣābat al-Ghajar.* Qaylūb (Egypt): Maṭābi' al-Ahrām al-Tijāriyyah, 1991.

al-Ḥaffār, Nādirah Barakāt. *Al-Ghurūb al-Akhīr.* Damascus: Ittiḥād al-Kuttāb al-'Arab, 1984.

———. *Imra'ah fī 'Uyūn al-Nās.* Damascus: Dār Ṭlās, 1988.

———. *Al-Hāwiyah.* Damascus: Ittiḥād al-Kuttāb al-'Arab, 1990.

al-Ḥaffār, Salmā. See al-Kuzbarī, Salmā al-Ḥaffār.

Ḥajj 'Ubayd, Malak. See 'Ubayd, Malak Ḥajj.

Ḥalīm, Asmā. *Ḥikāyat 'Abd al-Raḥmān*. Cairo: Dār al-Thaqāfah al-Jadīdah, 1977.

———. *Mu'jizat al-Qadar*. Cairo: Dār al-Thaqāfah al-Jadīdah, 1985.

———. *Ikhwān al-Ṣafā wa-Khillān al-Wafā*. Cairo: Dār al-Sha'b, 1990.

Ḥamdāh, Umayyah, *Wa-Antaẓir*. Beirut: Al-Maktabah al-'Aṣriyyah, n.d.

———. *Majnūn Shānyah*. Beirut Dār al-Ittiḥād, 1972.

———. *Al-Azraq al-Qādim ma'a al-Rīḥ*. Beirut Dār al-Āfāq al-Jadīdah, 1980.

Ḥamdī, Nājiyah Aḥmad. *4 Nisā'*. Baghdad: Maṭba'at al-Ma'ārif, 1955.

Ḥammād, 'Ā'ishah. *Imra'ah min 'Aṣrinā*. Jedda: Dār al-Mahrajān li-al-I'lān wa-al-'Alāqāt al-'Āmmah, 1990.

Ḥammūdah, Laylā. *Nabḍat Kā'in Ḥayy*. Cairo: Al-Hay'ah al-Miṣriyyah al-'Āmmah li-al-Kitāb, 1991.

Ḥamzah, Jīlān. *Qalb Bilā Qinā'*. Cairo: Dār al-Fikr al-'Arabī, 1960.

———. *Al-Lu'bah wa-al-Ḥaqīqah*. Cairo: Dār al-Fikr al-'Arabī, [1970].

———. *Qadar al-Ākharīn*. Cairo: Al-Hay'ah al-Miṣriyyah al-'Āmmah, [1974].

———. *Al-Zawjah al-Hāribah*. Cairo: Mu'assasat Akhbār al-Yawm, 1974.

———. *Zawj bi-al-Mazād*. Cairo: Mu'assasat Dār al-Sha'b, 1976.

———. *Musāfirah ma'a al-Jirāḥ*. Mu'assasat Akhbār al-Yawm, 1974.

———. *Al-Ḥabībah*. Cairo: Mu'assasat Akhbār al-Yawm, 1988.

———. *Ulamlim 'Iqdī bi-Ghaḍab*. Beirut: Dār al-Kitāb al-'Arabī, n.d.

Ḥannā, Hudā. *Ṣawt al-Malājī'*. Damascus: Maṭba'at Dimashq, n.d.

Ḥannūsh, Georgette. *Dhahaba Ba'īdan*. Beirut: Dār al-Andalus, [1961].

———. *'Ashīqat Ḥabībī*. Beirut: Al-Maktab al-Tijārī, [1965].

al-Ḥasanī, Amīrah. *Al-Azāhīr al-Ḥumr*. Damascus: Maṭābi' Ibn Khaldūn, 1962.

———. *Al-Qalb al-Dhahabī*. Damascus: Dār Ibn Zaydūn, 1963.

———. *Lahīb*. Damascus: Maṭābi' Ibn Khaldūn, 1962. (Published under the pseudonym Bint Baradā.)

———. *Al-Qalb al-Dhahabī*. Damascus: Maṭābi' Ibn Khaldūn, 1963. (Published under the pseudonym Bint Baradā.)

al-Ḥasanī, Mayy. *Wa-Inḥasara al-Ẓalām*. Beirut: Dār al-Balāghah, 1987.

Hāshim, 'Aliyyah. *Ṣirā' min al-A'māq*. Cairo, 1967.

Hāshim, Labībah. *Qalb al-Rajul*. Cairo: Maṭba'at al-Ma'ārif, 1904.

al-Ḥifnāwī, Hālah. *Al-'Abīr al-Ghāmiḍ*. Cairo: Mu'assasat Fann al-Ṭibā'ah, n.d.

———. *Hal Akhla' Thawbī*. 2nd ed., Beirut: Al-Maktab al-Tijārī li-al-Ṭibā'ah wa-al-Nashr wa-al-Tawzī', 1969. 3rd ed., 1979.

———. *Al-Rajul Yuḥibb Marratayn*. Cairo: Mu'assasat Rūz al-Yūsuf, 1977.

———. *Wasīṭ al-Jinn: Dustūr Yā Asyādī*. 2nd ed., Riyadh: Al-Sharikah al-Sharqiyyah al-'Ālamiyyah, 1982.

al-Ḥūmānī, Balqīs. *Ḥayy al-Lujā*. Beirut: Manshūrāt Ḥamad, 1969.

Ḥusayn, Bahījah. *Rā'iḥat al-Laḥāẓāt*. Cairo: Dār al-Thaqāfah al-Jadīdah, 1992.

al-Ḥusaynī, Suhaylah. *Antum Yā Man Hunāka*. Beirut: Dār al-Ittiḥād li-al-Ṭibā'ah wa-al-Nashr, 1972.

Ibrāshī, 'Azīzah. *Iṣlāḥ*. 3rd ed., Beirut: Dār al-Fikr li-al-Ṭibā'ah wa-al-Nashr wa-al-Tawzī', n.d. (The first two editions were published with the name of Ni'mat Dhuhnī as a coauthor. The latter admitted that she did not participate in writing the novel; she only paid for the expenses of publishing the book.)

'Īd, Nāhid, *Ashjān*. Cairo: Al-Mu'assasah al-Miṣriyyah al-'Āmmah li-al-Ta'līf wa-al-Anbā' wa-al-Nashr, [1965].

Idilbī, Ilfah. *Dimashq Yā Basmat al-Ḥuzn*. Damascus: Wizārat al-Thaqāfah wa-al-Irshād al-Qawmī, 1980. 2nd ed., Damascus: Dār Ṭlās, [1989].

———. *Ḥikāyat Jaddī*. Damascus: Dār Ṭlās, 1991.

Idrīs, Buthaynah. *Usrah fī al-Ẓalām*. Al-Zarqā' (Jordan), 1984.

'Indānī, Ṣabīḥah. *I'tirā'āt Imra'ah Fāshilah*. Beirut: Dār al-Rā'id, 1983.

al-Iryānī, Ramziyyah 'Abbās. *Ḍaḥiyyat al-Jasha'*. Taizz (Yemen): Al-Dār al-Ḥadīthah li-al-Ṭibā'ah wa-al-Nashr, n.d.

Isḥīq, Malīḥah. *Rā'i'ah*. Cairo, 1952.

Jabbūr, Munā. *Fatāh Tāfihah*. Beirut: Dār Maktabat al-Ḥayāh, n.d.

———. *Al-Ghirbān wa-al-Musūḥ al-Bayḍā'*. Beirut: Dār Maktabat al-Ḥayāh, 1966.

Jād, Hudā. *al-Washm al-Akhḍar*. Cairo: Al-Dār al-Qawmiyyah li-al-Ṭibā'ah wa-al-Nashr, 1965.

———. *'Aynāka Khaḍrāwān*. Cairo: Dār al-Hilāl, 1974.

———. *Jarīmah lam Turtakab*. Cairo: Dār al-Hilāl, 1976.

———. *Bayna Shāṭi'ayn*. Cairo: Al-Hay'ah al-Miṣriyyah al-'Āmmah li-al-Kitāb, 1986.

Jalāṣī, Zahrah. *In'ikāsāt 'inda al-Zāwiyah*. Tunis: Al-Dār al-Tūnisiyyah li-al-Nashr, 1990.

Juwaydī, Imtithāl. *Shjarat al-Ṣubayr*. Beirut: Dār al-Ṭalī'ah, 1972.

———. *Hijrat al-'Abīr*. N.p., 1972.

Kaḥlūnī, Samīḥah. *'Adhdhabūnī*. [Beirut], n.d.

———. *Imra'ah Ḍā'i'ah*, 2nd ed. Beirut: Al-Dār al-'Ālamiyyah li-al-Kitāb, 1972.

———. *I'tirāfāt Qāḍin*. Beirut: Dār al-Jīl, 1972.

Kan'ān, Evelyne Ḥittī. *Bayḍā'*. Beirut: Dār Majallat Shi'r, 1963.

Karam, 'Afīfah. *Badī'ah wa-Fu'ād*. New York: Maṭba'at Jarīdat al-Hudā, 1906.

———. *Fāṭimah al-Badawiyyah*. New York: Maṭba'at Jarīdat al-Hudā, n.d.

———. *Ghādat 'Amshīt*. New York: Maṭba'at Jarīdat al-Hudā, [1914].

Kāyid, Rawḍah, *Risālah fī al-Ṭarīq*. Damascus: Maṭba'at Dār al-Ḥayāh, 1973.

Khafājī, Umaymah. *Ṭāwūs fī al-Ẓalām*. Cairo: Maṭba'at Qāṣid Khayr, 1980.

Khalīfah, Saḥar. *Lam Na'ud Jawārī Lakum*. Cairo: Dār al-Ma'ārif, 1974. 2nd ed., Beirut: Dār al-Ādāb, 1988.

———. *Al-Ṣubbār*. Jerusalem: Galileo, 1976; Damascus: Dār al-Jalīl, 1984. Translated into English by Trevor LeGassick and Elizabeth Fernea as *Wild Thorns* (London: Al-Saqi Books, 1985). 2nd ed., New York: Interlink, 1991.

———. *'Abbād al-Shams*. Beirut: Munaẓẓamat al-Taḥrīr al-Filasṭīniyyah, 1980. Jerusalem: Dār al-Kātib, 1980; Damascus: Dār al-Jalīl, 1984.

———. *Mudhakkirāt Imra'ah ghayr Wāqi'iyyah*. Beirut: Dār al-Ādāb, 1986.

———. *Bāb al-Sāḥah*. Beirut: Dār al-Ādāb, 1990.

al-Khānī, Malīḥah. *Khaṭawāt fī al-Ḍabāb*. Damascus: Ittiḥād al-Kuttāb al-'Arab, 1984.

Kharīs, Samīḥah 'Alī. *al-Madd*. Amman: Dār al-Shurūq li-al-Nashr wa-al-Tawzī', 1989.

al-Kharsānī, Ghādah. *Lu'bat al-Qadar*. Cairo: Maṭābi' al-Ahrām al-Tijāriyyah, [1974].

———. *Ḥarīq fī al-Jannah*. Cairo: Maṭābi' al-Ahrām al-Tijāriyyah, 1976.

Khāshuqjī, Samīrah [Samīrah Bint al-Jazīrah al-'Arabiyyah]. *Dhikrayāt Dāmi'ah*. Alexandria: Dār Lūrān li-al-Ṭibā'ah wa-al-Nashr, 1962. 4th ed., Beirut: Al-Maktab al-Tijārī, 1967. Another edition, Beirut: Manshūrāt Zuhayr Ba'labakkī, 1979.

———. *Barīq 'Aynayka*. Beirut: Al-Maktab al-Tijārī li-al-Ṭibā'ah wa-al-Nashr wa-al-Tawzi', 1963. 2nd. ed., 1967.

———. *Wadda'tu Āmālī*. Beirut: Manshūrāt Zuhayr Ba'labakkī, 1971.

———. *Warā' al-Ḍabāb*. Beirut: Manshūrāt Zuhayr Ba'labakkī, 1971.

———. *Qaṭarāt min al-Dumū'*. 2nd ed., Beirut: al-Maktab al-Tijārī, 1973.

———. *Ma'tam al-Wurūd*. Beirut: Manshūrāt Zuhayr Ba'labakkī, 1973. 2nd ed., Beirut: Dār al-Āfāq al-Jadīdah, 1977.

———. *Wādī al-Dumū'*. Beirut: Manshūrāt Zuhayr Ba'labakkī, 1979.

Khayrī, Wafiyyah. *Al-Ḥayāh fī Khaṭar*. Cairo: Dār al-Ḥurriyyah, 1983.

al-Khūrī, Colette Suhayl. *Ayyām Ma'ahu*. Beirut: Al-Maktab al-Tijārī li-al-Ṭibā'ah wa-al-Nashr wa-al-Tawzī', 1959. 2nd ed., April, 1960. 3rd. ed., October, 1960. 4th ed., 1967.

———. *Laylah Wāḥidah*. Beirut: Al-Maktab al-Tijārī li-al-Ṭibā'ah wa-al-Nashr wa-al-Tawzī', 1961.

———. *Kiyān*. Beirut: Manshūrāt Zuhayr Ba'labakkī, 1968.

———. *Al-Marḥalah al-Murrah*. Beirut: Manshūrāt Zuhayr Ba'labakkī, 1969. 2nd ed., Damascus: Al-Maṭba'ah al-Ta'āwuniyyah, 1970.

———. *Dimashq Baytī al-Kabīr*. Beirut: Manshūrāt Zuhayr Ba'labakkī, 1970.

———. *Wa-Marra Ṣayf*. Damascus: Ittiḥād al-Kuttāb al-'Arab, 1975.

———. *Da'wah ilā al-Qunayṭirah*. Damascus: Ittiḥād al-Kuttāb al-'Arab, 1976.

———. *Ayyām ma'a al-Ayyām*. Damascus: Maṭba'at al-Kātib al-'Arabī, 1980.

al-Khush, Umaymah. *Zahrat al-Lūtūs*. Damascus: Dār al-Mustaqbal, 1993.

Kīlānī, Nādiyah. *Ḥubb Lam Ya*'rifhu al-Bashar. Cairo: Maktab al-Nīl li-al-Ṭibā'ah wa-al-Nashr, 1987.

Kīlānī, Qamar. *Ayyām Maghribiyyah*. Beirut: Dār al-Kātib al-'Arabī, 1965.

———. *Bustān al-Karaz*. Damascus: Ittiḥād al-Kuttāb al-'Arab, 1977.

———. *Al-Hawdaj*. Damascus: Ittiḥād al-Kuttāb al-'Arab, 1979.

———. *Ṭā'ir al-Nār*. Damascus: Ittiḥād al-Kuttāb al-'Arab, 1980.

———. *Al-Darrāsah*. Damascus: Dār al-Ba'th, 1980.

———. *Al-Ashbāḥ*. Tripoli (Libya): Al-Mansha'ah al-Sha'biyyah li-al-Nashr wa-al-Tawzī' wa-al-I'lān, 1981.

———. *Ḥubb wa-Ḥarb*. Damascus: Maṭābi' al-Kuttāb al-'Arab, 1982.

———. *Al-Dawwāmah*. Damascus: Wizārat al-Thaqāfah wa-al-Irshād al-Qawmī, 1983.

———. *Ḥulm 'alā Judrān al-Sujūn*. Tripoli (Libya): Al-Dār al-'Arabiyyah li-al-Kitāb, 1985.

al-Kuzbarī, Salmā al-Ḥaffār. *Yawmiyyāt Hālah*. Beirut: Dār al-'Ilm li-al-Malāyīn, 1950.

———. *'Aynān min Ishbīliyah*. Beirut: Dār al-Kātib al-'Arabī, 1965.

———. *Al-Burtuqāl al-Murr*. Beirut: Dār al-Nahār li-al-Nashr, 1974.

———. *'Anbar wa-Ramād*. Beirut: Dār Bayrūt, 1970 (autobiography).

Mahrān, Fawziyyah. *Bayt al-Ṭālibāt*. Cairo: Mu'assasat Rūz al-Yūsuf, 1961.

———. *Jiyād al-Baḥr*. Cairo: Mu'assasat Rūz al-Yūsuf, 1987.

———. *Ḥājiz Amwāj*. Cairo: Mu'assasat Rūz al-Yūsuf, 1988.

Mahrān, Rashīdah. *'Ashrat Ayyām Takfī*. Alexandria: Maṭba'at al-Jīzah, 1980.

———. *Al-Ḥubb wa-al-Nūr*. Beirut: Manshūrāt Filasṭīn al-Muḥtallah, 1981.

al-Makkāwī, Jīhān. *Mashrū' Zawāj*. [Cairo]: Dār Usāmah li-al-Ṭibā'ah, n.d.

Mamdūḥ, 'Āliyah. *Laylā wa-al-Dhi'b*. Baghdad: Dār al-Rāṣid, 1981.

———. *Ḥabbāt al-Naftālīn*. Cairo: Al-Dār al-Miṣriyyah al-'Āmmah li-al-Kitāb, 1986.

al-Māni', Samīrah. *Al-Sābiqūn wa-al-Lāḥiqūn*. Beirut: Dār al-'Awdah, 1972.

———. *Ḥabl al-Surrah*. London: Al-Ightirāb al-Adabī, 1990.

Mansī, Su'ād. *Al-Dimā'*. [Cairo]: Maṭba'at al-Ḥurriyyah, 1942.

Manṣūr, Ilhām. *Ilā Hibā: Sīrah Ūlā*. Dār al-Fārābī, 1991.

al-Masālmah, In'ām. *Al-Ḥubb wa-al-Waḥl*. Damascus: Dār al-Thaqāfah, [1963].

Mash'al, Miriam. *Fatāt al-Nakbah*. Amman: Maṭba'at al-Sha'b, 1957.

al-Mashārī, Ṣabīḥah Khālid. *Qaswat al-Aqdār*. Kuwait, 1959.

al-Maslūl, Ẓāfirah. *Wa-Māta Khawfī*, Riyadh: Iṣdārāt al-Nakhīl, 1990.

al-Ma'ūshī, Ibrīzā. *Hal Aghfir Lahu*. Beirut: Dār al-Thaqāfah, 1962.

———. *Anā min al-Sharq*. Beirut: Dār Lubnān li-al-Ṭibā'ah wa-al-Nashr, 1966.

———. *Al-Thalj al-Aswad*. [Beirut], 1980.

———. *Wa-Yabqā al-Su'āl*. Beirut, n.d.

al-Mu'ashshir, Īmān Salāmah. *Dam'ah Mughaṭṭāh bi-Ibtisāmah*. Amman: Dār al-Nahḍah, 1986.

———. *Al-Munḥarif*. Amman: Dār al-Nahḍah, 1986.

Mu'awwaḍ, Īmān. *Barā'ah Qatalathā al-Mukhaddirāt*. Jedda: Tihāmah, 1410 A.H. (novella, 66pp.).

Muḥammad, Ḥarbiyyah. *Jarīmat Rajul*. Baghdad: Maṭba'at al-Jāmi'ah, 1953.

———. *Man al-Jānī*. Baghdad: Maṭba'at al-Jāmi'ah, 1954.

Mukhtār, Āmāl. *Nakhb al-Ḥayāh*. Beirut: Dār al-Ādāb, 1993.

Murād, Mājidah 'Aṭṭār. *Murāhiqah*. Beirut: Dār al-Rawā'i', 1966.

———. *Fī al-Bad' Kāna al-Ḥubb*. Beirut: Dār al-Āfāq al-Jadīdah, 1978.

Mustaghānmī, Aḥlām. *Dhākirat al-Jasad*. Beirut: Dār al-Ādāb, 1993.

al-Na''ās, Murḍiyah. *Shay' min al-Dif'*. Tripoli (Libya): Maktabat al-Fikr, 1982.

al-Nālūtī, 'Arūsiyyah. *Marātīj*. Tunis: Dār Sarās li-al-Nashr, 1985.

Na'na', Ḥamīdah. *Al-Waṭan fī al-'Aynayn*. Beirut: Dār al-Ādāb, 1979.

———. *Man Yajru' 'alā al-Shawq*. Beirut: Dār al-Ādāb, 1989.

al-Nashawātī, Khadījah al-Jarrāḥ and Hiyām Nuwaylātī. *Arṣifat al-Sa'am*. [Damascus]: Maṭba'at al-Amn al-Qawmī, 1970.

Naṣrallāh, Emily. *Ṭuyūr Aylūl*. Beirut: Al-Mu'assasah al-Ahliyyah li-al-Ṭibā'ah wa-al-Nashr, 1962. 2nd ed., 1967. 3rd ed., 1977. 4th. ed., 1979. 6th ed., 1986.

———. *Shajarat al-Diflā*. Beirut: Maṭba'at al-Najwā, 1968. 2nd ed., 1975. 3rd ed., 1979. 4th ed., 1981.

———. *Al-Bāhirah*. Beirut: Mu'assasat Nawfal, 1977. 2nd ed., 1980. 3rd ed., 1985.

———. *Al-Rahīnah*. Beirut: Mu'assasat Nawfal, 1974. 2nd ed., 1980. 3rd ed., 1986.

———. *Tilka al-Dhikrayāt*. Beirut: Mu'assasat Nawfal, 1980. 2nd ed., 1986.

———. *Al-Iqlā' 'Aksa al-Zaman*. Beirut: Mu'assasat Nawfal, 1980. 2nd ed., 1984. Translated to English by Issa J. Boullata as *Flight Against Time* (Charlottetown: Ragweed Press, 1987).

Ni'mah, Rajā'. *Ṭaraf al-Khayṭ*. Dār al-Āfāq al-Jadīdah, 1983.

———. *Kānat al-Mudun Mulawwanah*. Cairo: Dār al-Hilāl, 1990.

Nuwayhiḍ, Jamāl Salīm. *Ghurbah fī al-Waṭan*. Amman: Dār al-Jalīl and al-Dār al-'Arabiyyah, 1988.

———. *'Urs fī al-Jannah*. Beirut, 1992.

———. *Mawkib al-Shuhadā'*. Beirut, n.d.

Nuwaylātī, Hiyām. *Fī al-Layl*. Damascus: Maṭba'at al-Ṣarkhah, [1959].

Nuwaylātī, Hiyām, and Khadījah al-Jarrāḥ al-Nashawātī. *Arṣifat al-Sa'am*. [Damascus]: Maṭba'at al-Amn al-Qawmī, 1970.

al-Qalamāwī, Suhayr. *Aḥādīth Jaddatī*. Cairo: Lajnat al-Ta'lif wa-al-Tarjamah wa-al-Nashr, 1935. 2nd ed., Cairo: al-Dār al-Qawmiyyah li-al-Ṭibā'ah wa-al-Nashr, 1959. 3rd ed., Cairo: Dār al-Hilāl, 1978.

Qaṣabjī, Ḍiyā'. *Imra'ah fī Dā'irat al-Khawf*. Tripoli (Libya): Al-Mansha'ah al-'Āmmah li-al-Nashr wa-al-Tawzī', 1985.

al-Qazwīnī, Khawlah. *Jirāḥāt fī al-Zaman al-Radī'*. Beirut: Dār al-Ṣaḥwah, 1993.

Qumayrah, Sulaymā. *Qabla al-Awān*. [Beirut], n.d.

al-Rāfi'ī, Salwā. *Jāsūs Raghma Anfih*. Cairo: Dār al-Ḥurriyyah, 1982.

———. *Kārithah Taḥta al-Tashṭib*. Cairo: Dār al-Ḥurriyyah, 1983.

———. *Raṣāṣah fī al-'Aql*. Cairo: Al-Hay'ah al-Miṣriyyah al-'Āmmah li-al-Kitāb, 1988.

al-Raḥabānī, Salwā. *Wajhī al-Ākhar*. Beirut: Dār al-Fikr al-Lubnānī, 1992.

Rashīd, Fawziyyah. *Taḥawwulāt al-Fāris al-Gharīb fī al-Bilād al-'Āribah*. Beirut: Al-Mu'assasah al-'Arabiyyah li-al-Dirāsāt wa-al-Nashr, 1990.

———. *Al-Ḥiṣār*. Cairo: Sīnā li-al-Nashr, 1993.

al-Rashīd, Hudā 'Abd al-Muḥsin al-Ṣāliḥ. *Ghadan Sa-Yakūn al-Khamīs*. Cairo: Mu'assasat Rūz al-Yūsuf, 1977.

———. *'Abath*. Cairo: Maṭābi' Rūz al-Yūsuf, 1980.

al-Rāwī, Fāṭimah. *Ghadan Tatabaddal al-Arḍ*. N.p.: Al-Maṭābi' al-'Āmmah, 1967.

al-Rāwī, Sharqiyyah. *'Aynāk 'Alamatānī*. Kuwait: Maṭābi' Dār al-Siyāsah, 1972.

Riḍa, Jalīlah. *Taḥta Shajarat al-Jummayz*. Cairo: Al-Majlis al-A'lā li-al-Thaqāfah; Al-Hay'ah al-'Āmmah li-Shu'ūn al-Maṭabi' al-Amīriyyah, 1980.

al-Rubay'ī, Mā'idah. *Jannat al-Ḥubb*. Najaf (Irāq): Maṭba'at al-Gharrī al-Ḥadīthah, 1968.

———. *Ḥubb wa-Ghufrān*. Najaf: Maṭba'at al-Najaf, 1971.

Rustum, Durriyyah. *Thalāth Ṣadīqāt*. Cairo: Dār al-Qāhirah li-al-Ṭibā'ah, 1958.

———. *Ahlan Bi-al-'Adhāb*. Cairo: Maktabat al-Anglo al-Miṣriyyah, 1964.

———. *Sayyidat al-Matā'ib*. Cairo: Maktabat al-Anglo al-Miṣriyyah, 1965.

———. *Qiṣṣat Raqṣat al-Thu'bān*. Cairo: Maktabat al-Anglo al-Miṣriyyah, 1967.

———. *Wa-Ikhtafā al-Shayṭān*. Cairo: Maktabat al-Anglo al-Miṣriyyah, 1970.

———. *Al-Mudibb al-Akbar wa-Daḥ wa-Baḥ*. Cairo: Maktabat al-Anglo al-Miṣriyyah, 1972.

———. *Qiṣṣat Arānib Bayt Salāmāt*. Cairo: Dār al-Sha'b, 1972.

———. *Fī al-Ẓill*. Cairo: Dār al-Sha'b, 1972.

———. *Al-Ba'ḍ Yufaḍḍilūnahā 'Āriyah*. Cairo: Dār al-Sha'b, 1972.

al-Sa'dāwī, Nawāl. *Mudhakkirāt Ṭabībah*. Cairo: Dār al-Ma'ārif, 1965. 2nd ed., 1985. Translated into English by Catherine Cobham as *Memoirs of a Woman Doctor* (London: Saqi Books, 1988; San Francisco: City Light Books, 1989).

———. *Al-Ghā'ib*. Cairo: Al-Hay'ah al-Miṣriyyah al-'Āmmah li-al-Kitāb, 1970. 2nd ed., Cairo: Maktabat Madbūlī, n.d. Translated into English by Shirley Eber as *Searching* (London and Atlantic Highlands, N.J.: Zed Books, 1991).

———. *Ughniyat al-Aṭfāl al-Dā'iriyyah*. 2nd ed., Cairo: Maktabat Madbūlī, 1983. (1st ed., 1978.) Translated into English by Marilyn Booth as *The Circling Song* (London and Atlantic Highlands, N.J.: Zed Books, 1989).

———. *Mawt al-Rajul al-Waḥīd ʿalā al-Arḍ*. Beirut: Dār al-Ādāb, 1976. 2nd ed., Cairo: Maktabat Madbūlī, 1978. 3rd ed., 1983. Translated into English by Sherif Hetata as *God Dies by the Nile* (London: Zed Books, 1985).

———. *Imraʾah ʿinda Nuqṭat al-Ṣifr*. Beirut: Dār al-Ādāb, 1977. 2nd ed., 1979. Translated into English by Sherif Hetata as *Woman at Point Zero* (London: Zed Books, 1983).

———. *Imraʾatān fī Imraʾah*. 4th ed., Cairo: Maktabat Madbūlī, 1983. Translated into English by Osman Nusairi and Jana Gough as *Two Women in One* (London: Al-Saqi Books, 1985; Seattle: Seal Press, 1986).

———. *Suqūṭ al-Imām*. Cairo: Dār al-Mustaqbal al-ʿArabī, 1988. Translated into English by Sherif Hetata as *The Fall of the Imam* (London: Methuen, 1988).

———. *Jannāt wa-Iblīs*. Beirut: Dār al-Ādāb, 1992.

———. *Al-Ḥubb fī Zamān al-Nafṭ*. Cairo: Maktabat Madbūlī, 1993.

al-Saddānī, Nūriyyah Ṣāliḥ. *Al-Ḥirmān*. Kuwait: Muʾassasat al-Saddānī, 1972.

———. *Wāḥat al-ʿUbūr*. Kuwait: Muʾassasat al-Saddānī, 1972.

Ṣādiq, Zaynab. *Yawm baʿda Yawm*. Cairo: Dār al-Hilāl, [1969].

———. *Lā Tasriq al-Aḥlām*. Cairo: Muʾassasat Rūz al-Yūsuf, 1978.

al-Ṣadr, Āminah Ḥaydar. *Al-Khālah al-Ḍāʾiʿah*. 2nd ed., Beirut: Dār al-Taʿāruf li-al-Maṭbūʿāt, 1978 (1st ed., 1970).

———. *Al-Faḍīlah Tantaṣir*. Najaf (Iraq), 1964. (Published under the initials A. Ḥ.). 2nd ed., Baghdad: Maṭbaʿat Offset al-Mīnāʾ, 1977. 3rd ed., n.p.: Al-Dār al-Islāmiyyah al-Kubrā, 1978.

———. *Imraʾatān wa-Rajul*. Baghdad: Dār al-Anwār li-al-Maṭbūʿāt, 1977.

———. *Laytanī Kuntu Aʿlam*. Beirut: Dār al-Taʿāruf li-al-Maṭbūʿāt, 1977.

———. *Liqāʾ fī al-Mustashfā*. 3rd ed., Beirut: Dār al-Taʿāruf li-al-Maṭbūʿāt, 1980.

———. *Al-Bāḥithah ʿan al-Ḥaqīqah*. 2nd ed., Beirut: Dār al-Taʿāruf li-al-Maṭbūʿāt, 1980.

———. *Al-Majmū'ah al-Qaṣaṣiyyah al-Kāmilah*, 3 vols. Beirut: Dār al-Ta'āruf, n.d.

al-Sa'dūn, Nāṣirah. *Law Dāmat al-Afyā'*. Baghdad: Maṭba'at Bābil, 1986.

———. *Dhākirat al-Madārāt*. Baghdad: Bayt Sīn li-al-Kutub, 1989.

al-Sa'īd, Amīnah. *Al-Jāmiḥah*. Cairo: Dār al-Ma'ārif, 1950. 2nd ed., 1960.

———. *Ākhir al-Ṭarīq*. Cairo: Dār al-Hilāl, 1959.

Sakākīnī, Widād. *Bayna al-Nīl wa-al-Nakhīl*. Cairo: Dār al-Fikr al-'Arabī, [1947].

———. *Arwā Bint al-Khuṭūb*. Dār al-Fikr al-'Arabī, [1950].

———. *Al-Ḥubb al-Muḥarram*. Dār al-Fikr al-'Arabī, [1952].

Salāmah, Fawziyyah. *Shāri' Wahdān*. Cairo: Dār Akhbār al-Yawm, 1992.

Salāmah, Hind. *Alḥān Ḍā'i'ah*. Beirut: Maṭābi' al-Istiqlāl, n.d.

———. *Zallat al-Jasad*. Beirut, n.d.

———. *Al-Dumā al-Mutaḥarrikah*. Beirut: Al-Maktab al-Tijārī li-al-Ṭibā'ah wa-al-Nashr wa-al-Tawzī', 1968.

Ṣāliḥ, Sālimah. *Al-Nuhūḍ*. Beirut: Maṭba'at al-Ra'y al-Jadīd, 1975.

Salmān, Nūr. *Fa-Ḍaḥikat*. Beirut: Dār al-Nashr li-al-Jāmi'iyyīn, 1961.

Samārah, Nuhā. See Ṣaydānī, Nuhā Samārah.

Samīr, Wiṣāl. *Zaynah*. Damascus: Al-Ahālī li-al-Ṭibā'ah wa-al-Nashr wa-al-Tawzī', 1992.

al-Sammān, Dīmah Jum'ah. *Al-Ḍil' al-Mafqūd*. Jerusalem: Dār al-'Awdah, 1992.

———. *Al-Qāfilah*. Kafr Qar' (Israel): Dār al-Hudā, 1992.

al-Sammān, Ghādah. *Bayrūt 75*. Beirut: Dār al-Ādāb, 1975. 2nd ed., Beirut: Manshūrāt Ghādah al-Sammān, 1977. 3rd ed., 1979. 4th ed., 1983. 5th ed., 1987.

———. *Kawābīs Bayrūt*. Dār al-Ādāb, 1976. 2nd ed., Beirut: Manshūrāt Ghādah al-Sammān, 1977. 3rd ed., 1979.

———. *Laylat al-Milyār*. Beirut: Manshūrāt Ghādah al-Sammān, 1985. 2nd ed., 1991.

Ṣanbar, Īlyānā. *Banafsajah li-al-'Ā'id*. Beirut: Dār Majallat Shi'r, [1965].

Ṣawālḥah, Julia. *Salwā*. Amman: Maṭba'at al-Tawfīq, 1979.

———. *Al-Nashamī*. Amman: Jam'iyat 'Ummāl al-Maṭba'ah al-Ta'āwuniyyah, 1979.

———. *Hal Tarji'īn*. Amman, 1979.

———. *Al-Ḥaqq al-Ḍā'i'*. Amman: Maṭba''at Shāhīn, 1984.

———. *Nār wa-Ramād*. Amman, 1984.

Ṣawāyā, Labībah Mīkhā'il. *Ḥasnā' Sālūnīk*. Damascus: Al-Maṭba'ah al-Baṭriyarkiyyah al-Urthūdhuksiyyah, 1909.

Ṣaydāwī, Nuhā Samārah. *Fī Madīnat al-Mustanqa'*. Beirut: Manshūrāt Zuhayr Ba'labakkī, 1983.

Sha'bān, Nādiyā Ẓāfir. *Raḥalat al-Ṭiflah*. Beirut: Dār al-Āfāq al-Jadīdah, 1991.

Shalash, Su'ād. *Lā Taqul Lī Wadā'an*. Cairo: Al-Hay'ah al-Miṣriyyah al-'Āmmah li-al-Kitāb, 1990.

Shallāsh, Salmā. *Al-Ḥubb qabla al-Khubz Aḥyānan*. Cairo: Mu'assasat Rūz al-Yūsuf, 1975.

———. *Bint al-Safīr*. Cairo: Mu'assasat Rūz al-Yūsuf, [1979].

Sharābī, Fawziyyah. *Uqtulū Waladī*. Cairo: Mu'assasat al-Khānjī, 1967.

Shaṭṭā, Amal Muḥammad, *Ghadan Ansā*. Jedda: Tihāmah, 1980.

———. *La 'Āsha Qalbī*. Jedda: Sharikat al-Madīnah li-al-Ṭibā'ah wa-al-Nashr, 1990.

Al-Shaykh, Ḥanān. *Intiḥar Rajul Mayyit*. Beirut: Dār al-Nahār li-al-Nashr, 1970.

———. *Faras al-Shayṭān*. Beirut: Dār al-Nahār li-al-Nashr, 1976.

———. *Ḥikāyat Zahrah*. Beirut, 1980. 2nd ed., Beirut: Dār al-Ādāb, 1989. Translated into English as *The Story of Zahra* (New York; London: Quartet Books, 1989). Translated into French as *Histoire de Zahra* (Paris: Lattès, 1980).

———. *Misk al-Ghazāl*. Beirut: Dār al-Ādāb, 1988. Translated into English by Catherine Cobham as *Women of Sand and Myrrh* (London: Quartet Books, 1989).

———. *Barīd Bayrūt*. Cairo: Dār al-Hilāl, 1992.

Shaykh al-'Arab, Thurayyā. *Lastu Dumyah Yā Ummī*. Baghdad: Wizārat al-Thaqāfah wa-al-I'lām, 1981.

Ṣidqī, Jādhibiyyah. *Ummunā al-Arḍ*. Cairo: Al-Dār al-Qawmiyyah li-al-Ṭibā'ah wa-al-Nashr, [1966]. (Republished under the tiltle *Ṣābirīn*, Cairo: Mu'assasat Akhbār al-Yawm, 1985. Cairo: Dār al-Kitāb al-Miṣrī al-Lubnānī, 1987).

———. *Anta Qāsin*. Cairo: Al-Dār al-Qawmiyyah li-al-Ṭibā'ah wa-al-Nashr, 1966. 2nd ed., Cairo: Dār al-Kitāb al-Miṣrī al-Lubnānī, 1987.

———. *Al-Baladī Yu'kal*. Cairo: Mu'assasat Akhbār al-Yawm, 1976.

al-Tabāyiniyyah, Natīlah. *Al-Mawt wa-al-Ba'th wa-al-Ḥadīth*. Tunis: Al-Dār al-Tūnisiyyah li-al-Nashr, 1990.

al-Ṭabbā', Masarrah Nu'mān. *Qulūb min Zujāj*. Cairo: Maktabat al-Anglo al-Miṣriyyah, 1971.

al-Tābi'ī, 'Alyā'. *Zahrat al-Ṣubbār*. Tunis, 1993.

Taqiyy al-Dīn, Nawāl. *Shams Khalfa al-Ḍabāb*. Damascus: Maṭba'at al-Kātib al-'Arabī, 1985.

Taymūr, 'Ā'ishah. *Natā'ij al-Aḥwāl fī al-Aqwāl wa-al-Af'āl*. Cairo: Al-Maṭba'ah al-Bahiyyah, 1887/88.

al-Taymūriyyah, 'Ā'ishah. See Taymūr, 'Ā'ishah.

Thābit, Kātyā. *Wa-Lā 'Azā' li-al-Sayyidāt*. Cairo: Dār al-Hilāl, 1979.

Ṭurbayh, Andrée. See 'Akkāwī, Andrée Ṭurbayh.

'Ubayd, Malak Ḥājj. *Al-Khurūj min Dā'irat al-Intiẓār*. Damascus: Ittiḥād al-Kuttāb al-'Arab, 1983.

Umm 'Iṣām. See al-Nashawātī, Khadījah al-Jarrāḥ.

'Usayrān, Laylā. *Lan Namūt Ghadan*. Beirut: Dār al-Ṭalī'ah, 1962.

———. *Al-Ḥiwār al-Akhras*. Beirut: Dār al-'Awdah, 1963.

———. *Al-Madīnah al-Fārighah*. Beirut: Maktabat al-Ḥayāh, 1966.

———. *'Aṣāfīr al-Fajr*. Beirut: Dār al-Ṭalī'ah, 1968.

———. *Khaṭṭ al-Af'ā*. Beirut: Dār al-Fatḥ, 1972.

———. *Qal'at al-Usṭah*. Beirut: Dār al-Nahār li-al-Nashr, 1979.

———. *Jisr al-Ḥajar*. Beirut: Dār al-'Awdah, 1982.

———. *Al-Istirāḥah*. Beirut: Sharikat al-Maṭbī'āt li-al-Tawzī' wa-al-Nashr, 1989.

al-'Uthmān, Laylā. *Al-Mar'ah wa-al-Qiṭṭah*. Beirut: Al-Mu'assasah al-'Arabiyyah li-al-Dirāsāt wa-al-Nashr, 1985.

———. *Wasmiyyah Takhruj min al-Baḥr*. Al-Ṣafāh (Kuwait): Sharikat al-Rubay'ān li-al-Nashr wa-al-Tawzī', 1986.

Wanīsī, Zuhūr. *Min Yawmiyyāt Mudarrisah Ḥurrah*. Algiers: Al-Sharikah al-Waṭaniyyah li-al-Nashr wa-al-Tawzī', 1979.

al-Yāfī, Laylā. *Thulūj Taḥta al-Shams*. Cairo: Dār al-Fikr al-'Arabī, [1961].

al-Yamāmah. See 'Abbāsī, Nihād Tawfīq.

Ya'qūb, Lucy. *Amjad Yawm fī al-Tārīkh*. Cairo: Al-Hay'ah al-Miṣriyyah al-'Āmmah li-al-Kitāb, 1988.

———. *Awtār al-Shajan*. Cairo: Al-Hay'ah al-Miṣriyyah al-'Āmmah li-al-Kitāb, 1988.

Yārid, Nāzik Sābā. *Nuqṭat al-Dā'irah*. Beirut: Dār al-Fikr al-Lubnānī, n.d.

———. *Al-Ṣadā al-Makhnūq*. Beirut: Mu'assasat Nawfal, 1986.

———. *Kāna al-Ams Ghadan*. Beirut: Mu'assasat Nawfal, 1988.

———. *Taqāsīm 'alā Watar Ḍā'i'*. Beirut: Mu'assasat Nawfal, 1992.

Yūsuf, Fawziyyah Jirjis. *Ayyām min Nār*. Cairo: Al-Maṭba'ah al-'Arabiyyah al-Ḥadīthah, 1972.

al-Zāmilī, Su'ād 'Alī. *Khafāyā al-Qadar*. Najaf: Maṭba'at al-Gharrī al-Ḥadīthah, 1970.

al-Zayyāt, 'Ināyāt. *Al-Ḥubb wa-al-Ṣamt*. Cairo: Dār al-Kātib al-'Arabī li-al-Ṭibā'ah wa-al-Nashr, 1967.

al-Zayyāt, Laṭīfah. *Al-Bāb al-Maftūḥ*. Maktabat al-Anglo al-Miṣriyyah, 1960. 2nd ed., Cairo: Al-Hay'ah al-Miṣriyyah al-'Āmmah li-al-Kitāb, 1989.

———. *Ḥamlat Taftīsh Awrāq Shakhṣiyyah*. Cairo: Dār al-Hilāl, 1992.

Zuhayr, Su'ād. *I'tirāfāt Imra'ah Mustarjilah*. Cairo: Al-Kitāb al-Dhahabī, 1961.

Notes

Introduction

1. An important pioneering study written on Arab women's fiction was that of Evelyne Accad, *Veil of Shame: The Role of Women in the Contemporary Fiction of North Africa and the Arab World* (1978). In this book Accad discusses women's novels in both Arabic and French in the Arab East as well in North Africa. Miriam Cooke's *War's Other Voices: Women Writers on the Lebanese Civil War* (1987a) also includes works written in French.

Chapter One. Women in Arab Society: A Historical Perspective

1. This is true despite certain aspects of Muḥammad's life story, which were matrilineal or matrilocal. His mother Amīnah spent her life with her family and his father used to pay her visits from time to time. Muḥammad lived with his mother until her death. After that he joined his paternal grandfather ʿAbd al-Muṭṭalib (Riencourt 1974: 188).

2. See also Watt (1956: 381).

3. The *Kitāb al-Aghānī* describes the custom whereby a woman could dismiss her husband: "women in the *Jahīliyyah*, or some of them, had the right to dismiss their husbands, and the form of the dismissal was this. If they lived in a tent, they turned it round, so that if the door had faced east, it now faced west, and when the man saw this he knew that he was dismissed and did not enter" (Watt 1956: 381; Riencourt 1974: 187). See also Dīb (1980: 114).

4. Some of these women are mentioned in Ibn Hishām (n.d.: 87, 88, 89, 160) (see also ʻA. Ḥasan 1970: 123). Even after the Prophet died, a woman known by the name of Sajāḥ from the tribe of Tamīm claimed to be a prophetess and led an army assembled from several Arab tribes to fight the Muslims (al-Ḥūfī 1963: 437–438)..

5. When the Prophet took power in Mecca, he had to struggle to obtain the key to the Kaʻbah from yet another woman, Umm ʻUthmān ibn Ṭalḥah (ʻA. Ḥasan 1970: 123).

6. For the different types of marriage in the *Jāhiliyyah*, see W. R. Smith (n.d.). An excellent source of data on marriage in pre-Muslim Arabia is the eighth volume of *Kitāb al-Ṭabaqāt al-Kubrā*, by Ibn Saʻd, a compilation of biographical information about the first women converts (Ibn Saʻd 1958). Stern (1939) presents a systematic analysis of Ibn Saʻd's book. See also Mernissi (1976: 29–41).

7. "And if ye fear that ye will not deal fairly by the orphans, marry of the women, who seem good to you, two or three or four; and if ye fear that ye cannot to justice (to so many), then one (only). . . . Thus it is more likely that ye will not do justice (regarding the treatment of more than one wife at the same time)" (Pickthall n.d.: 3).

8. This *fatwā* was published in *al-Manār* of ʻAbduh's disciple Muḥammad Rashīd Riḍā (1927). The text is also published in ʻAmārah (1972: vol. 2, 90–95; 1975: 111–118).

9. Bint al-Shāṭi' (a pseudonym of ʻĀ'ishah ʻAbd al-Raḥmān), in her *al-Qur'ān wa-al-Tafsīr al-ʻAṣrī* (ʻAbd al-Raḥmān 1970: 257–258), attacked Muṣṭafā Maḥmūd's interpretation of Sūrah 4:3, in which he argued for restricting marriage to one wife, since it is impossible to achieve absolute justice among multiple wives. Bint al-Shāṭi' did not believe that God would contradict himself by allowing up to four wives and then maintaining that one wife was all he meant (Smith 1980: 73). A similar approach was taken in Wāfī (n.d.: 122–155).

10. This religious trend is represented by a former shaykh at al-Azhar, Maḥmūd Shaltūt (n.d.: 190–209), and the Shaykh al-Islam in the Ottoman Empire Muṣṭafā Ṣabrī (1935: 5–22).

11. ʻĀ'ishah recounted that when the *Sūrat al-Nūr*, in which God called upon women believers to wear veils (*khumur*), was revealed, the women of Medina rushed to veil themselves (al-Ḥūfī 1963: 372).

12. Wāfī (n.d.: 26) states that ʻĀ'ishah was able to read but not to write, while al-Kattānī mentions that she could write (Kaḥḥālah 1977: vol. 1, 32).

13. For more details, see al-Numnum (1993).

14. This textbook remained in use in the Egyptian schools until the British occupation of Egypt (1882), when its use in the schools was banned (S. Mūsā n.d.: 73).

15. In his book *Manāhij al-Albāb al-Miṣriyyah*, al-Ṭahṭāwī urged parents to teach their daughters reading and the principles of religion in addition to sewing and embroidery (Badawī 1959: 322).

16. (Cairo, 1894). This book was translated into Arabic for the first time by Muḥammad al-Bukhārī and published in ʿAmārah (1976: vol. 1, 249–348).

17. *Taḥrīr al-Mar'ah* was first published in three installments in the newspaper *al-Mu'ayyad* on May 15, 20, and 28, 1899 (al-Shinnāwī 1982: 43).

18. In 1894, Murqus Fahmī al-Muḥāmī wrote a book entitled *al-Mar'ah fī al-Sharq*, in which he discussed the Egyptian women's cause and was the first to call for elimination of the veil, social mingling of the sexes, extending the right of divorce to women as well as men, outlawing polygamy, and legalization of intermarriage between Muslims and Copts (Khamīs 1978: 73; Sufūrī 1928: 685). However, al-Muḥāmī's book was totally overlooked, presumably because he was a Christian Copt.

19. Qāsim Amīn's wife disclosed that her husband did not believe in sudden innovations. He advocated a gradual abandonment of the veil. She remained veiled, and he did not try to force her to discard the veil. However, he saw to it that his daughters remained unveiled (Khākī 1973: 99).

20. Muḥammad ʿAbduh was singled out as the most likely possibility for the role of Qāsim's unknown assistant. In Cairo in the early 1880s, Amīn and ʿAbduh both belonged to a distinguished group of intellectuals who were dedicated to the task of reforming various aspects of Egyptian society. It included Jamāl al-Dīn al-Afghānī, Saʿd Zaghlūl, ʿAbdallāh Nadīm, and Adīb Isḥāq (Bahā' al-Dīn 1970: 12). When al-Afghānī and ʿAbduh were exiled to Paris, they formed an association called al-ʿUrwah al-Wuthqā and published a newspaper by the same name. Qāsim Amīn was an avid reader of the newspaper and was so greatly influenced by its teachings that he joined the association and became ʿAbduh's French tutor and translator. Furthermore, Qāsim Amīn met ʿAbduh in Geneva in 1898 and read from *Tahrīr al-Mar'ah* in the presence of both Saʿd Zaghlūl and Aḥmal Luṭfī al-Sayyid (M. Ḥ. Fahmī 1963: 47–49, 158–159). The book's style and content strongly suggest that ʿAbduh did

indeed collaborate, especially in writing the section that deals with religious affairs (see the argument for this in 'Amārah 1976: vol. 1, 70, 138). This conclusion becomes even more likely if we compare the ideas expressed therein with those 'Abduh expressed in his own writings. See, for example, 'Abduh's views concerning polygamy in his *fatwā* on this matter in 'Amārah (1976: vol. 2, 90–95). See also Riḍā (n.d.: 67–68); 'Abd al-Rāziq (1967: 320–325).

21. This fact has been overlooked by some scholars who tried to document the history of Arab women's liberation back to its earliest beginnings. See, for example, Philipp (1978: 277–294, especially 285–286).

22. More than 100 books were written in response to these two by Qāsim Amīn (Nāṣif 1962: 49). Most of the response was hostile, and Qāsim Amīn became the target of a heated campaign in which rumors were spread about his motives. Muṣṭafā Kāmil (1874–1908), the founder of the Nationalist Party in Egypt, opposed Amīn's proposals, fearing that they represented a British-inspired attempt to undermine the unity of the national cause. Kāmil's newspaper *al-Liwā'* became "an archenemy of Qāsim [Amīn] and his ideas, and an arena for the fiercest calumnies against him" (Haykal 1929: 125). Kāmil went so far as to publish a news article claiming that the British in India had begun a campaign to spread Amīn's works among the Indian people to defame Islam (Khamīs 1978: 78). Another prominent figure who fiercely campaigned against Amīn was Ṭal'at Ḥarb (d. 1941). Ḥarb wrote two books attacking Amīn's works: *Tarbiyat al-Mar'ah wa-al-Ḥijāb* (*The Education of Women and the Veil*, 1912) in response to *Taḥrīr al-Mar'ah*, and *Faṣl al-Khiṭāb fī al-Mar'ah wa al-Ḥijāb* (*The Final Word Concerning Women and the Veil*, 1901), a rebuttal of *al-Mar'ah al-Jadīdah*. Ḥarb maintained that women were inferior to men in intelligence and sensibility and accused Western imperialists of trying to destabilize Muslim society by changing the status of women (Ḥarb 1901: 7; Ḥarb 1912: 14–16).

The verbal battle extended beyond the borders of Egypt. Mukhtār ibn Aḥmad Mu'ayyad Pasha al-'Aẓmī, a distinguished religious leader in Syria, wrote his rebuttal of Amīn in *Faṣl al-Khiṭāb aw Taflīs Iblīs min Taḥrīr al-Mar'ah wa-Raf' al-Ḥijāb* (*The Final Word or Bankrupting the Devil from Liberating Women and Discarding the Veil*, 1900). He saw in Amīn's call for women's education and unveiling a violation of the Qur'ān and the *ḥadīth*; it was an innovation (*bid'ah*) in Islam (al-'Aẓmī 1900: 21). Al-'Aẓmī declared that women were inferior by nature (*fiṭrah*) and that nothing could be done to change this inherited defect (57, 85). They must be denied education in accordance with the teaching of Islam (52). Qāsim Amīn's principles regarding Muslim women's emancipation still draws criticism. See, for example, al-Muqaddim (n.d.: 19–40) and Kishk (1990: 13–57).

23. In 1911, while Aḥmad Luṭfī al-Sayyid was the rector of the Egyptian University (al-Jāmi'ah al-Ahliyyah, founded in 1908), a special program was set up to enable female students to attend night classes. Al-Sayyid tried to keep this plan as secret as possible, knowing it would draw fire from conservative circles. It was soon disclosed and groups of men gathered at the entrance to the university to prevent women from entering the campus. Al-Sayyid's program, however, remained intact (Khalīfah 1973: 84).

24. *Al-Jarīdah,* March 14, 1909 ('Awaḍ 1966: 76). For more details of al-Sayyid's conception of a happy marital life, see (al-Sayyid 1937: 76–77).

25. These articles were also published in Nāṣif (1910). Nāṣif saw the first volume of her book *al-Nisā'iyyāt* published in 1910. It consisted of twenty-four articles (published previously in the newspaper *al-Jarīdah*), two lectures, and one poem, in addition to an introduction written by Aḥmad Luṭfī al-Sayyid. After her death, the book was republished in 1920 in two parts (one volume) after adding the following new material: Nāṣif's correspondence with Mayy Ziyādah, a biography written by Nāṣif's brother Majd al-Dīn Ḥifnī Nāṣif, and a selection of speeches given at the commemorative ceremony after Nāṣif's death (Nāṣif 1962: 37–38). Cooke states incorrectly that *al-Nisā'iyyāt* was published in 1910 in two volumes (Cooke 1992: 446).

26. 'Abd al-Ḥamīd Ḥamdī was more vocal than Qāsim Amīn in his opposition to the veil. He published a newspaper called *al-Sufūr* (*The Unveiling*) to promote the cause of discarding the veil. However, Ḥamdī's wife remained veiled as Qāsim's did (Kaḥḥālah 1977: vol. 2, 178).

27. Nāṣif's marriage to 'Abd al-Sattār al-Bāsil, a tribal chief in Egypt's al-Fayyūm desert, had been arranged by a family friend. Then, to her amazement, Nāṣif discovered that her husband already had another wife and a daughter in his household (Nāṣif n.d.: vol. 1, 8–17; 1962: 63–65). Miriam Cooke, without revealing her sources, claims that Nāṣif's husband was homosexual (Cooke 1992: 446).

28. *Christian Science Monitor* (Boston), June 2, 1926 (Arafa 1973: 2).

29. *Al-Mu'ayyad*: vol. 6, 138 (August 7, 1910).

30. The last words of the passage make an explicit reference to polygamy in the Qur'ān (4:3). The text of al-Zahāwī's article was reprinted in al-Ṣāliḥ (1972: 53–59).

31. See also Woodsmall (1936: 69); al-Darbandī (1968: vol. 1, 24–25).

32. Some claimed that al-Zahāwī tried in vain to deny responsibility for that article after he was so fiercely attacked for it (al-Hilālī 1972: 14).

33. See, for instance, the chapter devoted to the cause of women in al-Zahāwī (1972: 316–328). See also al-Zahāwī (1934: 22, 179, 291). For English translations of some of al-Zahāwī's poetry, see Khouri (1971).

34. See the section entitled "*al-Nisā'iyyāt*" in al-Ruṣāfī (1972: vol. 2, 125–159).

35. Muṣṭafā al-Qāḍī compiled polemical articles on the veil in his book *Mukhtārāt fī al-Sufūr wa-al-Ḥijāb* (1924).

36. Examples are Jawād al-Shabībī and 'Abd al-Ḥusayn al-Arzī (Fahmī 1963: 173–174).

37. The text of al-Bustānī's speech was published in al-Bustānī (1950). Notwithstanding his call for women's education, al-Bustānī was critical of the excessive freedom of Europeans in their dealings with women (Hourani 1962: 100).

38. There is some evidence that Christian as well as Jewish women followed the steps of their Muslim counterparts. In Iraq, for example, both Christian and Jewish women wore the veil in some towns through the nineteenth century (Ghunaymah 1918: 172–173. See also al-Darbandī 1968: vol. 1, 16). Even by the 1930s Syrian Christian women in Aleppo, Ḥamāh, and Damascus "veiled to avoid being conspicuous" (Woodsmall 1936: 50, 51). In the town of al-Salṭ in Jordan, Christian women too practiced the veil. In Egypt, Christian women in some conservative towns were not only veiled by the 1930s, they also wore the *habera*, the traditional Egyptian garment (Woodsmall 1936: 53–54).

39. This was published for the first time in 1924 in *al-Hilāl* 33, no. 3: 249.

40. This book was translated into Urdu by 'Abd al-Ḥamīd al-Nu'mānī and Asrār Aḥmad al-Sahrawardī, and into Pushtu by Ṣalāh al-Dīn Saljūqī (Bayhum 1962: 10).

41. This book was translated by Muḥammad Jawād Mashkūr into Persian under the title *Zanva Tamaddon-e Jadid* (Bayhum 1962: 10).

42. Naẓīrah Zayn al-Dīn was born to a Druze family in B'aqlīn, a small village in Lebanon. The family moved to Beirut where Naẓīrah was educated, first at the Nazarene School and then at al-Kulliyyah al-'Almāniyyah (The Secular College), where she obtained the French and Lebanese baccalaureates. She furthered her studies at the American University in Beirut, majoring in English. It has been claimed that she wrote some poetry, but none of it was published (Ibrāhīm 1966: 113–114;

Ḥamdān 1928; al-Ghalāyīnī 1928; Nuwayhiḍ 1986: 94–99; 'Abd al-Rāziq 1928: 1190–1192; al-Yasū'i 1928: 366–374; Zeidan 1986: 127–128).

43. See also (50, 225).

44. Naẓīrah over-emphasized the role of reason (*'aql*) in understanding Islam (46, 50–51, 55). She took as a repeated theme 'Alī ibn Abī Ṭālib's saying: "Reason is a law (*shar'*) from inside, and law is a reason from outside" (Zayn al-Dīn 1928: 56).

45. See al-Ghalāyīnī (1928: 5, 15, 22); Ḥamdān (1928: 1); al-Jundī (n.d.: 15).

46. See also al-Ghalāyīnī (1928: 58–67) and Ṣabrī (1935: 76).

47. Immediately following the publication of Naẓīrah's work in 1928, many works (in addition to the books of al-Ghalāyīnī and Ḥamdān already cited) were written to attack her views. Among them were: Sa'īd Iyās, *al-Qawl al-Ṣawāb fī Mas'alat al-Ḥijāb*; Maḥmūd al-Shāmitillī, *al-Qawl al-Ṣawāb fī al-Radd 'alā A'dā' al-Ḥijāb*; Aḥmad Muḥīy al-Dīn al-Azharī, *al-Adillah al-Jaliyyah fī al-Ḥijāb wa-al-Madaniyyah*; Ṣalāh al-Dīn al-Za'īm, *Faṣl al-Khiṭāb fī al-Ḥijāb*; Sā'id al-Jābī, *Kashf al-Niqāb 'an Asrār Kitāb al-Sufūr wa-al-Ḥijāb*; and 'Abd al-Qādir, *al-Mar'ah fī Naẓar al-Islām* (Zayn al-Dīn 1929: vol. 4, 1).

48. Among those who responded positively to Naẓīrah's book were 'Abd al-Qādir al-Maghribī (Syria) (Zayn al-Dīn 1929: vol. 2, 9–13); 'Alī 'Abd al-Rāziq (Egypt) (13–15); Hudā Sha'rāwī (Egypt) (29); Amīn al-Rīḥānī (Lebanon) (35–36); and Khalīl Muṭrān (Egypt) (36–37). Ma'rūf al-Ruṣāfī wrote a special poem praising Naẓīrah (al-Ruṣāfī 1972: 157–158).

49. See reviews of Naẓīrah's book in *al-Nisr* (Brooklyn) (Zayn al-Dīn 1929: vol. 2, 40–46); *al-Sā'iḥ* (New York) (55–57); *Mir'āt al-Gharb* (83–84); *al-Shams* (U.S.A.) (101–103); *al-Rafīq* (Mexico) (88–89); *al-Khawāṭir* (Mexico) (116).

50. See reviews of Naẓīrah's book in *Jarīdat al-Ittiḥād al-Lubnānī* (Buenos Aires) (Zayn al-Dīn 1929: vol. 2, 69–71), *Fatāt Lubnān* (São Paulo) (75–78), *al-'Adl* (Rio de Janeiro) (99–100), *Abū al-Hawl* (São Paulo) (115), and *al-Zamān* (Buenos Aires) (117).

51. See 'Alī's review in Ṣalībā (1958: 143).

52. See, for instance, Muḥammad al-Buzum (1877–1955) in al-Daqqāq (1971: 366).

53. See, for instance, Adīb al-Taqīyy in Ṣalībā (1958: 144), and in M. Ḥ. Fahmī (1963: 185).

54. Among al-Ḥaddād's critics were Muḥammad al-Ṣāliḥ ibn Murād, *al-Ḥidād 'alā Imra'at al-Ḥaddād* (Tunis, 1931), and 'Umar al-Birrī al-Madanī, *Sayf al-Ḥaqq 'alā mā lā Yarā al-Ḥaqq* (Tunis, 1931). For more on al-Ḥaddād, see Khālid (1967); Karrū (1957).

55. For more details on this school, see Khalīfah (1973: 101–104). After the Egyptian Revolution of 1952, the government involved itself more deeply in the field of education. It enacted a law requiring primary education for both boys and girls, and education at all levels became tuition free. The number of female students in various educational institutions rose dramatically ('Abd al-Raḥmān 1977: 121–122). The last fortress of conservatism surrendered in 1962 when al-Azhar University began to admit female students into most of its faculties. By 1965, 533 women were studying there, and in 1968–1969 the number was 1,812 (Khalīfah 1973: 126).

56. Jirjis Salāmah (1963: 53–68) says that even Orthodox Copts were suspicious of the religious activities of these schools and of their attempts to convert the Copts either to Catholicism or to Protestantism. This may explain the Copts' efforts to establish their own local schools, beginning at the end of the last century (see also D. Shafīq 1955: 85).

57. See also Khalīfah (1973: 100).

58. According to the Egyptian *Government Almanac of 1935*, there were the following numbers of secondary schools for girls: four in Cairo, one in Alexandria, and a secondary section in Asyūṭ and Ṭanṭā. The number of pupils in 1933–1934 was 1,420. The Girls' College at al-Jīzah in 1933–1934 had 158 students and its kindergarten had 55 (Woodsmall 1936: 176).

59. For more details and statistics, see Khalīfah (1973: 126); Mūsā (n.d.: 5); 'Abd al-Raḥmān (1977: 121–122).

60. The French had 500 schools, the British had 100, and Americans had 88, not to mention those established by the Germans, Russians, Italians, and others (Ṭūbī 1966: 21).

61. It is a little-known fact that Egyptian women took part, however marginally, in 'Urābī's uprising against the British in 1882. A group of women volunteered to circulate secret leaflets in some parts of Egypt ('Abd al-Bāqī 1977: 271).

62. Hudā Sha'rāwī admitted this fact in an interview published in *al-Hilāl* (Sha'rāwī 1929: 650–654). See also al-Jawharī and Khayyāl (1980: 256).

63. The Egyptian Feminist Union's principal aims were to raise the intellectual and moral level of Egyptian women to enable them to realize political and social equality with men, from the legal as well as the moral point of view; to demand free access to all schools of higher education for girls desiring to continue their educations; to reform marriage customs to enable the two parties to get to know each other before they became engaged; to try to amend certain laws concerning marriage and divorce to protect the wife from the injustice done to her by the practice of polygamy for no good reason and to defend her from being renounced by her husband without thought or serious motive; to demand a law fixing the minimum age of marriage at sixteen for girls and eighteen for boys; to agitate for public hygiene and sanitation; to encourage virtue and fight immorality; to combat certain superstitions, cults, and customs that do not conform to common sense; and to propagate the principles of the Feminist Union through the medium of the press (Arafa 1973: 4–5; ʻAbd al-Bāqī 1977: 279).

64. Hudā Shaʻrāwī's account of what went on was as follows: "I and my secretary Sīzā Nabarāwī removed the veil, and stepped onto the ship's ladder unveiled. We looked around to see the effect of an unveiled face on people who were seeing it for the first time. We did not see any response, however, because people were looking at Saʻd [Zaghlūl] eager to see his face" (Shafīq 1955: 137).

65. See the story in Zayn al-Dīn (1928: 164).

66. The two women were Amīnah Shukrī and Rāwiyah ʻAṭiyyah (Aḥmad 1964: 89).

67. Ḥikmat Abū Zayd was a professor of history at ʻAyn Shams University. The second woman to be appointed minister of social affairs, in 1974, was ʻĀ'ishah Rātib, a professor of international law at Cairo University (ʻAbd al-Bāqī 1977: 285).

68. *The National Charter* (Cairo), May 1962, p. 74.

69. For earlier philanthropic societies in Lebanon, see Ibrāhīm (1966: 12).

70. The club's executive committee included ʻAnbarah Salām, ʻĀdilah Bayhum, Amīnah Sharīf, Ibtihāj Qaddūrah, Waḥīdah Khālidī, and Widād Maḥmaṣānī (al-Khālidī 1978: 113–114).

71. The name was later changed to al-Ittiḥād al-Nisā'i al-ʻArabī (The Arab Feminist Union) (Ibrāhīm 1966: 100).

72. See Ibrāhīm (1966: 42–43) and *al-Nahār* (Beirut) vol. 28, no. 7, 712: 9 (January 25, 1961).

73. For more details, see Bayhum (1952: 117) and al-Razzāz (1975: 123).

74. For more details on Iraqi women's organizations, see al-Darbandī (1968: vol. 1, 223–289).

75. In the 1930s Ruth R. Woodsmall made the following observation: "There has been no concerted movement in Palestine against the veil. On the contrary, even though some have recognized it as a handicap, Moslem women leaders in Jerusalem have felt that the veil is necessary as a cultural defence and an evidence that Arab customs are not giving way under the pressure of Zionism" (1936: 52). Even after independence, veiling is still widely practiced in some Arab countries, especially in Saudi Arabia and the Persian Gulf states. In the aftermath of the Iranian Revolution of 1979, the call for reinstating the veil in the Arab world gathered steam. In a recent book, the Moroccan scholar Fatima Mernissi discusses the comeback of the veil (*ḥijāb*) at the end of the twentieth century to some Arab societies as self-defense against the threat of the West: "This look back into history, this necessity for us to investigate the *ḥijāb* through its interpretation in the centuries that followed, will help us understand its resurgence at the end of the twentieth century, when Muslims in search of identity put the accent on the confinement of women as a solution for a pressing crisis. Protecting women from change by veiling them and shutting them out of the world has echoes of closing the community to protect it from the West. Only by keeping in mind this double perspective—women's body as symbolic representation of community—can we understand what the *ḥijāb* signified in year 5 of the Hejira, what stakes it represented, and what stakes it brings into play in today's explosive, passionate, and sometimes violent debates" (1991: 99–100).

The Egyptian activist, Amīnah al-Sa'īd, provides an interesting theory to explain the comeback of the veil in Egypt, especially among university students on economic grounds. By wearing the veil (and the so-called Islamic attire), poor students spare themselves from competing with those students who wear expensive clothes and cosmetics (al-Sa'īd 1987: 31).

The Arab press is still publishing controversial books about the religious aspects of veiling (see, for example, al-Ghaffār 1977; al-Muḥaymid 1980; Kāẓim 1982; Ḥammād 1984; al-Ṭībī 1990) as well as its political dimension (see, for example, al-'Arabī 1989). For criticism of the call for reinstating the veil, see al-Fanjarī (1987); S. al-Miṣrī (1989); Nūr al-Dīn (1993).

Chapter Two. The Pioneering Generation

1. See, for example, the views of Muḥammad Mahdī (Mubārak 1926: 627); Aḥmad Muḥammad al-Ḥūfī (1963: 604–605); 'Ā'ishah 'Abd al-Raḥmān (1962: 134–135; 1963: 8–13).

2. Pre-Islamic poetry was transmitted orally, and much of it was not written down for generations after its composition. We know that much of this poetry was lost, and it is highly probable that some of what is missing was women's poetry (Bayhum 1962: 64; al-Ḥūfī 1963: 605). Among the evidence for this loss is the fact that Abū Nuwās (757–814) knew and used to recite the works of sixty pre-Islamic female poets (Bayhum 1962: 64).

3. Tamāḍir bint 'Amr al-Ḥārith, otherwise known by her nickmane al-Khansā', was already a well-established poet before the emergence of Islam. She was particularly famous for her elegies bewailing her brothers Mu'āwiyah and Ṣakhr, who were killed in tribal clashes. After the deaths of her brothers, al-Khansā' converted to Islam. Her four sons were killed in the battle of al-Qādisiyyah (635). For more details, see Nicholson (1969: 126–127); Fernea and Bezirgan (1977: 3–6); al-Ḥūfī (1963: 626–627); Ḥasan (1970: 15–17; 1969: 81); 'Abd al-Raḥmān (1963a).

4. This link between female poets and elegy remained alive at least until the 1930s. Fadwā Ṭūqān, the Palestinian poet, writes in her autobiography about the manner in which she had been trained. Her brother started this process by giving her an elegy of a woman lamenting her brother's death, chosen from Abū Tammām's *al-Ḥamāsah*, asking her to memorize it (Ṭūqān 1985: 68–69). The first poem she saw published, Ṭūqān recalls, followed the rhyme and meter of an elegy composed by the Abbasid poet Ibn al-Rūmī (Ṭūqān 1985: 83–84).

5. Mayy Ziyādah refers to one example in Arabic grammar (agreement between nouns and adjectives) to demonstrate discrimination against women: "No mind, no matter how biased to men, can comprehend the reason for using masculine plural adjectives to modify a group that consists of 999 healthy and sound women . . . if they have with them only one man who is infirm and insane" (Ziyādah 1931: 11).

This accusation against the Arabic language was also heard during the 1940s when the Arab Feminist Conference, held in Cairo in 1944 at Hudā al-Sha'rāwī's initiative, recommended to the Arab Language Academy in Cairo that the Arab world eliminate the *Nūn al-Niswah* (the subject-marker of plural feminine on Arabic verbs) ('Abduh and Shafīq 1945: 147–148). It is interesting to note that both English and French have been also accused of being discriminatory languages. In the case of English, for example, Germaine Brée noted that "the term 'feminime' carries with it connotations clearly enshrined in Webster: 'tender, soft' as oppoeed to 'robust, strong, male'. Although 'feminine' quite properly designates only 'a feminine expression', it has acquired a militant color. Whereas 'male', Webster informs us, besides referring to sex, denotes 'an intensity or superiority of the characteristic qualities of anything'" (Brée 1973: 5). In French, the definitions are even more revealing: "'*Female*, animal of feminine sex: the female of the monkey.... Used correctly when speaking disparagingly of women'. '*Male*, he who belongs to the sex physiologically characterized by the presence of the fecundating principle... a vigorous man, physically and morally'" (Brée 1973: 85). For more details on the attitude of English vis-à-vis women, see Lakoff (1975).

6. 'Ā'ishah 'Abd al-Raḥmān believes that the critics ignored al-Akhyaliyyah, who excelled in love poetry, because she overstepped the boundaries they had laid down for female poets, that is, elegy ('Abd al-Raḥmān 1963b: 12).

7. Born in Ḥāṣbayyah, Lebanon. Her father was killed in the religious massacre of 1860 when she was only a few days old. Her mother moved with her to Beirut. Maryam was educated first in Jerusalem and then in Beirut, where she graduated in 1877. She was married to Shāhīn Makāriyūs and their house became a center where educated men and women gathered. Her activities in Bākūrat Sūriyā included a lecture on al-Khansā' that was later published in *al-Muqtaṭaf* (vol. 9, no. 9, 1885: 265–271). She was involved in a debate over the intellectual capacity of women. She defended her sex in this debate, claiming that women were superior to men in feeling, virtue, and perceptivity (see Fawwāz 1894–1895: 497–510; Kaḥḥālah 1977: vol. 5, 44–48; 1979: vol. 2, 310–311; Zeidan 1986: 271–272).

8. A book that contains the constitution of this association and some of the lectures delivered was printed in Beirut in 1881 (Zaydān n.d.: 71).

9. The Executive Committee included Mrs. Nūr Ḥamādah (president) and Mrs. Qusṭanṭīn Thābit (vice president).

10. See Appendix 1 for a listing of these journals.

11. A good number of women's journals, nevertheless, were published in Lebanon itself between 1896 and the late 1950s. See Appendix 2 for a listing of these journals.

12. For instance, in 1898 Alexandra Avierinoh published in her journal *Anīs al-Jalīs* statistics about the rate of illiteracy among women in

Egypt. Whereas the rate of literacy among men was 3.6 percent, the rate of literacy among women was only 0.05 percent (Khalīfah 1973: 111). Another statistic about the same subject was published in *al-Nahḍah al-Nisā'iyyah*, from which we learn that the rate of literacy among the Egyptian women in 1917 reached 1.8 percent, and even in 1937 the rate did not exceed 2 percent (Khalīfah 1973: 112).

13. The Egyptian government distributed *Fatāt al-Sharq* in its schools (Khalīfah 1973: 51).

14. In fact, the first Egyptian woman to contribute to the press was Jalīlah Tamrahān (d. 1899) in one of the earliest magazines in Egypt, *Ya'sūb al-Ṭibb* (established in 1865 by Dr. Muḥammad 'Alī al-Baqlī). She was one of the first graduates of the School of Midwives founded by Muḥammad 'Alī, and later served as an instructor in the same school. She wrote on medical issues (Khalīfah 1973: 23, 74–75, 104, 132; Kaḥḥālah 1977: vol. 5, 307–308).

15. Some scholars were led astray by this device, believing that Maryam Maẓhar was a real person. Even as late as 1939 we see one of them refer to her as the late Maryam Maẓhar who was "the first woman journalist Egypt knew" (Khalīl 1939: 110). However, Salīm Sarkīs himself had already unveiled this fact in 1907, claiming that he had chosen to publish *Mir'āt al-Ḥasnā'* under a fictitious name because he was a *persona non grata* in the Ottoman Emire due to his hostile political views and he feared that this journal would be banned in Syria if he published it under his real name (al-Ṭamāwī 1989: 180; al-Jundī n.d.: 7; 1979: 339–343). This story does not, however, explain why he chose a female rather than a male name. Most probably, Sarkīs resorted to this device for commercial reasons, since publishing a women's magazine under a female name would understandably attract more readers among women as well as men. Sarkīs himself admitted that *Mir'āt al-Ḥasnā'* achieved a great deal of success, especially among women (al-Jundī 1979: 343).

16. Mary 'Ajamī (1888–1965) was born and educated in Damascus at the Russian and Irish schools. She taught in Damascus and Alexandria and contributed to many journals in Egypt, Syria, and Lebanon. She was a poet and translator and also a political activist who worked against the Ottomans. For more details, see Dāghir (1972: vol. 3, part 1, 803–805); al-Razzāz (1975: 175–176); al-Kayyālī (1968: 226–236); Fattūḥ (1966: 2–6); Sakākīnī and Tawfīq (1959: 93–100); Zeidan (1986: 202–204).

17. Nāzik al-'Ābid was born in Damascus to a very wealthy and influential family. Her father was a *vali* (governor) in the Ottoman imperial districts of al-Karak and al-Mawṣil. She learned Arabic, Turkish, French,

and German in Damascus. After her return from exile in Turkey with her family in 1918, she established a feminist society, a cultural club, a school for orphaned girls, and a magazine. During King Faisal's short reign in Damascus, al-'Ābid was very active in the resistance against the French, even on the battlefield, for which King Faisal awarded her a military title. For more details, see Kaḥḥālah (1977: vol. 5, 320–321; 1979: vol. 2, 116–117); Sakākīnī and Tawfīq (1959: 25–35); Ṭarābīshī (1980: 97–102).

18. For a listing of women's journals published in Iraq, see Appendix 3.

19. For more details on women's literary salons in France, see Brée (1973: 25).

20. Maryānā Marrāsh was the first Syrian female poet to publish a collection of poetry; her *Bint Fikr* (*An Idea*) was printed in Beirut in 1893. Marrāsh obtained a permit from the Ottoman government to print her book after composing a poem in which she had praised the Sultan 'Abd al-Ḥamīd (al-Rifā'ī 1969: 198).

21. Unfortunately, we do not know with certainty any details regarding her tour in France. Some scholars, however, came up with the baseless theory that Maryānā Marrāsh created her salon after seeing similar salons in France (al-Miṣrī and Wa'lānī (1988: 31). Her salon did not start from scratch; most of the participants were regular visitors to her family's home, where they used to meet with her father and two brothers (al-Kayyālī 1957b: 566, 570).

22. For more details on Maryānā Marrāsh, see al-Kayyālī (1957a: 138–140; 1957b: 565–574; 1968: 93–99); Kaḥḥālah (1977: vol. 5, 34–36; 1979: vol. 2, 308–309); Ṭarrāzī (1913: vol. 1, 241–245); Dāghir (1956: vol. 2, part 1, 697–698); Fattūḥ (1962: 28–29); Zeidan 1986: 364–365.

23. It has been alleged that Nāzlī Fāḍil was the one who paved the road for Sa'd Zaghlūl to be the prominent politician he later became. Nāzlī Fāḍil's warm relations with the British occupiers in Egypt, especially with Lord Cromer, the British High Commissioner in Cairo, are beyond dispute (see, for example, Storrs 1937: 98; al-Jundī 1979: 303–304; Ramaḍān 1976: 124). This fact put Nāzlī Fāḍil in a special position to influence the political fortunes of some rising Egyptian politicians. Sir Ronald Storrs, a high-ranking British official in Egypt who visited Nāzlī Fāḍil's salon, wrote in his memoirs: "Sa'd Zaghlūl was her lawyer and it was at her advice or command—they were not easy to distinguish, that the *Azhar* student had learnt French and generally rendered himself *ministrabile* and, in the end, *papabile* "(Storrs 1937: 92–93). She also arranged Zaghlūl's marriage to

Ṣafiyyah, the daughter of Muṣṭafā Fahmī (who held the post of premier in Egypt for fifteen years), an act that led to Zaghlūl's entering the political arena as a minister (al-Shinnāwī 1982: 45; Sufūri 1928: 686–687; Khamīs 1978: 74; al-Jundī 1979: 304, 308–309, 362).

24. A journalist and political writer, al-Muwayliḥī was born and died in Cairo. He established the newspaper *Miṣbāḥ al-Sharq*.

25. Born in Damascus, Isḥāq died in Beirut. He spent most of his life in Egypt and was associated with 'Abduh and al-Afghānī. He founded the newspaper *Miṣr* and wrote some plays. After his death, some of his writings were collected in a volume called *al-Durar*.

26. Born in Lebanon, Nimr immigrated to Egypt, where he founded the two journals *al-Muqaṭṭam* and *al-Muqtaṭaf* in cooperation with his friend Ya'qūb Ṣarrūf.

27. A Lebanese journalist, Barakāt immigrated to Egypt, where he edited the newspaper *al-Ahrām* after the death, in 1901, of its founder Salīm Taqlā.

28. Originally her first name was Mary. She herself admitted that her mother changed the name to Mayy (Fahmī 1955: 98; Ḥasan 1964: 20). Mayy, in a letter to Jubrān Khalīl Jubrān, revealed that her mother had chosen Mayy for her because she remembered, when she was still a student, taking part in Corneille's *Horace*, in which the name of the character Camille was changed to Mayy (Sa'd 1983: 16). (Most probably Mayy's mother was referring to Salīm al-Naqqāsh's version of *Horace*, which was first performed in 1868 and was known by its Arabicized title *Mayy*.) But Farīd (1979b: 177) quoted Ḥāfiẓ Maḥmūd's claim that Dāwūd Barakāt was the one who chose the name Mayy. This claim is also mentioned in R. Mūsā (n.d.: 16).

She was born in Nazareth to a Lebanese father and a Palestinian mother. Mayy Ziyādah received her primary education first at missionary schools in her home town (1892–1899) and thereafter at a boarding school in 'Aynṭūrah in Lebanon (1900–1903). She continued her education at a French school in Beirut. In 1908 the family migrated to Cairo, where Mayy Ziyādah's father bought and ran the newspaper *al-Maḥrūsah* (an agnomen for Cairo) in the beginning of 1909. When he died in October 1929, Mayy Ziyādah took over the editorship of this paper, changing it into a weekly publication.

29. Mayy was fascinated by the role Madame de Sévigné played in the literary life of France. See Mayy's article about Madame de Sévigné in Ziyādah (1975e: 49–64); for her admiration of Madame de Staël, see Jabr (1960: 106).

30. Mayy relates the story of the beginning of her salon: in 1913 she was asked to read Jubrān Khalīl Jubrān's address at a gathering to honor the poet Khalīl Muṭrān, which was initiated by the Egyptian University and sponsored by the Khedive 'Abbās Ḥilmī. After reading Jubrān's address, Mayy gave her own address, which was received warmly by the audience. At the end of the ceremony Mayy invited some intellectuals to meet at her house weekly (Ziyādah 1930: 400–410; Ḥasan 1964: 96).

31. Ṭāhir al-Ṭanāḥī states that Mayy's salon lasted until 1929 (al-Ṭanāḥī 1974: 26). Fatḥī Raḍwān, however, recalls visiting Mayy's salon in 1931 commenting: "It seems to me that I reached this salon in its last days" (Raḍwān 1967: 329). Raḍwān's estimation is supported by Salāmah Mūsā, a close friend of Mayy, who maintains that Mayy kept the salon up until her mother's death (1932) (Mūsā 1961: 156).

32. Among the non-Arabs who visited the salon were the American writer Henry James and Longfellow's son (S. 1928: 660).

33. Fū'ād Ṣarrūf, a close friend of Mayy, mentions that Mayy was a gifted musician and that she knew how to play several musical instruments (Ḥasan 1964: 111). Ṭāhā Ḥusayn reveals that after the participants of the salon would leave, he and a few others would stay behind to enjoy Mayy's conversation, literature, music, and singing (Sa'd 1983: 182).

34. Ismā'īl Ṣabrī was very impressed by Mayy's performance in the gathering held by the Egyptian University to honor Khalīl Muṭrān in 1913 (see n. 30). Ṭāhir al-Ṭanāḥī states that Ṣabrī requested Mayy's father to introduce him to his daughter (al-Ṭanāḥī 1974: 33). With his rich experience in conducting literary salons (he was at the center of Alexandra Avierinoh's salon in Alexandria almost two decades before) he was placed in charge of running the discussion at the beginning of Mayy's salon. This was a training period for Mayy, because Ṣabrī was adamant in using Classical Arabic in the salon discussions (Ziyādah 1930: 400–401).

35. Muṣṭafā al-Shihābī left us an account of his experience attending Mayy's salon for the first time: "As if I were in the sublime temple of literature and the shrine of brilliancy and genius. . . . It seemed to me that I was in the presence of angels about whom I used to read in the works of the greatest French writers" (Sakākīnī 1969: 85).

36. The poets who were in love with Mayy and reflected this sentiment in their poetry included Ismā'īl Ṣabrī, Aḥmad Shawqī, Walīyy al-Dīn Yakan, and al-'Aqqād. In fact, Mayy was involved in a love affair with the *Mahjari* writer Jubrān Khalīl Jubrān, although they never met in person. For more details on this relationship see Gibran and Gibran (1974: 367–369); Sakākīnī (1969: 140–167); al-Ṭanāḥī (1974: 114–116); Sa'd (1973: 65–68, 118–120, 177–184, 203–205); Ḥasan (1964: 142–143).

37. It is believed that Mayy inspired Muṣṭafā Ṣādiq al-Rāfi'ī to write his major prose works *Rasā'il al-Aḥzān, al-Saḥāb al-Aḥmar,* and *Awrāq al-Ward* (Sakākīnī 1969: 127).

38. The writers who exchanged letters with Mayy included Aḥmad Luṭfī al-Sayyid (see copies of his letters in al-Ṭanāḥī 1962a: 15–22; *Ākhir Sā'ah* (Cairo), January 7, 1981: 47–49; al-Ṭanāḥī 1974: 155–176; also one of Mayy's letters to al-Sayyid is in Ḥasan 1964: 259–262); Anṭūn al-Jumayyil (see his letters to Mayy in al-Ṭanāḥī 1962b: 120–125); and al-'Aqqād (al-Ṭanāḥī 1974: 78–113). For the correspondence between Mayy and Jubrān Khalīl Jubrān, see al-Kuzbarī and Bishrū'ī (1984); al-Ṭanāḥī (1974: 114–150); Sakākīnī (1969: 140–167); Sa'd (1973: 361–362); Ḥasan (1964: 245–251); 'Awwād (1981: 91–92). See also al-Ṭanāḥī (1962c: 29–33); al-Ṭanāḥī (1962d: 154–160). For letters sent to Mayy by other intellectuals of her age, Arab and non-Arab alike, see al-Kuzbarī (1982).

39. Al-Sayyid, for example, originally opposed the publication of the letters he had exchanged with Mayy (Sakākīnī 1969: 170).

40. Jamīlah al-'Alāyilī later wrote about her ordeal: "I was raised in a very conservative and religious environment. The mere act of publishing [under] my name in a small local magazine would have caused a sort of mourning in the family, since they considered that [act] a violation of tradition and *status quo* and an invitation for slandering the family reputation. . . . I used to write secretly after locking myself in my private room while my family was asleep. I would hide the papers in which I had published one of my articles" (al-Jundī 1970: 23).

41. This collection of poems was expanded and published again twice: in Beirut in 1887 and in Cairo in 1914 (Ziyādah 1975f: 19; Ibrāhīm 1964: 24). Maskūni (1947: 124) wrongly claims that *Hadīqat al-Ward* was republished in 1881 and 1913. The same claim is mentioned in Dāghir (1972: vol. 3, part 2, 1414).

42. In addition to Arabic, Umm Nizār is believed to have had a limited knowledge of Persian (Ṭabbānah 1974: 53).

43. These two books were never published because they were lost after 'Ā'ishah Taymūr's death (Ziyādah 1975a: 55–56).

44. 'Ā'ishah Taymūr recalled her father's warning when she was still at the beginning of her literary career: "reading much love poetry will eliminate your studies from your memory" (Ziyādah 1975a: 66).

45. See, for example, Taymūr (1952: 205, 207, 260–264).

46. In an article published in the Egyptian daily *al-Afkār* (1923), the writer hints at a literary circle (salon?) that used to meet regularly for years

at 'Ā'ishah Taymūr's house (Ziyādah 1975a: 94–96). This claim surfaces again in another article (1928), where this alleged circle is referred to as a salon that used to meet after 1882 (Fulān 1928: 48). Ḥanīfah al-Khaṭīh goes a step further and, without referring to any source, mentions the names of the most prominent participants: Ṣafiyyah Zaghlūl, Hudā al-Sha'rāwī, and Bāḥithat al-Bādiyah (Malak Ḥifnī Nāṣif) (al-Khaṭīb 1984: 39). Mayy Ziyādah questioned the validity of this claim and cited Ismā'īl Taymūr's denial that his sister used to hold such a salon (Ziyādah 1975a: 96).

47. Manṣūr 1955: 38; Shammūsh 1942: 586; Muḥammad (n.d.: part 1, 95).

48. This article was first published in the newspaper *al-Ādāb* in 1888. It was later published in Fawwāz (1894–1895: 306–308), and in Kaḥḥālah (1977: vol. 3, 170–174).

49. Ironically, feminists in the West made similar observation about men there. In *A Room of One's Own*, Virginia Woolf wrote: "Women have served all these centuries as looking-glasses possessing the magic and delicious power of reflecting the figure of man at twice its natural size" (1957: 35).

50. Later in this chapter we will see that the attempt to record the oral narratives (which belong largely to the female cultural domain) was repeated by Suhayr al-Qalamāwī in her book *Aḥadīth Jaddatī* (see pp. 78–79 in this chapter). This phenomenon deserves close study to identify the different oral components of the cultural legacy of Arab women and the ways by which they were carried on to succeeding generations. In a passing reference to the role of women in preserving some aspects of oral culture, Ibrāhīm 'Abd al-Qādir al-Māzinī states, "Woman serves as a memory for the human race. She is the one who has preserved fables, fairy tales, group songs, stories, anecdotes, and proverbs. Without exaggerating, I think that all of us as children have sat down by our female relatives, maids, or other women, listening to their recollections and to their tales and anecdotes about demons, evil spirits, monsters and human beings" (al-Māzinī 1992: 46). Al-Māzinī argues that by preserving and passing on this culture, women have been able not only to preserve the language, but also to contribute toward its growth and expansion (46–47).

51. 'Abd al-Muḥsin Ṭ. Badr in his comprehensive study about the emergence and development of the Arabic novel in Egypt does not refer at all to Taymūr's *Natā'ij al-Aḥwāl* in the text; he only lists it in the appendix (Badr 1968). On the other hand, Hamilton A. R. Gibb fails even to mention Taymūr's name while dealing with Arabic narrative in the nineteenth century (Gibb 1982).

52. Al-Ṭahṭāwī undertook the translation of Fénelon's work during his stay in the Sudan between 1850–1854. Ḥusayn F. al-Najjār indicates that the rendition was published in Beirut in 1867 (al-Najjār 1987: 180). Jack Tājir, on the other hand, gives the impression that al-Tahṭāwī's rendition was printed once before it came out in Beirut, although he fails to mention the publication place and date (Tājir n.d.: 56).

53. The novel as a genre in Arabic could be said to date either to Jubrān Khalīl Jubrān's *al-Ajniḥah al-Matakassirah* (1912) or to Muḥammad Ḥusayn Haykal's *Zaynab* (1913).

54. There is disagreement about when Zaynab Fawwāz was born. Emily Fāris Ibrāhīm (1966: 107) mentions that Zaynab was born in 1850, while Dāghir (1956: vol. 2, part 1, 637) claims that she was born in 1846. Most sources, however, agree that she was born in 1860 (see Fahmī 1955: 48; Kaḥḥālah 1977: vol. 2, 82; Muḥammad n.d.: part 1, 116; Najm 1961: 117). Although all these sources give the date of Zaynab's death as 1914, Sa'īdah Ramaḍān claims that she died in 1909 (Ramaḍān 1976: 122).

55. Leila Ahmed's statement that Zaynab Fawwāz was Christian is an apparent error (Ahmed 1992: 141). For Fawwāz's family background see Fawwāz (1984: 12–13). The fact that Zaynab Fawwāz was Muslim qualified her to be an insider, whereas Christian Syro-Lebanese women in Egypt remained, to a great extent, outsiders unwelcomed to discuss thorny questions such as the status of women in Islam (see, for example, Mayy Ziyādah's experience in this regard, n. 86 in this chapter). Fawwāz, almost a century before Fatima Mernissi (Mernissi 1991) raised the issue of authenticity regarding some misogynous sayings attributed to the Prophet Muḥammad (e.g., see Fawwāz 1910: 116–117).

56. The sources also contradict each other about Zaynab's early married life. Fāṭimah Ḥusayn Fawwāz, in an unpublished study, concluded that Zaynab was married to an illiterate relative of hers who served as a falcon trainer and stableman at the prince's palace. According to this story, Zaynab later managed to divorce him because they did not get along. Another version has it that a relative of Zaynab's wanted to force her to marry him, but that she fled to a nearby forest where she was picked up by a group of merchants who took her with them to Beirut. In Beirut, Zaynab once again worked as a maid, this time for an Egyptian family, and eventually moved to Alexandria with them. These two accounts are quoted in Fā'ūr (1980: 66).

57. Zaynab Fawwāz showed her gratitude to Fāṭimah al-Khalīl by including her among the famous women whose biographies appeared in her *Kitāb al-Durr* (Fawwāz 1894–1895: 427–428).

58. Fawwāz's tutors included Muḥammad Shiblī, who taught her the basics of reading and writing, Muḥyī al-Dīn al-Nabhānī, who taught her grammar and composition, and Ḥasan Huṣnī al-Ṭūwayrānī, who taught her rhetoric, prosody, and history (al-Jundī n.d.: 82). See also Fā'ūr (1980: 67).

59. Such as "Lisān al-Ḥāl, al-Nīl", "al-Mu'ayyad", "al-Ittiḥād al-Miṣri", "al-Bustānī", "al-Ustādh", "al-Fatā", "al-Fatāh", "al-Muhandis", and "al-Ahālī" (Fā'ūr 1980: 67). Fawwāz's articles are collected in Fawwāz (1910).

60. Hanā Kasbānī Kūrānī was born in Kafr Shīmā, Lebanon, to a family of Syrian origin. She was educated both in government and missionary schools. She contributed to many Lebanese periodicals, among them *Lisān al-Ḥāl* and *al-Fatāh*. In 1892 she represented Syria and Lebanon at the International Women's Conference held in Chicago. Hanā remained in the United States for three years, giving a series of lectures on the subject of "the Eastern woman." She died at the age of twenty-nine, after falling ill with tuberculosis. Her works included *Risālah fī al-Akhlāq wa-al-'Ādāt* (*A Treatise on Manners and Customs*), for which she was awarded a medal from Sultan 'Abd al-Ḥamīd. In addition, she translated three novels into Arabic from English (*Fāris wa-Ḥimāruhu, Zuqāq al-Miqlāh*, and *al-Ḥaṭṭāb wa-Kalbuhu Bārūd*). For more details, see Kaḥḥālah (1979: vol. 2, 311–312; 1977: vol. 5, 213–215); Dāghir (1972: vol. 3, part 2, 1091–1092); Ibrāhīm (1964: 47–56); Muḥammad (n.d.: part 2, 95–112); Zeidan (1986: 256–257).

61. Kūrānī's article was published in the newspaper *Lubnān* (Beirut). For excerpts, see Ibrāhīm (1964: 32); Kaḥḥālah (1979: vol. 2, 296–297).

62. Fawwāz's article was first published in 1892 in the newspaper *al-Nīl*, no. 151. It was republished in Fawwāz (1910: 19–25).

63. Fawwāz's *dīwān* was never published. For samples of her poetry, see Muḥammad (n.d.: part 1, 154–160); Kaḥḥālah (1977: vol. 5, 82–83); Nāṣif (1962: 297–313).

64. It is interesting to note that Zaynab Fawwāz considered the idea of sending a copy of this book to the women's section of the World's Columbian Exposition, which was held in Chicago in 1893, as a sign of support to the exposition. In July 1892 she wrote a letter to Bertha Honoré Palmer, the chairperson of the exposition's Board of Managers, inquiring as to how she could send a copy of her book and apologizing for not being able to personally attend the exposition for religious reasons, because she was a Muslim woman who could not travel abroad alone. (See Fawwāz's

letter in Fawwāz 1910: 31–32, and Palmer's reply on 63–64.) It is, however, doubtful that Fawwaz's book made it in time for the exposition, because it was published only in 1894–1895. Nāṣif (1910: 43) mentioned that Wāṣif Ghālī translated Fawwāz's book into French as *Les Perles Eparpillées.*

65. Fā'ūr (1980: 69) said that this novel was published in 1899; Najm (1961) mentions two different dates: 1895 (117) and 1899 (295).

66. For the technique of popular narrative, especially as in *Sīrat al-Ẓāhir Baybars* see (Yūnus 1960).

67. Zaynab Fawwāz was an enthusiastic supporter of the then nascent Arab theater. In one of her articles, she encourages theater-going in order not to fall victim to alcohol and forbidden pleasure (Fawwāz 1910: 60–63). Drama is the literary genre contributed to least by Arab women. Among the entire pioneering generation, only one, Zaynab Fawwāz, wrote a play—*Al-Hawā wa-al-Wafā'* (*Love and Faithfulness*, 1893). In Egypt, a very limited number of female playwrights emerged, starting from the 1960s, among them are Saniyyah Qurā'ah (Zeidan 1986: 242), Jādhibiyyah Ṣidqī (Zeidan 1986: 170–172), and Fatḥiyyah al-'Assāl (Zeidan 1986: 211–212; 'Abd al-Ghanīyy n.d.: 193–197, 240). However, the most celebrated female playwright has been Nihād Jād (d. 1989), who received her M.A. degree from Indiana University in the United States. Her controversial play *'a al-Raṣīf* (*On The Pavement*) was staged with tremendous success in Cairo in the summer of 1986 (see, for example, al-Jayyār 1986, Muntaṣir 1986, and Hilāl 1986). This play was published in 1989. Nihād Jād's second published play was *'Adīlah wa-Maḥaṭṭat al-Utūbīs* (Cairo, n.d.) and was translated into English as *Adila and the Bus Stop* (1987). In his book *Ḥarakat al-Ta'līf al-Masraḥī fī Sūriyyah Bayna 1945–1967*, Aḥmad Ziyād Muḥabbak does not list any Syrian women playwrights who produced works during the period 1945–1967 (1982: 409–411; see also al-Miṣrī and Wa'lānī 1988: 16–17). In the rest of the Arab world the harvest is no more abundant. However, among the few promising female playwrights is the Saudi Arabian writer Rajā' Muḥammad al-'Ālim.

68. Kaḥḥālah (1977: vol. 5, 290) says that Labībah Hāshim was born in Kafr Shīmā. Other sources say that she was born in Beirut (see Ibrāhīm 1964: 72; Dāghir 1972: vol. 3, part 2, 1365).

69. For more details on Labībah Mikhā'īl Ṣawāyā, see Kaḥḥālah (1979: vol. 2, 306–307); (1977: vol. 4, 288–290) and Ibrāhīm (1964: 65–69).

70. Farīdah 'Aṭiyyah was born in Tripoli, Lebanon, where she was educated in the American School. After graduating, she taught for a while

at this same school. She contributed to Lebanese periodicals and newspapers, and translated the *Ayyām Bambay al-Akhīrah* (*The Last Days of Pompeii*) from English into Arabic (Kaḥḥālah 1979: vol. 2, 305–306; 1977: vol. 3, 169; Zeidan 1986; 216–217).

71. For more details see Ibrāhīm, (1964: 95–104; 1966: 110); al-Jundī (n.d.: 47–48); Dāghir (1956: vol. 2, part 1, 661–662); al-'Aqīqī (1976: vol. 2, 343); Kaḥḥālah (1977: vol. 3, 307–316 1977: vol. 2, 302–305); Zeidan 1986: 251–252); Nuwayhiḍ (1986: 216–219).

72. In 1913 Karam replaced Mukarzil for six months in editing *al-Hudā* while he attended the Arab Congress in Paris. As an expression of gratitude for Mukarzil's help, Karam dedicated her second novel, *Fāṭimah al-Badawiyyah,* to him.

73. The issue of the first "real" or "artistic" novel written in Arabic remains highly controversial among scholars. Buthaynah Sha'bān (Sha'bān 1993: 215; Qabbānī 1993: 19) tries to give this discussion another dimension when she raises the possibility that perhaps *Badī'ah wa-Fu'ād* was the first novel in Arabic because it was published eight years [sic] before Muḥammad Ḥusayn Haykal's *Zaynab,* which is considered by many scholars to be the first novel in Arabic (see, for example, M. M. Badawi's argument in Badawi 1993: 109–110). Indeed, some scholars trace the beginning of the Arabic novel to 1865 with the publication of the philosophical novel *Ghābat al-Ḥaqq fī Tafṣīl al-Akhlāq al-Fāḍilah* (*The Forest of Truth in Detailing Cultured Manners,* Aleppo, 1865), written by the Syrian writer Fransīs Fatḥ Allāh Marrāsh (1836–1873) in 1862 (see, for example the discussion in Moreh 1988: 62). Even in terms of social novels there are earlier works. The Lebanese Salīm al-Bustānī (1848–1884) wrote a number of novels serialized in his magazine *al-Jinān* (1870–1887) in Beirut, dealing with social issues. His first work was *al-Hayām fī Jinān al-Shām* (*Love in Syrian Gardens,* 1870). Before 'Afīfah Karam's *Badı'ah wa-Fu'ād,* Salīm Sarkīs wrote *al-Qulūb al-Muttaḥidah fī al-Wilāyāt al-Muttaḥidah* (*Hearts United in the United States,* 1904), a novel that also portrays the life of Syrian immigrants to America. Even in the sphere of women's novels, we can point to much earlier works than Karam's, such as Alice Buṭrus al-Bustānī's *Ṣā'ibah* (1891), Zaynab Fawwāz's *Ḥusn al-'Awqib aw Ghādah al-Zāhirah* (1899), and Labībah Hāshim's *Qalb al-Rajul* (1904).

Perhaps because of the social, religious, and political criticism they contained, *Badī'ah wa-Fu'ād,* as well as Karam's other novels, were not widely available in the Arab world and therefore did not have a great impact on the development of the Arabic novel. Contrary to other Syro-Lebanese emigrant writers, Karam's works were never reprinted in any

Arab country. The Lebanese scholar Emily Fāris Ibrāhīm, for example, complains that she could find none of Karam's works (Ibrāhīm 1964: 98).

74. In her introduction to the second novel, *Fāṭimah al-Badawiyyah*, Karam discloses that, after sending the manuscript of *Badī'ah wa-Fu'ād* to *the al-Hudā* Publishing House, she changed her mind and requested that the manuscript be sent back to her. The reason for this change of mind was Karam's feeling that the novel was a worthless work. The owner of the press, Na''ūm Mukarzil, refused Karam's request and printed the novel (Karam n.d.: 1).

75. The solidarity is exhibited when Alice, an American woman, grants shelter and aid to Fāṭimah and her baby without having been previously acquainted with them. In this novel an entire chapter (Chapter 45, pp. 236–241) is entitled "The Woman Does Not Know Herself Unless She is in the Presence of Another Woman."

76. At one point in the novel Fāṭimah complains about Salīm's treatment of her: "He was the one who snatched me away from pure nature and threw me into the waves of the corrupt city.... He was educated and I was illiterate. He was the one who seduced me" (261–262).

77. In his discussion of 'Afīfah Karam, Louis Cheikho, a Jeusit scholar, makes a point of blaming her for "some false criticism against religion and its represntatives" (Cheikho 1926: 116).

78. Karam, although criticizing the methods of education employed by nuns in their schools, provides us with an autobiographical segment: "Although this writer has been educated by nuns to whom she confesses their favor on the world... despite that, she would not forbid her pen from criticizing them in one regard, i.e., raising and educating girls. They grant them only a religious education and they teach them how to unquestionably obey their parents and superiors" (1914: 48).

79. Sawsan embodies the theme of women's solidarity in *Ghādat 'Amshīt*. She is Farīdah's friend from school who has been preparing herself to become a nun. After Farīdah's forced marriage Sawsan comes to live in her household in order to help her through her miserable life. Sawsan nurses Farīdah at a time when everybody else has abandoned her.

80. There is conflicting information regarding Karam's works. Dāghir (1956: 662) lists the three novels in Arabic that have been discussed here, as well as five translated works: *Malikah li-Yawm*, *Nancy Stāyir* (?), *Muḥammad 'Alī Bāshā wa-Ibnuh*, *Cleopatra*, and *Ibnat Nā'ib al-Malik*. Sha'bān (1993: 233) lists the same works (with slight variations in some titles) without differentiating between the original works and the

translated ones. Although I was successful in obtaining access to Karam's three novels discussed here, all my attempts to locate her other works in the Middle East and the United States remained fruitless.

81. Selections from this collection of poems were translated into Arabic by Jamīl Jabr as *Azāhīr Ḥulm* (Ziyādah 1952).

82. This pseudonym was both an interpretation and a translation of Mayy Ziyādah's name. *Isis*, Mayy explained, had the same symbolic meaning as the name of the Virgin Mary, while *Copia* is the Latin translation of *Ziyādah* (Sa'd 1973: 10).

83. Quoted in Sa'd (1973: 54–55). See also Sakākīnī (1969: 45), and al-Ṭanāḥī (1974: 153–154).

84. See also Sakākīnī (1969: 47–48).

85. Ziyādah translated *Rujū' al-Mawjah* (*Le retour du flot* by Brada) from French, *Ibtisāmāt wa-Dumū' (Deutsche Liebe* by F. Max Müller) from German, and *al-Ḥubb fī al-'Adhāb* (*The Refugees: A Tale of Two Continents* by Sir Arthur Conan Doyle) from English.

86. Mayy Ziyādah worked for this cause under a fundamental handicap. She remained, in essence, an outsider in Egypt and generally refrained from tackling sensitive issues related to Islam. Salāmah Mūsā, a close friend of Mayy, writes about her: "For she well knew that if she actually had propagated the emancipation of women and struggled for that end, she would have faced a wall of opposition because she was not Egyptian, and not a Muslim woman herself" (Mūsā 1961: 247). In fact, Mayy Ziyādah once was fiercely attacked by the Egyptian writer Muḥammad Lutfi Jum'ah because she had claimed that divorce among Muslims was easy and widespread. Jum'ah accused Ziyādah of being influenced by foreign writers who had unrealistically dealt with the status of Muslim women: "Mayy today protrays the Egytian woman as if she is portraying a barbarian woman" (Jum'ah 1923b: 179). She was again criticized by the same writer because, while dealing with Bahithat al-Bādiyah's religious sentiment, she had concluded that among Muslims religion is blended with social and national sentiments. Jum'ah states "This is again a foreign notion that Mayy adopted from Westerners. If we can understand the motivation of foreigners we cannot accept that from someone who is considered to be one of us" (1923c: 203).

87. Quoted in Ghurayyib (1978: 141–142); Sa'd (1973: 193–194).

88. See, for example, the confession of the Egyptian poetess Jamīlah al-'Alāyilī: "My family, which was conservative in matters of religion and

customs, wanted to prepare me to master the domestic skills... then Mayy's literary articles attracted my attention and I started reading them.... I found myself yearning to write" (Mandūr 1958: 43).

89. Mayy Ziyādah's published books number thirteen in all. In addition to *Fleurs de Rêve*, the three biographies mentioned, and the three translated novels (see n. 85), she wrote the following works: *Sawāniḥ Fatāh, Bayna al-Madd wa-al-Jazr, al-Ṣaḥā'if, Ẓulumāt wa-Ashi''ah, Kalimāt wa-Ishārāt*, and *al-Musāwāh*. Two of her lectures were published: Ghāyat al-Ḥayāh and Risālat al-Adīb ilā al-Ḥayāh al-'Arabiyyah. Some references have been made to a story in English entitled "The Shadow on the Rock," which she published in *Sphinx*, an Egyptian review (R. Mūsā n.d.: 84; M. 'A. Ḥasan 1964: 53): despite several attempts, I have failed to locate this story. Other researchers have faced the same difficulty (see, for example, Khemiri and Kampffmeyer 1930: 27). It is believed that Mayy left some unpublished works, among the most referred to being *Layālī al-'Uṣfūriyyah* (*The Madhouse Nights*) (Mūsā n.d.: 84; Jabr 1974: 16). Mayy wrote this work in the late 1930s while she was hospitalized in an insane asylum in Lebanon. Al-Kuzbarī believes that this manuscript is in the possession of Mayy's relatives in Lebanon (al-Kuzbarī 1987: vol. 1, 215). Jamīl Jabr mentions that a French general who visited Mayy at the mental hospital reported that Mayy was preparing a work on the Phoenicians in Homer's poetry (Jabr 1974: 17).

90. One of Mayy's short plays was *'Alā al-Ṣadr al-Shafīq* (*On the Compassionate Breast*), published in *al-Hilāl* (Ziyādah 1923: 67–78), and later republished in Sa'd (1973: 714–731). The other was a supplement to her treatise on equality (Ziyādah 1975d: 129–149).

91. This short story was later reprinted in Sa'd (1973: 689–696).

92. This story was later reprinted in Sa'd (1973: 697–705).

93. This story was later reprinted in Sa'd (1973: 706–711).

94. For more details on Suhayr al-Qalamāwī, see Sakākīnī and Tawfīq (1959: 37–46); Muṣṭafā (1978: 57–58); Farīd (1979a: 71); al-Hilālī (1966: 22–23); Kaḥḥālah (1979: vol. 2, 332–333); Zeidan (1986: 246–248).

95. For more information see her autobiography, *'Alā al-Jisr* (*On the Bridge*, 1986). See also al-Hilālī (1966: 37–38); Kaḥḥālah (1979: vol. 2, 334); 'Abd al-Ḥayy (1966: 119–120); Farīd (1979a: 70–71); Muṣṭafā (1978: 59–61).

96. For a list of Bint al-Shāṭi''s scholarly works, see Zeidan (1986: 184–187).

97. Bint al-Shāṭi', in her autobiogrpahy *'Alā al-Jisr*, refers repeatedly to either Destiny (e.g., pp. 59, 122, 148) or God and Heavenly Power interchangeably (e.g., pp. 84–85, 90, 97) to explain various major events that have shaped her life, such as the course of her studies and marriage. The reader is left with the impression that Bint al-Shāṭi' has been a mere spectator and not an actor vis-à-vis her own life.

98. It is interesting to note that this device was also used in Western women's literature. Among women writers of the Victorian Age (1837–1901), for example, "the height and the trademark of female role-playing was the male pseudonym. Primarily a way of obtaining serious treatment from critics, the pseudonym also protected women from the righteous indignation of their own relatives" (Showalter 1977: 57–58). In the United States "women exploited the feminine stereotype with pastoral pseudonyms like Grace Greenwood, Fanny Forrester, and Fanny Fern, but in the 1880s the Tennessee novelist Mary N. Murfee used the name 'Charles Egbert Breddock' and deceived even her publisher for six years" (Showalter 1977: 59).

99. See *al-'Irfān* (Beirut), vol. 37, no. 3 (March 1950).

100. See *al-Ḥasnā'* (Beirut), no. 608 (April 20, 1973).

101. Bint al-Shāṭi' told the story behind her use of this pseudonym: "It happened when I published my first article in the daily *al-Ahrām* in 1936. It was the first in a long series of articles about the Egyptian countryside. When I finished writing the article, I was at a loss: should I sign my name? This was not logical. I was raised in a conservative environment and grew up with a mystical *Azhari* villager father who venerated tradition. I looked for a name behind which I could hide, and could find none but the playground of my youth and the place of my inspiration. I could find none but the beach of Dumyāṭ" ('Abd al-Ḥayy 1966: 123).

102. See the story of her failed marriage in Ibrāhīm (1954: 41–49).

103. Sīzā al-Nabarāwī served as a secretary to Hudā Sha'rāwī who headed the Egyptian Feminist Union. She was also the editor of *L'Egyptienne*.

104. Zaynab Fawwāz was married to Adīb Naẓmī, a Syrian who already had three wives at the time (Ibrāhīm 1964: 38).

105. This situation is not unique to this group of women. Western feminist writers and literary critics have also observed, as Carolyn Heilburn does, that "of the great women writers, most have been unmarried, . . . [and

few] have had children" (Showalter 1977: 6). This conflict between writing and marriage in the case of the Arab women writers remained alive almost a century later. The Bahraini fiction writer Fawziyyah Rashīd (b. 1954) states, "The beloved cursed writing made me a human being lacking equilibrium and stability.... It made me unable to stay married or think about marriage because all husbands, without exception, ask for a quiet wife who is successful as a housewife and a child raiser who can set up the house the way the best hotels and restaurants are set up" (Rashīd 1992: 58).

106. In her book *Ṣuwar min Ḥayātihinna*, Bint al-Shāṭi' told the tragic stories of some of her female acquaintances who were among the first women to join the university ('Abd al-Raḥmān 1959).

107. See also Muṣṭafā (1978: 57–58).

108. Mayy acknowledges the impact of Baḥithat al-Bādiyah's book *Al-Nisā'iyyāt* on her at an early stage of her literary career, admitting that it provided her "with warm female spirit" (Ziyādah 1930: 17).

109. Only part of this volume was published in 1879. The author died before finishing her project (Kaḥḥālah 1979: vol. 2, 310).

110. Nāṣif established personal relationships with some non-Arab influential women such as the Turkish and nationalist writer Khālidah Adīb (1883–1964) (Halidé Edib Adivar) whom she first met during her visit to Turkey in 1908. She also corresponded with a Muslim princess in India advising her regarding the education of Muslim women (Nāṣif 1962: 59). She also helped the American writer Elizabeth Cooper, who visited her in the desert, to better understand Egyptian women. As a token of gratitude, Cooper dedicated her book to Nāṣif (Cooper 1914). Nāṣif had extended a similar service to the British writer Charlotte Cameron who also wrote about the Egyptian woman (Cameron 1913).

111. Khayr al-Dīn al-Ziriklī discloses that Alexandra Avierinoh showed him personally the manuscript of her collection of poetry (al-Ziriklī 1979: vol. 2, 8).

112. Al-Miṣrī and Wa'lānī (1988: 20) state that, in the process of writing their book, they came across some unpublished works written by Syrian women who, for "compelling reasons," chose not to publish.

113. Another instance is the Iraqi poet Rabāb al-Kāẓimī (b. 1918) whose poetry, some critics claim, was composed by her father, 'Abd al-Muḥsin al-Kāẓimī (Ṭabbānah 1974: 42).

114. For more on al-'Aqqād's views about women, see Diyāb (1969), 'Abdallāh (1976: 7–36), and Muḥammad (1975).

115. Al-Ḥakīm was attacked by some writers for his views vis-à-vis women. See, for example, Mandūr (n.d.: 10), 'Awaḍ (1974: 70), and 'Aṭiyyah (1979: 26–27). For an interesting study of al-Ḥakīm's attitude toward women see 'Īd (1979). See also 'Abdallāh (1976; 89–127).

116. See, for example, Nochlin (1971).

117. For a rebuttal of al-Ḥakīm's philosophy see F. F. B. (1939) (the author was likely a woman who signed her articles with her initials).

118. This article, "al-Mar'ah wa-al-Lughah," was published in the periodical *al-Mar'ah al-Jadīdah* in 1924. It was republished in al-Māzinī's *Qabḍ al-Rīh* (Cairo, 1926). This article was the basis of a lecture entitled Athar al-Mar'ah 'alā al-Lughah given by al-Māzinī (most probably in 1949) and was published with a note by Midḥat al-Jayyār in *Ibdā'* 10, no. 4 (April, 1992): 39–48.

Chapter Three. The Quest for Personal Identity

1. For a psychoanalytical interpretation of *al-Jāmiḥah*, see Ṭarābīshī (1987: 242–277).

2. Ḥadīth ma'a Mu'allifat *Anā Aḥyā* (1960: 4).

3. Ibid.

4. One of the women novelists who was profoundly influenced by Laylā Ba'labakkī's *Anā Aḥyā* is Munā Jabbūr. In fact, her novel *Fatāh Tāfihah* was influenced by Ba'labakkī's novel almost to the point of plagiarism. Nadā, the heroine of Jabbūr's novel, is almost a copy of Ba'labakkī's Līnā: she rebels against her father, who does not hide his sympathy with the French and who opposes Nadā's desire to work because he considers working to be shameful for a member of a wealthy family like his. He, like Līnā's father, carries on an extramarital affair. Nadā and Līnā both despise their mothers for accepting their husbands' authority without question. Even more reminiscent of Līnā, Nadā feels superior to her colleagues at school, referring to them as "pigs" (Jabbūr n.d.: 7). She also contemplates suicide (30) and is disgusted at the sight of a pregnant woman (73), both of which are true of Līnā as well. Nadā's rebellion ultimately fails, and she becomes desperate to get married to any man to have a child and satisfy her urge to become a mother (218). In the end, Nadā, like Līnā, is forced to return home despite an agonizing sense of

alienation from her family (again we see the theme of the vicious circle: home → outside world → home).

Not only does Jabbūr borrow the framework of her novel from Ba'labakkī's *Anā Aḥyā*, she also copies some of Ba'labakkī's expressions and images from that novel. She uses the same unusual expression, *yastamidd . . . ladhdhah*, "to derive pleasure from," to refer to men staring lustfully at her (Jabbūr n.d.: 108, as compared to Ba'labakkī 1964: 140). And Nadā's urge to degrade her father by rubbing his nose with her high-heeled shoes (65) mirrors Līnā's urge to do the same to her own father (Ba'labakkī 1964: 28).

5. Ḥadīth ma'a Mu'allifat *Anā Aḥyā* Laylā Ba'labakkī—al-Wujūdiyyah al-Kubrā" (1960).

6. Ḥadīth ma'a Mu'allifat *Anā Aḥyā* Laylā Ba'labakkī—al-Wujūdiyyah al-Kubrā" (1960).

7. Jabrā I. Jabrā describes *Anā Aḥyā* as "fragmented and loose." Although he praised the novel as a whole, he wished that Ba'labakkī had cut the length of it by a quarter or a half (Jabrā 1962: 216).

8. In 1963 Laylā Ba'labakkī used this collection of short stories to enter a contest sponsored by the Book Friends Society in Lebanon. The periodical *Ḥiwār* disclosed that there were rumors that *Safīnat Ḥanān ilā al-Qamar* did not win the prize, even though the judicial committee had voted unanimously to grant Ba'labakkī the prize because the work "has a certain degree of freedom not yet customary in Arabic literature to the extent that the Committee can make the State [Lebanon] bear the responsibility for [granting] the prize" (*Difā'an 'an al-Ḥuriyyah* 1964: 176).

9. For an account of Laylā Ba'labakkī's trial, see Ba'labakkī (1964b: 5–26). For an English translation of this account, see Fernea and Bezirgan (1977: 280–290).

10. Translated in Fernea and Bezirgan (1977: 280).

11. For a review of this work see al-Sharābī (1958: 50–51). Al-Khūrī came back to writing poetry almost thirty years later with the publication of her collection of Arabic poetry *Ma'aka 'alā Hāmish Riwāyātī* (Damascus, 1987).

12. Interestingly, Western feminists have found negative portrayals of marriage to be a pattern in feminist novels in the West. As Judi M. Roller observes, "Marriage is the worst of all confinements in the feminist novel. . . . Marriage is presented as a microcosm of patriarchy and capitalism" (1986: 158).

13. For Ziyād's role as a father figure for Rīm, see also (60–61, 86, 144).

14. See al-Khāzin and Ilyān (1970: 90).

15. See *al-Mirṣād* (Tel Aviv) n.v. (September 2, 1966: 4).

16. In his study about the significant role of place in *Ṭuyūr Aylūl*, the Lebanese scholar Nadīm Da'kūr notices the tendency of both male and female characters to conceive of the village as a narrow and locked place. He counted thirty-one references to the expression *al-āfāq al-ba'īdah*, "the faraway horizons," used in the context of most characters in their attempts to free themselves from the suffocating atmosphere of the village (Da'kūr 1987: 10).

17. See pp. 150–152 for a discussion of the significance of the birth of a girl in Arab culture.

18. In 1962, Emily Naṣrallah won an award from the Book Friends Society in Lebanon for her novel *Ṭuyūr Aylūl*. She also won Sa'īd 'Aql's prize for the same novel ('Uthmān 1974: 38).

19. In Naṣrallāh's third novel, *al-Rahīnah* (*The Hostage*, 1974), fate is not an abstract force hovering above the characters' heads and lives, but rather a force that is personified in a powerful feudal lord named Namrūd. Namrūd's victim, Rāniyah, is promised at birth to him as a wife by her poor and powerless mother in an attempt to spare Rāniyah from poverty when she is grown. Although Namrūd gives her some freedom of movement, even allowing her to pursue her university studies in Beirut, Rāniyah finds herself forced to come back to the village to marry Namrūd. 'Afīf Farrāj rightly indicates that the difference between Naṣrallāh's first two novels (*Ṭuyūr Aylūl* and *Shajarat al-Diflā*), on one hand, and *al-Rahīnah*, on the other, is that, although oppression in the first two novels is basically realistic and human inflicted (the struggle against it, therefore, being still within the realm of human capability), the oppression in *al-Rahīnah* is fate inflicted (rendering any human resistance futile) (Farrāj 1980: 68–69).

20. For a critique of her views, see 'Aṭawī (1979: 45–54). See also Jāsim (1980: 135–193).

21. Al-Sa'dāwī expanded upon these subjects in later books, among them 1974; 1977a; 1977c; 1978b.

22. This work was translated by Catherine Cobham and published in 1988 with the title *Memoirs of a Woman Doctor*. All citations will be from the English edition, cited as El Saadawi (1988).

23. See Malti-Douglas (1991: 111–129) for a clever discussion of the parallels between *Memoirs of a Woman Doctor* and the classic autobiography, Ṭāhā Ḥusayn's *al-Ayyām* (*The Days*). Calling *Memoirs of a Woman Doctor* a feminist response to *al-Ayyām* (128), which al-Sa'dāwī read early on and found to be a misogynist text, Malti-Douglas explains how these two works are parallel in important ways, particularly in light of the "paradigmatic relationship" in Arab-Islamic culture "in which women and blind become interchangeable phenomena" (125), due to their "physical marginality" (117).

24. Although the Arabic *al-ghā'ib* may be literally translated as "the absent one," the English edition of this novel, translated by Shirley Elber and published in 1991 is entitled *Searching*. All quotations will be from the English edition.

25. This highlights another, more intimate connection between Fouada and the heroine of *Memoirs of a Woman Doctor*, making it possible to view *Searching* as an answer to questions the physician asks herself in *Memoirs of a Woman Doctor*. Consider the quote by that heroine, as she begins to despair of her loneliness ever coming to an end (as Fouada's never does): "What do you want? A man who only exists in your imagination and doesn't walk about the earth? A man who talks, breathes and thinks but doesn't have a body like other men? . . . Why don't you shut yourself up in your prison cell and go back to sleep?" (El Saadawi 1988: 85). Fouada is, in a sense, that heroine's literary double, living a life that could have been almost identical to the physician's if it were not for the latter's successful search for a partner and meaning in her work.

26. Translated into English by Basil Hatim and Elizabeth Orsini and published as *Woman Against Her Sex* in 1988. Quotations will be from this English edition.

27. Quotations will be from the English edition, translated from the Arabic by Marilyn Booth and published in 1989 as *The Circling Song* by El Saadawi.

28. For various views regarding the artistic value of this novel, see Nadwah (symposium) 1978: 123–128.

29. In a recent interview, al-Sa'dāwī referred to the wide fame she has achieved in the West to defend the artistic merits of her fiction in the face of criticism coming from Arab male critics. She praises Western critics for being "objective," implying that their Arab counterparts lack this characteristic. Furthermore, al-Sa'dāwī claimed that she is not interested in what the Arab critic has to say, because he is not qualified to

appreciate her personality. She believes that she is different from other personalities that the Arab critic has been heretofore accustomed to dealing with (al-'Uwayṭ 1992: 9).

30. For more information about 'Ināyāt al-Zayyāt, see Zeidan (1986: 119).

31. But a rejection of one's femininity was by no means the only response by these novels' protagonists to their plight. Isīs, the heroine of 'Alyā' Dālātī's *Khada'atnī al-Mir'āh* (*The Mirror Deceived Me,* 1969) responds in the opposite way and becomes almost narcissistic about her body: "O God, how beautiful is this body. I went closer to the mirror and started kissing myself.... I discovered that night that I was wonderful" (11). Her marriage, however, proves to be nothing more than a form of rape; in fact, her husband literally rapes her on her wedding night to prove his right to possess her (39).

32. Al-Ḥifnāwī repeated the same theme (using almost exactly the same words) in her short story "al-Salāsil" ("The Chains") (1969b: 57).

33. El Saadawi (1980: 45). See also (1970: 79).

34. Work as a symbol of freedom for women is a characterstic these novels shared with Western feminist ones, according to Judi M. Roller (1986: 139).

35. Again, al-Sa'dāwī's work is an exception to that of her contemporaries. This is undoubtedly due, in part, to the fact that al-Sa'dāwī has not lived a "cramped" life, but is highly educated and has been involved in public life through her medical practice as well as through her political activism. As she became more experienced herself, her novels seem to have improved, especially in terms of character development and political sophistication.

36. After all, immediate success on men's terms by women authors would have been very threatening to the establishment and failure due to a lack of experience and education would be, and was, held up as evidence of women's lack of ability and talent.

37. A major difference, though, exists between Western feminist novels and the ones discussed in this chapter. According to Roller, in Western feminist novels the heroine "generally [has] some control over her destiny" and is "partially responsible for the end of the novel" (1986: 131). In Arab women's novels, however, this is not usually the case: "destiny" becomes an explanation for events over which the heroine has no control. This difference may be the result of a much greater degree of cynicism and

a sense of powerlessness on the part of Arab women novelists—but this reliance on "destiny" or "fate" as the mover of events could be read as undermining any attempt to change images of women from psssive and helpless to autonomous, strong, and responsible.

38. Showalter defines this language, known as "ecriture feminine," as "the inscription of the female body and female difference in language and text" and briefly describes the status of the discussion around it (Showalter 1985: 249).

39. This is by no means an argument for a universal female consciousness, but neither should we forget that many aspects of these cultures have common historical origins or aspects adopted from each other due to intercultural contact.

40. This shows clearly the influence of Rimbaud's sonnet "Voyelles," in which the French poet associates a specific color with each of the vowel sounds.

Chapter Four. The Quest for National Identity

1. In Munā Jabbūr's *Fatāh Tāfihah* (46), the heroine takes the same attitude toward her father, who benefits financially from the French mandate in Lebanon.

2. Quotations will be from the English edition, which was translated by Osman Nusairi and Jane Gough and published in 1986 under the title *Two Women in One.*

3. One of Bahiah's reactions to her father's treatment of her is to associate him in her mind with a police officer she often sees on her way to and from school, himself a striking symbol of masculine authority, and with a teacher at school who keeps a strict, watchful eye on her (another important authority figure in her life). These associations are manifested in Bahiah's drawings, in which her father appears with a handlebar moustache (like the policeman) and carries a large stick (like the one the teacher keeps in the classroom). On some level, although Bahiah believes she does not fit in with other girls, she knows that she is at the mercy of these powerful men partly because she is female.

4. Bahiah recalls that when she was still little, "[h]er mother used to gasp when she saw her jumping the stairs. Then Bahiah would hear her heart thumping. She would tense the muscles of her legs, bring her thighs tightly together, and walk towards her mother with that familiar girl's

gait: legs bound together, barely separated from one another. She felt that if they separated, something would tumble down like glass" (75–76).

5. The same kind of image, of leaving the earth and moving to a higher point, appears as Bahiah goes to Salim's house for the first time. He lives on a mountain (al-Muqaṭṭam) and therefore Bahiah experiences a sense of elevation on her way to visit him. This internal experience is also manifested outwardly: "her feet strode steadily and quickly over the asphalt, and her eyes searched the jungle of streets for the protruding arm stretching between the horizon's heart and the blue sky caught between the buildings and the mountain" (61). Literally and figuratively, Bahiah has lived her life virtually on one horizontal plane. Her apartment is on the ground floor and she needs to climb only four steps to get to it. She needs to climb one or two steps to get to the train, and only three to reach the auditorium. The greatest number of steps she has ever climbed is six, to reach the laboratory. Now, to reach Salim's house, she has to climb a whole mountain. For a further analysis of al-Saʿdāwī (1975), see Ṭarābīshī (1978: 10–50).

6. Literally *The Death of the Last Man on Earth* and published in Sherif Hetata's English translation in 1985 as *God Dies by the Nile*. Quotations will be from the English edition.

7. For a further discussion of al-Saʿdāwī's criticism of practiced religion in this novel see Farrāj (1980: 274–275).

8. Twenty years after the publication of *al-Bāb al-Maftūḥ*, al-Zayyāt was at liberty to admit the autobiographical aspects of the novel. She acknowledged that Laylā, the heroine of the story, possesses some of her personal traits, although she has made Laylā younger by ten years (Laṭīfah al-Zayyāt 1993: 57). *Al-Bāb al-Maftūḥ* was later made into a movie starring Fātin Ḥamāmah and Ṣāliḥ Salīm. Al-Zayyāt complained that the end of the movie differed from that of the novel; a change that affected the general meaning of the story. In the novel the heroine achieves liberation through the self and the action that solidifies the self. In the movie, al-Zayyāt notes, this liberation is realized through a man ("Ḥawla al-Iltizām al-Siyāsī" 1990: 145).

9. This representation is illustrated by his reactionary attitude toward women and their roles in society and his lack of patriotic sentiment demonstrated by his ridiculing Laylā for volunteering in the National Guard and his opposition to the nationalization of the Suez Canal Company by Nasser.

10. Female characters in the novel have internalized the patriarchal notions of that culture at that time regarding the position of women in

society. For example, Laylā's female school principal tries to persuade her students not to participate in a demonstration by saying, "The function of a woman is to be a mother and home is her place. Weapon and struggle are man's" (42).

11. Al-Zayyāt disclosed in 1993 that she wrote this novel between 1957 and 1960 and that when it was published (1960) she was already thirty-seven years old. She also revealed that her academic specialization in literature coupled with teaching it at the university (since 1952) influenced her attitude toward writing. Writing, to her, was not only a matter of being talented and sensitive; it required studying, training, and a comprehensive outlook on things that transforms details and fractions into symbols and ideas. Therefore, she made sure to read fiction masterpieces and studies on the technique of the novel before embarking on the writing her novel *al-Bāb al-Maftūḥ*. Among the novelists whose works she read were the Russians Ivan Turgenev, Anoton Chekhov, and Leo Tolstoy (Laṭīfah al-Zayyat 1993: 56).

12. This division is not always strictly observed. Sometimes al-Zayyāt mixes successfully the two levels of the language in narration (see, for example, p. 46). Al-Zayyāt states that her language in *al-Bāb al-Maftūḥ* was the reason for not receiving the State Encouragement Prize for fiction in Egypt because ʻAbbās Maḥmūd al-ʻAqqād, who held a high position in the Ministry of Education, was critical of the free employment of the colloquial language in the novel and threatened to resign if al-Zayyāt's novel was awarded the prize (Laṭīfah al-Zayyāt 1993: 57).

13. Like some of the authors discussed in Chapter Three, al-Zayyāt uses color in the context of clothes to allow Laylā to convey a nonverbal message to her cousin and lover, ʻIṣām: "Laylā stood in front of the wardrobe and, unconsciously, her hand reached to the most beautiful dress, her red dress of the color of watermelon. Her aunt had told her that it brought out the beauty of her skin. No, she would not wear this dress. She is not going to dress up for him. She would not strive to regain him. Laylā took her hand away from the dress and chose a pink blouse and a simple black skirt and combed her hair carelessly and went up to her aunt's apartment . . ." (61).

14. This is referred to again on p. 257.

15. Fu'ād Duwārah argues that al-Zayyāt, by dwelling on the detailed description of the Suez battle at the end of the story, avoids having to tackle Laylā's personal problems, such as the inevitable confrontation with her fiancé and her father, who represents the reactionary forces in her society (Duwārah 1968: 154).

16. The Arab defeat in the 1967 war deepened al-Zayyāt's conviction that the "woman question" is strongly tied to the national one. At the time that Sinai was still under Israeli occupation, al-Zayyāt was asked why she, with all her qualifications, did not lead a feminist movement. She replied, "There are always priorities. I am of the opinion that liberating the homeland is a societal issue, and that women will never attain their freedom unless the society attains its. . . . Although the woman question has its own particularity to which I need to pay special attention. This attention, however, does not totally preoccupy me because I direct my attention to the homeland with its men and women" (al-Zayyāt fī Mir'āt 1993: 58).

17. For more details regarding the Arabic novel and the Palestinian problem, see Zeidan (1989: 58–82).

18. See, for example, Widād's elegy for her father (90–91). It is interesting to note that this dialectic relation between land (*arḍ*) and honor (*'irḍ*) remained alive in novles written about the 1967 war. For example, in his novel *Ḥārat al-Naṣārā* (Beirut, 1969), the Palestinian novelist Nabīl Khūrī portrays, through the heroine Salmā, the transition from occupying Jerusalem in 1967 to violating a woman's body as only a natural process. Once one loses his land, he ends up losing his honor. Salmā turns to her murdered husband for help: "Why have you left me? Why don't you rise up from the dead to protect me from that man who stretched his hand out wanting to touch me? Where are you to repel the hand that grabbed me under the threat of a gun? Nobody except you has ever touched me! How could that filthy man touch me? Where are you to protect me? . . . Did you know that he who conquers the city and the neighborhood will try to replace you and put his hand in the place of your hand?" (13. See Zeidan 1989: 72, 75).

In the Syrian novelist Mamdūḥ 'Adwān's *al-Abtar* (Damascus, 1970), we read this dialogue between Syrian villagers in the Golan Heights during the Israeli invasion:

> — Where are you going folks?
> — Our turn will come.
> — And the land?
> — What can we do? May God provide for us. What is important is the safety of honor and the children. (23)

In his study *al-Naqd al-Dhātī ba'da al-Hazīmah* (Beirut, 1969), Ṣādiq Jalāl al-'Aẓm concludes that the issue of saving honor was one of the main reasons causing Palestinians to flee the West Bank during the 1967 wars (see Māḍī 1978: 94). For further discussion of the concept of land and honor in the Palestinian culture, see Warnock (1990: esp. 22–24).

19. Al-Juwaydī's obsession with political commentaries and pure historical details throughout the whole novel is rightly considered by Muṣṭafā Karkūtī to be a major artistic flaw. He describes this novel as "a news film supported by pictures illuminating the events" (Abū Maṭar 1980: 152–153).

20. It is interesting to note that Khalīfah did not start writing before gaining her personal freedom: after thirteen years of painful marriage at an early age (she was eighteen) she left her husband who was working abroad. Reflecting on this frustrating experience Khalīfah confesses, "The biggest mistake of my life was that I got married in order to escape the oppressive society of Nablus [her home town]... sometimes... I pity myself that I had to spend so many years in a failing marriage" (Lenṭin 1982: 17).

21. Muhammad Siddiq acknowledges similar shortcomings in this novel and calls it "more a project for a novel than an accomplished work" (1986: 144).

22. Quotations will be from the English edition, entitled *Wild Thorns*, translated by Trevor LeGassick and Elizabeth Fernea and published in its second edition in 1991.

Khalīfah explains, "The word *al-ṣubbār* ["cactus"] has many literary connotations due to its symbolism, the cactus being a plant capable of surviving in the harshest conditions. Its fruit is sweet and bitter at the same time. It is thorny on the outside, yet sweet on the inside" (Lenṭin 1982: 12).

23. All quotations will be from the English edition, translated by Catherine Cobham and published in 1989.

24. Badr recalls that she was sent to this orphanage, where she stayed for three years, due to the tough financial situation of her family caused by her father's frequent imprisonments as a result of his political activism (Badr 1992: 235).

25. For example, in the novel, Jinan's father is arrested, as was Badr's. Also, as Jinan is evacuated during the Arab-Israeli War in 1967, being told that it will be for only a few days, she realizes that she will never be back, and she chooses to take with her a pen and a photograph of her deceased mother. This was the very situation that Badr experienced during that war as a girl, as she describes it to Shaaban (1991: 159).

26. Badr explains the dialectic relationship between her own experience in life (exile) and the structure of this novel: "When I started writing my novel *A Compass for the Sunflower* in 1976, I tried to bring the image of exile into the text. I structured my novel in the shape of squares

crossing vertically and horizontally in order to draw the complete picture. It was like a crossword puzzle. Does not exile represent something like this in our lives? Time is interrupted and places are separated or connected in a particular pattern" (Badr 1992: 239).

27. This is represented metaphorically in the novel, as Jinan considers the oleander flower: "Shade-loving plants are known for their amazing ability to grow and divide. They need only a little water... soil is unimportant to them, although without it their growth can be neither normal nor continuous" (Badr 1989: 9).

28. Badr describes her mother as a feminist and tells Shaaban how influential this was for her as she was growing up (Shaaban 1991: 156–157).

29. In the novel, Jinan recalls that her father managed to obtain an ancient rifle to fight the Israelis during the 1967 war, "but a friend of his came on foot from Ramallah and said to him, 'You're free to decide that you want to stay. But what about the girls? They're a big responsibility'" (Badr 1989: 75). Badr reveals a similar experience in her own family, adding a new detail: her father's friend who pressured him to flee with his daughter to protect his honor was religious (Badr 1992: 236).

30. For further discussion of this issue see al-Ikhtiyār (1991: esp. pp. 76–81).

31. See similar views on pp. 55, 164, 252, and 276.

32. This is an allusion to T. S. Eliot's poem "The Love Song of J. Alfred Prufrock," which starts with

> Let us go then, you and I,
> When the evening is spread out against the sky
> Like a patient etherised upon a table (1958: 3)

Al-Sammān's intention was to evoke the atmosphere of boredom and futility that dominates Eliot's poem.

33. In an interview, Ghādah al-Sammān discussed her dilemma in determining Yāsmīnah's fate while writing the novel. At first she had intended to make Yāsmīnah become a prostitute, but during the process of writing the novel the character "rebelled and decided she preferred a life of poverty and challenge to society" (al-Sammān 1980: 198).

34. Al-Sammān noted that she began writing *Bayrūt 75* on October 9, 1974, and prepared it for publication on November 22 of the same year (al-Sammān 1975: 108). It came out in March 1975, only one month before the outbreak of the Lebanese civil war.

35. Al-Sammān claims that she started writing this novel during the war. When her apartment in Beirut was hit and set on fire, she succeeded in salvaging the manuscript of *Kawābīs Bayrūt* (al-Sammān 1980: 45).

36. This exerpt of al-Sammān's writing contradicts some of Miriam Cooke's conclusions in her book, *War's Other Voices: Women Writers on the Lebanese Civil War*. In that work, Cooke focuses on a group of Arab women writers who she calls the *Beirut Decentrists*. Some of their common characteristics, according to her, include a refusal of explanations of the Lebanese civil war as political or economic (26) and the fact that they (and other women writers) "did not attempt to identify an enemy" (118). Cooke herself characterizes the war as having defined no "sides" as we usually understand that word. However, the preceding indicates that al-Sammān saw the war as political and economic. The heroine took an active part in getting the war started, because she saw something needed to be accomplished. She identified enemies and took sides, and this is portrayed positively by al-Sammān in the novel.

37. The Syrian critic, Muḥyī al-Dīn Ṣubḥī, notes rightly that the heroine, due to her emotional and intellectual attachment to the library, cannot comprehend the event of its burning all at once; she rather does that in stages. She first sees the fire in the library, then hears the fire sound, and at the end she realizes that the library is one fire (Ṣubḥī 1979: 128–129).

38. Publication of al-Sammān's *Kawābīs Bayrūt* began at the beginning of 1976 in the form of installments in a Lebanese magazine. By August of that year the first 160 nightmares had been published (al-Sammān 1979: 6).

39. T. S. Eliot explained his theory of the "objective correlative" as follows: "The only way of expressing emotion in the form of art is by finding an objective correlative; in other words, a set of objects, a situation, a chain of events which shall be the formula of that particular emotion, such that when the external facts, which must terminate in sensory experience, are given, the emotion is immediately evoked" (Eliot 1932: 145).

40. See 'Afīf Farrāj's interpretation of this dream, which I found particularly helpful (Farrāj 1980: 138–139).

41. A number of critics have refused to recognize *Kawābīs Bayrūt* as a full-fledged novel, considering it rather a reportage or a diary. See, for example, Khūst (1977: 127–128). 'Abd al-'Azīz Shubayl, on the other hand, argues that this work is "a real novel," although it may not conform to conventional forms. It consists, Shubayl believes, of the basic components of a novel, such as the element of narration, time and place

frameworks, events, major and minor characters, dialogue, and flashback (Shubayl 1987: 41). Samar R. al-Fayṣal indicates that *Kawābīs Bayrūt* was the first Syrian novel to depart from the classical form (al-Fayṣal 1979: 414).

42. Quotations will be from the English edition, published in 1989.

43. This is particularly significant because Zahra's mother used to escape to the bathroom when her father became violent. Women have been allowed so little privacy that they have developed very specific survival techniques. Did Zahra "learn" this one from her mother or would anyone in her position realize that locking herself in the bathroom was her only option?

44. Interestingly, "destiny" is not used to explain outcomes in this novel—another reason to read *The Story of Zahra* as significant in its approach to accountability.

45. Regarding this change in attitude, Cooke writes the following: "Codes of shame and honor lose significance in comparison with the immensity and majesty of nature. It is a majesty that seems capable of stripping men of their past, of their importance, of their separateness. Africa is a sea that drowns all difference" (Cooke 1987a: 51). I would argue just the opposite—that Africa reminds Majed of his "difference," so much so that his cultural beliefs and practices seem not only out of place there, but even meaningless because the community support that gives them meaning is absent. The "codes" in question become insignificant, not *in spite* of difference, but *because* of it. Those in power almost always claim that absolute truth or necessity justifies oppressive conditions, but Majed begins to understand that "wrongness" and "immorality," are merely culturally negotiated value judgments and are, therefore, relative.

46. Although Cooke uses the term *rape* to describe the first sexual experience, I wonder whether that is appropriate. Zahra's *plan* is to distract Sami from killing, and her first attempt is by parading half-dressed on the roof across from the one on which he is sleeping. When he seems interested in her, she goes to visit him, and her narration of that first sexual experience with him indicates neither fear nor reluctance. There is no passion on her part, either, mentioned in that account, but when she arrives home afterwards, she hardly sounds like a victim: "A thread of happiness ran through me" (128). This statement is followed immediately by descriptions of their subsequent meetings, which we learn are the only times when she feels pleasure. Was Zahra raped then or did she plan that first sexual contact? Could this be read as a victory for Zahra in her efforts to help stop the killing? Perhaps Sami does not have any reason to think he is not

raping the strange woman who enters his room, but even so, Zahra's perspective of the event ought not be dismissed as irrelevant. If she visits Sami with the intention of having sexual intercourse with him, naming it *rape* oversimplifies the situation and privileges his point of view (which is especially problematic in a discussion of this subject).

47. The best illustration of this in the novel is Ahmad's revelation to Zahra of what the war means to him: "Whenever I hear it said that this war is almost over without anything being accomplished, I freeze. The end of the war means I will become a shadow in the streets where, with my rifle, I have been master, room by room, building by building, tree by tree. I have been master of the nights as well as the days . . . I don't wish for this war to end. I don't want to have to worry about what to do next. The war has structured my days and nights, my financial status, my very self" (143–144).

48. Recall the discussion in Chapter Three of escape and confinement in women's literature.

49. This, added to the novel's structure and various narrating characters, is reminiscent of many novels discussed in Chapter Three in which this kind of "fragmentation" is a common literary device. Al-Shaykh carefully portrays the conflicts between the external constraints placed on Zahra and her own beliefs and desires, which Roller cites as an important reason for fragmentation in women's novels (Roller 1986: 68). These conflicts are so great that Zahra occasionally breaks down or experiences fragmentation of her Self. Likewise, the point of view is fragmented in the novel when Hashem and Majed each narrate a chapter, a format that Roller also examines in her discussion (Roller 1986: 68).

50. Recall Zahra's description of her father on p. 7, quoted earlier in this discussion.

51. Laylā 'Usayrān discloses the autobiographical nature of this novel. It is the story of her house in Beirut, which was destroyed in 1976, and the subsequent death of her cook ('Usayrān 1985: 137).

52. Quotations will be made from the English edition, published in 1987.

53. This is illustrated by the raven who appears outside Radwan's window on the morning when he learns of Saleem's death. At first, when he hears the raven, he tries to reassure himself that this is Canada, and "if the cry of a black raven is a bad omen pronouncing evil in your country, its story is different here, like many other things you have discovered"

(185). However, just after hearing the raven, Radwan learns of Saleem's death.

54. Again I contradict Miriam Cooke, who distinguishes between "patriotism" and "nationalism" in Western terms. Cooke sees the Beirut Decentrists (including 'Usayrān and al-Sammān) as "defining a new patriotism," and contrasts them with male Arab writers whose "fiction bore the mark of nationalism" (Cooke 1987a: 165). However, in the Arab world, nationalism is about the hope for reuniting the Arab countries that have been arbitrarily divided against the Arabs' will and is not about establishing superiority of, or domination by, the Arab nation. And "patriotism," to many Arabs, is a betrayal of the nationalist movement because it would involve supporting those arbitrary boundaries between the now-recognized Arab countries. Note al-Sammān's statement: "I insist that I am an Arab writer, and do not accept being labelled as a Syrian or Lebanese writer" (1980: 138). Of course, part of the problem here is definition—it could be argued that Miriam Cooke and I simply have different definitions for the same terms, and we each make valid arguments based on them. But in referring to some male writers as writing in a nationalist vein under her definition, because they "wrote of revolution, of just causes, of enemies within and without" (165), Cooke is taking their work out of context. After all, al-Sammān also "wrote of revolution, of just causes, of enemies within and without," and yet Cooke refers to her work as "patriotic." This, then, becomes more than a problem of definition. Cooke's notion of nationalism involves the desire and attempt to dominate others, and the Arabs' situation involves the desire and attempt to free themselves of domination by others. This is not to argue that there were not significant differences between men's and women's writing on the subject of Arab national identity, or that women writers did not have an especially valuable perspective or analysis of the civil war; but I must disagree that one of these differences is that men were "nationalist" and women were "patriotic" according to Cooke's definitions.

Chapter Five. Conclusions

1. The term *the literature of long nails* was used earlier, interestingly enough, in an article about Arab women's fiction published in the women's magazine *Sayyidatī* (*Ṣūrat al-Rajul* 1983).

2. Arab women writers had to confront the issue of getting their works published in an industry dominated exclusively by men until very recently. Perhaps Zaynab Fawwāz was the first one to leave us an account regarding troubles with her publisher. In a letter to the editor of *Al-'Irfān*,

Fawwāz discloses, not without sorrow, that the publisher of her novel *Al-Malik Qūrūsh aw Malik al-Furs* (Cairo, 1905) took the freedom to alter her work without consulting her; he condensed the last chapters and removed all the poetry (Fawwāz 1984: 33), an act that devastated her work and exposed it to some negative reviews. Fawziyyah Fawwāz suggests that, most probably, Zaynab Fawwāz's other books were subject to the same treatment (Fawwāz 1984: 33). In other cases the publishers took financial advantage of women writers; Laylā Ba'labakkī decided, after her agonizing experience with the publisher of her first book, to publish her novel *Al-Ālihah al-Mamsūkhah* on her own. Although Ba'labakkī had paid the printing costs, the owner of the press sold the book to another publisher while she was abroad. Ba'labakkī describes this episode as "frightful," causing her to feel "disgusted, frightened, and saddened" whenever she completes a book (Ba'labakkī 1965: 10–11). Nowadays, there are a number of publishing houses founded by women writers for the purpose of publishing their own works. Several such publishing houses include that of Ghādah al-Sammān and Hudā al-Na'mānī in Beirut, 'Ā'ishah Abū al-Nūr in Cairo, and Su'ād al-Ṣabbāḥ in Kuwait and Cairo. In Cairo at least one publishing house (Sīnā li-al-Nashr) is owned and run by a woman (Rāwiyah 'Abd al-'Aẓīm). It publishes a wide variety of books, some of them being controversial like Sanā' al-Miṣrī's feminist book *Khalfa al-Ḥijāb: Mawqif al-Jamā'āt al-Islāmiyyah min Qaḍiyyat al-Mar'ah* (Behind the Veil: The Attitude of Islamic Organizations Regarding the Question of Women, 1989), which was recently banned in Egypt after being attacked by religious authorities. On the other hand, some publishing houses have discovered the commercial value of publishing women's works, especially novels revolving around love affairs, and are making a point of printing the authors' photos on the back covers of their books.

As early as 1963, the Syrian critic George Ṭarābīshī criticized the commercialization of women's novels at the expense of the artistic aspects: "Despite this grave artistic weakness, publishing houses take unusual interest in publishing women's novels. I am absolutely certain that if the author were a male the majority of these novels would not be published. . . . The women in our country write in order that people see the feminine [feature] (*unthā*) in her. Publishing houses are interested in her and readers clap hands for her for no reason other than that she is a woman. Our women writers today resemble movie stars and their pictures and whereabouts occupy prominent places in newspapers and magazines" (Tarābīshī 1963: 49).

3. These difficulties were not by any means restricted to those authors being dealt with in this book. The Egyptian short story writer Alīfah Rif'at, for example, started her literary career using pennames (such as Bint Banhā, 'Āyidah, and Alīfah Ṣādiq) not to arouse her husband's

wrath. When he found out in 1960 about his wife's endeavors, he gave her a choice: either she would refrain from writing and being published or else they would divorce and she would lose custody over her young daughter. It was not until 1971, after she had suffered serious mental distress, that her husband let her resume writing (see Fawzī 1987: 34, 194). Another Egyptian, the novelist Su'ād Zuhayr found herself clashing with her entire family when her novel *Yawmiyyāt Imra'ah Mustarjilah* (*The Diary of a Masculine Woman*, published in book form in 1961) began being published in installments in the weekly *Rūz al-Yūsuf*. Accusing her of tarnishing the family's reputation by writing such a "real" story, her family threatened to sue her if she did not stop the series. To put an end to this hostility. Zuhayr had to declare openly that the story of the novel was not autobiographical, but rather was a diary that she had received by mail from an anonymous women (Sha'bān 1962: 59).

4. For more details, see al-Ḥakīm (1939a: 18); Zeidan (1989: 59).

5. This is known to many feminists as the Eve-Madonna dichotomy, a common phenomenon in patriarchal cultures (and widely documented in Western societies), which divides images of women, and actual women by extension, into categories labeled *good* and *bad* women. "Good" women are docile, obedient, motherly, and self-sacrificing. "Bad" women are sexual and independent and are thus suspected of being evil and wanting to dominate and hurt men. For a discussion of this issue, see Ruth (1980).

6. Salwā Bakr, an Egyptian female fiction writer, states: "The creative writer suffers from the repression of three restrictive regimes: religion, sex and politics. As far as the woman writer is concerned, the language is an added oppressor—the language which contains in its coffin the inherited male terms and expressions and which does not allow but a narrow margin to enable the woman writer to express her inner world as a female" (Bakr 1992: 154).

Appendix 1. Women's Journals in Egypt

1. Main sources: Al-Jarā'id al-'Arabiyyah fī al-'Ālam, *al-Hilāl* 12 (October 15, 1903): 49–57; Cheikho (1926); al-Jundī (n.d.); Dāghir (n.d.); Diyāb (1981); Jum'ah (1982); Kaḥḥālah (1979: vol. 2); Khalīfah (1973); Subkī (1986); Ṭarrāzī (1913: vol. 2).

An asterisk marks journals founded by male journalists or publishing houses but designated for female readership.

2. It turned out that "Maryam Maẓhar" was actually the pen name of a male writer, Salīm Sarkīs (1867–1926), a Lebanese living in Egypt who

founded the newspaper *Raj' al-Ṣadā* and the magazine *Majallat Sarkīs* (al-Jundī n.d.: 7; 1979: 340–343; al-Ṭamāwī 1989: 5–9).

3. Most sources state that this magazine was discontinued in 1904 (Dāghir 1972: vol. 3, part 1, 137–138; Shumays 1985: 12; Yūsuf 1969: 10). Al-Jundī (n.d.: 39) claims that the magazine was discontinued in 1908. Al-Ṭamāwī mentions 1907 as the year in which *Anīs al-Jalīs* came to its end (al-Ṭamāwī 1989: 128).

4. Alexandra Khūrī Avierinoh (1872–1927) was born in Beirut and educated in missionary schools there. At the age of ten she moved with her family to Alexandria, where she learned Arabic, French, and Italian. She was married to an Italian named Avierinoh at the age of sixteen. In addition to *Anīs al-Jalīs*, she published the journal *Lotus* in French. She was very active in public affairs; in 1900 she represented Egypt at the Peace Conference in Paris. Sultan 'Abd al-Ḥamīd and the Shah of Iran, Muẓaffar al-Dīn, both granted her orders of merit. She was assisted in editing *Anīs al-Jalīs* by Najīb al-Ḥaddād (1867–1899) and his brother Amīn al-Ḥaddād (1868–1912). Amīn al-Ḥaddād, in his memories of the year 1904, published in *Muntakhabāt Amīn al-Ḥaddād* (Alexandria, 1913), discloses that some of the poetry published in *Anīs al Jalīs* and attributed to Alexandra Avierinoh was written by him in exchange for a fee (Yūsuf n.d.: 11). Al-Jundī's claim that Avierinoh did not know Arabic well and wrote no works in that language (n.d.: 6), is contradicted by her five chapter play, *Amānat al-Ḥubb* (*The Fidelity of Love*), which was written although not performed (Muḥammad n.d.: part 2, 93), and her translation into Arabic of the novel, *The Suffering of Mothers* (*Shaqā' al-Ummahāt*) (Kaḥḥālah 1977: vol. 5, 303). For more details, see E. Ibrāhīm (1964: 57–64); Dāghir (1972: vol. 3, part 1: 137–139); Zeidan (1986: 239–240).

5. Esther Azhari Moyāl (1873–1948) was born to a Jewish family in Beirut, where she was educated in a missionary school. After her marriage in 1894 she moved to Cairo and began her literary and journalistic activities. In addition to writing articles for Egyptian periodicals, such as *al-Ahrām* and *al-Hilāl*, Moyāl translated a number of Emile Zola's stories into Arabic. She died in Jaffa, Palestine. For more details see Dāghir (1983: 683–685).

6. It included a section in Turkish and another in French (Kaḥḥālah 1977: vol. 2, 149).

7. Nabawiyyah Mūsā (1890–1951) was an outstanding educator and the first woman to become an inspector in Egypt. She was fired after a dispute with the minister of education because she criticized girls' curricula. She established her private schools, the Madāris Banāt al-Ashrāf (The Schools for Nobles' Daughters) in Cairo and Alexandria. In her

important book, *al-Mar'ah wa-al-'Amal* (*Women and the Labor Force*, 1920), she called for equality of the sexes, and expressed her conviction that only education could bring it about. She also published a collection of poetry in 1938 (Dāghir 1972: vol. 3, part 2, 1131; Kaḥḥālah 1979: vol. 2, 128–129; Mikhail 1979: 29–36; Maskūnī 1970: 52–54; Zeidan 1986: 281–282).

8. Fāṭimah (Rose) al-Yūsuf (1898–1958) was born in Tripoli, Lebanon, where she started her education. At the age of ten she moved to Alexandria. She showed her talent as an actress at an early age, working with different theatrical groups. Despite her tremendous success on the stage, she switched to political and artistic journalism. She was the first woman in Egypt to found a publishing house, from which she published (in addition to *Rūz al-Yūsuf*) the weekly *Ṣabāḥ al-Khayr* (Dāghir 1977: vol. 3, no. 1, 155; Maḥmūd 1980: 76–77; Ḥannā 1979: 34–37; Muṣṭafā 1978: 61; Zeidan 1986: 305–306).

9. In addition to *al-Amal*, Munīrah Thābit published a French journal entitled *l'Espoir* for a short period (Maḥmūd n.d.: 87).

10. Munīrah Thābit (1902–1967) was born in Alexandria, Egypt, where she learned French and English in addition to Arabic. She moved to Cairo and founded her journals *al-Amal* in Arabic and *l'Espoir* in French. For more details see al-Jundī (n.d.: 63–65); Yūsuf (1969: 494–496); Zeidan (1986: 64).

11. Durriyyah Shafīq was one of the first female graduates of the Egyptian University and one of the first Egyptian women to study abraod. After obtaining her doctorate in France, she returned to Egypt and became active in promoting women's rights (see al-Jawharī and al-Khayyāl 1980: 258; Nelson 1986: 15–31); Ahmed (1992: 202–207).

12. Zaynab al-Ghazālī al-Jubaylī (b. 1917) was born in Cairo to an *Azhari* father, who granted his daughter an intensive Islamic education. In 1936 she founded *Al-Markaz al-'Āmm li-al-Sayyidāt al-Muslimāt* (The General Headquarters of Muslim Women), which cooperated closely with the Muslim Brotherhood. She was jailed during Nasser's regime and wrote about that experience in *Ayyām min Ḥayātī* (*Days of My Life*). For more details about al-Jubaylī, see Ibn al-Hāshimī (1989: 17–23); Boullata (1990: 123–127); Hoffman (1975: 233–254); Ahmed (1992: 197–202); Harlow (1992: 127–129); Zuhur (1992: 45–48).

13. The first issue was published under the name *Nūn* (May 1989) as a quarterly magazine. The Egyptian government refused to grant this publication a permit as a magazine, and consequently, it was not put on public sale. The publication became a newsletter (*nashrah*) of the Arab

Women's Solidarity Association, AWSA (*Jam'iyyat Taḍāmun al-Mar'ah al-'Arabiyyah*) starting with the May 1990 issue. The AWSA was dissolved by the Egyptian government in 1991, and its newsletter was discontinued.

Appendix 2. Women's Journals in Lebanon

1. Main sources: Cheiko (1926); Dāghir (n.d.); Diyāb (1981); Ibrāhīm (1964; 1966); Jum'ah (1982); Kaḥḥālah (1973; 1979, vol. 2); al-Khaṭīb (1984); Ṭarrāzī (1913: vol. 2).

An asterisk marks journals founded by male journalists or publishing houses but designated for female readership.

2. Abī al-Luma' resumed the publication of this journal in Paris (Dāghir n.d.: 214).

3. Ḥabbūbah Ḥaddād (1897–1957) was born in al-Bārūk, Lebanon. She studied economics and political science at the American University in Beirut. In 1920 she began a two-year trip through France and the United States. Most of her writings have been lost (Ibrāhīm 1964: 181–197; Zeidan 1986: 75).

4. First published in Paris with Faraḥ Anṭūn (1861–1922) as an editor. Between 1922 and 1929 Ḥaddād herself published and edited this magazine in Beirut (Ibrāhīm 1964: 184–185).

5. Jūlyā Ṭu'mah Dimashqiyyah (1880?–1954) was born in al-Makhtārah, Lebanon. She was educated in the American School for Girls in Sidon and in a teachers' school in al-Shuwayfāt. Later she taught in Palestine, Egypt, and Lebanon. In 1918 she established "Jāmi'at al-Sayyidāt" (The Ladies' League), which was involved in philanthropic activities (Dāghir n.d.: vol. 2, part 1, 369–370; Zeidan 1986: 103).

6. In 1916 Mary Yannī ('Aṭallāh) started publishing a written pamphlet under the same name for a small group of friends (Nuwayhiḍ 1986: 274).

Appendix 3. Women's Journals in Iraq

1. Main sources: al-Darbandī (1968; 1970); Dāwūd (1958); Diyāb (1981); Ibrāhīm (1982); Jum'ah (1982).

Appendix 4. Women's Journals in Syria

1. Main sources: al-Khaṭīb (1984); al-Miṣrī and Wa'lānī (1988); Nuwayhiḍ (1986); Zeidan (1986); Razzāz (1975); Rifā'ī (1969).

Appendix 5. Women's Journals in the Rest of The Arab World and Abroad

1. Salwā Aṭlas Salāmah (1883–1949) was born in Homs, Syria. She immigrated to Brazil where she distinguished herself as an eloquent speaker. Some of her speeches were published in *Ḥadīqat Khuṭab* (São Paulo, 1928). For further details, see Ṣaydaḥ (1964: 604); al-'Aqīqī (1976: 211); Zeidan (1986: 143–144).

2. Bilingual; Arabic and Portuguese.

3. For more information about Maryānā Da'būl Fākhūrī, see Ibrāhīm (1966: 130–132); Ṣaydaḥ (1966: 69–80; 1964: 55); Zeidan (1986: 228).

4. Samīrah Khāshuqjī (1940–1986) is widely known by her penname Samīrah bint al-Jazīrah al-'Arabiyyah (Samīrah, the Daughter of the Arabian Peninsula). Born in Mecca, she was educated in Egypt, where she obtained a B.A. degree in economics. She wrote seven novels and one collection of short stories, in addition to a study about the Saudi woman. For more details, see *Dalīl al-Kātib* (1984: 101); Amīn (1973: 507–510); al-Fawzān (1971: 1090–1092); Zeidan (1986: 85–88).

5. Ghunaymah Fahd al-Marzūq (1941–) was born in Kuwait. After receiving a degree from Cairo University in Egypt she returned home and worked in journalism. For more details, see Ismā'īl (1980: 144–145); Ṣāliḥ (1978: 65–74); 'Abdallāh (1973: 397–400); Zeidan (1986: 256–266).

6. Journals founded by male journalists or publishing houses but intended for female readership are marked with an asterisk.

7. Khanāthah Banūnah (1937–) was born in Fez, Morocco, where she received her primary and secondary schooling. After graduating from a teachers' training college in Casablanca, she returned to her home town to teach. So far she has written one novel and six short story collections. She was the first woman to found a woman's periodical in Morocco. For more details, see al-'Awfī (1980: 225–235); al-Mudaynī (n.d.: 398–426); al-Nassāj (n.d.: 248–262; 1977: 347–357); Accad (1982: 18–34); Zeidan (1986: 57).

Appendix 6. Novels Written by Arab Women (1887–1993)

1. Nihād Ṭawfīq 'Abbāsī has written at least two other novels: *Jazīrat al-'Adālah* and *Muḥākamat Yamāmah 'Arabiyyah* (an autobiography). I failed to obtain bibliographical details on these two works.

References

European Language Sources

Accad, Evelyne. 1990. *Sexuality and War: Literary Masks in the Middle East*. New York: New York University Press.

———. 1982. "Women's Voices from the Maghreb." In *Arab Literature in North Africa: Critical Essays and Annotated Bibliography*, pp. 18–34. Cambridge: Dār Mahjar.

Ahmed, Leila. 1992. *Women and Gender in Islam: Historical Roots of a Modern Debate*. New Haven, Conn., and London: Yale University Press.

Arafa, Bahiga. 1973. *The Social Activities of the Egyptian Feminist Union*. Cairo: Elias' Modern Press.

Badawi, M. M. 1993. *A Short History of Modern Arabic Literature*. Oxford: Clarendon Press.

———, ed. 1992. *Modern Arabic Literature*. Cambridge: Cambridge University Press.

Badr, Liana [see also Badr, Liyānah]. 1989. *A Compass for the Sunflower*, trans. Catherine Cobham. London: Women's Press.

Badran, Margot, and Miriam Cooke, eds. 1990. *Opening the Gates: A Century of Arab Feminist Writing*. Bloomington: Indiana University Press.

Baym, Nina. 1987. "The Madwoman and Her Languages: Why I Don't Do Feminist Literary Theory." In *Feminist Issues in Literary Scholar-*

ship, ed. S. Benstock, pp. 45–61. Bloomington and Indianapolis: Indiana University Press.

Benstock, S., ed. 1987. *Feminist Issues in Literary Scholarship*. Bloomington; Indianapolis: Indiana University Press.

Boullata, Issa J. 1990. *Trends and Issues in Contemporary Arab Thought*. Albany: State University of New York Press.

Brée, Germaine. 1973. *Women Writers in France: Variations on a Theme*. New Brunswick, N.J.: Rutgers University Press.

Cameron, Charlotte. 1913. *A Woman's Winter in Africa: A 26,000-Mile Journey*. London: Stanley Paul.

Cooke, Miriam. 1992. "Arab Women Writers." In *Modern Arabic Literature*, ed. M. M. Badawi, pp. 443–462. Cambridge: Cambridge University Press.

———. 1987a. *War's Other Voices: Women Writers on the Lebanese Civil War*. New York: Cambridge University Press.

———. 1987b. *Women Write War: The Centering of the Beirut Decentrists*. Oxford: Centre for Lebanese Studies.

Cooper, Elizabeth. 1914. *The Women of Egypt*. London: Hurst and Blackett.

Donovan, Josephine, ed. 1987. "Toward a Women's Poetics." In *Feminist Issues in Literary Scholarship*, ed. S. Benstock, pp. 98–109. Bloomington and Indianapolis: Indiana University Press.

Elliot, T. S. 1958. *The Waste Land and Other Poems*. New York: Harcourt, Brace and World.

———. 1932. *Selected Essays*. London: Faber and Faber.

El Saadawi, Nawal [see also al-Sa'dāwī, Nawāl]. 1991. *Searching*, trans. Shirley Elber. London and Atlantic Highlands, N.J.: Zed Books.

———. 1989. *The Circling Song*, trans. Marilyn Booth. London and Atlantic Highlands, N.J.: Zed Books.

———. 1988. *Memoirs of a Woman Doctor*, trans. Catherine Cobham. London: Saqi Books.

———. 1986. *Two Women in One*, trans. Osman Nusairi and Jane Gough. Seattle: Seal Press.

———. 1985. *God Dies by the Nile*, trans. Sherif Hetata. London: Zed Books.

———. 1980. *The Hidden Face of Eve: Women in the Arab World,* trans. and ed. Sherif Hetata. London: Zed Press.

Fayad, Mona. 1987. *The Road to Feminism: Arab Women Writers.* East Lansing: Michigan State University.

Fénelon, François de Salignac de la Mothe-. 1774. *The Adventures of Telemachus, the Son of Ulysses,* trans. Percival Proctor. London: G. Kearsly.

Fernea, Elizabeth W., ed. 1985. *Women and the Family in the Middle East.* Austin: University of Texas Press.

——— and Basima Q. Bezirgan, eds. 1977. *Middle Eastern Muslim Women Speak.* Austin and London: University of Texas Press.

Gibb, Hamilton A. R. 1982. *Studies on the Civilization of Islam.* Princeton, N.J.: Princeton University Press.

Gibran, Jean, and Kahlil Gibran. 1974. *Kahlil Gibran, His Life and World.* Boston: New York Graphic Society.

Gilbert, Sandra M., and Susan Gubar. 1979. *The Madwoman in the Attic: The Woman Writer and the Nineteenth-Century Literary Imagination.* New Haven, Conn.: Yale University Press.

Gubar, Susan. 1985. "'The Blank Page' and the Issues of Female Creativity." In *The New Feminist Criticism: Women, Literature, and Theory,* ed. E. Showalter, pp. 292–313. New York: Pantheon Books.

Hafez, Sabry. 1989. "Intentions and Realisation in the Narrative of Nawal El-Saadawi." *Third World Quarterly* 11, no. 3 (July): 188–198.

Harlow, Barbara. 1992. *Women, Writing, and Political Detention.* Middletown, Conn.: Wesleyan University Press; Hanover, N.H.: University Press of New England.

Hirsch, Marianne. 1983. "Spiritual Bildung: The Beautiful Soul as Paradigm." In *The Voyage In: Fictions of Female Development,* ed. E. Abel, M. Hirsh, and E. Langland, pp. 23–48. Hanover, N.H.: University of New England Press.

Hoffman, Valerie. 1985. "An Islamic Activist: Zaynab al-Ghazali." In *Women and the Family in the Middle East,* ed. E. W. Fernea, pp. 233–254. Austin: University of Texas Press.

Hourani, Albert. 1962. *Arabic Thought in the Liberal Age, 1798–1939.* London; New York: Oxford University Press.

Jessup, Henry H. 1873. *The Women of the Arabs.* New York: Dodd and Mead.

Khalifeh, Sahar [see also Khalīfah, Saḥar]. 1991. *Wild Thorns,* 2nd. ed., trans. Trevor LeGassick and Elizabeth Fernea. New York: Interlink.

Khemiri, Tahir, and G. Kampffmeyer. 1930. *Leaders in Contemporary Arabic Literature: A Book of Reference,* part 1. Hamburg: Veröffentlichung de Seminars für Geschichte und Kultur de Vorderen Orients.

Khouri, Mounah A. 1971. *Poetry and the Making of Modern Egypt.* Leiden: E. J. Brill.

Lakoff, Robin. 1975. *Language and Woman's Place.* New York: Harper and Row.

Mahmoud, Fatma M. 1976. *Women in the Arabic Novel in Egypt.* Cairo: GEBO.

Malti-Douglas, Fedwa. 1991. *Woman's Body, Woman's Word.* Princeton, N.J.: Princeton University Press.

Mernissi, Fatima. 1991. *Women and Islam: An Historical and Theological Enquiry,* trans. Mary Jo Lakeland. Oxford: Basil Blackwell.

———. 1976. *Beyond the Veil: Male-Female Dynamics in a Modern Muslim Society.* Cambridge, Mass.: Schenkman.

Mikhail, Mona N. 1979. *Images of Arab Women.* Washington, D.C.: Three Continents Press.

Moreh, Shmuel. 1988. *Studies in Modern Arabic Prose and Poetry.* Leiden: E. J. Brill.

Mūsā, Salāmah. 1961. *The Education of Salāma Mūsā,* trans. L. O. Schuman. Leiden: E. J. Brill.

Naṣrallāh, Emily. 1987. *Flight Against Time,* trans. Issa J. Boullata. Charlottetown: Ragweed Press.

Nelson, Cynthia. 1986. "The Voices of Doria Shafik: Feminist Consciousness in Egypt, 1940–1960." *Feminist Issues* 6, no. 2: 15–31.

Nicholson, Reynold A. 1969. *A Literary History of the Arabs.* Cambridge, Mass.: Harvard University Press.

Nochlin, Linda. 1971. "Why Are No Great Women Artists?" In *Women in Sexist Society: Studies in Power and Powerlessness,* ed. Vivian

Gornick and Barbara K. Moran, pp. 480–510. New York: New American Library.

Philipp, Thomas. 1978. "Feminism and Nationalist Politics in Egypt." In *Women in the Muslim World*, ed. L. Beck and N. Keddie, pp. 277–294. Cambridge, Mass.: Harvard University Press.

Pickthall, Mohammed M., trans. N.d. *The Meaning of the Glorious Koran*. New York: New American Library.

Riencourt, Amaury de. 1974. *Sex and Power in History*. New York: David McKay.

Rigney, Barbara Hill. 1980. *Madness and Sexual Politics in the Feminist Novel: Studies in Brontë, Woolf, Lessing, and Atwood*. Madison: University of Wisconsin Press.

Roller, Judi M. 1986. *The Politics of the Feminist Novel*. Westport, Conn.: Greenwood Press.

Ruth, Sheila. 1980. "Images of Women in Patriarchy: The Male Identified Woman." In *Issues in Feminism: A First Course in Women's Studies*, ed. S. Ruth, pp. 83–97. Boston: Houghton Mifflin.

Sakākīnī, Widād. 1949. "The Evolution of the Syrian Woman." *United Asia* 1: 531–535.

Shaaban, Bouthaina. 1991. *Both Right and Left Handed: Arab Women Talk About Their Lives*. Bloomington and Indianapolis: Indiana University Press.

al-Shaykh, Ḥanān. 1989. *The Story of Zahra*. New York and London: Quartet Books.

Showalter, Elaine, ed. 1985a. *The New Feminist Criticism: Women, Literature, and Theory*. New York: Pantheon Books.

———. 1985b. "Toward a Feminist Poetics." In *The Feminist Criticism: Women, Literature, and Theory*, ed. E. Showalter, pp. 125–143. New York: Pantheon Books.

———. 1977. *A Literature of Their Own: British Women Novelists from Brontë to Lessing*. Princeton, N.J.: Princeton University Press.

Siddiq, Muhammad. 1986. "The Fiction of Sahar Khalifah: Between Defiance and Deliverance." *Arab Studies Quarterly* 8, no. 2 (Spring): 143–160.

Siddiqi, Muhammad M. 1952. *Women in Islam*, 3rd ed. Lahore: Institute of Islamic Culture.

Smith, Jane I., ed. 1980. *Women in Contemporary Muslim Societies.* Lewisburg, Penn.: Bucknell University Press.

Smith, W. Robertson. N.d. *Kinship and Marriage in Early Arabia*, reprint of 1903 ed. Boston: Beacon Press.

Stern, Gertrude. 1939. *Marriage in Early Islam*. London: The Royal Asiatic Society.

Storrs, Ronald. 1937. *The Memoirs of Sir Ronald Storrs*. New York: G. P. Putnam's Sons.

Tarabishi, Georges [see also Ṭarābīshī, George]. 1988. *Woman Against Her Sex: A Critique of Nawal El-Saadawi*, trans. Basil Hatim and Elizabeth Orsini. London: Saqi Books.

Warnock, Kitty. 1990. *Land Before Honour: Palestinian Women in the Occupied Territories*. Basingstoke: Macmillan.

Watt, W. Montgomery. 1956. *Muhammad at Medina*. Oxford: Clarendon Press.

Woodsmall, Ruth R. 1936. *Moslem Women Enter a New World*. New York: Round Table Press.

Woolf, Virginia. 1957. *A Room of One's Own*. New York and London: Harcourt Brace Jovanovich.

Zeidan, Joseph. 1989. "The Image of the Jew in the Arabic Novel 1920–1973." *Shofar* 7, no. 3 (Spring): 58–82.

Zuhur, Sherifa. 1992. *Revealing Reveiling: Islamist Gender Ideology in Contemporary Egypt*. Albany: State University of New York Press.

Non-European-Language Sources

'Abd al-Bāqī, Zaydān. 1977. *Al-Mar'ah bayna al-Dīn wa-al-Mujtama'*. Cairo: Maṭba'at al-Sa'ādah.

'Abd al-Ghaniyy, Muṣṭafā. N.d. *Masraḥ al-Thamānīnāt: Dirāsah fī al-Naṣṣ al-Masraḥī al-Miṣrī*. Cairo: Dār al-Wafā' li-al-Nashr.

'Abd al-Ḥayy, 'Abd al-Tawwāb. 1966. *'Aṣīr Ḥayātī, Ḥayāt 31 Shakhṣiyyah 'Arabiyyah Hāmmah Sabaqatka ilā Taḥqīq Ṭumūḥihā*. Cairo: Al-Dār al-Qawmiyyah li-al-Ṭiba'āh wa-al-Nashr.

'Abd al-Raḥmān, 'Ā'ishah [Bint al-Shāṭi']. 1986a. *'Alā al-Jisr: Bayna al-Ḥayāh wa-al-Mawt: Sīrah Dhātiyyah*. The Complete Works, vol. 3. Cairo: Al-Hay'ah al-Miṣriyyah al-'Āmmah li-al-Kitāb.

———. 1986b. *Wuqūd al-Ghaḍab, Imra'ah Khāṭi'ah, Raj'at Fir'awn*. The Complete Works, vol. 2. Cairo: Al-Hay'ah al-Miṣriyyah al-'Āmmah li-al-Kitāb.

———. 1970. *Al-Qur'ān wa-al-Tafsīr al-'Aṣrī*. Cairo: Dār al-Ma'ārif.

———. 1963a. *Al-Khansā'*, 2nd ed. Cairo: Dār al-Ma'ārif.

———. 1963b. *Al-Shā'irah al-'Arabiyyah al-Mu'āṣirah*. Cairo: Jāmi'at al-Duwal al-'Arabiyyah; Ma'had al-Dirāsāt al-'Arabiyyah al-'Āliyah.

———. 1962. "Al-Adab al-Niswī al-'Arabī al-Mu'āṣir." In *Al-Adab al-'Arabī al-Mu'āṣir: A'māl Mū'tamar Rūmā al-Mun'aqid fī Tishrīn al-Awwal Sanat 1961*, pp. 132–169. Paris: Aḍwā'.

———. 1960a. "Ayyām Ma'ahu." *Al-Ahrām* 86, no. 26721 (February 9): 6.

———. 1960b. "Al-Qiṣṣah wa-al-Kātib, al-Mar'ah al-Jadīdah fī Qiṣaṣihim wa-Qiṣaṣihā." *Al-Ahrām* 76, no. 27046 (December 3): 5.

———. 1959. *Ṣuwar min Ḥayātihinna*. Cairo: Al-Sharikah al-'Arabiyyah li-al-Ṭibā'ah wa-al-Nashr.

———. 1958. *Sukaynah Bint al-Ḥusayn*. Cairo: Dār al-Hilāl.

———. 1945. "Al-Kalimah Lahā." *Al-Kitāb* 1, no. 1 (November): 45–47.

———. 1942. *Sayyidat al-'Izbah: Qiṣṣat Imra'ah Khāṭi'ah*. Cairo: Maṭba'at al-Ma'ārif.

'Abd al-Raḥmān, 'Awāṭif. 1977. "Al-Ṣiḥāfah al-Miṣriyyah wa-Dawr al-Mar'ah fī al-Tanmiyah." *Dirāsāt 'Arabiyyah* 13, nos. 10–11 (August–September): 120–143.

'Abd al-Rāziq, Muṣṭafā. 1967. "Athar al-Mar'ah fī Ḥayāt al-Shaykh Muḥammad 'Abduh." *Al-Hilāl* 75, no. 12 (December): 320–325.

'Abd al-Rāzaq, 'Alī. 1928. "Al-Sufūr wa-al-Ḥijāb." *Al-Hilāl* 36, no. 10 (August): 1190–1192.

'Abdallāh, Muḥammad Ḥasan. 1973. *al-Ḥarakah al-Adabiyyah wa-al-Fikriyyah fī al-Kuwayt*. Kuwait: Rābiṭat al-Udabā' fī al-Kuwayt.

'Abdallāh, Ṣūfī. 1976. *Ḥawwā' wa-Arba'āt 'Amāliqah*. Cairo: Al-Hay'ah al-Miṣriyyah al-'Āmmah li-al-Kitāb.

'Abduh, Ībrāhīm, and Durriyyah Shafīq. 1945. *Taṭawwur al-Nahḍah al-Nisā'iyyah min 'Ahd Muḥammad 'Alī ilā 'Ahd al-Fārūq*. Cairo: Maktabat al-Adāb.

Abū Maṭar, Aḥmad. 1980. *Al-Riwāyah fī al-Adab al-Filasṭīnī 1950–1975*. Baghdad: Dār al-Rashīd li-al-Nashr.

Abū al-Shabāb, Wāṣif K. 1977. *Ṣūrat al-Filasṭīnī fī al-Qiṣṣah al-Filasṭīniyyah al-Mu'āṣirah min Sanat 1948 ilā Sanat 1973*. Beirut: Dār al-Ṭalī'ah li-al-Ṭibā'ah wa-al-Nashr.

'Adwān, Mamdūḥ. 1970. *Al-Abtar*. Damascus: n.p.

'Afīfī, 'Abdallāh. N.d. *Al-Mar'ah al-'Arabiyyah fī Ẓilāl al-Islām*. Beirut: Dār al-Kātib al-'Arabī.

Aḥmad, Aḥmad Ṭ. 1964. *Al-Mar'ah Kifāḥuhā wa-'Amaluhā*. Cairo: Dār al-Jamāhīr.

'Ajamī, Mary. 1969. *Dawḥat al-Dhikrā*, Introduction by 'Afīfah Ṣa'b. Damascus: Wizārat al-Thaqāfah wa-al-Siyāḥah wa-al-Irshād al-Qawmī.

'Amārah, Muḥammad. 1980a. *Qāsim Amīn wa-Taḥrīr al-Mar'ah*. Cairo: Dār al-Hilāl.

———. 1980b. *Qāsim Amīn wa-Taḥrīr al-Mar'ah*, 2nd ed. Beirut: Al-Mu'assasah al-'Arabiyyah li-al-Dirāsāt wa-al-Nashr.

———, comp. 1976. *Qāsim Amīn: al-A'māl al-Kāmilah*. Beirut: Al-Mu'assasah al-'Arabiyyah li-al-Dirāsāt wa-al-Nashr.

———. 1975. *Al-Islām wa-al-Mar'ah fī Ra'y al-Imām Muḥammad 'Abduh*. Cairo: Al-Qāhirah li-al-Thaqāfah al-'Arabiyyah.

———, comp. 1972–1974. *Muḥammad 'Abduh: al-A'māl al-Kāmilah*, 6 vols. Beirut: Al-Mu'assasah al-'Arabiyyah li-al-Dirāsāt wa-al-Nashr.

Amīn, Bakrī Shaykh. 1973. *Al-Ḥarakah al-Adabiyyah fī al-Mamlakah al-'Arabiyyah al-Sa'ūdiyyah*. Beirut: Dār Ṣādir.

Amīn, Qāsim. 1970. *Taḥrīr al-Mar'ah*, includes an Introduction by Aḥmad Bahā' al-Dīn. Cairo: Dār al-Ma'ārif.

al-'Aqīqī, Najīb. 1976. *Min al-Adab al-Muqārin*, vol. 2, 3rd ed. Cairo: Maktabat al-Anglo al-Miṣriyyah.

al-'Aqqād, 'Abbās Maḥmūd. N.d. *Shu'arā' Miṣr wa-Bī'ātuhum fī al-Jīl al-Māḍī*. Cairo: Nahḍat Miṣr li-al-Ṭibā'ah wa-al-Nashr wa-al-Tawzī'.

———. 1969. *Al-Majmū'ah al-Kāmilah (al-'Aqqād wa-al-Madhāhib 2)*, vol. 12. Beirut: Dār al Kitāb al-'Arabī.

———. 1962. "Rijāl ḥawla Mayy." *Al-Hilāl* 70, no. 3 (March): 84–89.

al-'Arabī, Shahrazād. 1989. *Al-Bu'd al-Siyāsī li-al-Ḥijāb*. Cairo: Al-Zahrā' li-al-I'lām al-'Arabī.

al-'Ashrī, Jalāl. 1967. "Ghādah al-Sammān wa-Azmat al-Qiṣṣah al-Qaṣīrah." *Al-Fikr al-Mu'āṣir* 27 (May): 54–63.

al-Aṣmā'ī, 'Abd-Mālik ibn Qurayb. 1971. *Fuḥūlat al-Shu'ārā'*, ed. Charles C. Torrey. N.p.: Dār al-Kitāb al-Jadīd.

'Aṭawī, Muḥsin. 1979. *Al-Mar'ah fī al-Taṣawwur al-Islāmi*. Beirut: Al-Dār al-Islāmiyyah.

'Aṭiyyah, Aḥmad M. 1979. *Tawfīq al-Ḥakīm al-lā-Muntamī: Dirāsah fī Fikr al-Ḥakīm al-Siyāsī*. Cairo: Dār al-Mawqif al-'Arabī.

'Aṭiyyah, Farīdah Y. 1912. *Bayna 'Arshayn*. Tripoli (Lebanon): Maṭba'at al-Najāḥ.

'Aṭṭār, Mājidah. 1966. *Murāhiqah*. Beirut: Dār al-Rawā'i'.

'Awaḍ, Lewis. 1966. *Al-Mu'aththirāt al-Ajnabiyyah fī al-Adab al-'Arabī al-Ḥadīth*, part 1: *Qaḍiyyat al-Mar'ah*. Cairo: Dār al-Ma'rifah.

'Awaḍ, Ramsīs. 1974. *Tawfīq al-Ḥakīm Alladhī lā Na'rifuhu*. Cairo: Tawzī' Dār al-Sha'b.

al-'Awfī, Najīb. 1980. *Darajat al-Wa'y fī al-Kitābah: Dirāsāt Naqdiyyah*. Casablanca: Dār al-Nashr al-Maghribiyyah.

'Awwād, Simon, ed. 1981. *Min Adab Mayy Ziyādah*. Beirut: Dār 'Awwād li-al-Ṭibā'ah wa-al-Nashr.

al-'Aẓmī, Mukhtār P. 1900. *Faṣl al-Khiṭāb wa Taflīs Iblīs min Taḥrīr al-Mar'ah wa-Raf' al-Ḥijāb*. Beirut: Al-Maṭba'ah al-Adabiyyah.

B., F. F. 1939. "Al-Mar'ah la Tanquṣuhā Ayyat Mawhibah Fanniyyah." *Al-Thaqāfah* 1, no. 12 (March): 27–28.

Badawī, Aḥmad A. 1959. *Rifā'ah Rāfi' al-Ṭahṭāwī*, 2nd ed. Cairo: Lajnat al-Bayān al-'Arabī.

Badr, 'Abd al-Muḥsin Ṭāhā. 1968. *Taṭawwur al-Riwāyah al-'Arabiyyah al-Ḥadīthah fī Miṣr, 1870–1938*, 2nd ed. Cairo: Dār al-Ma'ārif.

Badr, Liyānah [see also Badr, Liana]. 1992. "Shajarat al-Kalām: Al-Ḥurriyyah fī al-Ḥayāh wa-fī al-Ibdā'." *Fuṣūl* 11, no. 3 (Autumn): 233–241.

———. 1979. *Būṣlah min ajl 'Abbād al-Shams*. Beirut: Dār Ibn Rushd.

Bahā' al-Dīn, Aḥmad. 1970. "Taṣdīr." In *Taḥrīr al-Mar'ah*, by Qāsim Amīn, pp. 5–24. Cairo: Dār al-Ma'ārif.

Bakr, Salwā. 1992. "Shihādah." *Fuṣūl* 11, no. 3 (Autumn): 154–155.

Ba'labakkī, Laylā. 1965. *Al-Ālihah al-Mamsūkhah*, 2nd ed. Beirut: Al-Maktab al-Tijārī li-al-Ṭibā'ah wa-al-Nashr.

———. 1964a. *Anā Aḥyā*, 2nd ed. Beirut: Al-Maktab al-Tijāri li-al-Ṭibā'ah wa-al-Tawzī' wa-al-Nashr.

———. 1964b. *Safīnat Ḥanān ilā al-Qamar*. Beirut: Al-Mu'assasah al-Waṭaniyyah li-al-Ṭibā'ah wa-al-Nashr.

———. 1960. *Al-Ālihah al-Mamsūkhah*. Beirut: Dār Majallat Shi'r.

———. 1959. *Naḥnu bi-lā Aqni'ah*. Beirut: Manshūrāt al-Nadwah al-Lubnāniyyah.

———. 1958. *Anā Aḥyā*. Beirut: Dār Majallat Shi'r.

———. 1954. "Kufr." *Al-'Irfān* 41, no. 6 (April): 693.

al-Bannā, Salwā. 1972. *'Arūs Khalfa al-Nahr*. Beirut: Dār al-Ittiḥād.

Bayhum, Muḥammad Jamīl. 1962. *Al-Mar'ah fī Ḥaḍārat al-'Arab wa-al-'Arab fī Tārīkh al-Mar'ah*. Beirut: Dār al-Nashr li-al-Jāmi'iyyīn.

———. 1952. *Fatāt al-Sharq fī Ḥaḍārat al-Gharb*. Beirut: Matba'at Qulfāṭ.

Bint al-Shāṭi' [see 'Abd al-Raḥmān, 'Ā'ishah].

al-Bustānī, Alice Buṭrus. 1891. *Ṣā'ibah*. Beirut: Al-Maṭba'ah al-Adabiyyah.

al-Bustānī, Fu'ād Ifrām, ed. 1950. *Al-Mu'allim Buṭrus al-Bustānī*, 2nd ed. Beirut: Al-Maṭba'ah al-Kathūlīkiyyah.

Cheikho, Louis. 1926. *Tārīkh al-Adāb al-'Arabiyyah fī al-Rub' al-Awwal min al-Qarn al-'Ishrīn*. Beirut: Maṭba'at al Ābā' al-Yasū'iyyīn.

Dāghir, Yūsuf As'ad. 1983. *Maṣādir al-Dirāsah al-Adabiyyah: A'lām al-Nahḍah al-Qarnān al-Tāsi' 'Ashar wa-al-'Ishrīn*, vol. 4. Beirut: Al-Jāmi'ah al-Lubnāniyyah.

———. 1972. *Maṣādir al-Dirāsah al-Adabiyyah: Al-Fikr al-'Arabī al-Ḥadīth fī Siyar A'lāmihi*, vol. 3, 2 parts. Beirut: Al-Jāmi'ah al-Lubnāniyyah.

———. 1956. *Maṣādir al-Dirāsah al-Adabiyyah: al-Fikr al-'Arabī fī Siyar A'lāmihi*, vol. 2, part 1. Beirut: Jam'iyyat Ahl al-Qalam fī Lubnān.

———. N.d. *Qāmūs al-Ṣiḥāfah al-Lubnāniyyah 1858–1974*. Beirut: Al-Jāmi'ah al-Lubnāniyyah.

Da'kūr, Nadīm. 1987. "Al-Makān fī *Ṭuyūr Aylūl*: Al-Qaryah Ittiṣālan wa-Mu'āyashah." *Al-Anwār* 28, no. 9507 (July 26): 10.

Dālātī, 'Ālyā Hūghū. 1969. *Khada'atnī al-Mir'āh*. Beirut: Manshūrāt 'Ashtārūt.

Dalīl al-Kātib al-Sa'ūdī. 1984. Riyadh: Al-Jam'iyyah al-'Arabiyyah al-Sa'ūdiyyah li-al-Thaqāfah wa al-Funūn.

al-Daqqāq, 'Umar. 1971. *Funūn al-Adab al-Mu'āṣir fī Sūriyyā (1870–1970)*. Aleppo, Syria: Dār al-Sharq.

al-Darbandī, 'Abd al-Raḥmān S. 1968 *al-Mar'ah al-'Irāqiyyah al-Mu'āṣirah*, vol. 1. Baghdad: Maktabat Dār al-Baṣrī.

———. 1970. *Al-Mar'ah al-'Irāqiyyah al-Mu'āṣirah*, vol. 2. Baghadad: Dār al-Baṣrī.

Dāwūd, Ṣabīḥah al-Shaykh. 1958. *Awwal al-Ṭarīq ilā al-Nahḍah al-Niswiyyah fī al-'Irāq*. Baghdad: Maṭābi' al-Rābiṭah.

al-Dayrī, Ilyās. 1960. "*Al-Ālihah al-Mamsukhah*." *Al-Nahār* 27, no. 7583 (August 26): 4.

Dīb, Farjallāh Ṣāliḥ. 1980. "'An al-Umūmah wa-al-Usrah 'inda al-'Arab." *Dirāsāt 'Arabiyyah* 17, no. 1 (November): 108–121.

Difā'an 'an al-Ḥurriyyah: Laylā Ba'labakkī. 1964. *Ḥiwār* 5–6 (September–October): 176–182.

Diyāb, 'Abd al-Ḥayy. 1969. *Al-Mar'ah fī Ḥayāt al-'Aqqād*. Cairo: Dār al-Sha'b.

Diyāb, Ḥāmid al-Shāfi'ī. 1981. "Qā'imah Bibliyūgrāfiyyah bi-al-Dawriyyāt al-Ṣādirah fī al-Waṭan al-'Arabī." *'Ālam al-Kutub* 2, no. 3: 448–456.

al-Durdunjī, Hiyām Ramzī. 1970. *Ilā al-Liqā' fī Yāfā*. Tripoli, Libya: Al-Maṭba'ah al-Lībiyyah.

Duwārah, Fu'ād. 1968. *Fī al-Riwāyah al-Miṣriyyah*. Cairo: Dār al-Kitāb al-'Arabī.

Fahmī, Māhir Ḥasan. 1963. *Qāsim Amīn*. Cairo: Al-Mu'assasah al-Miṣriyyah al-'Āmmah li-al-Ta'līf wa-al-Tarjamah wa-al-Ṭibā'ah wa-al-Nashr.

Fahmī, Manṣūr. 1955. *Muḥāḍarāt 'an Mayy Ziyādah ma'a Rā'idāt al-Nahḍah al-Nisā'iyyah al-Ḥadīthah*. Cairo: Ma'had al-Dirāsāt al-'Arabiyyah al-'Āliyah.

al-Fanjarī, Aḥmad Shawqī. 1987. *Al-Niqāb fī al-Tārīkh, fī al-Dīn, fī 'Ilm al-Ijtimā'*. Cairo: Al-Hay'ah al-Miṣriyyah al-'Āmmah li-al-Kitāb.

Farīd, Amānī. 1979a. "Adībāt Miṣriyyāt Mu'āṣirāt." *Al-Hilāl* 87, no. 12 (December): 70–73.

———. 1979b. "Al-Ṣālūnāt al-Adabiyyah al-Nisā'iyyah fī Miṣr." *Al-Hilāl* 87, no. 5 (May): 116–119.

Farrāj, 'Afīf. 1980. *Al-Ḥurriyyah fī Adab al-Mar*'ah, 2nd ed. Beirut: Dār al-Fārābī.

Fattūḥ, 'Īsā. 1966. "Mary 'Ajamī." *Al-Adīb* 25, no. 4 (April): 2–6.

———. 1964. "Adībāt min Sūriyyā." *Al-Adāb* 12, no. 6 (June): 52–55.

———. 1962. "Maryānā Marrāsh Shā'irat Ḥalab." *Al-Adīb* 21, no. 5 (May): 28–29.

Fā'ūr, Kāmil. 1980. "Al-Baḥth 'an Zaynab Fawwāz." *Al-Masīrah* 1, no. 2 (February): 65–69.

Fawwāz, Zaynab. 1984. *Ḥusn al-'Awāqib, al-Hawā wa-al-Wafā'*. Beirut: Al-Majlis al-Thaqāfī li-Lubnān al-Janūbī.

———. 1910. *Al-Rasā'il al-Zaynabiyyah*. Cairo: Al-Maṭba'ah al-Mutawassiṭah.

———. 1894–1895. *Kitāb al-Durr al-Manthūr fī Ṭabaqāt Rabbāt al-Khudūr*. Būlāq, Egypt: Al-Maṭba'ah al-Amīriyyah.

Fawzān, Ibrāhīm ibn Fawzān. 1971. *Al-Adab al-Ḥijāzī al-Ḥadīth bayna al-Taqlīd wa-al-Tajdīd*, vol. 2. Cairo: Maktabat al-Khānjī.

Fawzī, Maḥmūd. 1987. *Adab al-Aẓāfir al-Ṭawīlah*. Cairo: Dār Nahḍat Miṣr li-al-Ṭibā'ah wa-al-Nashr.

al-Fayṣal, Samar R. 1979. *Malāmiḥ fī al-Riwāyah al-Sūriyyah*. Damascus: Ittiḥād al-Kuttāb al-'Arab.

Fulān [pseudonym]. 1928. "Al-Ṣālūnāt al-Adabiyyah wa-Ātharuhā fī al-Ruqiyy al-Fikrī: 'Alā Dhikr Ba'ḍ Ṣālūnāt Miṣriyyah." *Al-Mar'ah al-Misriyyah* 9, no. 1: 48–49.

al-Ghaffār, 'Abd al-Rasūl 'Abd al-Muḥsin. 1977. *Al-Mar'ah al-Mu'aṣirah*. Beirut: Dār al-Zahrā'.

al-Ghalāyīnī, Muṣṭafā. 1928. *Naẓārāt fī Kitāb al-Sufūr wa-al-Ḥijāb al-Mansūb ilā al-Ānisah Naẓīrah Zayn al-Dīn*. Beirut: Maṭābi' Quzmā.

Ghunaymah, Yūsuf Rizqallāh. 1918. "Al-Mar'ah fī al-'Irāq." *Al-Muqtaṭaf* 52, no. 3 (March): 169–173.

Ghurayyib, Rūz. 1980. *Nasamāt wa-A'āṣīr fī al-Shi'r al-Nisā'ī al-Mu'āṣir*. Beirut: Al-Mu'assasah al-'Arabiyyah li-al-Dirāsāt wa-al-Nashr.

———. 1978. *Mayy Ziyādah al-Tawahhuj wa-al-Ufūl: Ḥayātuhā, Shakhṣiyyatuhā, Adabuhā, Fannuhā*. Beirut: Mu'assasat Nawfal.

al-Ḥaddād, al-Ṭāhir. 1972. *Imra'atunā fī al-Sharī'ah wa-al-Mujtama'*, 2nd ed. Tunis: Al-Dār al-Tūnisiyyah li-al-Nashr.

"Ḥadīth ma'a Mu'allifat *Anā Aḥyā* Laylā Ba'labakkī—al-Wujūdiyyah al-Kubrā." 1960. *Al-Yawm* (Tel Aviv) 12, no. 3702 (November 16): 4.

al-Ḥakīm, Tawfīq. 1939a. "Athar al-Mar'ah fī Udabā'inā al-Mu'āṣirīn." *Al-Thaqāfah* 1, no. 20 (May 16): 43–44.

———. 1939b. "Hal Tanquṣ al-Mar'ah Ba'ḍ al-Mawāhib al-Fanniyyah." *Al-Thaqāfah* 1, no. 9 (February 28): 6–8.

Ḥamdān, Salīm. 1928. *Al-Madaniyyah wa-al-Ḥijāb*. Beirut: Maṭābi' Quzmā.

Ḥamdān, Umayyah. N.d. *Wa-Antaẓir*. Beirut: Al-Maktabah al-'Aṣriyyah.

———. 1980. *Al-Azraq al-Qādim ma'a al-Rīḥ*. Beirut: Dār al-Āfaq al-Jadīdah.

Ḥammād, Suhaylah Zayn al-'Ābidīn. 1984. *Al-Mar'ah bayna al-Ifrāṭ wa-al-Tafrīṭ*, 2nd ed. Jedda: Al-Dār al-Sa'ūdiyyah li-al-Nashr wa-al-Tawzī'.

Ḥannā, Īliyyā Ḥ. 1979. "Ma'a al-Sayyidah Fāṭimah al-Yūsuf fī Dhikrayātihā al-Ṣuḥufiyyah." *Al-Adīb* 38, nos. 7–8 (July – August): 34–37.

Ḥarb, Muḥammad Ṭal'at. 1912. *Tarbiyat al-Mar'ah wa-al-Ḥijāb* (*The Education of Women and the Veil*), 2nd ed. Cairo: Maṭba'at al-Manār.

———. 1901. *Faṣl al-Khiṭāb fī al-Mar'ah wa al-Ḥijāb* (*The Final Word Concerning Women and the Veil*). Cairo: Maṭba'at al-Taraqqī.

Ḥasan, 'Alī Ibrāhīm. 1970. *Nisā' lahunna fī al-Tārīkh al-Islāmī Naṣīb*, 2nd ed. Cairo: Maktabat al-Nahḍah al-Miṣriyyah.

Ḥasan, Muḥammad 'A. 1974. "Shā'irat al-Rithā' wa-Adwār al-Ghinā' 'Ā'ishah al-Taymūriyyah." *Al-Hilāl* 82, no. 4 (April): 14–23.

———. 1964. *Mayy: Adībat al-Sharq wa-al-'Urūbah.* Cairo: 'Ālam al-Kutub.

"Ḥawla al-Iltizām al-Siyāsī wa-al-Kitābah al-Nisā'iyyah: Muqābalah ma'a Laṭīfah al-Zayyāt." 1990. *Alif* 10:134–150.

Haykal, Muḥammad Ḥ. 1929. *Tarājim Miṣriyyah wa Gharbiyyah.* Cairo: Maṭba'at al-Siyāsah.

al-Ḥifnāwī, Hālah. 1969a. *Hal Akhla' Thawbī*, 2nd ed. Beirut: Al-Maktab al-Tijārī li-al-Ṭibā'ah wa-al-Nashr wa-al-Tawzī'.

———. 1969b. *Laylah fī Sarīr Rajul*, 2nd ed. Beirut: Al-Maktab al-Tijārī li-al-Ṭibā'ah wa-al-Nashr wa-al-Tawzī'.

Hilāl, Yūsuf. 1986. "Jalāl al-Sharqāwī Yudāfi' 'an Nafsihi." *Rūz al-Yūsuf* 61, no. 3034 (August 4): 44–45.

al-Hilālī, 'Abd al-'Azīz. 1966. *Udabā' al-Mu'tamar.* Baghdad: Wizārat al-Thaqāfah wa-al-Irshād.

al-Hilālī, 'Abd al-Razzāq, ed. 1972. "Al-Shā'ir al-Faylasūf Jamīl Ṣidqī al-Zahāwī." In *Al-Dīwān*, by J. Ṣ. al-Zahāwī, vol. 1, pp. 1–48. Beirut: Dār al-'Awdah.

al-Ḥūfī, Aḥmad Muḥammad. 1963. *Al-Mar'ah fī al-Shi'r al-Jāhilī*, 2nd ed. Cairo: Dār al-Fikr al-'Arabī.

al-Ḥūmānī, Salwā. 1954. "Al-Mar'ah al-'Arabiyyah Nahḍatuhā Ijtimā'iyyah wa-'Ilmiyyah." *Al-'Irfān* 41, no. 6 (April): 641–647.

Ḥusayn, Ṭāhā. 1939. "Ḥarīm li-al-Sayyidah Qūt al-Qlūb al-Dirmirdāshiyyah." *Al-Thaqāfah* 1, no. 15 (April 11): 7–11.

Ibn al-Hāshimī. 1989. *Al-Dā'iyah Zaynab al-Ghazālī: Masīrat Jihād wa-Ḥadīth min al-Dhikrayāt min Khilāl Kitābātihā*. Cairo: Dār al-I'tiṣām.

Ibn Hishām, Muḥammad 'A. N.d. *Al-Sīrah al-Nabawiyyah*, vol. 1. ed. Maḥammad Fahmī al-Sarjānī. Cairo: Al-Maktabah al-Tawfīqiyyah.

Ibn Ismā'īl, Muḥammad Ibn Aḥmad. N.d. *'Awdat al-Ḥijāb: Ma'rakat al-Ḥijāb wa-al-Sufūr*, comp. Muḥammad Aḥmad al-Muqaddim. Riyadh: Dār Ṭībah li-al-Nashr wa-al-Tawzī'.

Ibn Sa'd, Muḥammad. 1958. *Kitāb al-Ṭabaqāt al-Kubrā*, vol. 8. Beirut: Dār Ṣādir.

Ibrāhīm, Emily F. 1966. *Al-Ḥarakah al-Nisā'iyyah al-Lubnāniyyah*. Beirut: Dār al-Thaqāfah.

———. 1964. *Adībāt Lubnāniyyāt*. Beirut: Dār al-Rayḥānī li-al-Ṭibā'ah wa-al-Nashr.

———. 1954. *Salmā Ṣā'igh Āhah min Bilādī*. Beirut: Manshūrāt Ahl al-Qalam.

'Īd, Muḥammad S. 1979. "Tawfīq al-Ḥakīm 'Adaw li-al-Mar'ah am Ṣadīq?" *Al-Kātib* 19, no. 215 (April): 62–72.

Ibrāhīm, Zāhidah. 1986. *Al-Jarā'id wa-al-Majallāt al-'Irāqiyyah 1869–1987*. 2nd ed. Kuwait: Dār al-Nashr wa-al-Maṭbū'āt al-Kuwaytiyyah.

Idrīs, 'Āyidah. 1961. "Al-Ālihah al-Mamsūkhah." *Al-Jadīd* 8, no. 8 (August): 55–60.

al-Ikhtiyār, Najlā' Nasīb. 1991. *Taḥarrur al-Mar'ah 'abra A'māl Simone de Beauvoir wa-Ghādah al-Sammān*. Beirut: Dār al-Ṭalī'ah.

Ismā'īl, Ismā'īl Fahd. 1980. *Al-Qiṣṣah al-'Arabiyyah fī al-Kuwayt*. Beirut: Dār al-'Awdah.

al-Jabartī, 'Abd al-Raḥrmān. 1904–5. *'Ajā'ib al-Āthār fī al-Tarājim wa-al-Akhbār*, vol. 1. Cairo: Al-Maṭba'ah al-'Āmirah al-Sharqiyyah.

al-Jabartī, 'Abd al-Raḥmān. 1961. *Muẓhir al-Taqdīs bi-Dhahāb Dawlat al-Faransīs*, vol. 2, ed. A. 'Aṭiyyah, 'A. 'Āmir, and M. 'Abd al-Laṭīf. Cairo: Al-Hay'ah al-'Āmmah li-Shu'ūn al-Maṭābi' al-Amīriyyah.

Jabbūr, Munā. N.d. *Fatāh Tāfihah*. Beirut: Dār Maktabat al-Ḥayāh.

Jabr, Jamīl. N.d. *Mudhakkirāt Mayy Ziyādah*. Beirut: Dār al-Rīḥānī li-al-Ṭibā'ah wa-al-Nashr.

———. 1974. "Mayy Ziyādah fī al-'Uṣfūriyyah." *Al-Ḥasnā'* 680 (July 5): 16–17.

———. 1960. *Mayy Ziyādah fī Ḥayātihā wa-Adabihā*. Beirut: Al-Maṭba'ah al-Kāthūlīkiyyah.

———. 1950. *Mayy wa-Jubrān*. Beirut: Dār al-Jamāl.

Jabrā, Jabrā I. 1962. "Al-Riwāyah wa-al-Qiṣṣah al-Qaṣīrah wa-al-Masraḥiyyah wa-Dawruhā fī al-Mujtama' al-'Arabī." In *Al-Adab al-'Arabī al-Mu'āṣir: A'māl Mū'tamar Rūmā al-Mun'aqid fī Tishrīn al-Awwal Sanat 1961*, pp. 215–237. Paris: Aḍwā'.

Jād, Nihād. N.d. *'a al-Raṣif*. Cairo: Maktabat Gharīb.

———. 1989. *'Adīlah wa-Maḥaṭṭat al-Ūtūbis*. Cairo: Al-Hay'ah al-Miṣriyyah al-'Āmmah li-al-Kitāb. Translated into English by Angele B. Samaan as *Adilah and the Bus Stop* (Cairo: General Egyptian Book Organization [1987]).

Jammūl, Yumnā Ni'mah. 1973. "Emily Naṣrallāh, al-Adab wa-al-Shi'r 'Indahā Qaṭrat Nadā." *Al-Ḥasnā'* (Beirut) 637 (November 16): 52–53.

Jāsim, 'Azīz al-Sayyid. 1980. *Ḥaqq al-Mar'ah bayna Mushkilat al-Takhalluf al-Ijtimā'ī wa-Mutaṭallabāt al-Ḥayāh al-Jadīdah Ru'yah Thaqāfiyyah Ijtimā'iyyah Jinsiyyah*. Beirut: Al-Mu'assash al-'Arabiyyah li-al-Dirāsāt wa-al-Nashr.

al-Jawharī, Maḥmūd M., and Muḥammad 'A. Khayyāl. 1980. *Al-Akhawāt al-Muslimāt wa-Binā' al-Usrah al-Qur'āniyyah*. Alexandria: Dār al-'Awdah.

al-Jayyār, Sawsan. 1986. "Al-Kātibah al-Ṣuḥufiyyah Nihād Jād Tatasā'al." *Rūz al-Yūsuf* 61, no. 3034 (August 4): 52–54.

al-Jindī, Anwar [see al-Jundī, Anwar].

Jubrān, Jubrān Khalīl. 1922. *Al-Ajniḥah al-Matakassirah*. Cairo: Maṭba'at al-Hilāl.

Jum'ah, Muḥammad Luṭfī. 1923a. "Bāḥithat al-Bādiyah wa-al-Ānisah Mayy." *Majallat al-Nahḍah al-Nisā'iyyah* 2, no. 6 (January): 145–146.

———. 1923b. "Bāḥithat al-Bādiyah wa-al-Ānisah Mayy." *Majallat al-Nahḍah al-Nisā'iyyah* 2, no. 7 (February): 173–180.

———. 1923c. "Bāḥithat al-Bādiyah wa-al-Ānisah Mayy." *Majallat al-Nahḍah al-Nisā'iyyah* 2, no. 8 (March): 203–204.

Jum'ah, Sa'īd. 1982. "Qā'imah bi-al-Dawriyyāt al-Ṣādirah 'an al-Mar'ah fī al-Waṭan al-'Arabī." *'Ālam al-Kutub* 2, no. 4: 808–811.

al-Jumaḥī, Muḥammad ibn Sallām. N.d. *Ṭabaqāt al-Shu'arā'*. Beirut: Dār al-Nahḍah al-'Arabiyyah.

al-Jundī, Anwar. N.d. *Adab al-Mar'ah al-'Arabiyyah*. Cairo: Maṭba'at al-Risālah.

———. 1979. *Ṣafaḥāt Majhūlah fī al-Adab al-'Arabī al-Mu'āṣir*. Cairo: Maktabat al-Anglo al-Miṣriyyah.

———. 1970. "Jamīlah al-'Alāyilī." *Al-'Ulūm* 15, no. 1 (January): 22–24.

Juwaydī, Imtithāl. 1972. *Shajarat al-Ṣubbayr*. Beirut: Dār al-Ittiḥād.

Kaḥḥālah, 'Umar Riḍā. 1979. *Al-Mar'ah fī al-Qadīm wa-al-Ḥadīth*, vol. 2. Beirut: Mu'assasat al-Risālah.

———. 1978. *Al-Mar'ah fī al-Qadīm wa-al-Ḥadīth*, vol. 1. Beirut: Mu'assasat al-Risālah.

———. 1977. *A'lām al-Nisā' fī 'Ālamay al-'Arab wa-al-Islām*, 3rd ed., 5 vols. Beirut: Mu'assasat al-Risālah.

Karam, 'Afīfah. 1914. *Ghādat 'Amshit*. New York: Maṭba'at Jarīdat al-Hudā.

———. 1906. *Badī'ah wa-Fu'ād*. New York: Maṭba'at Jarīdat al-Hudā.

———. N.d. *Fāṭimah al-Badawiyyah*. New York: Maṭba'at Jarīdat al-Hudā.

Karrū, Abū al-Qāsim Muḥammad. 1957. *Al-Ṭāhir al-Ḥaddād Rā'id al-Ḥurriyyah wa-Naṣīr al-Mar'ah*, 2nd ed. Tunis: Al-Maṭba'ah al-'Aṣriyyah al-Kayyālī, Sāmī. 1968. *Al-Adab al-'Arabī al-Mu'āṣir fī Sūriyyā*, 2nd ed. Cairo: Dār al-Ma'ārif.

———. 1957a. *Muḥāḍarāt 'an al-Ḥarakah al-Adabiyyah fī Ḥalab 1800–1950*. Cairo: Ma'had al-Dirāsāt al-'Arabiyyah al-'Āliyah.

———. 1957b. "Maryānā Marrāsh." *Al-Ḥadīth* 31, no. 9 (September): 565–574.

Kāẓim, Ṣāfī Nāz. 1982. *Fī Mas'alat al-Sufūr wa-al-Ḥijāb*. Cairo: Maktabat Wahbah.

Khākī, Aḥmad. 1973. *Qāsim Amīn, Tārīkh Ḥayātihi al-Fikrī*. Cairo: Maktabat al-Anglo al-Miṣriyyah.

Khālid, Aḥmad. 1967. *Al-Ṭāhir al-Ḥaddād wa-al-Bī'ah al-Tūnisiyyah fī al-Thulth al-Awwal min al-Qarn al-'Ishrīn*. Tunis: Al-Dār al-Tūnisiyyah li-al-Nashr.

al-Khālidī, 'Anbarah S. 1978. *Jawlah fī al-Dhikrayāt bayna Lubnān wa-Filasṭīn*. Beirut: Dār al-Nahār.

Khalīfah, Ijlāl. 1973. *Al-Ḥarakah al-Nisā'iyyah al-Ḥadīthah: Qiṣṣat al-Mar'ah al-'Arabiyyah 'alā Arḍ Miṣr*. Cairo: Al-Maṭba'ah al-'Arabiyyah al-Ḥadīthah.

Khalīfah, Saḥar [see also Khalifeh, Sahar]. 1980. *'Abbād al-Shams*. Beirut: Munaẓẓamat al-Taḥrīr al-Filasṭīniyyah.

———. 1976. *Al-Ṣabbār*. Jerusalem: Galileo.

———. 1974. *Lam Na'ud Jawārī Lakum*. Cairo: Dār al-Ma'ārif.

Khalīl, 'Alī Muḥammad. 1939. "Al-Ṣiḥāfah al-Niswiyyah bi-Miṣr bi-Munāsabat Dukhūl Majallat al-Mar'ah al-Miṣriyyah fī 'Āmihā al-'Ishrīn." *Majallat al-Mar'ah al-Miṣriyyah* 20, no. 3 (March): 109–113.

Khamīs, Muḥammad A. 1978. *Al-Ḥarakāt al-Nisā'iyyah wa-Ṣilatuhā bi-al-Isti'mār wa-Ra'y al-Jam'iyyāt al-Nisā'iyyah wa-al-Hay'āt al-Islāmiyyah wa-Kibār al-'Ulamā' fī Miṣr fī Ishtighāl al-Mar'ah bi-al-Ṣiyāsah wa-al-A'māl al-'Āmmah*. Cairo: Dār al-Anṣār.

al-Khaṭīb, Ḥanīfah. 1984. *Tārīkh Taṭawwur al-Ḥarakah al-Nisā'iyyah fī Lubnān wa-Irtibāṭuhā bi-al-'Ālam al-'Arabī 1800–1975*. Beirut: Dār al-Ḥadāthah.

al-Khāzin, William, and Nabīh Ilyān. 1970. *Kutub wa-Udabā'*. Beirut: Al-Maṭba'ah al-'Aṣriyyah.

al-Khūlī, al-Bahiyy. N.d. *Al-Islām wa-al-Mar'ah al-Mu'āṣirah*, 3rd ed. Kuwait: Dār al-Qalam.

al-Khūrī, Colette S. 1987. *Ma'aka 'alā Hāmish Riwāyātī*. Damascus: Ittiḥād al-Kuttāb al-'Arab.

———. 1967. *Ayyām Ma'ahu*, 4th ed. Beirut: Al-Maktab al-Tijārī li-al-Ṭibā'ah wa-al-Nashr wa-al-Tawzī'.

———. 1961. *Laylah Wāḥidah*. Beirut: Al-Maktab al-Tijārī li-al-Ṭibā'ah wa-al-Nashr wa-al-Tawzī'.

Khūrī, Nabīl. 1969. *Ḥārat al-Naṣārā*. Beirut: Dār al-Nahār.

Khūst, Nādiyah. 1977. "Ghādah al-Sammān fī Kawābīs Bayrūt." *Al-Mawqif al-Adabī* 72 (April): 127–138.

Kishk, Muḥammad Jalāl. 1990. *Jahālāt 'Asr al-Tanwīr: Qirā'ah fī Fīkr Qāsim Amīn wa-'Alī 'Abd al-Rāziq*. Cairo: Maktabat al-Turāth al-Islāmī.

al-Kuzbarī, Salmā al-Ḥaffār. 1987. *Mayy Ziyādah aw Ma'sāt al-Nubūgh*, 2 vols. Beirut: Mu'assasat Nawfal.

———, ed. 1982. *Mayy Ziyādah wa A'lām 'Aṣrihā: Rasā'il Makhṭūṭah Lam Tunshar 1912–1940*. Beirut: Mu'assasat Nawfal.

——— and Suhayl Bishrū'ī. 1984. *Al-Shu'lah al-Zarqā': Rasā'il Jubrān Khalīl Jubrān ilā Mayy Ziyādah*, 2nd ed. Beirut: Mu'assasat Nawfal.

Laṭīfah al-Zayyāt fī Mir'āt Laṭīfah al-Zayyāt. 1993. *Ibdā'* 11, no. 1 (January): 54–58.

Lenṭin, Ronit. 1982. *Siḥot 'im Nashim Palesṭiniyot*. Jerusalem: Mifras.

Māḍī, Shukrī 'Azīz. 1978. *In'ikās Hazīmat Ḥuzayrān 'alā al-Riwāyah al-'Arabiyyah*. Beirut: Al-Mu'assasah al-'Arabiyyah li-al-Dirāsāt wa-al-Nashr.

Maḥmūd, Ḥāfiẓ 1980. "Sayyidāt fī Balāṭ Ṣāḥibat al-Jalālah al-Ṣiḥāfah." *Al-Hilāl* 88, no. 5 (May): 74–77.

Makāriyūs, Maryam. 1885. "Al-Khansā'." *Al-Muqtaṭaf* 9, no. 9 (June): 265–271.

al-Malā'ikah, Nāzik. 1973. *Ma'ākhidh Ijtimā'iyyah 'alā Ḥayāt al-Mar'ah al-'Arabiyyah*. Damascus: n.p.

———. 1970. "Ma'ākhidh Ijtimā'iyyah 'alā al-Mar'ah al-'Arabiyyah." *Al-Adāb* 18, no. 4 (April): 89–93.

———. 1953. "Al-Mar'ah bayna al-Ṭarafayn al-Salbiyyah wa-al-Akhlāq." *Al-Adāb* 1, no. 12 (December): 66–69.

Mandūr, Muḥammad. N.d. *Masraḥ Tawfīq al-Ḥakīm*. Cairo: Jāmi'at al-Duwal al-'Arabiyyah.

———. 1958. *Muḥāḍarāt fī al-Shi'r al-'Arabī ba'da Shawqī*, vol. 3. Cairo: Maktabat Nahḍat Miṣr.

Mannā', Haytham. 1980. *Al-Mar'ah fī al-Islām*. N.p.

Manṣūr, Fahmī. 1955. *Muḥāḍarāt 'an Mayy Ziyādah Ma'a Rā'idāt al-Nahḍah al-Nisā'iyyah.* Cairo: Jāmi'at al-Duwal al-'Arabiyyah, Ma'had al-Dirāsāt al-'Āliyah.

al-Maqdisī, Anīs. 1967. *Al-Ittijāhāt al-Adabiyyah fī al-'Ālam al-'Arabī al-Ḥadīth,* 4th ed. Beirut Dār al-'Ilm li-al-Malāyīn.

Maskūnī, Yūsuf Y. 1970. "Al-Murabiyyah Nabawiyyah Mūsā." *Al-Aqlām* 6, no. 8 (May): 52–54.

———. 1947. *Min 'Abqariyyāt Nisā' al-Qarn al-Tāsi' 'Ashar,* vol. 1, 2nd ed.
Baghdad: Maṭba'at al-Ma'ārif.

Ma'ūshī, Ibrīzā. 1962. *Hal Aghfīr Lahu?* Beirut: Dār al-Thaqāfah.

al-Māzinī, Ībrāhīm. 1992. "Athar al-Mar'ah 'alā al-Lughah." *Ibdā'* 10, no. 4 (April): 39–48.

———. 1926. *Qabḍ al-Rīḥ.* Cario: Dār al-Sha'b.

al-Miṣrī, Marwān, and Muḥammad 'Alī Wa'lānī. 1988. *Al-Kātibāt al-Sūriyyāt 1893–1987.* Damascus: Al-Ahālī li-al-Ṭibā'ah wa-al-Nashr wa-al-Tawzī'.

al-Miṣrī, Sanā'. 1989. *Khalfa al-Ḥijāb: Mawqif al-Jamā'āt al-Islāmiyyah min Qaḍiyyat al-Mar'ah.* Cairo: Sīnā li-al-Nashr.

Mubārak, Zakī. 1926. "Kuttāb al-'Ahd al-Māḍī." *Al-Muqtaṭaf* 68, no. 6 (June): 625–636.

al-Mudaynī, Aḥmad. N.d. *Fann al-Qiṣṣah al-Qaṣīrah bi-al-Maghrib fī al-Nash'ah wa-al-Taṭawwur wa-al-Ittijāhāt.* Beirut: Dār al-'Awdah.

Muḥabbak, Aḥmad Z. 1982. *Ḥarakat al-Ta'līf al-Masraḥī fī Sūriyyah Bayna 1945–1967.* Damascus: Ittiḥād al-Kuttāb al-'Arab.

al-Muḥāmī, Murqus Fahmī. 1894. *Al-Mar'ah fī al-Sharq.* Cairo: n.p.

Muḥammad, Aḥmad Sayyid. 1975. "Al-'Aqqād wa-al-Mar'ah." *Al-Hilāl* 83, no. 9 (September): 98–107.

Muḥammad, Fatḥiyyah. N.d. *Balāghat al-Nisā' fī al-Qarn al-'Ishrīn,* 2 parts. Cairo: Ḥusayn Ḥasanayn.

al-Muḥaymīd, Khadījah 'Abd al-Hādī. 1980. *Ḥarakāt Taghrīb al-Mar'ah al-Kuwaytiyyah.* Beirut: Al-Dār al-Islāmiyyah.

Muntaṣir, Zaynab. 1986. "Al-Bāshawāt Yaḥtafilūn bi-Thawrat Yūlyū 'a al-Raṣīf." *Rūz al-Yūsuf* 61, no. 3034 (August 4): 50–51.

al-Muqaddim, Muhammad A., ed. N.d. *'Awdat al-Ḥijāb*, vol. 1. Riyadh: Dār Ṭībah.

Mūsā, Ra'ūf S. N.d. *Mayy: Ḥayātuhā wa-Ṣālūnuhā wa-Adabuhā*. Alexandria: Dār Maṭābi' al-Mustaqbal; Beirut: Mu'ssasat al-Ma'ārif li-al-Ṭibā'ah wa-al-Nashr.

Mūsā, Salāmah. N.d. *Al-Mar'ah Laysat Lu'bat al-Rajul*. Cairo: Salāmah Mūsā li-al-Nashr wa-al Tawzī'.

Muṣṭafā, 'Āṭif. 1978. "A'lām 'alā Ṭarīq al-Nahḍah al-Nisā'iyyah fī Miṣr." *Al-Hilāl* 86, no. 4 (April): 54–61.

Nadwah. 1978. *Ughniyat al-Aṭfāl al-Dā'iriyyah* Anḍaj Riwāyāt Nawāl al-Sa'dāwī. *Dirāsāt 'Arabiyyah* 14, no. 11 (September): 123–128.

al-Najjār, Ḥusayn F. 1987. *Rifā'ah al-Ṭahṭāwī Rā'id Fikr wa-Imām Nahḍah*. Cairo: Al-Hay'ah al-Miṣriyyah al-'Āmmah li-al-Kitāb.

Najm, Muḥammad Y. 1961. *Al-Qiṣṣah fī al-Adab al-'Arabī al-Ḥadīth 1870–1914*, 2nd ed. Beirut: Al-Maktabah al-Ahliyyah.

———. 1967. *Al-Masraḥiyyah fī al-Adab al-'Arabī al-Ḥadīth 1847–1914*. Beirut: Dār al-Thaqāfah.

Nāṣif, Majd al-Dīn Ḥ., ed. 1962. *Athār Bāḥithat al-Bādiyah Malak Ḥifnī Nāṣif 1886–1917*. Egypt: Al-Mu'assasah al-Miṣriyyah al-'Āmmah li-al-Ta'līf wa-al-Tarjamah wa-al-Ṭibā'ah wa-al-Nashr.

———. N.d. "Mu'assisat al-Nahḍah al-Niswiyyah bi-Miṣr Malak Ḥifnī Nāṣif." In *Balāghat al-Nisā' fī al-Qarn al-'Ishrīn*, Pt. 1, by Fatḥiyyah Muḥammad, pp. 4–26. Cairo: Ḥusayn Ḥasanayn.

Nāṣif, Malak Ḥ. [penname: Bāḥithat al-Bādiyah]. 1910. *Al-Nisā'iyyāt*, vol. 1. Alexandria: Maṭba'at al-Jarīdah.

Naṣrallāh, Emily. 1986. *Nisā' Rā'idāt min al-Sharq wa-al-Gharb*. Beirut: Mu'assasat Nawfal.

———. 1984. *Al-Iqlā' 'Aksa al-Zaman*, 2nd ed. Beirut: Mu'assasat Nawfal.

———. 1980. *Tilka al-Dhikrayāt*. Beirut: Mu'assasat Nawfal.

———. 1968. *Shajarat al-Diflā*. Beirut: Maṭba'at al-Najwā.

———. 1962. *Ṭuyūr Aylūl*. Beirut: Al-Mu'assasah al-Ahliyyah li-al-Ṭibā'ah wa-al-Nashr.

al-Nassāj, Sayyid Ḥamīd. 1977. *Al-Adab al-'Arabī al-Mu'āṣir fī al-Maghrib al-Aqṣā 1963–1975*. Cairo: Dār al-Turāth al-'Arabī li-al-Ṭibā'ah.

———. N.d. *Adab al-Taḥaddī al-Siyāsī fī al-Maghrib al-'Arabī*. Beirut: Dār al-Ra'y.

Ni'mah, Rajā'. 1973. *Ṭaraf al-Khayṭ*. Beirut: Dār al-Āfāq al-Jadīdah.

Numnum, Ḥilmī. 1993. "Al-Mar'ah al-Miṣriyyah wa-al-Ḥamlah al-Faransiyyah: Thawrat al-Nisā' qabla Thawrat al-Qāhirah." *Al-Hilāl*, no. 5. (May): 15–21.

Nūr al-Dīn, 'Abd al-Salām. 1993. "Al-Judhūr al-Wathaniyyah Li-al-Ḥijāb." *Adab wa-Naqd* 89 (January): 45–60.

Nuwayhiḍ, Nādiyah al-Jirdī. 1986. *Nisā' min Bilādī*. Beirut: Al-Mu'assasah al-'Arabiyyah li-al-Dirāsāt wa-al-Nashr.

Qabbānī, Ghāliyah. 1993. "Buthaynah Sha'bān Tuḥīl Nash'at al-Riwāyah al-Nisā'iyyah ilā Lubnāniyyah Muhājirah: *Badī'ah wa Fu'ād* Sabaqt *Zaynab*." *Al-Sharq al-Awsaṭ* 15, no. 5230 (March 24): 19.

al-Qāḍī, Muṣṭafā. 1924. *Mukhtārāt fī al-Sufūr wa-al-Hijāb*. Baghdad: N.p.

al-Qalamāwī, Suhayr. N.d. *Aḥādīth Jaddatī*. Cairo: Lajnat al-Ta'līf.

———. 1978. "Ma'a Awwal Sayyidah Tafūz bi-Jā'izat al-Dawlah (Interview)." *Al-Hilāl* 86, no. 4 (April): 66–67.

———. 1965. "'Ṭuyūr Aylūl." *Al-Hilāl* 73, no. 6 (June): 148–153.

———. 1964. *Al-Shayāṭīn Talhū*. Cairo: Dār al-Qalam.

Qumayrah, Sulaymā. N.d. *Qabla al-Awān*. N.p.

Raḍwān, Fatḥī. 1967. *'Aṣr wa-Rijāl*. Cairo: Maktabat al-Anglo al-Miṣriyyah.

Ramaḍān, Sa'īdah. 1976. "Al-Ḥarakah al-Nisā'iyyah al-Ḥadīthah: Qiṣṣat al-Mar'ah 'alā Arḍ Miṣr." *Al-Thaqāfah* 3, no. 32 (May): 122–127.

Rashīd, Fawziyyah. 1992. "U'ānī Kawnī Imra'ah min al-Khalīj." *Al-Ādāb* 40, no. 11 (November): 56–59.

al-Razzāz, Nabīlah. 1975. *Mushārakat al-Mar'ah fī al-Ḥayāh al-'Āmmah fī Sūriyyā mundhu al-Istiqlāl 1945 wa-ḥattā 1975*. Damascus: Wizārat al-Thaqāfah wa-al-Irshād al-Qawmī.

Riḍā, Muḥammad Rashīd. 1975. *Ḥuqūq al-Nisā' fī al-Islām*. Beirut: Al-Maktab al-Islāmī.

———. 1932. *Nidā' ilā al-Jins al-Laṭīf Yawm al-Mawlid al-Nabawī al-Sharīf*. Cairo: Maṭba'at al-Manār.

Riḍā, Muḥyī al-Dīn. 1924. *Balāghat al-'Arab fī al-Qarn al-'Ishrīn*. Cairo: Al-Maṭba'ah al-Raḥmāniyyah.

Rifā'ī, Shams al-Dīn. 1969. *Tārīkh al-Ṣiḥāfah al-Sūriyyah: Al-Ṣihāfah al-Sūriyyah fī al-'Ahd al-'Uthmānī 1800–1918*. Cairo: Dār al-Ma'ārif.

al-Rīḥānī, Albert, ed. 1966. *Al-Rīḥānī wa-Mu'āṣirūh: Rasā'il al-Udabā' ilayhi*. Beirut: Dār al-Rīḥānī li-al-Ṭibā'ah wa-al-Nashr.

al-Rīḥānī, Amīn. 1967. "Ra'y Amīn al-Rīḥānī fī al-Mar'ah al-Sharqiyyah." *Al-Hilāl* 75, no. 12 (December): 139–140.

al-Rubay'ī, 'Abd al-Raḥmān Majīd. 1984. *Aṣwāt wa-Khaṭawāt: Maqālāt fī al-Qiṣṣah al-'Arabiyyah*. Beirut: Al-Mu'assasah al-'Arabiyyah li-al-Dirāsāt wa-al-Nashr.

al-Ruṣāfī, Ma'rūf. 1972. *Dīwān Ma'rūf al-Ruṣāfī*, 2 vols. Beirut: Dār al-'Awdah; Baghdad: Maktabat al-Nahḍah.

S. 1928. "Ḥadīth ma'a al-Ānisah Mayy." *Al-Hilāl* 36, no. 4 (April): 658–661.

Ṣabrī, Muṣṭafā. 1935. *Qawlī fī al-Mar'ah wa-Muqāranatuhu bi-Aqwāl Muqallidāt al-Gharb*. Cairo: Al-Maṭba'ah al-Salafiyyah.

Sa'd, Fārūq. 1983. *Bāqāt min Ḥadā'iq Mayy*, 3rd ed. Beirut: Dār al-Āfāq al-Jadīdah.

———. 1973. *Bāqāt min Ḥadā'iq Mayy*. Beirut: Manshūrāt Zuhayr Ba'labakkī.

al-Sa'dāwī, Nawāl [see also El Saadawi, Nawal]. 1988. *'An al-Mar'ah*. Cairo: Dār al-Mustaqbal al-'Arabī.

———. 1978a. "Kayfa Tarā al-Mar'ah al-'Arabiyyah Nafsahā." *Dirāsāt 'Arabiyyah* 14, no. 8 (June): 3–19.

———. 1978b. *Al-Rajul wa-al-Jins*. Beirut: Al-Mu'assasah al-'Arabiyyah li-al-Dirāsāt wa-al-Nashr.

———. 1977a. *Al-Mar'ah wa-al-Ṣirā' al-Nafsī*. Beirut: Al-Mu'assasah al-'Arabiyyah li-al-Dirāsāt wa-al-Nashr.

———. 1977b. *Qaḍiyyat al-Mar'ah al-Miṣriyyah al-Siyāsiyyah wa-al-Jinsiyyah*. Cairo: Dār al-Thaqāfah al-Jadīdah.

———. 1977c. *Al-Wajh al-'Ārī li-al-Mar'ah al-'Arabiyyah*. Beirut: Al-Mu'assasah al-'Arabiyyah li-al-Dirāsāt wa-al-Nashr.

———. 1975. *Imra'atān fī Imra'ah.* Beirut: Dār al-Ādāb.

———. 1974. *Al-Unthā Hiya al-Aṣl.* Beirut: Al-Mu'assasah al-'Arabiyyah li-al-Dirāsāt wa-al-Nashr.

———. 1972. *Al-Mar'ah wa-al-Jins,* 2nd ed. Beirut: Al-Mu'assasah al-'Arabiyyah li-al-Dirāsāt wa-al-Nashr.

———. 1970. *Al-Ghā'ib.* Cairo: Al-Hay'ah al-'Āmmah li-al-Ta'līf wa-al-Nashr.

———. 1965. *Mudhakkirāt Ṭabībah.* Cairo: Dār al-Ma'ārif.

al-Sa'īd, Amīnah. 1987. "Hal Ta'ūd al-Mar'ah ilā 'Aṣr al-Ḥarīm." *Al-Hilāl* 95, no. 9 (September): 30–35.

———. 1950. *Al-Jāmiḥah.* Cairo: Dār al-Ma'ārif.

Ṣā'igh, Salmā. 1964. *Ṣuwar wa-Dhikrayāt,* 2nd ed. Beirut: Dār al-Ḥaḍārah.

Sakākīnī, Widād. 1980. "Ẓāhirat al-Kibar fı Bidāyāt Jadīdāt." *Al-Adīb* 39, nos. 11–12 (November–December): 21–22.

———. 1969. *Mayy Ziyādah fī Ḥayātihā wa-Āthārihā.* Cairo: Dār al-Ma'ārif.

———. 1965. *Qāsim Amīn.* Cairo: Dār al-Ma'ārif.

——— and Tamāḍir Tawfīq. 1959. *Nisā' Shahīrāt min al-Sharq wa-al-Gharb.* Cairo: Maktabat al-Anglo al-Miṣriyyah.

Salāmah, Hind. 1968. *Al-Dumā al-Ḥayyah.* Beirut: Al-Maktab al-Tijārī li-al-Ṭibā'ah wa-al-Nashr wa-al-Tawzī'.

Salāmah, Jirjis. 1963. *Tārīkh al-Ta'līm al-Ajnabī fī Miṣr fī al-Qarnayn al-Tāsi' 'Ashar wa-al-'Ishrīn.* Cairo: Al-Majlis al-A'lā li-Ri'āyat al-Funūn wa-al-Adāb wa-al-'Ulūm al-Ijtimā'iyyah.

Ṣalībā, Jamīl. 1958. *Muḥāḍarāt fī al-Ittijāhāt al-Fikriyyah fī Bilād al-Shām wa-Atharuhā fī al-Adab al-'Arabī al-Ḥadīth.* Cairo: Ma'had al-Dirāsāt al-'Arabiyyah al-'Āliyah.

Ṣāliḥ, Laylā Muḥammad. 1978. *Adab al-Mar'ah fī al-Kuwayt.* Kuwait: Dhāt al-Salāsil.

al-Ṣāliḥ, Ṣāliḥ A. 1972. *Jamīl Ṣidqī al-Zahāwī, Tarjamat Ḥayātihi, Atharuhu, Dirāsah 'anhu.* Damascus: N.p.

al-Sammān, Ghādah. 1980. *Al-Qabīlah Tastajwib al-Qatīlah.* Beirut: Manshūrāt Ghādah al-Sammān.

———. 1979. *Kawābīs Bayrūt,* 3rd ed. Beirut: Manshūrāt Ghādah al-Sammān.

———. 1975. *Bayrūt 75*. Beirut: Manshūrāt Ghādah al-Sammān.

———. 1973a. *La Baḥr fī Bayrūt,* 2nd ed. Beirut: Dār al-Adāb.

———. 1973b. *Ḥubb*. Beirut: Dār al-Adāb.

———. 1966. *Layl al-Ghurabā'*. Beirut: Dār al-Adāb.

———. 1962. *'Aynak Qadarī*. Beirut: Dār al-Adāb.

Ṣaydaḥ, George. 1964. *Adabunā wa-Udabā'unā fī al-Mahājir al-Amrīkiyyah,* 3rd ed. Beirut: Dār al-'Ilm li-al-Malāyīn.

———. 1966. "Adab al-Mahjar fī Mabādhilih." *Al-Ma'rifah* 5, no. 50 (April): 61–80.

al-Sayyid, Aḥmad L. 1937. *Al-Muntakhabāt*. Part 1. Cairo: Dār al-Nashr al-Ḥadīth.

———. 1910. "Muqaddamah." In *Bāḥithat al-Bādiyah: Al-Nisā'iyyāt,* ed. M. Nāṣif, pp. 4–8. Alexandria: Maṭba'at al-Jarīdah.

Sha'bān, Buthaynah. 1993. "Al-Riwāyah al-Nisā'iyyah al-'Arabiyyah." *Mawāqif* 70 and 71 (Spring): 211–233.

Sha'bān, Fawzī. 1962. "Ḥawla Adabinā al-Nisā'i." *Al-Ādāb* 10, no. 11 (November): 59–60.

Shafīq, Aḥmad. 1934. *Mudhakkirātī fī Niṣf Qarn,* vol. 1. Egypt: Maṭba'at Miṣr.

Shafīq, Durriyyah. 1955. *Al-Mar'ah al-Miṣriyyah min al-Farā'inah ilā al-Yawm*. Cairo: Maṭba'at Miṣr.

Shaltūt, Maḥmūd. N.d. *Al-Islām 'Aqīdah wa-Sharī'ah*. Cairo: Al-Idārah al-'Āmmah li-al-Thaqāfah al-Islāmiyyah bi-al-Azhar.

Shammūsh, Isḥāq. 1942. "Al-Sayyidah 'Ā'ishah 'Iṣmat Taymūr." *Al-Risālah* 10, no. 465 (June 1): 584–586.

al-Sharābī, Kamāl Fawzī. 1958. "'Ishrūn 'Āman." *Al-Adīb* 17, no. 3 (March): 50–51.

Sha'rāwī, Hudā. 1929. "Interview." *Al-Hilāl* 35: 650–654.

al-Shaykh, Ḥanān. 1980. *Ḥikāyat Zahrah,* 2nd ed. Beirut: Dār al-Ādāb.

———. 1970. *Intiḥār Rajul Mayyit.* Beirut: Dār al-Nahār li-al-Nashr.

al-Shinnāwī, al-Sayyid Fahmī. 1982. "Ṣālūn Nāẓlī Hānum." *Al-Hilāl* 90, no. 9 (September): 40–48.

Shubayl, 'Abd al-'Azīz. 1987. *Al-Fann al-Riwā'i 'inda Ghādah al-Sammān.* Sūsah, Tunisia: Dār al-Ma'ārif li-al-Ṭibā'ah wa-al-Nashr.

Shukrī, Ghālī. 1977. *Ghādah al-Sammān bi-lā Ajniḥah.* Beirut: Dār al-Ṭalī'ah.

Shumays, 'Abd al-Mun'im. 1985. "Al-Amīrah Alexandra Ṣāḥibat Awwal Ṣālūn fī Miṣr." *Al-Hilāl* 93 (May): 12.

Ṣubḥī, Muḥyī al-Dīn. 1979. "Kawābīs Bayrūt li-Ghādah al-Sammān bayna Tajāwuz al-Wāqi' wa-Tajāwuz al-Adab." *Dirāsāt 'Arabiyyah* 15, no. 5 (March): 126–142.

———. 1978. *Muṭāraḥāt fī Fann al-Qawl: Muḥāwarāt ma'a Udabā' al-'Aṣr.* Damascus: Ittiḥād al-Kuttāb al-'Arab.

———. 1974. *'Awālim min al-Takhyīl.* Damascus: Wizārat al-Thaqāfah wa-al-Irshād al-Qawmī.

al-Subkī, Āmāl Kāmil B. 1986. *Al-Ḥarakah al-Nisā'iyyah fī Miṣr mā bayna al-Thawratayn 1919 wa 1952.* Cairo: Al-Hay'ah al-Miṣriyyah al-'Āmmah li-al-Kitāb.

Sufūrī [pseudonym]. 1928. "Dhikrā Qāsim Amīn wa-Nahḍat al-Mar'ah al-Miṣriyyah, Dhikrayāt Tārīkhiyyah." *Al-Muqtaṭaf* 72, no. 6 (June): 684–688.

"Ṣūrat al-Rajul fī Adab al-Aẓāfir al-Ṭawīlah." 1983. *Sayyidatī* 2, no. 101 (February): 16–19.

Ṭabbānah, Badawī. 1974. *Adab al-Mar'ah al-'Irāqiyyah fī al-Qarn al-'Ishrīn,* 2nd ed. Beirut: Dār al-Thaqāfah.

al-Ṭahṭāwī, Rifā'ah R. N.d. *Takhlīṣ al-Ibrīz ilā Talkhīṣ Bārīz.* Beirut: Dār Ibn Zaydūn; Cairo: Maktabat al-Kulliyyāt al-Islāmiyyah.

———. 1912. *Mabāhij al-Albāb al-Miṣriyyah fī Manāhij al-Adāb al-'Aṣriyyah,* 2nd ed. Cairo: Maṭba'at Sharikat al-Raghā'ib.

———. 1872. *Al-Murshid al-Amīn li-al-Banāt wa-al-Banīn.* Cairo: Maṭba'at al-Madāris al-Malakiyyah.

Tājir, Jack. N.d. *Ḥarakat al-Tarjamah bi-Miṣr Khilāl al-Qarn al-Tāsi' 'Ashar.* Cairo: Dār al-Ma'ārif.

al-Ṭamāwī, Aḥmad Ḥusayn. 1989. *Fuṣūl min al-Ṣiḥāfah al-Adabiyyah.* Cairo, Tripoli, and London: Dār al-Farjānī.

al-Ṭanāḥī, Ṭāhir. 1974. *Aṭyāf min Ḥayāt Mayy.* Cairo: Dār al-Hilāl.

———. 1962a. "Gharām Luṭfī al-Sayyid." *Al-Hilāl* 70, no. 1 (January): 15–22.

———. 1962b. "Adībān fī Gharām Mayy." *Al-Hilāl* 70, no. 4 (April): 120–125.

———. 1962c. "Qiṣṣat Gharām Mayy wa-Jubrān Khalīl Jubrān." *Al-Hilāl* 70, no. 8 (August): 29–33.

———. 1962d. "Gharām Mayy wa-Jubrān." *Al-Hilāl* 70, no. 9 (September): 154–160.

Taqrīr. 1951. Cairo: Jam'iyyat al-Ittiḥād al-Nisā'ial-Miṣri.

Ṭarābīshī, George [see also Tarabishi, Georges]. 1963. "Al-Istilāb fī al-Riwāyah al-Nisā'iyyah al-'Arabiyyah." *Al-Ābāb* 11, no. 3 (March): 43–49.

———. 1987. *'Uqdat Ūdīb fī al-Riwāyah al-'Arabiyyah.* Beirut: Dār al-Ṭalī'ah.

———. 1984. *Unthā ḍidda al-Unūthah: Dirāsah fī Adab Nawāl al-Sa'dāwī 'alā Ḍaw' al-Taḥlīl al-Nafsī.* Beirut: Dār al-Ṭalī'ah li-al-Ṭibā'ah wa-al-Nashr.

———. 1980. "Muḥammad Jamīl Bayhum wa-Qaḍiyyat al-Mar'ah." *Dirāsāt 'Arabiyyah* 17, no. 2 (December): 77–115.

———. 1978. *Al-Adab min al-Dākhil.* Beirut: Dār al-Talī'ah.

Ṭarrāzī, Philip dī. 1913. *Tārīkh al-Ṣiḥāfah al-'Arabiyyah,* vols. 1 and 2. Beirut: Al-Maṭba'ah al-Adabiyyah.

Taymūr, 'Ā'ishah. 1952. *Ḥilyat al-Ṭirāz.* Cairo: Dār al-Kitāb al-'Arabī.

———. 1887/8. *Natā'ij al-Aḥwal fī al-Aqwāl wa-al-Af'āl.* Cairo: Al-Maṭba'ah al-Bahiyyah.

al-Taymūriyyah, 'Ā'ishah [see Taymūr, 'Ā'ishah].

al-Ṭībī, 'Ākāshah 'A. 1990. *Muḥajjabāt li-Mādhā.* Cairo: Maktabat al-Turāth al-Islāmī.

Ṭūbī, Asmā. 1966. *'Abīr wa-Majd.* Beirut: Matba'at Qulfāṭ.

al-Ṭunnāhī, Ṭāhir [see al-Ṭanaḥī, Ṭāhir].

Ṭūqān, Fadwā. 1985. *Riḥlah Ṣa'bah Riḥlah Jabaliyyah.* Acre (Israel): Dār al-Aswār.

'Usayrān, Laylā. 1985. "Yawm fī Ḥayāt Laylā 'Usayrān al-Ḥāfiẓ: Falajatnī Bayrūt." In *Al-Awrāq al-Dhahabiyyah: Mukhtārāt min Afḍal mā Nasharathu al-Ṣiḥāfah wa-al-Dawriyyāt fī 'Ām Kāmil,* pp. 137–138. Nicosia, Cyprus: Mu'assasat Masters li-al-Nashr wa-al-Ittiṣāl.

———. 1979. *Qal'at al-Usṭah.* Beirut: Dār al-Nahār li-al-Nashr.

———. 1972. *Khaṭṭ al-Af'ā.* Beirut: Dār al-Fatḥ.

———. 1968. *'Aṣāfīr al-Fajr.* Beirut: Dār al-Ṭalī'ah.

———. 1966. *Al-Madīnah al-Fārighah.* Beirut: Dār Maktabat al-Ḥayāh.

———. 1963. *Al-Ḥiwār al-Akhras.* Beirut: Dār al-Ṭalī'ah.

———. 1962. *Lan Namūt Ghadan.* Beirut: Dār al-Ṭalī'ah.

'Uthmān, Hāshim. 1974. "Al-Adab al-Niswī fī Lubnān." *Al-Hilāl* 82, no. 4 (April): 36–41.

al-'Uwayṭ, 'Aql. 1992. "Lā Ahtamm bi-Maqālāt al-Nuqqād, al-Qurrā' Hum Alladhīn Ṣana'ūnī." *Al-Anwār* 33, no. 11245 (July 18): 9.

Wāfī, 'Alī 'A. N.d. *Al-Mar'ah fī al-Islām.* Cairo: Maktabat Gharīb.

Wajdī, Muḥammad Farīd. 1936. "Hal li-al-Mar'ah an Tata'allam al-'Ulūm al-'Āliyah wa-an Tukhāliṭ al-Rijāl wa-Tushārikahum fī al-A'māl." *Majallat al-Azhar* 6: 485–492.

al-Yāfī, Laylā. N.d. *Thulūj taḥta al-Shams.* Cairo: Dār al-Fikr al-'Arabī.

al-Yasū'ī, Lamens. 1928. "Nidā' Islāmī li-Taḥrīr al-Mar'ah." *Al-Mashriq* 36, no. 5 (May): 366–374.

Yūnus, 'Abd al-Ḥamīd. 1960. *Al-Ẓāhir Baybars fī al-Qiṣaṣ al-Sha'bī.* Cairo: Dār al-Qalam.

Yūsuf, Niqūlā. 1969. *A'lām min al-Iskandariyyah.* Alexandria: Munsha'at al-Ma'ārif.

———. 1963. Alexandra Avierinoh Ṣāḥibat *Anīs al-Jalīs. Al-Adīb* 22, no. 1 (January): 9–11.

al-Zahāwī, Jamīl Ṣ. 1972. *Al-Dīwān,* 2 vols., ed. with an Introduction by 'Abd al-Razzāq al-Hilālī. Beirut: Dār al-'Awdah.

———. 1934. *Al-Awshāl.* Baghdad: Maṭba'at Baghdad.

Zaydan, Joseph [see Zeidan, Joseph].

Zaydān, Jurjī. N.d. *Tārīkh Adāb al-Lughah al-'Arabiyyah,* vol. 4. Cairo: Dār al-Hilāl.

Zayn al-Dīn, Aḥmad M. 1979. "Al-Mar'ah kamā Tarā Nafsahā fī al-Riwāyah al-Lubnāniyyah." *Dirāsāt 'Arabiyyah* 15, no. 3 (January): 70–99.

Zayn al-Dīn, Naẓīrah. 1929. *Al-Fatāh wa-al-Shuyūkh, Naẓarāt wa-Munāẓarāt fī al-Sufūr wa-Taḥrīr al-'Aql wa-Taḥrīr al-Mar'ah wa-al-Tajaddud al-Ijtimā'ī fī al-'Ālam al-Islāmī.* Beirut: Maṭābi' Quzmā.

———. 1928. *Kitāb al-Sufūr wa-al-Ḥijāb Muḥāḍarāt wa-Naẓarāt Marmāhā Taḥrīr al-Mar'ah wa-al-Tajaddud al-Ijtimā'ī fī al-'Ālam al-Islāmī.* Beirut: n.p.

al-Zayyāt, 'Ināyāt. 1967. *Al-Ḥubb wa-al-Ṣamt.* Cairo: Dār al-Kitāb al-'Arabī li-al-Ṭibā'ah wa-al-Nashr.

al-Zayyāt, Laṭīfah. 1992. "Al-Kātib wa-al-Ḥurriyyah." *Fuṣūl* 11, no. 3 (Autumn): 227–232.

———. 1989. *Min Ṣuwar al-Mar'ah fī al-Qiṣaṣ wa-al-Riwāyāt al-'Arabiyyah.* Cairo: Dār al-Thaqāfah al-Jadīdah.

———. 1986. *Al-Shaykhūkh wa-Qiṣaṣ Ukhrā.* Cairo: Dār al-Mustaqbal.

———. 1960. *Al-Bāb al-Maftūḥ.* Cairo: Maktabat al-Anglo al-Miṣriyyah.

Zeidan, Joseph. 1986. *Maṣādir al-Adab al-Nisā'ī fī-al-'Ālam al-'Arabī al-Ḥadīth.* Jedda: Al-Nādī al-Adabī al-Thaqāfī.

al-Ziriklī, Khayr al-Dīn. 1979. *Al-A'lām: Qāmūs Tarājim li-Ashhar al-Rijāl wa-al-Nisā' min al-'Arab wa-al-Musta'ribīn wa-al-Mustashriqīn,* vol. 2, 4th ed. Beirut: Dār al-'Ilm li-al-Malāyīn.

Ziyādah, Mayy. 1982. *Al-Mu'allafāt al-Kāmilah,* 2 vols., ed. Salmā al-Ḥaffār al-Kuzbarī. Beirut: Mu'assasat Nawfal.

———. 1975a. *'Ā'ishah Taymūr Shā'irat al-Ṭalī'ah.* Beirut: Mu'assasat Nawfal.

———. 1975b. *Bayna al-Jazr wa-al-Madd.* Beirut: Mu'assasat Nawfal.

———. 1975c. *Kalimāt wa-Ishārāt.* Beirut: Mu'assasat Nawfal.

———. 1975d. *Al-Musāwāh.* Beirut: Mu'assasat Nawfal.

———. 1975e. *Al-Ṣaḥā'if*. Beirut: Mu'assasat Nawfal.

———. 1975f. *Wardah al-Yāzijī*. Beirut: Mu'assasat Nawfal.

———. 1967. *Ẓulumāt wa-Ashi''ah*. 2nd ed. Beirut: Dār al-Andalus.

———. 1952. *Azāhīr Ḥulm*, trans. Jamīl Jabr. Beirut: Dār Bayrūt.

———. 1935. "Al-Sirr al-Muwazza'" ["The Uncovered Secret"]. *Al-Risālah* (March 4): 327–328.

———. 1934a. "Al-Ḥubb fī al-Madrasah" ["Love in School"]. *Al-Hilāl* 43, nos. 1 (November): 5–10.

———. 1934b. "Al-Sham'ah Taḥtariq" ["The Candle Is Burning"]. *Al-Hilāl* 42, no. 3 (January): 258–262.

———. 1934c. "Fī al-Dhikrā al-Sādista 'Ashrata li-Bāḥithat al-Bādiyah." *Majallat al-Mar'ah al-Miṣriyyah* 15, nos. 10–11 (November–December): 397–401.

———. 1931. "'Mitr' Yvonne Nietter fī Miṣr." *Majallat al-Mar'ah al-Miṣriyyah* 12, nos. 1 and 2 (January and February): 11–12.

———. 1930. "Zafāf Karīmat Ḥifnī bīk wa-Shaqīqat Bāḥithat al-Bādiyah." *Majallat al-Mar'ah al-Miṣriyyah* 11, nos. 1 and 2 (February 15): 16–17.

———. 1923. "'Alā al-Ṣadr al-Shafīq [On the Compassionate Breast]." *Al-Hilāl* 32, nos. 1–2 (November): 67–78.

INDEX

A

C

D

E

G

H

I

K

L

M

N

O

P

al-Sa'īd, Premier Nūri, 38
Sa'īd, Khedive, 59
Ṣā'igh, Salmā, 52, 53, 83
saj' (rhymed prose), 57, 66–68, 70
Sakākīnī, Widād, 86
Salāmah, Hind, 142
Sarkīs, Rāmiz, 52
Sarkīs, Salīm (Maryam Maẓhar), 49, 53
salons, 4, 44, 50–55, 74, 82, 83
al-Sammān, Ghādah, 191–205, 221, 227, 229, 232, 324, 236
al-Saqqāf, Khadījah, 55
Ṣarrūf, Ya'qūb, 43, 75
Saudi Arabia, 1
Ṣawāyā, Labībah Mikhā'īl, 68–69, 87, 89
al-Sayyid, Aḥmad Luṭfī, 20, 21, 31, 52, 53, 74
seclusion of women, 11, 30, 150
segregation of the sexes, 16, 25, 32, 44, 82, 101, 105
self-centeredness, 175, 227, 229
self-determination, 235
self-expression, 93
self-fulfillment, 20, 96, 97, 114–16, 140, 157, 167, 226
Self-Other dichotomy, 154
de Sévigné, Madame, 53
sex objects, 107, 154
sexism, 4, 136, 137, 142, 144, 147, 193
sexual equality, 11, 26, 78, 88, 146, 219
sexual freedom, 105
sexual identity, 160, 161
sexual maturity, 166
sexuality, 103, 110, 113, 128, 137, 144, 149, 158, 159, 163, 207–08, 211–13, 215–17, 228
Shaaban, Bouthaina, 186
Shafīq, Durriyyah, 36, 48
Shakespeare, 195
Shakkūr, Madame Manṣūr, 24
Sham'ūn, Labībah, 47
Sha'rāwī, 'Alī, 34
Sha'rāwī, Hudā, 33–35, 53, 75, 83, 87, 94
Shawkat, Dr. Sāmī, 24
Shawqī, Aḥmad, 53
al-Shaykh, Ḥanān, 205–17, 228–29, 236
short stories, 1, 77, 79, 80, 96, 103, 192–94, 205
Showalter, Elaine, 140, 141, 149, 151
Shukrī, Ghālī, 195
Shumayyil, Shiblī, 53, 74
Siddiq , Muhammad, 182
Ṣidqī, Ismā'īl, 48
social change, 75, 179, 235, 236
social class, 33, 35, 38, 39, 54, 114–16, 125, 149, 181, 199, 208
social conservatism, 124
social constraints, 88, 104
social criticism, 63, 93
social customs, 13, 95, 99, 101, 104, 120, 123, 142, 145, 167, 178
social injustice, 196, 198
social issues, 50, 81, 130, 133
social structure, 163, 188
solidarity, 5, 66, 72, 126, 130, 132, 162
Solomon, King, 204
South America, 29, 71
Spencer, Herbert, 16
de Staël, Madame, 53
status of women, 9, 10, 14, 23, 39, 42, 43, 62, 65, 80, 235
Storrs, Ronald, 83
stream-of-consciousness, 102, 133, 155, 171, 187

Y

Z

CPSIA information can be obtained at www.ICGtesting.com
Printed in the USA
BVOW070036080812

297310BV00001B/6/A

9 780791 42172